book takes a new look at all the crucial questions of man's ability to survive in the decades to come. In the context of past and future, he writes of water, land, and air pollution, of the pillage of mineral resources, of radioactive contamination, of plundered wildlife and woodlands, of the crescendo of environmental noise and the stresses of urban crowding. He attacks current policies of economic growthmanship as well as long-held collective attitudes toward reproduction. Restraint of man's fertility—most significant to the future of the Third World—is Dr. Loraine's primary concern, and in this study he reviews new concepts of population control in sociological and medical thinking.

The Death of Tomorrow is a warning and a challenge. The author writes: "Only when the gravity of the current situation is appreciated by a sufficient number of people throughout the world will rational solutions to mankind's predicament be forthcoming."

THE DEATH OF TOMORROW

THE DEATH OF TOMORROW

JOHN A. LORAINE

In association with
R. D. E. Rumsey

WITH A FOREWORD BY
His Royal Highness
THE DUKE OF EDINBURGH

J. B. Lippincott Company
Philadelphia

U.S. Library of Congress Catalog Card No: 72–3986

ISBN 0–397–00917 8

Printed in Great Britain

To Diana

FOREWORD

by His Royal Highness The Duke of Edinburgh

The choice which confronts mankind in the last third of the twentieth century is a difficult one. Problems of overpopulation, environmental pollution, depletion of finite resources and the threat of widespread starvation are becoming more obvious every day.

There are those who maintain that family planning will cure the population explosion, that policies of economic growth will not irretrievably wreck the environment, that the quality of life is not in jeopardy and that the 'green revolution' in agriculture is the answer to our chronic food shortages. Others maintain that only drastic measures can save man from himself. Indeed the gulf between official optimism on the one hand and informed scientific pessimism on the other is so wide as to be almost unbridgeable.

In this book Dr. John A. Loraine takes a hard and critical look at the contemporary world scene. He writes of polluted air, of troubled waters, of intolerable cacophony, of the ever-increasing threat of radioactive contamination and of our fast-vanishing resources of metals and fossil fuels. He criticises current economic doctrine for its fixation with the growth of production and consumption. But first and foremost he stresses the perils of overpopulation and makes it abundantly clear that in his view unless reproductive activities are controlled there can be no future for mankind.

Dr. Loraine deals with his subject in a broad historical perspective and sets out his case with a powerful and dispassionate clarity. The conclusions which he draws are ominous, but it is only when there is a widespread recognition of the existence of such problems that solutions for humanity will be forthcoming. Dr Loraine is to be congratulated for giving such a vivid picture of the dilemma and the choice facing mankind.

1972

PREFACE

This book is about the world of the 1970's. It is concerned with four major and closely interconnected themes—environmental pollution, destruction of natural resources, economics and, above all, overpopulation. It has sought to paint the canvas of contemporary life with a broad brush, and it has dealt with topics as diverse as afforestation and abortion, contraception and the Common Market, fluoridation and family planning, hydrology and homosexuality, inflation and the internal combustion engine, pesticides and prostaglandins, wild life and Women's Liberation. For me the preparation of this book has been an experience of consuming interest in the course of which I have been transported far from my original training in the practice of medicine and in biomedical research.

Human activities, particularly in the spheres of reproduction and environmental spoilation, have already placed our planet in jeopardy. The maladies which afflict us are complex and deepseated. Their palliation much less their cure will be exceedingly difficult and will demand from us qualities of resourcefulness, magnanimity, tolerance and ingenuity seldom witnessed in mankind's long and turbulent history. I believe that unless we act now the prognosis for tomorrow will be bleak indeed.

Edinburgh,   John A. Loraine
January 1972

AUTHOR'S ACKNOWLEDGEMENTS

Grateful acknowledgement is made to R. D. E. Rumsey, for his contributions to the preparation of Chapters I, II, III, XI and XII, and the bibliography; for helpful advice on specific chapters, to Dr. R. H. Best (IX), N. H. Fairbairn (XVI), Professor G. M. Howe (VIII), Dr. A. W. G. Manning (VII), and W. D. C. Wright (XIII); to the Medical Research Council in Edinburgh, for their support in connection with studies described in Chapter XVI; to Druscilla T. Rodger, who also helped with the bibliography; and to Helen G. Campbell and others of the secretarial staff.

My wife has been a tower of strength throughout the writing of this book and the dedication conveys my gratitude.

J.A.L.

CONTENTS

There was a time when the countless tribes of men, dispersed over the world though they were, were oppressing the surface of the deep-bosomed earth; and Zeus seeing it took pity and in his wise heart resolved to lighten the all-nurturing earth of men, having fanned the flame of great strife in the Trojan war, that the load of death might empty the world. And so the heroes were slain at Troy, and the counsel of Zeus was fulfilled.

Stasinus, *Cypria*   fragment 1
? Seventh century BC

I

AIR CAN BE DANGEROUS

Fair is foul, and foul is fair;
Hover through the fog and filthy air.

Macbeth

Air pollution is not new. It has existed from very early times, even as far back as the days of the Babylonian and Roman Empires.

In the Europe of the early Middle Ages most of the heat generated was derived from wood. However, by the early part of the thirteenth century woodlands and forests throughout that continent had been largely destroyed and it became increasingly necessary to find an alternative source of fuel supply. Eyes were hopefully turned towards Asia where following the journeys of explorers such as Marco Polo, there were exciting reports of the burning of coal.

From the very beginning coal was seen to foul the air due to the emission of smoke, soot and the choking fumes of sulphur dioxide. The Church was violently opposed to coal in the early stages, designating it an unnatural fuel and seeing in its fumes a likeness of the brimstone which accompanied Hell Fire! In 1257 AD Queen Eleanor, wife of Henry III of England, was forced to leave the city of Nottingham because she could not tolerate the smoke liberated from coal fires, and in 1273 Edward I enacted a law designed to prevent the use of the soft form of coal for domestic heating. The law was far from being a formality; on the contrary it was rigorously enforced, and in 1306 a citizen of London was tried and executed for burning coal within the confines of the city.

Later monarchs notably Richard II and Henry V introduced further legislation in an attempt to regulate coal usage and

prevent noxious odours; indeed Henry V went so far as to
establish a commission to superintend the movement of coal
into the city of London. But in spite of these draconian
measures the situation steadily worsened. So much so that by
Tudor times industrial activity had reached such a peak of
intensity that the whole of London was enveloped in smoke,
and travellers to Elizabethan England from overseas were
amazed and disgusted at the degree of contamination. In the
sixteenth and seventeenth centuries industry continued to
proliferate in London, and between 1580 and 1660 imports of
goods into the city increased by a factor of 25. By 1660, the
year of the Restoration of King Charles II, Britain was producing two million tons of coal annually, this being some five
times more than the whole of the rest of the world combined.

Mercantilists and industrialists were reluctant to take any
steps which might jeopardise an economy based on coal and
becoming steadily more lucrative. However, protests came from
other quarters. The renowned English physician, Thomas
Sydenham, who was responsible for the description of a number
of diseases including a form of St Vitus Dance, remarked that
'the sulphur and fumes of sea coals gave occasion for thought',
while in 1661 John Evelyn, the noted naturalist, provided a
detailed description of some of the sources of atmospheric
pollution, stressed the ill effects which might accrue from this
form of contamination and even suggested possible remedies for
it. Evelyn was apparently well ahead of time, for his improvements included the resiting of offending industries and the
planting of trees and shrubs to form the modern equivalent of
green belts.

The Industrial Revolution of the late eighteenth and nineteenth centuries greatly intensified the problem of atmospheric
pollution as it did other types of environmental contamination.
The birth place of the revolution was England, that 'workshop
of the world', but soon it spread to other countries. By 1850 it
was overtaking France, Belgium, Imperial Germany and the
USA; by 1900 Tsarist Russia, Sweden and even far off Japan.
Mineral resources, especially coal and metals such as iron, were
the life blood of the Industrial Revolution. Factories proliferated, demands for coal escalated, and as a consequence

prodigious amounts of smoke and flyash were liberated indiscriminately and haphazardly into the atmosphere. Air pollution became a blight on nineteenth century England. Not only was the health of factory workers gravely impaired, but those who happened to reside near to industrial sites were also exposed to significant health hazards. Even that redoubtable English statesman, Lord Palmerston, a man not generally noted for his espousal of social causes, was critical, and in 1852, addressing an audience of Sussex farmers, he averred 'the country should purify the towns and the towns should fertilise the country—we allow decomposed substances in towns to pollute the atmosphere, to ruin health, to cause premature misery, to be pestilent and destructive of existence'.

A major event occurred in 1859, for in August of that year in Titusville, Pennsylvania, USA, Edwin Drake opened the world's first oil well. Almost overnight a new era was ushered in. Oil meant money, and a feverish rush for its exploitation was initiated. The process rapidly gained momentum, and as a result the towering giants of modern times, the petroleum and petrochemical industries, came into existence. The air was further fouled. Now a whole host of new pollutants, man-made and frequently undetectable to eyes and nose, were loosed into the atmosphere. Health problems arose on every side as populations, spurred on by the heightening tempo of industrialisation, crowded themselves into ever larger cities.

The scenario for an air pollution disaster had already been written in England by the second half of the nineteenth century. The first occurred in London in 1873; meteorological conditions were favourable, a thick cloud of pollution enveloped the city and over 1,000 people died. There were similar episodes in London in January 1880, February 1882, December 1891 and December 1892. In the autumn of 1909 Glasgow was threatened by recurrent bouts of air pollution. In 1911 a local physician, Harold Antoine Des Voeux, provided a description of this episode, noted its deleterious effects on the health of his patients, and introduced into the English language the word *smog*, this being a contraction for a mixture of smoke and fog.

By the opening of the twentieth century in Britain much had been learned about the causes of atmospheric pollution, and

there was a large measure of agreement amongst experts as to
how the problem could be tackled. However, there was
continued apathy in governmental circles, and this prevented
any positive action being taken to diminish the dismal
smokiness of British cities. True, a programme of smoke
abatement was initiated in 1912 by the Liberal Government led
by H. H. Asquith, and ever since then measurements have been
made of the content of smoke and sulphur dioxide in the air
over a number of our major towns. However, progress in the
field of atmospheric pollution received a sharp set back due to
the outbreak of the First World War, and although scientific
interest in the subject grew steadily in the 1920's and 1930's,
the economic climate of these years was not propitious to
governmental expenditure in this area. Indeed in the UK the
first Clean Air Act did not appear on the statute book until as
late as 1956, and even then it was mainly a consequence of the
renowned London smog of 1952. As will be pointed out in
Chapter XIII, during the 1950's and 1960's British politicians of
all parties were obsessed with the necessity for economic
growth, and in an era of growthmanship associated with the
rapid spread of industry, it is hardly surprising that the situation
with respect to atmospheric pollution was slow to improve.
Eventually in the late 1960's protection of the environment
against pollution of all types received governmental support,
although it must be emphasised that this topic was given scant
consideration even as late as the General Election of June 1970.

The USA and other nations which experienced the Industrial
Revolution were increasingly afflicted with the same malady as
Britain. By the latter part of the nineteenth century the
combination in the USA of rapid industrialisation, an entrenched dogma of growthmanship, and a laissez-faire free
enterprise type of economy were producing predictable results.
Between 1900 and 1914 the smoke situation of a number of
major cities was carefully investigated—Pittsburg in 1902, St.
Louis in 1907 and Chicago in or about 1910. These surveys
clearly demonstrated the presence of health hazards; unfortunately, they did not produce any action on the political front.
Then in the early 1940's a new phenomenon made its
appearance in the city of Los Angeles. This was photochemical

smog, a condition bearing some resemblance to but still distinct from that described by the Glaswegian Des Voeux. A product of rapid industrialisation, heavy automobile ownership, over-population and unusual meteorological conditions, photo-chemical smog merits special attention later in this chapter.

By the early 1960's the situation with respect to atmospheric pollution in the major cities of the USA had become well nigh intolerable. Officialdom finally became convinced that action was necessary, and in 1967 Lyndon Johnson's Democratic Administration passed the first Air Quality Act. When signing the Act into law the President was forthright in his condemna-tion of the current scene and commented 'either we stop poisoning our air, or we become a nation in gas masks, groping our way through dying cities and a wilderness of ghost towns'. The Republican Administration of Richard Nixon, elected in 1968, also pledged itself to a clean air programme, and in his State of the Union message of January 1970 Nixon gave an assurance that the Federal Government would combat atmos-pheric pollution with all the means at its disposal.

*   *   *

This history of atmospheric pollution is studded with national disasters. Three of them have received widespread publicity, and as a result political and legislative action have ensued. The first occurred in the valley of the River Meuse in Belgium in 1931 when over 60 persons died as a result of breathing polluted air. This episode stimulated interest in atmospheric pollution in the French-speaking countries of Europe, and there were debates on the subject in the French parliament of that time. The second disaster took place in the USA in October 1948. This time those exposed were the inhabitants of the small but heavily industrialised city of Donora in Pennsylvania (population 12,300). The air over the city was heavy with smoke and fog belched from its numerous factories and plants; but in addition there was present what meteorologists call a thermal inversion, and which is charac-terised by the presence of a layer of warm air above one of colder air. As a consequence of this climatic abnormality fog and smoke were trapped over the city for some days. Fifteen men and five women died while hundreds were incapacitated due to illnesses affecting the respiratory tract. At last the conscience of the nation was stirred, and the US Public Health Service made an extensive study of the disaster with a view to preventing its repetition elsewhere.

The site of the third major disaster was London and the time December 1952. Here, as in Donora, the major factors were fog, smoke and a thermal inversion. A notable feature of the disaster was the precipitous rise in the atmospheric content of sulphur dioxide and particulate matter which took place during the five days throughout which the smog invested the city. Some 4,000 people are thought to have died, those with respiratory illnesses and heart diseases being the most severely affected. A public enquiry ensued, and as a result of its recommendations the Clean Air Act of 1956 reached the statute book.

*   *   *

The reasons for the great increase in atmospheric pollution throughout the world and especially since the end of the Second World War are readily discernible. One major factor has been the population explosion which has brought in its train urbanisation on a unique scale. Clustered throughout our planet in innumerable cities and towns, under conditions which range from spectacular opulence to abysmal poverty, the world's citizenry proceed to pollute the air in a variety of ways. They must heat their places of abode; they must dispose of their refuse often by incineration. Above all, in an era which has been dubbed as one of rising expectations, they desire to drive their own motor cars. Much of the populace work in factories and plants, which tend to proliferate in areas of high population density there to constitute potent sources of atmospheric pollution. And the overall situation is likely to worsen because not only is the world population rising rapidly, but the dynamic behind industrial expansion shows no sign of slackening.

Hand in hand with overpopulation and industrialisation as causes of atmospheric pollution goes the condition of affluence. Affluence is characteristic of the Western world—of Europe,

North America and Australasia; it is not in evidence in the Third World of Africa, Asia and Latin America where the living standards of the majority of the people remain abysmally low. Affluence and economic growth have proved to be natural bedfellows. A rising Gross National Product has come to be regarded as a highly sensitive index of national success and our age has been one in which materialistic concepts and criteria have been paramount. The philosophy of growthmanship has found much favour in political circles and until very recently has gone virtually unchallenged. Who can wonder therefore that, in the presence of such a powerful and all-pervasive dogma, the floodgates to atmospheric pollution have been opened on an unprecedented scale? Thus the 'average' family man in a developed country wishes to be equipped with labour-saving devices of all kinds including washing machines, vacuum cleaners, refrigerators and even garbage grinders. He watches his television screen with avidity and he may well still be a lover of radio. Many of the devices which he uses are operated by electricity, and as a result demands for this commodity have soared. Indeed, since the end of the Second World War, the demand has been doubling every 10 years and is likely to continue to do so for the foreseeable future. Coal, coke, oil and gas—the so-called fossil fuels—provide the great majority of the energy necessary to meet our needs and to power the industrial colossus of the West. But at the very same time as they provide such energy these fuels contribute on a grand scale to the problem of atmospheric pollution.

The role of the motor car in the genesis of air pollution will receive consideration later, but at this stage it is useful to emphasise the rather obvious fact that the spread of ownership of motor vehicles is closely linked to the affluence of the populace. Indeed in many areas of the developed world of the 1970's the 'one car family' has become an anachronism. Instead in its place we have the 'multi car family' in which not only the parents but also the children own and drive automobiles.

Overpopulation, industrialisation, affluence—these are at the root of atmospheric pollution. But what substances foul the air and cause the damage? Unfortunately, they are both many and varied as I shall now proceed to show.

Villains of the Air

Two categories of air pollution exist—*natural* and *man-made*. Within the former group are included volcanic eruptions, naturally occurring hazes, wind-blown dust and pollen, smoke from forest fires and air-borne bacteria and other micro organisms. The latter category, reflecting human activities, constitutes the major topic of the remainder of this chapter. Such forms of pollution are highly diverse; moreover, they play a notable role in contaminating our general environment and reducing the quality of our lives.

As mentioned previously atmospheric pollution reaches its zenith over large industrial cities. Prevailing weather conditions can also predispose to the condition. Normally air currents above cities are unstable; this allows any hot air generated to rise and tends to prevent the build up of pollutants by carrying away the noxious particles into the upper atmosphere. Sometimes, however, and particularly under conditions of windlessness, thermal inversions occur and, as noted earlier, these have proved to be of great importance in the production of natural disasters resulting from air pollution. Thermal inversions make their appearance at night when the ground cools more rapidly than the air; consequently by morning the layer of air in closest proximity to the ground has become less warm than that above it. The circulation of air is thus inhibited and pollutants tend to accumulate at a level in the atmosphere at which they can be inhaled by the population. Normally the sun will 'burn away' the inversion by heating the ground once again to a temperature higher than the upper layers of the atmosphere. Sometimes, however, it fails to do so in time, especially in large cities where there is a plentitude of automobiles during the morning rush hour. Certain geographical locations such as river valleys predipose to thermal inversions. They are of frequent occurrence in the central region of the Soviet Union, while in the USA they are mainly encountered in the area between the Appalachian and Rocky Mountains and between the Rockies and the Sierra Nevadas.

There are four main constituents to air pollution—*gases, vapours, liquid droplets* and *solid particles.* Heavier particles and droplets tend to fall in areas immediately affected; on the other hand, vapours and gases may be dispersed widely depending on meteorological conditions and can affect other countries and even other continents.

SULPHUR AND ITS OXIDES

These are probably the most widely distributed of all the artificial gaseous pollutants and have certainly been the most extensively studied. The gas sulphur dioxide (SO_2) is the most important member. It is produced by the combustion of fuels containing sulphur, numbering amongst them coal, oil and natural gas. Industrial plants which manufacture sulphuric acid belch forth large amounts of the gas and it is also liberated during the making of steel. When materials such as wood, rubber tyres, paper, cardboard and certain solid wastes are incinerated the air becomes contaminated with sulphur dioxide.

During the conversion of sulphur to sulphur dioxide small amounts of another gas known as sulphur trioxide, are produced. In the presence of moisture sulphur trioxide forms sulphuric acid. The latter is responsible for the bluish white plumes of smoke so typical of the air above areas of heavy industry, and it is also believed by many to have been a major culprit in the air pollution disasters in the Meuse Valley, Donora and London. Normally, the conversion of sulphur dioxide to the trioxide is slow, but the process is hastened in the presence of bright sunshine.

Sulphur dioxide is highly injurious to vegetation especially to plant life. At relatively low concentrations it inhibits the process of photosynthesis whereby the plant obtains its nourishment, and if the exposure is continued for any length of time the leaves change colour, becoming yellow and then white. At higher concentrations of the gas the delicate cells of the plant are killed and its whole structure disintegrates. Plants with thin leaves are especially susceptible to the noxious effects of sulphur dioxide. Alfalfa, cotton and grapes have shown major changes, as have many favourite varieties of garden plants, including sweet peas, verbenas, asters, violets, hollyhocks, zinnias, marigolds, begonias and nasturtiums.

Plants are not the only sufferers. Sulphur dioxide and sulphuric acid hasten the corrosion and deterioration of a number of metals including iron, steel, copper, nickel and aluminium. Building materials such as limestone, marble, roofing slates and mortar are attacked by sulphur dioxide and trioxide, while the former can make paper unduly brittle, reduce the strength of leather and bring about the deterioration of natural and synthetic fibres such as cotton, wool and nylon.

CARBON MONOXIDE

The saga of carbon monoxide (CO) as an air pollutant is closely bound up with that of the motor car and the internal combustion engine. The gas is colourless and odourless, and largely because of these properties it can be a very dangerous poison. Carbon monoxide is reasonably stable in the atmosphere but through time it becomes oxidised to carbon dioxide.

Effects produced by carbon monoxide on human health will be discussed in Chapter III. However, at this stage it is worth recalling that concentrations of just over 1,000 parts per million will produce rapid death. At the much lower level of 100 parts per million—generally considered to be the upper limit of safety in industrial practice—symptoms of poisoning including giddiness, headaches and undue lassitude are likely to make their appearance in susceptible individuals. Levels of carbon monoxide in the atmosphere have been monitored in certain areas of the world for some time, and the results obtained are of interest. Thus in a busy street in Cincinnati, Ohio, readings ranged between 0 and 55 parts per million with an average of 9.5. In Los Angeles, levels as high as 72 parts per million have been reported, while in London's Oxford Street in 1960 a peak concentration of 100 parts per million was recorded.

As will be emphasised in Chapter II the USA with its high affluence and burgeoning car ownership leads the world with respect to carbon monoxide pollution. Thus the three million cars on the roads of Los Angeles each day in the early 1960's produced 8,000 tons of the gas, and this figure transcends anything seen elsewhere in the Western world. But in Los Angeles and in other cities the automobile is not the sole culprit. Industry also plays its part, major offenders being mills producing iron, steel, wood pulp and paper.

CARBON DIOXIDE

This is a close relative of carbon monoxide; however it is much less poisonous to the human race. Carbon dioxide (CO_2) is essential for the life and wellbeing of all green plants. The latter remove it from the air by photosynthesis, this essentially being the process whereby the sun's energy is trapped in the plant cells and is used therein to build up the highly complicated organic substances necessary for growth.

Nature permits carbon dioxide to enter the atmosphere in various ways. Thus it is a normal waste product of respiration in all animal species including man and it is produced when living tissues decompose. How is it removed from the atmosphere? Here the pathways are less well established, and much research remains to be carried out in this important area. However, it is virtually certain that the oceans of the world have a large part to play in the process, absorbing the gas and storing it in the form of carbonates of magnesium and sodium.

Does carbon dioxide produce any local effects? It does but fortunately these are much milder than is the case with sulphur and its oxides. However, it has now been established that the gas can cause deterioration of building stones such as limestone and can corrode magnesium and possibly other metals as well.

Definite evidence now exists that the carbon dioxide content of the atmosphere is rising, and recent figures supporting this view were quoted in the first report of the British Royal Commission on Environmental Pollution published early in 1971. Thus in the 1890's the atmospheric concentration of the gas was 290 parts per million; by 1960 it had risen to 312 parts per million; by 1969 to 320 parts per million, and by 2000 AD, if present trends continue, a figure as high as 360 parts per million could well be attained. One is therefore safe in concluding that the concentration of carbon dioxide in the air has risen by almost 10 per cent since the 1890's, almost half of this increase taking place since the end of the Second World War. What has been the reason for this dramatic change? There is little doubt that the most important factor in its causation has been the sustained increase in industrial activity and especially the combustion of prodigious amounts of fossil fuels.

Carbon dioxide is a focus of major interest at the present time. The interest arises from the possibility that rising levels of the gas in the atmosphere might alter our weather irrevocably and might even cause a global catastrophe, the effects of which could well be irreversible. Is there any basis for such fears? Precise information is exceedingly difficult to obtain because of the paucity of reliable and objective data. Theoretically it is possible that excessive quantities of carbon dioxide could augment what has been termed the 'greenhouse effect', this being the ability of certain gases in the upper atmosphere to act as a heat trap and so to prevent the earth's heat from radiating back into space. Furthermore, the increasing amount of heat generated by conventional as well as by nuclear power stations might warm the earth's surface directly. Possibly due to a combination of such phenomena the temperature all over the world could rise, bringing in its train the thawing of polar icecaps, a rise in sea levels and widespread flooding. Will humanity ever observe such an effect? An unequivocal answer cannot be provided. However, at present, a catastrophe of this type appears to be unlikely especially in view of the fact that over the past three decades meteorologists inform us that, probably due to the increased atmospheric content of particulate matter, the temperature of the earth has tended to cool rather than to rise.

And what effects will there be on our climate when supersonic aircraft such as the Anglo-French Concorde and the Russian Tupolev come into general commercial use? Will such planes by their well-known propensity to consume oxygen and to liberate large amounts of carbon dioxide increase the greenhouse effect? Will they through the formation of cirrus clouds alter the weather in distant areas of our planet? Again we do not know the precise answers to these important questions, and as a result speculation, sometimes with highly alarmist overtones, is rife. One point is however crystal clear and that is the clamant need for detailed and meticulous research in this vital area. How unfortunate it is that such investigative work was not initiated years ago rather than now when the juggernaut of social and political pressure may make the termination of what could well turn out to be an ill-designed and highly expensive project, difficult or impossible.

OXIDES OF NITROGEN

In many parts of the world such oxides constitute an important source of atmospheric pollution. They are produced in large quantities during the high temperature combustion of coal, oil and gas, and in the USA these fuels are responsible for the emission of some three million tons of nitrogen oxides annually. Other forms of industry are also notable contributors, one of the most important being that involving the manufacture of artificial fertilisers. However, as in the case of carbon monoxide, the internal combustion engine is probably the richest source of nitrogen oxide pollution especially in cities such as Los Angeles where car ownership is almost universal.

The first oxide of nitrogen to be formed is nitric oxide. This combines with atmospheric oxygen to form nitrogen dioxide, the latter having a yellowish brown colour. The conversion of nitric oxide to nitrogen dioxide is hastened by the presence of sunlight, and as will be emphasised later, this is an important factor in the development of photochemical smog. In rural areas of the USA and elsewhere concentrations of nitrogen oxide in the atmosphere are quite low, seldom exceeding one part per million. However, in the streets of Los Angeles concentrations as high as 3.5 parts per million have been recorded.

In contrast to carbon dioxide there appears little likelihood that a generalised increase in the atmospheric content of nitrogen oxides will take place. This is because such substances can all be converted into nitrates and the latter, being readily soluble in water, are rapidly removed from the atmosphere by rain.

LEAD AND FLUORIDES

Lead is a metal highly toxic to mankind, and some of the symptoms which can arise through overdosage with it are discussed in Chapter III. Lead poisoning has a very long history. Indeed it is said to have contributed to the downfall of the Roman Empire by killing off many of its leading citizens who drank their wine in leaden pots, ingested the metal, and concentrated it in their bones.

In industrial areas smelters emit large quantities of lead. The combustion of certain fuels, especially coal, also contributes as do dusts and sprays containing lead arsenate and various typs of paint. In some industrial areas in our planet the lead content of the soil has been stated to be as high as 12,000 parts per million, and drinking water has been reported to contain up to 0.04 parts per million of the metal.

As with carbon monoxide and oxides of nitrogen the internal combustion engine is a potent source of atmospheric pollution by lead. Lead is added to petrol in the form of its tetra ethyl and tetra methyl salts. These increase what are termed the 'anti knock' properties of petrol, and thus make it possible to improve the octane rating of the fuel used in modern high compression engines (see also Chapter II). When the lead salts are exposed to heat they rapidly decompose either in the combustion chamber of the vehicle or in its carburettor. They are then spewed into the air generally in the form of bromides or chlorides, these salts forming minute particles which are readily dispersable.

Since the end of the First World War there has been a huge increase in the amount of lead used by the automobile industry. Thus in the USA in 1924 the consumption of tetra ethyl lead in various types of petrol was less than a million pounds per annum; by 1968 the corresponding figure was 700 million pounds. Silcock, writing in the *Sunday Times* in April 1971, states that at present American vehicles discharge from their exhausts into the atmosphere approximately a quarter of a million tons of lead each year; in Britain with its smaller population and less widespread car ownership the corresponding figure is some 10,000 tons per annum.

We are exposed to contamination by lead not only through the air but also in our food and drink. Indeed it is estimated that our dietary intake of the metal may reach the figure of one third of a milligramme per day, and that this way well be in excess of the quantity which we inhale as a result of atmospheric pollution.

Studies on the Greenland icecap have demonstrated that

there are dangers of global contamination by lead. Such investigations were performed during the 1960's by a research team from the California Institute of Technology, and in the course of the work samples of snow and ice were analysed for their lead content using new and sophisticated techniques. It was concluded that between 800 BC and 1750 AD there had been a slow but steady rise in the content of lead deposited in the icecap. However, after 1750 a marked increase in the tempo of deposition took place, and between 1750 and 1940 amounts increased some four fold. Subsequent to 1940 the rise was even more spectacular and between that year and 1965 levels increased by approximately 300 per cent. What were the reasons behind this marked change? The proliferation of industrial activity probably accounted for the rise between 1750 and 1940, while between 1940 and 1965 the additional factor could well have been the abundance of automobiles.

Conditions near the South Pole also came under the scrutiny of the Californian research team. However, in this geographical location the results obtained were quite different. Lead levels were very low indeed, being actually less than those found in the Greenland icecap long before the 1st century AD. One of the most plausible theories offered for the contrast between Greenland and Antarctica is that lead smelting and motor car ownership, prime factors in lead contamination, are mainly activities of the Northern Hemisphere. So far the Southern Hemisphere has had the great good fortune of being shielded from this man-made type of pollution. The reasons behind its immunity are complex but it is probable that climatic factors have played the predominant role.

Water pollution by fluorides will be mentioned in Chapter V, but at this stage it is worth recalling that this element can also contaminate the air. Fluorides are liberated during the combustion of coal; they are widely used in the ceramics, aluminium and fertiliser industries and they are discharged during the smelting of iron and non-ferrous metals.

Fluorides can cause profound damage to plants because of their unfortunate propensity to concentrate the metal. Plants which are especially sensitive to fluoride intoxication include gladioli, apricots and peaches; the young needles of pines and other conifers are also very susceptible. Fluoride, particularly in gaseous form, makes its prime attack upon the leaves; like sulphur dioxide it prevents photosynthesis and eventually the cells of the leaf collapse and die. On the other hand, roots, stems and flowers are affected to a relatively small extent by the metal. Livestock in fluoride-contaminated areas ingest the metal in their forage. In small quantities it is beneficial to their bones and teeth. However, when large amounts are eaten deleterious effects such as mottling of teeth, retardation of growth, loss of weight, and in cattle, reduction of milk yields, are apt to make their appearance.

POLLUTION BY PARTICLES

Particulate pollution is both widespread and important. Larger particles such as dust, coarse dirt and flyash are usually solid; because of this they settle rapidly out of the air. Particles in fumes and smoke can be either solid or liquid; they are smaller in diameter, do not settle out of the atmosphere as do their larger brethren and tend to be blown around by the wind or by air currents. They consist mainly of carbon combined with tarry organic materials of a complex nature. Not infrequently they have a metallic component which may be silicon, aluminium, iron, copper, zinc, manganese or arsenic.

Three main sources of particulate pollution exist—*industrial activity, the motor car and domestic fuel consumption.* In the industrial field major offenders are iron, steel and cement mills, power plants and oil refineries. The industrial contribution to particulate pollution is enormous, and in the USA in the late 1960's such enterprises expelled into the atmosphere each year some three million tons of particulate matter along with one million tons of hydrocarbons. Automobile exhausts generally emit fine particles of small diameter; in the USA over a million tons of such pollutants reach the air each year in this way. Domestic heating particularly by coal makes a notable contribution; so does the incineration of garbage. Many of the ill effects of particulate pollution are produced by what are known as aerosols, these being clouds of fine solid or liquid particles. Acidic constituents of air pollution tend to be more dangerous when suspended in the form of aerosols. Car exhausts containing dissolved oxides of nitrogen pose special problems, as do aerosols emitted from industrial plants particularly if they contain oxides of sulphur and sulphuric acid.

Air transport too is contributing to particulate pollution, and the exhausts of modern jet aircraft are capable of pouring tons of these substances each year into the skies. The effects produced are naturally most noticeable in the vicinity of the world's large international airports, the numbers of which are increasing by leaps and bounds. Dr John Middleton, Commissioner of the US National Air Pollution Control Administration, has expressed anxiety that a very significant percentage of aircraft fuel is consumed within an altitude of 3,000 to 5,000 feet, this being an area of concern from the point of view of public health. Unhappily new pollution-free jet engines, although now available for commercial use, are being installed into aircraft at a rather slow rate. Perhaps the recent report that the US Attorney General has decided to prosecute 11 international airlines for polluting the air over New York City will speed the changeover to cleaner power units for jet airliners.

In the air over many industrial cities there is a cycle of particulate pollution throughout the 24 hours. Such a cycle has been noted, for example, in Tokyo, New York City, Los Angeles, San Francisco and London. The most frequent pattern is one in which there are low values for the pollution during the night with two daytime peaks, one in the early morning and the other in the late afternoon. However, such a cycle is by no means invariable. For example, in cities in which 24-hour shifts are worked and where there is little or no wind by night, the second daytime peak tends to make its appearance in the early rather than in the late afternoon.

New York City and Tokyo experience a peak of particulate pollution at about 8 a.m. On the other hand, Berkeley in California shows a somewhat smaller peak just before noon. The reason for the difference is not entirely clear, but could well be related to the fact that the first two cities burn coal as the mainspring of industry, while in Berkeley this fuel has now been mainly superseded by oil and natural gas. Many factors probably contribute to the daily fluctuations in particulate pollution. Sunlight is certainly important as is the degree of air turbulence. Working hours play their part, and since the introduction of the five-day week the cycle has become much less prominent at weekends than during weekdays. The season of year is also relevant especially in coal-burning areas where levels of particulate pollution may be two or three times higher in winter than in summer.

PHOTOCHEMICAL POLLUTION

This is also known as photochemical smog and, as mentioned earlier, it first came into prominence in Los Angeles in the 1940's. Since then it has spread widely and has been observed over many large industrial cities including San Francisco, New York, Baltimore, Philadelphia, London, Tokyo, São Paulo and Sydney.

Los Angeles remains the ideal geographical location for the development of photochemical pollution. Weather conditions favour it—there are frequent thermal inversions, there is windlessness and there is bright sunshine for much of the day. The outward manifestations of the pollution are the haze and decreasing visibility, much of this being due to the formation of aerosols. Foremost amongst the pollutants are oxides of nitrogen, hydrocarbons, aldehydes and a variety of aromatic substances. Complex chemical reactions take place in the atmosphere of a smog-invested city. Thus the gas, ozone, tends to be produced in excessive quantities as do ammonia and ammonium sulphate. Other toxic salts also make their appearance and especially prominent members of this coterie are compounds known as peroxyacetyl nitrates.

As with many other types of air pollution the motor car is a major factor in the genesis of photochemical smog. Oxides of nitrogen are formed during combustion at high temperatures. They are emitted from vehicle exhausts especially during the acceleration and cruising phases of automobile operation, and in Greater Los Angeles alone some 500 tons of such materials are produced in this manner each day. Industrial enterprises, especially power plants, are also conspicuous offenders although in the case of Los Angeles their contribution must rate second to that of the automobile.

Photochemical smog produces marked biological effects. In humans it can cause eye irritations and discomfort. Plant life suffers to a marked extent; growth is stunted, while leaves become stippled in appearance, wither and finally die. Trees are affected and in the mountains overlooking Los Angeles 100,000 acres of pines have been destroyed. Crop damage can be extensive. In California it is believed to amount of $8 million per annum, while on the eastern seaboard of the USA the cost may be in the region of £18 million. Various materials degenerate as a result of exposure to photochemical smog. Thus the stretching of rubber is impaired and the fading of dyes is hastened.

Los Angeles well merits the accolade of the world's capital of air pollution. The saga of Los Angeles also demonstrates with some clarity the major effect which overpopulation has played in this type of environmental contamination. During the last few decades there was a huge influx of people into southern California as part of the westward migration so typical of social trends in the modern USA. More people mean more industrial activity, more automobiles, more domestic heating, and as a corollary, more atmospheric pollution. Indeed the viewpoint that population density bears an intimate relationship to the degree of air pollution in Los Angeles receives support from the results of a health survey conducted in California during 1956. In this survey 70 per cent of those questioned in Greater Los Angeles admitted to being inconvenienced or palpably distressed by the presence of photochemical smog. On the other hand, in the Bay Area of San Francisco, a region where weather conditions are not dissimilar but where the overall population density is considerably less, only 25 per cent of the populace voiced similar complaints.

*   *   *

The earth is enclosed by an envelope of air. Which areas of our planet are worst affected by atmospheric pollution, for what diseases is it responsible in our fellow men and how can this form of environmental contamination be controlled? These will be the major themes of the next two chapters.

References

AMERICAN ASSOCIATION FOR THE ADVANCEMENT OF SCIENCE (1965). *Air Conservation*. A report of the Air Conservation Commission of the American Association for the Advancement of Science, Publication No. 80, Washington DC.

AGRICULTURAL RESEARCH COUNCIL (1967). *The Effects of Air Pollution on Plants and Soil.* London, HM Stationery Office.

ALBONE, ERIC S. (1971). 'Pollution of the Air'. In *Can Britain Survive?* Edited by GOLDSMITH, EDWARD. London, Tom Stacey, pp. 143-154.

ARVILL, ROBERT (1969). *Man and Environment.* London, Penguin Books, Ch. 6.

BARR, JOHN (1970). *The Assaults on our Senses.* London, Methuen, Ch. 6.

CARR, DONALD E. (1965). *The Breath of Life.* London, Gollancz.

EHRLICH, PAUL R. and HOLDREN, JOHN P. (1971). 'Overpopulation and the Potential for Ecocide': In *Global Ecology,* Edited by EHRLICH, PAUL R. and HOLDREN, JOHN P. New York, Chicago, San Francisco, Atlanta, Harcourt Brace Jovanovich Inc., pp. 64-78.

LEWIS, HOWARD R. (1965). *With Every Breath You Take.* New York, Crown Publishers Inc.

MAUNDER, W. J. (Editor) (1969). *Pollution; What it is, what it does, what can be done about it.* Canada, University of Victoria.

MEETHAM, A. R. (1964). *Atmospheric Pollution—its origins and prevention.* London, Pergamon.

MINISTRY OF TECHNOLOGY, WARREN SPRING LABORATORY (1967). *The Investigation of Atmospheric Pollution.* London, HM Stationery Office.

ROYAL COMMISSION ON ENVIRONMENTAL POLLUTION—First Report (1971). London, HM Stationery Office.

SILCOCK, BRYAN (1971). 'Lead Pollution at Crisis Point'. *Sunday Times,* 25th April.

STERN, A. C. (Editor) (1968). *Air Pollution.* New York and London, Academic Press, Vols I, II, III.

WORLD HEALTH ORGANISATION, MONOGRAPH SERIES (1961). *Air Pollution.* No. 46, Geneva.

II

AIR INTERNATIONAL

The North American Continent

Atmospheric pollution reaches its apogee in the United States. However, this is also the country which has the most advanced and sophisticated machinery for dealing with the problem.

Americans are now acutely aware of air pollution, and undoubtedly the space race and particularly the lunar landings have contributed to this national mood. Indeed the astronauts themselves have been amongst the most vociferous protesters against contamination of the air. Thus Walter Schirra in Apollo 7 is said to have been greatly distressed by the cloud of photochemical smog which he observed over Southern California and extending eastward for 100 miles from the coast, while his mate Donn Eisele was shocked to note that the smog had infiltrated into the clouds, and was reported to have been 'most discouraged' by the extent and magnitude of the pollution.

For the scale of air pollution in the USA is daunting. Each year more than 170 million tons of man-made products are unceremoniously dumped into the atmosphere, the figure being not far short of one ton for every man, woman and child inhabiting the country. The earth is believed to produce each year a total quantity of atmospheric pollutants amounting to 800 million tons. Accordingly, the USA with less than 6 per cent of the planet's population contributes over 20 per cent of its air pollution!

The US Public Health Service is now extremely conscious of the country's predicament. The organisation states that an air pollution problem of varying severity exists in every community which has a population in excess of 50,000; smaller towns can also show the characteristic symptoms if they are highly industrialised and if motor car ownership is particularly heavy. Three hundred cities in the USA, containing the homes of 43 million citizens or roughly one-third of the total urban population of the nation, are stated to suffer from a major degree of air pollution. The Federal Government has recently listed the most severely affected areas. Pride of place goes to New York followed closely by Chicago, Philadelphia, Los Angeles, Cleveland, Pittsburg, Boston, Newark, Detroit and St Louis. Apart from the obvious feature of high population density, three other factors have over the past decade contributed to the increasing tempo of atmospheric pollution in such cities. These are the rising demand for electric power, the proliferation of the automobile and the enhanced disposal of garbage by incineration.

New York City provides a unique example. Its demands for electricity are soaring, and much of the one-and-a-half million tons of sulphur dioxide liberated annually into the atmosphere over it is derived from power stations. The monopoly in this field is held by the Consolidated Edison Company. Like all industrial concerns it is wedded to a philosophy of economic growth exemplified in its case by the need to build more and more power plants. Such policies had an ironic outcome during 1970. Towards the end of that summer there was a heatwave, and a thermal inversion extended along the whole of the eastern seaboard of the USA. New York was the prime target and soon the city found itself in the grip of a dense photochemical smog. As always under such circumstances automobiles had made a significant contribution; so much so that at one stage the Mayor, John Lindsay, came near to banning motor traffic from the centre of the city. However, at the root of the dilemma lay the activities of Consolidated Edison. The heatwave had been intense; it had caused domestic air conditioning plants to be used to their maximum capacity, and as a result there was widespread air pollution. But now another factor was added. Demand for electricity still exceeded supply and this occurred in spite of frantic attempts of Consolidated Edison to obtain electricity from as far away as Canada and Tennessee. So to the distress and potential health hazard caused by the photo-chemical smog there was added the further irritation of widespread power cuts. Was there a solution? Consolidated Edison had no doubt what the answer should be. More power plants must be constructed in order to contain demand and prevent further electricity cuts. But in reality the situation was much more complex, for the construction of such plants would merely exacerbate the already critical situation with respect to atmospheric pollution. A vicious circle specific for the latter part of the twentieth century had been created in New York City, and the analogy of the dog chasing its tail would not come amiss. Policies of growthmanship and technological wizardry had failed to provide solutions to the problem; nor are they likely to do in the future for New York and for other cities destined to be afflicted in a similar manner.

Other American conurbations show a high degree of air pollution. In Chicago, 25,000 tons of contaminants are liberated daily into the air, in Los Angeles 15,000 tons (including 1,000 tons of carbon monoxide), in Detroit 5,000 tons and in Buffalo 3,000 tons. Photochemical smog is no longer restricted to Los Angeles. Many other cities now show it even those such as San Francisco and Washington DC, which formerly prided themselves on their scenic beauty. In Denver, Colorado, views of the Rocky Mountains were once a feature of the city much admired by its inhabitants; now the panorama is frequently dimmed by haze. Tucson, Arizona, is renowned throughout the western part of the USA as a health resort. Now its air is polluted mainly as a result of the activities of the mining industry which has established itself in close proximity. The Tucson of yore was an ideal place in which to convalesce from heart disease and from conditions affecting the respiratory tract. Now the quality of the air has become impaired and the invalids have taken flight.

The smog of Los Angeles is legion. It has become almost continuous and can readily be observed in adjoining states such as Nevada and Arizona. Local radio stations in Los Angeles keep a watchful eye on the air; they act as policemen, warning of rising levels of air pollution and advising parents to keep their children indoors at such times. The city of St Louis was blanketed by smog for four consecutive days in August 1969; during this time dangerously high levels of atmospheric pollu-

tants were detected, and these made their appearance in spite of
the fact that the municipality had adhered strictly to recommended control procedures. In November of the same year
smog of a very similar type affected the general area of Chicago,
while in 1970 other major cities were likewise invested. Even far
off Hawaii, once described by Mark Twain as 'the loveliest fleet
of islands that lies anchored in any ocean' is not immune, its
capital Honolulu having been stricken by the malady. The days
have gone forever when the pilot of the jet aircraft bound for
Honolulu must carefully check his instruments and consult his
navigator in order to ascertain when he is approaching his
destination. He can now see the city from afar, enveloped as it
is in a murky pall of atmospheric pollution.

Some American authorities believe that in addition to
contaminating the air over cities and destroying general
amenity, protracted air pollution can in certain areas irrevers-
ibly alter the weather. Thus in Tulsa, Oklahoma, annual rainfall
has risen over the past 70 years, and its rate of increase has been
proportional to the rise in particulate pollution over that city.
Conversely, in cities such as Pittsburg, Louisville and Buffalo,
the closure of industrial complexes has been shown to be
associated with a diminution in the rainfall.

All are agreed that the automobile has played a Mephis-
tophelean role in the genesis of atmospheric pollution in the
USA. On a nationwide scale it accounts for 60 per cent of the
contamination. However, regional variations are also important.
For example, in Los Angeles where the car reigns supreme, 90
per cent of the pollution is derived from this source, while in
Buffalo, where industrial activities are pre-eminent, its contribution drops to 25 per cent. Ninety million tons of pollutants
especially substances such as carbon monoxide, hydrocarbons,
oxides of nitrogen and lead, are discharged each year into the
atmosphere by American cars; moreover, the total is rising
annually as car ownership reaches even greater heights. Who in
the USA will provide the threnody for the internal combustion
engine when it ultimately disappears from our planet? Certainly
not those to whom the environment is a precious and
non-renewable heritage.

The United Kingdom

The British scene with respect to atmospheric pollution differs markedly from that of the USA. In general it is better; in patches it is as bad or even worse. Our weather conditions tend to militate against a high degree of air pollution and in particular, the absence of strong sunshine provides us with some protection against the photochemical smog now so commonplace in many US cities. Moreover, we lack high mountain ranges such as the Rockies, and skyscrapers are not a major feature of our urban areas. The last two factors are of considerable importance because due to them atmospheric pollutants tend to become dispersed and are prevented from concentrating themselves in specific areas. As already noted in Chapter I the British authorities have for many years monitored atmospheric levels of smoke and sulphur dioxide at various sites. The decade of the 1960's saw a marked intensification of this process.

Even the most ardent doomwatcher is forced to admit that the overall situation with respect to air pollution has markedly improved in Britain over the past 15 years. The catalyst for this improvement was undoubtedly the passage into law of the Clean Air Act of 1956 which, amongst other provisions, called for the establishment of smokeless zones over industrial areas. Local authorities varied greatly in their response to the provisions of the Act. In the South Eastern region of England and particularly in Greater London the reaction was both rapid and effective, and this has been the part of the country in which the most striking betterment has taken place. However, in other regions notably in the dreary mining towns of the North of England and Scotland, the response of local authorities has been much more sluggish with the result that many cities in these areas, for example Middlesborough, Newcastle and Glasgow, still show a marked degree of air pollution with smoke as the major offender.

The improvements of the past two decades can be directly attributed to the striking drop in the overall amounts of smoke liberated into the atmosphere over the British Isles. For example in the London area smoke concentrations fell by a factor of three between 1958 and 1968. Moreover, the relative contributions of the sources responsible for smoke pollution have altered significantly. Thus in 1953 rather more than half of the smoke belched into the air came from domestic chimneys; industry contributed one-third, and surprisingly enough, railways were responsible for one-sixth. In 1968 the pattern had changed out of all recognition. Domestic chimneys were now responsible for 80 per cent of the pollution; the contribution of industry had fallen to 20 per cent and railways had been completely eliminated because diesel and electric locomotives had replaced the steam engines of bygone days. The reduction in atmospheric pollution has proceeded *pari passu* with the increasing use of smokeless fuels both in industry and in the home. Unfortunately, however, the rosy picture with respect to smokeless fuels may not be maintained, for in recent times, supplies of such materials have been considerably depleted, and if the deficit is not made good and other types of fuel have to be burnt serious environmental contamination could result.

What has been the saga of sulphur dioxide, that other stubborn air pollutant so typical of the British scene? During the past few years the overall rate of liberation of the gas into the atmosphere has remained relatively static and, if anything, levels have tended to decrease. However, black spots still remain, and London is one of them for the concentration of sulphur dioxide in its streets is almost double that of smoke-laden Middlesborough, Newcastle and Glasgow. An encouraging feature with respect to sulphur dioxide has been the sharp fall (amounting to 40 per cent between 1958 and 1968) which has taken place in the air which we breathe at ground level. This has mainly been due to better dispersal of the gas in the atmosphere, and here the construction of taller chimneys has probably played a major part. However, the increasing dispersal of the gas could have unforeseen effects. Sulphur dioxide is converted in the atmosphere into sulphates, and this could be one of the reasons for the production of 'acid rain' which is reported to be falling in increasing quantities in Scandinavia and other parts of Europe.

The improvement in air pollution in some of Britain's major industrial cities is to be greatly welcomed. However, it should certainly not lead to a mood of complacency, and unfortunately there is already evidence of such a reaction in some quarters. Three points are made by those who are traditionally euphoric and to whom the sun rises and sets on London. The first is that pollution by particulate matter has greatly diminished over our capital city in recent years; the second is that some 125 different kinds of birds have recently been identified within the confines of London. The third refers to the condition of the Thames and emphasises the return of certain types of fish to the river as a result of pollution abatement measures. These views frequently receive publicity in the national press, and could well lead to the assumption that Britain does not face an environmental problem of large dimension. However, in spite of the rhetoric, London is not Britain. Indeed it is far from typical of the United Kingdom as a whole, and an overall judgment based on such restricted and parochial criteria can only be deplored.

The European Continent and the USSR

Over much of the land mass of Europe there hangs the pall of air pollution. Destiny has decreed that the countries of the European Economic Community will experience it, for, after all, a prime purpose of the Community is to increase economic growth and as will be stressed later in this essay, such a policy can lead only in the long term to increasing pollution of air, water and land. Until quite recently there was great apathy in Western Europe with respect to the control of air contamination. Now there are stirrings. For example, the government of Federal Germany is currently monitoring a number of air pollutants and is stated to be especially worried about the emission of lead salts from automobile exhausts, while recently the world's press has carried reports that Italy, France, the Netherlands and Belgium are preparing to attempt to counteract growing air pollution in their cities.

The need for such control in Western Europe is clamant, for air pollution is widespread, although as yet it has not reached the formidable proportions characteristic of the United States. The air over the vast industrial complex of the Ruhr is now contaminated with a host of chemical substances and more recently industrial cities in Northern Italy and in the Po Valley have been similarly affected. Quite soon Western Europe could experience a photochemical smog similar in degree to that routinely observed by the citizens of Los Angeles. Indeed the prodromata for the malady have already made their appearance for during 1968 a combination of bright summer sunshine and gaseous pollutants in the atmosphere produced over part of the Netherlands a facsimile of the Californian scene. Undoubtedly many cities within the European Economic Community will ultimately prove vulnerable to this type of environmental contamination, Paris and Milan being amongst those especially susceptible because of their climatic conditions.

Greece is not yet a member of the European Common Market although she has aspirations for such an association. But, even now, Greece has a major problem with respect to atmospheric pollution. Indeed the Greek Chamber of Technology views the situation with much gravity and even goes so far as to state that unless appropriate remedial action is taken swiftly, the city of Athens might have to be abandoned within 10 years! This is certainly an alarmist prophecy and time will tell whether or not it will be fulfilled. However, already there is a haze and worsening visibility in Athens with the result that the view of the Acropolis from the centre of the city is frequently obscured.

                              *   *   *

The Europe of the early 1970's still remains split into two camps separated by the ideological barrier of the Iron Curtain. How do the Marxist countries behind that curtain fare in the sphere of atmospheric pollution? Information is somewhat meagre, but it is sufficient to enable us to conclude that, as in the capitalist West, air pollution poses a major threat to the environment.

Slovakia was the birth place of Alexander Dubcek that most undogmatic of communists; it is also the industrial heart of the

Czechoslovak state. Here a soft variety of brown coal is burned extensively, and because of this there is much air pollution arising mainly from smoke and sulphur dioxide. Industrial areas of Poland and of the German Democratic Republic still rely to a major extent on coal as a source of energy and as a result atmospheric pollution is prominent. The powerful propaganda machine of the Soviet Union congratulates itself on the fact that the air of Moscow is much sweeter than that of any comparable capital city in the West. The point may well be valid, but almost certainly dialectical considerations have had little or no part to play. Two major factors have operated to preserve the integrity of Moscow's air; the first is that the concentration of heavy industry in that city is not unduly high and the second is that as compared with Western capitals, the incidence of motor car ownership remains low. But Moscow is a somewhat special case and it is probable that most major Soviet cities have an air pollution problem. Thermal inversions are common in Tiblisi which is affected by smog for 6 out of the 12 months. The daylight in Leningrad is said to be 40 per cent less than in nearby Pavlosk, while in several Armenian cities for example Erevan, the quantity of carbon monoxide in the atmosphere exceeds the norms established by the Ministry of Health.

Countries in the Eastern bloc have legislated in an attempt to curb air pollution. Thus in the Soviet Union, Poland, Czechoslovakia and Rumania criteria for air quality were introduced some years ago. It could be argued that the Marxist type of government makes it easier to enact such laws as the state is the sole owner of plants and factories. However, Goldman, writing in *The Ecologist* in 1970, states that the Soviet government has been slow to deal with air pollution and that of all the factories acknowledged to be a source of this form of contamination only 14 per cent are fully equipped and 26 per cent partially equipped with facilities for purification.

Asia and Other Areas of the World

In the Third World of Asia, Africa and Latin America, industrialisation is on an exiguous scale as compared with that of the West. For most people affluence is a figment of the imagination and as a result the incidence of motor car ownership is low.

Nevertheless air pollution is present in many parts of the Third World. However, when one compares its place in the hierarchy of social ills with such overwhelming problems as overpopulation, rampant urbanisation, grinding poverty and near starvation, it pales into insignificance. It is therefore a matter of no surpise that the governments of the under-developed world place air pollution low on their list of priorities and show little or no interest in enforcing legislation designed to curb it. A major source of atmospheric contamination in the Third World is domestic heating. The cold of oriental and tropical nights can sometimes be severe; if coal is not available to warm the homes of the inhabitants then dried animal excreta are used, this practice being especially widespread in Asia and Africa. Unfortunately, animal dung, in addition to generating smoke, has a high sulphur content. Indeed its incineration on a large scale is thought to contribute markedly to the contamina-tion of the air over cities such as Singapore, Rangoon, Saigon, Bangkok, Calcutta, Bombay, Karachi and New Delhi.

Japan's situation is unique in Asia. The country is rich, technologically advanced, and its government takes pride in its burgeoning economic growth rate; Japan has also one of the most serious and intractable air pollution problems anywhere on earth. The mixture is as before, heavy industrialisation, a high population density and ever-increasing automobile owner-ship interacting to befoul the atmosphere. The industrialisation of Japan began in earnest during the American occupation of the country in the years immediately following the Second World War. Then in the early 1960's cheap Middle Eastern oil laden with sulphur replaced coal as the major source of industrial energy; soon it was being burnt widely in homes throughout the country. Since then the practice has resulted in the liberation into the atmosphere of 1.7 million tons of pollutants annually, a major constituent being sulphur dioxide.

Japan is also heavily overpopulated. This situation has arisen in spite of the fact that the country has had a liberal abortion law for over two decades and that in recent years the overall reaction of society to large families has been antagonistic. The current population density of the country (277 persons per square kilometre) ranks sixth in the list of nations, while Greater Tokyo with a population reputed to exceed 20 million is now the world's largest city. As numbers increase *pari passu* with living standards so car ownership soars, and in Tokyo at present there are said to be over 200,000 vehicles on the roads.

The Japanese scenario was inexorably set for an air pollution disaster, and sure enough, dramatic events occurred during the summer of 1970. Then Tokyo experienced a Los Angeles type of photochemical smog and was blanketed in a pall of atmospheric pollution for several days. Newspaper reports stated that the smog was of a particularly noxious variety containing as it did relatively large amounts of sulphur dioxide and sulphuric acid. Conditions in the city came to resemble those obtaining during the Second World War when air raid warnings were commonplace. Radio stations and television networks put out frequent announcements; loudspeaker vans toured the city ordering people to stay indoors and advising motorists either to abandon their cars or to leave them at home. Children were warned not to play out of doors for fear of contracting respiratory infections. Thousands had to be treated in hospitals for sore throats and eye complaints. Birds and animals dying in Tokyo Zoo during the episode were shown at post-mortem to have completely blackened lungs. There was a brisk trade in small portable oxygen generators. The trade was especially profitable amongst policemen on traffic duty who found it necessary to leave their posts at frequent intervals, inhale the gas, and thus attempt to cleanse their lungs of noxious pollutants.

Does the future hold out any prospect of amelioration for Tokyo? Not if one believes the Director of the Pollution Research Centre. He is frankly pessimistic. He predicts that pollution will increase 500 fold during the next 10 years and he foresees the day when pedestrians will carry gas masks as naturally as umbrellas!

Air Pollution—Taming the Tiger

There are now a multiplicity of highly specialised textbooks devoted to the control of air pollution, and obviously a detailed consideration of this highly complex topic would be inappropriate in this essay. The rest of this chapter will merely attempt to stress how sophisticated the science of air pollution has become and to mention briefly how the legislative machinery in some countries is attempting to grapple with the problem.

Industry is now in the forefront of research designed to preserve the quality of the air, and as a result scientists with a specialised training in this type of engineering are eagerly sought after both by private companies and by state-run organisations. Through the labours of such individuals a wealth of new technology has quite suddenly erupted as methods of manufacture and processes of combustion of fuels have come under ever increasing scrutiny.

There are numerous examples of technological progress in this field. For instance novel devices have been introduced to burn complex end products and so to render them harmless, to trap, separate and concentrate dust droplets and gases from the main exhaust flow, and to improve the dispersion of pollutants into the atmosphere. Facilities now exist for disposing of the concentrated materials so obtained, and not infrequently the profits accruing to the firm as a result of the resale of such products may more than compensate for the financial outlay involved in controlling the pollution. Good examples of worthwhile by-products obtained in this way are lead dust produced during the melting of scrap metal and hydrogen sulphide generated during the processing of gas and oil; even as apparently useless an item as flyash, obtained from electricity generating stations, is now being increasingly used in road making and in the building industry. A particularly heavy frontal attack has been mounted by large-scale commercial enterprises on pollution by particulate matter, and this operation, at least in some parts of the world, has met with striking success. Industry has also devoted time and energy to a study of noxious gases particularly sulphur dioxide, nitrogen oxides and carbon monoxide. Here, however, economic factors have loomed largely because these substances are generally present in quantities much smaller than is the case for particulate matter with the result that the costs of their removal are correspondingly increased.

Air pollution produced by motor vehicles has been constantly referred to in preceding pages, and its paramount importance in the genesis of photochemical smog and other types of atmospheric pollution has been repeatedly stressed. Emissions from automobiles are derived from two main sources—the exhaust and the crankcase. Proud automobile owners all over the world may be surprised to learn that the intrinsic efficiency of the petrol engine is not particularly high; in fact this is one of the major reasons for the air pollution produced. Between 5 and 7 per cent of the fuel is wasted and passes directly into the exhaust; 20 per cent blows past the pistons and into the crankcase while $1\frac{1}{2}$ per cent is lost by evaporation from the fuel tank and carburettor. But this is not the whole story for levels of exhaust pollution depend greatly on the mode of operation of the vehicle. Thus under conditions of full throttle and rapid acceleration, fuel combustion is reasonably complete and air pollution is slight; on the other hand when the engine of the car is 'idling', as it is forced to do in severe traffic congestion in cities, atmospheric pollution is at its maximum.

Techniques having as their aim the clean up of automobile exhausts have been under intensive scrutiny in recent years. This has been especially so in the USA where the Federal Government has shown increasing anxiety about the whole question of environmental pollution. Modifications to the petrol engine have now been devised. These include the technique of fuel injection designed to improve carburation, variable spark timing, and the redesigning of combustion chambers so that the engine fuel can be used more completely. Indeed the claim has recently been made that automobile manufacturers in Detroit, working in association with an oil company, have produced a prototype of automobile which is virtually pollution free. Unfortunately, the time interval elapsing between the development of such a vehicle and its introduction into general use is likely to be protracted, and accordingly, the 'dirty' unaesthetic car models of today are likely to remain with us for many years to come.

Lead is a highly toxic metal, injurious to man (see Chapter III). It increases the 'anti knock' properties of petrol along with its octane rating, and in its absence engine performance is notably impaired. If lead were eliminated from petrol, the octane rating of the fuel could still be restored by additional refining; however, this would almost certainly increase costs, and in Britain the price of petrol could rise by at least 1p per gallon. Here one has an example of the familiar situation in which it is necessary to strike a balance between economic considerations and the threat of a possible health hazard. Up to this point in history economic considerations have invariably triumphed. Unless a profound alteration in human attitudes takes place the process is likely to repeat itself in the case of the automobile.

Although the great majority of motor cars are propelled by the petrol engine, other types of transport rely on diesel engines. In this group are included heavy lorries and buses, together with certain types of locomotives and boats. The main pollutants emitted by diesel engines are oxides of nitrogen and unburnt hydrocarbons; however, relative to the petrol engine, the amount of carbon monoxide discharged by diesels is small. To many of us diesel exhausts are highly unattractive, and pedestrians and other road users object to them because of the large amounts of smoke which they liberate. Furthermore, the sickly sweet odour typical of their discharge and thought to be due to the presence of aldehydes, is much resented. However, perhaps we have been unduly critical of diesel engines because in terms of atmospheric pollution, they are certainly a much less baneful influence than is the petrol engine. Moreover, the efficiency of the diesel engine is superior to that of the latter, and indeed it is one of the best methods known for converting thermal energy into mechanical work. Pollution from diesel exhausts can readily be reduced by quite simple measures, these including good maintenance and efficient carburation. Legislation designed to make this type of care mandatory is long overdue.

Many authorities now aver that the days of the petrol engine are numbered. But what will take its place? Herein lies the dilemma, because research into alternative sources of traction remains at a very rudimentary stage. However, some suggestions have been offered. For example, the possibility of using electrically powered vehicles with batteries or overhead cables is currently being explored. Such a development would entail the generation of enormous amounts of electricity and its cost could well be prohibitive. An automobile powered by fuel cells is now on the drawing board but at present such a vehicle is a dream rather than a reality. However, even if the concept came to fruition it is already apparent that there would be complications, for unless the appropriate machine was meticulously maintained and serviced, the emission of pollutant gases might pose difficulties already all too familiar in the case of the internal combustion engine.

*   *   *

International agreement on standards which should be adopted to control air pollution is essential for it is now generally agreed that this type of contamination is increasing throughout the planet and that unless remedial action is taken, the health of the populace could suffer. The World Health Organisation has expressed its concern about the current situation and has selected six pollutants for intensive international study; these are sulphur dioxide, particulate matter, carbon monoxide, photochemical oxidants, nitrogen oxides and lead. The investigations sponsored by the WHO have three main aims in view—to pinpoint the areas of the earth which show the highest degree of air pollution, to determine the levels in the atmosphere at which pollutants begin to affect human health, and to establish recognised standards and criteria for the quality of the air. Unfortunately, as frequently occurs in such exercises, individual nations have been sluggish in following WHO's lead. Thus in the Western world only the USA and Federal Germany have adopted what would be generally regarded as satisfactory criteria for air quality, while in the Eastern bloc such standards have been introduced only in respect of the Soviet Union,

Poland, Rumania and Czechoslovakia. However, the situation could well change rapidly, and at the time of writing, there are reports in the world press that countries such as Italy, France, Belgium, Greece, Japan, India, South Africa and Australia are preparing to counteract growing air pollution, if necessary by legislative action. Chapter III of this book will indicate that controversy still exists as to the precise role played by air pollution in the genesis of disease in man, and until information on this important subject becomes more definite many governments are reluctant to authorise the expenditure of the large sums of money which would inevitably be required.

*   *   *

The USA and the UK are two countries which recognise the existence of an air pollution problem, and which, admittedly with slow and faltering steps, have endeavoured to mitigate it. The remainder of this chapter gives a brief account of some of the measures which their legislative systems have introduced.

The dynamic towards the control of air pollution in the USA gained momentum in the 1960's; prior to that decade little was achieved. Traditionally legislation against atmospheric pollution in the USA is enforced at a local level through city or country ordinances. The record of such ordinances has generally been poor and often they have been singularly ineffective. The city of St Louis provides a good example of the intractable nature of the problem. Here there has been continuous local agitation since the mid-1920's with the formation of smoke abatement societies. Nevertheless, in spite of this well-merited concern air pollution is still rampant, and during 1969 and 1970 St Louis experienced heavy bouts of photochemical smog.

Of all the states of the Union, California has taken the lead in attempting to combat air pollution. This attitude is understandable because of the transcendent nature of the problem in that part of the country. Over the years the Californian state legislature has drawn up a whole series of standards of air quality and pollutant emission and has made herculean efforts to grapple with the rapidly escalating pollution from vehicle exhausts. A three-tier structure for standards of air quality has been introduced. According to this classification 'adverse' levels produce sensory irritation, especially of the eyes, damage to vegetation and a reduction in visibility; 'serious' levels cause alterations in bodily functions and could well be responsible for various types of chronic disease, while 'emergency' levels produce the symptoms of acute illness in susceptible individuals and may even lead to death. Sulphur dioxide has been monitored in this way: its 'adverse' level has been fixed at 1 part per million for 1 hour, its 'serious' level at 5 parts per million and its 'emergency' level at double that figure. Standards for contaminants liberated from car exhausts have been adopted and the state refuses to register cars emitting higher levels than the standards. Unfortunately, the law applies only to new cars just off the production line and does not affect those already licensed and registered. Obviously any gains which may accrue from the legislation will be of a long rather than a short-term nature.

In recent years the US Federal Government has thrown its weight behind measures designed to control air pollution. It has put pressure on the individual states of the Union to enact appropriate legislation and it has made funds available for the promotion of research in this general field. The Clean Air Act of 1963 provided for a marked increase of Federal expenditure in the form of grants to local air pollution control agencies; it also encouraged close collaboration amongst various state legislatures with a view to co-ordinating the programme in its totality. The Air Quality Act of 1967 set up machinery designed to establish standards for air throughout the nation. However, it also insisted that such standards could only be adopted after the desires of the local populace as well as of local industrial concerns had been fully taken into account! In the USA the road to the Olympus of clean air will be long and arduous; however, at least it can be said that the Federal Government has now recognised that a problem of atmospheric pollution exists and that by its actions it has expressed its willingness to attempt to do something about it.

*   *   *

Great Britain was the first country in the world to enact legislation against air pollution, and between 1863 and 1906 a series of Alkali Acts (now known as Alkali etc. Works Regulation Acts) reached the statute book. These were originally designed to curb pollution by hydrogen chloride, a substance produced during the manufacture of sodium carbonate. Subsequently, the Acts were extended to include a whole variety of other industrial pollutants, and today enterprises such as chemical and cement works, ore smelting plants, iron and steel factories, power stations, gas works and oil refineries must be registered under the current Act. Registration certificates have to be renewed annually, and to enforce the Act there exists a highly qualified group of chemists and chemical engineers known as the Alkali Inspectorate. At present there are 26 such inspectors in England and Wales grouped in districts and responsible to the Minister for the Environment; in Scotland there are four inspectors responsible to the Secretary of State. In 1969, 412 complaints about air pollution emanated from local authorities and from other bodies. These were investigated by the Alkali Inspectorate; in 24 cases an infraction of the Act was deemed to have taken place, but in all but two of these infractions, appropriate remedies were taken without recourse to the courts.

The Alkali Acts were not originally intended to control pollution by smoke, which as noted earlier, had traditionally been much the most widespread and damaging air pollutant in Britain. Before the 1950's the control of smoke pollution was enforced through a series of Public Health Acts; these were administered by local authorities and were generally quite ineffectual in dealing with this type of nuisance. Then the great London smog of 1952 occurred and in the course of this 4,000 people died. Organisations such as the National Smoke Abatement Society made violent protests, and eventually the Conservative Government of the day established a Committee under the chairmanship of Sir Hugh Beaver to examine the whole question of air pollution.

The progeny resulting from the deliberations of the Beaver Committee was the Clean Air Act of 1956. The latter dealt mainly with smoke, and one of its stipulations was that 'dark smoke may not be emitted from a chimney of any building'. It was also concerned with the minimum height of chimneys in industrial practice, and it forbade new furnaces to be installed in industrial plants unless these were capable of operating continuously without emitting smoke. However, the Act will always be remembered for the power which it gave to local authorities to declare areas under their jurisdiction to be 'smokeless zones', and hence to designate the emission of smoke from the chimney of any building in that area as an offence. The Clean Air Act had obvious limitations. Pollutants other than smoke received little or no attention; nor did the motor car which in recent years has become a prime source of atmospheric contamination. Now further legislation in this area is needed because we live in an era of rising car ownership. Indeed if the internal combustion engine has not undergone significant modification by the early years of the twenty-first century, it is likely that by that time the amount of carbon monoxide liberated from the exhausts of our automobiles will have risen from its present 6 million to 14 million tons per annum.*

Much remains to be done in the UK in the field of air pollution. Better monitoring programmes for individual pollutants are required; further research is needed into the relationship between air pollutants and human disease, and special attention must be given to areas of the country in which local authority measures designed to curb atmospheric contamination have failed or have proved inadequate. The Government of the day must keep a watchful eye on the overall situation and must, if necessary, be prepared to act in the best interests of the community. If it fails to do so the improvement in the quality of the air over our islands which we have so laboriously won over the years will prove to be ephemeral and will melt like the snow with the advent of spring.

* This estimate could, of course, be quite academic if, as suggested in Chapter VIII, world oil supplies are exhausted by the early years of the twenty-first century.

40 THE DEATH OF TOMORROW

References

ALBONE, ERIC (1970). 'The Ailing Air'. *The Ecologist,* 1, No. 3, pp. 4-9.
AMERICAN ASSOCIATION FOR THE ADVANCEMENT OF SCIENCE
(1965). *Air Conservation.* A report of the Air Conservation Commission
of the American Association for the Advancement of Science,
Publication No. 80, Washington DC.
BARR, JOHN (1970). *The Assaults on our Senses.* London, Methuen, Ch.
6.
CROSBIE, A. J. (1970). 'How much air should we spoil?'. *Scotsman,* 17th
February.
EHRLICH, PAUL R. and EHRLICH, ANNE (1970). *Population,
Resources, Environment.* San Francisco, W. H. Freeman and Co.
GILPIN, ALAN (1963). *Control of Air Pollution.* London, Butterworth.
GOLDMAN, MARSHALL (1970). 'Russian Roulette, Environmental
Disruption in the Soviet Union'. *The Ecologist,* 1, No. 6, pp. 18-23.
HAWKES, NIGEL (Editor) (1971). 'The air we breathe'. *Daily Telegraph
Magazine,* 28th May.
HORNIG, ROBERTA and WELSH, JAMES (1970). 'A World in Danger'.
Washington Star, 11th to 18th January.
KELF-COHN, R. (1970). 'The smokeless fuel mystery'. *Daily Telegraph,*
29th July.
MAUNDER, W. J. (Editor) (1969). *Pollution; What it is, what it does,
what can be done about it.* Canada, University of Victoria.
MEETHAM, A. R. (1964). *Atmospheric Pollution—its origins and preven-
tion.* London, Pergamon.
ONE HUNDREDTH AND SIXTH ANNUAL REPORT OF ALKALI, ETC.
WORKS ACT 1969 (1970). London, HM Stationery Office.
ROYAL COMMISSION ON ENVIRONMENTAL POLLUTION—First
Report (1971). London, HM Stationery Office.
SMITH, PETER (1971). 'Japan: economic dream, ecological nightmare'.
The Ecologist, 1, No. 18, pp. 16-19.
THE TIMES (1970). 'The Polluters—Clean Air? We don't believe in it'.
25th March.
WORLD HEALTH ORGANISATION (1963). *Air Pollution, a survey of
existing legislation.* Geneva, WHO.
ZORZA, VICTOR (1970). 'A big stink in Russia'. *Guardian,* 11th
February.

III

MALADIES OF THE AIR

He went up to London, and took a great Cold etc., which he could never afterwards claw off again.

John Evelyn, *Fumifugium,* 1661 AD

Inflation has been labelled the British disease; but so also has chronic bronchitis, for the latter has traditionally been one of the major causes of death and morbidity in our islands. Each year chronic bronchitis costs us over £65 million due to losses in industrial production and the costs of medical care. The death rate from chronic bronchitis each year totals 30,000; in 1967 it caused 6.8 per cent of all male and 2.6 per cent of all female deaths.

Chronic bronchitis and the associated condition, emphysema, develop slowly and insidiously over a long period of time. First there is a persistent and hacking cough with the production of purulent spit. Then breathlessness makes its appearance and becomes progressively more disabling. Finally the heart fails, chronic invalidism supervenes and death ensues.

Air pollution undoubtedly plays an important role in the genesis of chronic bronchitis, and during the great London smog of 1952 the disease struck with unprecedented force. It had its impact mainly on the aged, many of whom died prematurely. But younger groups were also affected, so much so that in that year the number of people under the age of 45 dying from diseases of the respiratory tract was three times higher than normal.

When the content of smoke and sulphur dioxide in the atmosphere rises the incidence of chronic bronchitis follows the same trend, and there are many examples from the British scene and elsewhere testifying to this association. For instance, in the Second World War postmen in London who suffered from bronchitis were shown to be much more likely to be absent from work whenever fog and smoke blanketed the city and reduced the visibility to below 1,000 metres; in the same city the demand for hospital beds for patients with chest diseases traditionally soars during periods of air pollution. In the industrial centre of Salford near Manchester absence from work due to chronic bronchitis mounts with increasing concentrations of smoke in the atmosphere. Children in England and Wales have higher death rates from respiratory diseases, particularly chronic bronchitis, than do their counterparts anywhere else in Northern Europe; indeed their mortality figures are approximately double those of the Scandinavian countries. The reason for the discrepancy is not far to seek, our miasmic air and especially the dreary smokiness of our industrial cities being mainly responsible.

In the countryside the air is cleaner than in cities, and it would therefore be reasonable to expect that chronic bronchitis would be less prevalent in rural than in city dwellers. This viewpoint derives some support from the available evidence, although it has to be admitted that the differences between the two groups are not particularly striking. However, death rates from bronchitis are considerably higher amongst the unskilled working classes than in professional people, and one of the main reasons for this difference could well be the propensity of the latter group, due to their relative affluence, to eschew grimy and smoky cities as their places of residence. Cigarette smoking receives attention later; however, at this stage it is worth stressing that the practice has a malign effect on those already afflicted with chronic bronchitis, increasing the severity of the condition and decreasing the lifespan of the patient.

Chronic bronchitis and emphysema are the diseases in which the causative effects of air pollution are most pronounced. However, in the case of pneumonia a similar type of relationship also exists, and it is known that in London death rates from this condition tend to rise when there are prolonged periods of fog and when the weather is cold. The nigger in the woodpile in the case of lung cancer is undoubtedly the cigarette, a fact which has been sternly—almost brutally—re-emphasised in a recent report from the Royal College of Physicians of London. What role, if any, does air pollution play in the causation of lung cancer? Here expert opinion reserves judgment, and the Physicians' report is a model of discretion when it states that 'some element in the British urban environment seems to produce in those sufficiently exposed to it an increased liability to developing cancer'. The nature of the 'urban factor' remains mysterious; it is still an elusive will o'the wisp, and some aver that it may not even be an air pollutant.

The introduction of smokeless zones in Britain as recommended in the Clean Air Act of 1956 has been of great benefit in the fight against chronic bronchitis and other respiratory complaints. In Chapter II it was emphasised that the improvement has been especially marked in the southern and eastern regions of England where local authorities have shown a gratifying eagerness to comply with the provisions of the Act. The eagerness was duly rewarded. The winter of 1962 produced weather conditions not too dissimilar to those of the great London smog 10 years previously; the fog lasted for about the same length of time, and again there was a marked rise in the atmospheric content of sulphur dioxide. But there was one vital difference. In 1962 smokiness over the city was much less pronounced, and this could well be the reason why the death rate was only 700 as compared with over 4,000 10 years earlier.

*　　*　　*

When an attempt is made to correlate specific air pollutants with particular maladies, formidable difficulties are encountered. Throughout the practice of medicine we have become accustomed to equate cause and effect. Thus syphilis results from an infection with a specific type of spirochaete, tuberculosis from a bacterium, poliomyelitis from a virus, coronary thrombosis from the blockage of one of the blood vessels in the heart wall, and so on. But in the sphere of air pollution and disease the situation is much less clearcut. Indeed the whole subject is still at a very early stage of development and is undoubtedly one which will repay careful study in the future.

Research on air pollution and disease cannot be based on animal experimentation largely because of the well-nigh insuperable difficulties of extrapolating the findings in various animal species to the human situation. It is therefore necessary for us to direct our attention to man himself and our canvas of investigation must be broad. Thus we require to study large numbers of human subjects living under different environmental conditions and exposed to a variety of atmospheric pollutants. We require to delineate much more precisely than before the relationship of air pollution to smoking and in particular to determine why a combination of the two factors produces such deleterious effects on health. We require to tighten up our diagnostic criteria for the disease states known as chronic bronchitis and emphysema and to study the varying sympto- matology of these conditions from one country to another. Finally—and this could prove to be the toughest assignment of all—we require much more accurate methods than currently exist in order to measure the degree of atmospheric pollution to which a given individual is exposed. The air has thrown down the gauntlet to those whose interests lie in the field of environmental medicine. Will they grasp the nettle or will the problems be of such magnitude that they will defy solution?

*   *   *

When we breathe polluted air we can develop symptoms of illness. What do we currently know of the specific effects produced by individual pollutants?

SULPHUR COMPOUNDS
When sulphur dioxide is inhaled it irritates the tissues of the upper respiratory tract, constricts the fine air tubes in the lungs and produces a choking sensation. At concentrations of one part per million and below it produces little or no effect in healthy adults; however, even at that low level it can affect babies, children, the aged, and sufferers from chronic bron- chitis. Normal individuals exposed to five parts per million of sulphur dioxide for one hour generally complain of choking, while if the concentration rises to 10 parts per million for one hour they become severely distressed. In industrial practice the maximum 'permissible' limit for sulphur dioxide has been set at five parts per million; air over cities not infrequently contains levels of two parts per million.

Sulphur trioxide is always present in concentrations smaller than those of the dioxide; the gas readily combines with water to form sulphuric acid. Both in man and in experimental animals sulphur trioxide has been shown to be considerably more irritant than the dioxide causing choking sensations at much lower concentrations. 'Permissible' levels of sulphur trioxide in industrial practice and over urban areas remain to be established as do concentrations of sulphuric acid vapours. However, in spite of the lack of quantitative information, the dangers of exposure to sulphuric acid are not in doubt, and as indicated previously, it is believed that this substance played a major role in the air pollution disasters of the Meuse Valley, Donora and London.

CARBON MONOXIDE

This is a highly lethal gas, much favoured by those with suicidal intent. Car exhausts emit it in relatively large amounts and are likely to continue to do so until radical changes are made in the design of the internal combustion engine or until another form of traction is devised.

The toxicity of carbon monoxide mainly arises from the fact that it has a greater affinity for the blood pigment, haemoglobin, than has oxygen. Basically, carbon monoxide produces its effect by depriving body tissues of oxygen which is vital to their continued function. The heart reacts to this situation by attempting to increase the rate of blood flow throughout the body. This throws a considerable strain on the cardiac muscles and has prompted the suggestion that certain heart diseases, notably angina and coronary thrombosis, might be exacerbated in the presence of high blood levels of carbon monoxide. However, the heart is not the only organ affected. The brain shares in the intoxication, and it has now been demonstrated that inhalation of fumes from automobile exhausts can cause a generalised lack of mental alertness in drivers. In an era of burgeoning car ownership this must obviously be a potent cause for concern.

The 'permissible' level of carbon monoxide in industrial practice is 50 parts per million; in the air over urban areas a figure of 55 parts per million is often encountered. At levels of

100 parts per million most people experience dizziness, head-aches and lassitude; their mode of behaviour alters and their efficiency is notably impaired; at levels of 1,000 parts per million death occurs quite rapidly. In Los Angeles pollution by carbon monoxide has been given a status similar to that accorded to air raids during the Second World War; three levels of alert have been set—at concentrations of 100, 200 and 300 parts per million respectively. Californians do not leave their pollution at home. Instead they transport it with them, so much so that at the customs check-point at the border between California and Mexico atmospheric concentrations of carbon monoxide as high as 160 parts per million have been recorded, and customs officers searching the cars have been shown to have grossly elevated levels of the gas in their blood.

POLLUTANTS IN PHOTOCHEMICAL SMOG

Chapter I indicated that a variety of abnormal chemical substances were present in the air of smog-invested cities such as Los Angeles. There and elsewhere officials frequently express anxiety about the possibility that certain types of health hazard may result from such exposure. However, at present, it must be admitted that a correlation between specific chemical sub-stances and definite disease entities is difficult to discern.

Undoubtedly chronic eye irritations are common amongst the population of Southern California. Indeed, it is claimed that some two-thirds of the people of this region suffer in this way. Eye specialists are in great demand in California and many of them enjoy highly lucrative private practices. However, up till now, convincing evidence is lacking that any permanent visual damage results from exposure to the constituents of photo-chemical smog. Moreover, the actual chemical substances responsible for the eye irritation have yet to be delineated. The gas, ozone, was once thought to be the major culprit. However, in recent years this view has fallen out of favour, and expert opinion now inclines to the belief that the effects result from exposure to a mixture of substances including amongst their number formaldehyde, various types of peroxide and peroxy-acetyl nitrates.

Not only is nitrogen dioxide a poisonous gas; it is also a frequent constituent of photochemical smog. It can produce lung diseases in animals, and it is reported to have caused damage to the lungs of workmen in factories in the USSR. In industrial practice the 'safe' limit for nitrogen dioxide is generally placed at five parts per million; however some authorities question this figure regarding it as too high. In air over urban areas the presence of nitrogen dioxide in significant amounts is always unwelcome, and anxiety is felt if levels rise above 0.25 parts per million.

LEAD

The effects of lead pollution on health are difficult to assess. Frequently the subject is clouded with emotive overtones with the result that discussion of it generates considerably more heat than light! Widely divergent views exist amongst those who must be regarded as authorities in this highly specialised field. Thus, the Shell Oil Company—hardly a neutral observer—states 'there is no case against the present level of lead emission from gasoline on medical grounds'. On the other hand, a distinguished academic, Professor D. Bryce-Smith of Reading University holds that 'present levels of lead in blood are between 20 and 40 per cent of those known to cause overt symptoms of lead poisoning, which are themselves higher than those which cause long term effects'. Bryce-Smith backs up his opinion by writing in a chemical journal 'to the best of my knowledge no other toxic chemical pollutant has accumulated in man to average levels so close to the threshold for overt clinical poisoning'.

Lead toxicity has an insidious onset and its presence can readily be overlooked. Early symptoms are vague and non-specific. They include loss of weight and appetite, headaches and excessive fatigue; alterations in the functions of the liver and kidneys can occur at relatively low levels of exposure, and there is likely to be damage to the pigment haemoglobin carried by the red blood cells. More severe lead poisoning produces a variety of symptoms including colicky abdominal pain, paralysis of muscles, pigmentation of the gums and changes in the nervous system manifested by fits, lack of concentration and mental deterioration. Difficulties arise when one attempts to equate the symptoms of lead intoxication with the actual levels of the metal present in the circulating blood. This is especially so when the affection is mild, and it is probable that a great number of early cases never reach the point of diagnosis.

Controversy also exists with respect to the major sources of lead pollution. There is general agreement that food and water are important contributors, but the same harmony of opinion does not exist in the case of emissions from vehicle exhausts. The North American scene has provided cogent evidence implicating the automobile as a major source of contamination, this being borne out by the fact that the blood lead content of individuals such as traffic policemen, garage hands and road tunnel employees tends to be a good deal higher than that of city dwellers in other types of occupation. However, the tocsin of dissent to the viewpoint that lead pollution from car exhausts is pre-eminent has been sounded by scientists at the Medical Research Council's Air Pollution Unit in London. These investigators—and it has to be admitted that their studies have so far been conducted in a small number of individuals—have stated that the contribution of automobiles to air pollution is relatively minor, amounting to only 7 per cent of the amount of lead found in the bodies of British citizens. The opinions of this Unit were obviously important and received wide publicity in the British press. As might be expected, they had political implications being enthusiastically received by the Government, already under pressure to legislate against the addition of lead to petrol and well aware that the outcome of such an exercise would be to raise the costs to the consumer. What are we to conclude from this welter of conflicting evidence? Without doubt the clamant need is for more research designed to elucidate some of the more perplexing questions in relation to lead toxicity. However, in addition, we have the right to expect that the Government will remain vigilant, will be unimpressed by euphoric statements which lack the requisite evidence and will legislate swiftly and decisively should a definite health hazard from lead become apparent.

*   *   *

No chapter on diseases associated with air pollution can ignore the role of cigarette smoking. For undoubtedly this is the 'captain of the men of death' in the field of respiratory illness far outranking in this respect the lethality of atmospheric pollutants inhaled either singly or collectively.

Over the last one-and-a-half decades the saga of the cigarette has been ably recounted in numerous articles in the medical and scientific literature. The cigarette is one of the great scourges of modern society; its effects on health are almost wholly malevolent and the suffering which it causes is very great. Cigarette smokers are twice as likely to die during middle age as are non-smokers, and each year in the UK some 20,000 deaths of men in the prime of their lives arise directly from this cause. For the cigarette has been responsible for a new epidemic disease of global distribution, namely that of lung cancer. The incidence of this condition has risen strikingly in recent years in all parts of the world, and in England and Wales, if present smoking habits persist, it is predicted that by the 1980's the number of deaths per year attributable to the disease may well top the 55,000 mark. By that time the number of men dying annually from lung cancer could be in the neighbourhood of 40,000 while female deaths could amount to 15,000.

Cigarette smoking not only kills; it also causes much morbidity. Thus it is an important predisposing cause to chronic bronchitis and emphysema. It increases the liability to coronary heart disease and to strokes. It impairs the healing of gastric and duodenal ulcers, and if associated with a high consumption of alcohol, makes the individual more likely to contract lung tuberculosis and to develop cirrhosis of the liver. Certain types of cancer are more common in smokers, especially tumours affecting the mouth, larynx, gullet, bladder and pancreas. Even the pregnant woman is not spared, for if she smokes during her pregnancy her baby is likely to be smaller than normal, she has a greater tendency to miscarry and she may well see her child die during the first few days of life.

The only segment of British society which now eschews the cigarette is the medical profession. To doctors the evidence has come as a blinding light not unlike the apocalypse vouchsafed to St John on the island of Patmos during the first century AD.

A marked retreat from the cigarette has now taken place, and doctors who now wish to smoke generally rely on the cigar or the pipe both of which are much less injurious to health. The result has been that the incidence of lung cancer in the medical profession has plummeted in a most dramatic manner.

But what of the general population? Here the situation remains highly unsatisfactory. Indeed the warnings of the last 10 years have gone virtually unheeded—so much so that some 70 per cent of British males between the ages of 20 and 70 still smoke as do 50 per cent of females in the age range 20 to 45. The trauma which they inflict on themselves by this practice is massive, and in the presence of this truly monumental health hazard the effects produced by atmospheric pollutants pale into insignificance.

References

AIR POLLUTION 1969 (1970). *Hearing before the Sub-committee on Air and Water Pollution of the Committee on Public Works*—United States Senate, Washington, US Government Printing Office.

AMERICAN ASSOCIATION FOR THE ADVANCEMENT OF SCIENCE (1965). *Air Conservation*. A report of the Air Conservation Commission of the American Association for the Advancement of Science, Publication No. 80, Washington DC.

BRYCE-SMITH, D. (1971). 'Lead Pollution from Petrol'. *Chemistry in Britain*, **7**, pp. 284-286.

HEALTH EFFECTS OF AIR POLLUTION (1970). 'Report on a Symposium'. *Indust. Med.*, **39**, pp. 71-79.

HAWKES, NIGEL (Editor) (1971). 'The air we breathe'. *Daily Telegraph Magazine*, 28th May.

JOURNAL OF AIR POLLUTION RESEARCH ASSOCIATION (1969). *Toxicological and Epidemiological Basis for Air Quality Criteria*, **19**, pp. 629-732.

LAWTHER, P. J., MARTIN, A. E. and WILKINS, E. T. (1962). *Epidemiology of Air Pollution*—Report on Symposium, Geneva, World Health Organisation.

ROYAL COLLEGE OF PHYSICIANS (1970). *Air Pollution and Health*. London, Pitman Medical and Scientific.

ROYAL COLLEGE OF PHYSICIANS (1971). *Smoking and Health*. London, Pitman Medical and Scientific.

WALLER, R. E., LAWTHER, P. E. and MARTIN, A. E. (1969). *Clean Air and Health in London*. Proceedings of Clean Air Conference—National Society for Clean Air.

IV

WHENCE WATER?

Of water men have need in winter and summer, in sickness and health, by night and by day. Without water no man has ever thought life agreeable, or even possible.

Plutarch, Moralia 956

Life is completely dependent on water. Two-thirds of man's body is composed of it, and it is as vital to him as the air he breathes. Man can exist without food for some weeks—but starve him of water and he will die within a few days.

The lives of all of us are built around water. Vallentine in his book *Water in the Service of Man* had succinctly stated the situation when he remarks 'we admire it, drink it, wash with it, swim in it, fish in it, sail on it, pump it, extract power from it, grow food with it, ration it, waste it and pollute it'. In our overcrowded world we also fight about supplies of it and are likely to do so to an ever increasing extent in the future. Where does this precious commodity come from? What will be the pattern of demand for it in the future?

The surface of the globe is seven-tenths water. Unfortunately, 97 per cent of this total is in the form of salt water which with its 35 parts per 1,000 of dissolved salts is virtually undrinkable. The remaining 3 per cent is fresh water, but as much as three-quarters of this is incarcerated in the polar icecaps particularly in Greenland and Antarctica. And it is much to be hoped that it will remain there; for were it suddenly to be freed it would raise sea levels by over 200 feet, flood many of our major cities and cause a veritable orgy of destruction.

The remainder of the world's fresh water supplies exists in lakes and rivers, as underground water, as vapour in the atmosphere and as water contained in the upper layers of the soil. Underground water, commonly referred to as groundwater, accounts for most of it. This is our 'water capital', one of our most precious patrimonies. Much of the groundwater is located within half a mile of the earth's surface, and in many areas of our planet it is being removed at an alarming rate in an attempt to slake the thirst of millions and to satisfy the avarice of industry and commerce. Lakes contain about one-hundredth of our fresh water supplies, rivers and the atmosphere about one-three-thousandth and soil about double that of rivers and air. The relative amounts of fresh water present in lakes, rivers, air and soil may appear small, but in practice the quantities involved are very large indeed.

The water supply of the earth is in a continuous state of flux, and to this ceaseless movement beset with infinite complexities the term hydrological cycle is given. The oceans undoubtedly play a major role in the cycle. They cover some 70 per cent of the earth's surface, and they constitute the great reservoir on which our supplies of fresh water ultimately depend. The sun's energy causes water to evaporate from oceans and to some extent from lakes. The water is then transferred in the form of vapour over the land masses of the earth there to be precipitated as rain, hail, snow and dew. But the precipitation does not remain on the land; it ultimately returns to the oceans like a homing pigeon to its nest, and in the course of its pilgrimage it utilises a variety of routes including the run-off from streams and rivers, overland flow and the steady percolation of groundwater.

In reality the hydrological cycle is much more complex than the foregoing description would indicate. As much as 70 per cent of the water evaporated from the sea does not find its way back to its place of origin. Instead it returns to the atmosphere evaporating thither from lakes and rivers, from the soil, and through the transpiration of plants which remove it from soil and release it from their foliage in vaporous form. This fraction is sometimes designated 'lost' water because it does not complete the cycle by reaching surface streams, rivers and groundwaters. However, the appellation would appear to be somewhat pessimistic because in reality such water is of great importance playing a vital role in the growth of forests, crops and grasses of all types. Another feature of the hydrological cycle is that the return of water to seas and oceans may take a very long time indeed, even centuries. Thus the water can be stored for year upon year in the polar icecaps, or it can remain as snow on the earth's surface and even in the form of groundwater.

The amounts of water handled in the course of the hydrological cycle are enormous, and in spite of his much vaunted authority over nature, man's capacity to influence the cycle is very limited indeed. He must concentrate predominantly on the diversion of surface waters and of groundwater, although in recent years he has had the temerity to attempt to alter the precipitation stage of the cycle by rain making. Arvill in his *Man and Environment* is highly critical of man's interference with the hydrological cycle and has stressed particularly the harmful influence which he has exerted by altering the speed of movement of water in rivers and streams. Generally, if water is left in its natural state its rate of flow will not be unduly rapid. It will percolate in a leisurely fashion through soils, bogs, marshes and fens, and in the course of its journey it will protect delicate ecosystems and will fulfill its life-giving function with respect to flora and fauna. But when man intervenes by clearing forests, dredging rivers and constructing engineering works of all kinds the flow of water markedly accelerates. Now it hastens to the sea or reservoir, cannot dally within the ecosystems and can even become a marauding force removing precious topsoil, impoverishing agricultural land and flooding farms and townships.

*   *   *

Rain is a major source of water, and as any standard school atlas will show, rainfall varies greatly in different parts of the world. It can be negligible in areas such as the Sahara Desert, Central Asia, Central Australia and some parts of Latin America. On the other hand, it can be as high as 200 inches annually in North West Scotland around Loch Quoich, 163 inches per year in the foothills of the Himalayas and 100 inches in Assam and in parts of Central America. A vast country such as the Soviet Union has a very uneven rainfall. The western part of European Russia in closest proximity to the Atlantic Ocean is the wettest area; further east and especially in inland regions, rainfall diminishes markedly. East of the Volga River over the greater part of Kazakhstan rainfall is negligible with dry winds and droughts recurring at intervals of 4 to 5 years. In the far

eastern Pacific region of the country precipitation is compara-
tively small, although lands bordering on the Sea of Okhotsk
can have up to 27 inches per year. In addition to having an
uneven rainfall the water resources of the Soviet Union are
badly distributed in relation to its population. Hence the desire
of the Russian government, talked of even before the Second
World War, to divert the waters of north flowing rivers such as
the Ob and the Yenisei so that they could flow southwards,
ultimately enter the Caspian and Aral Seas and so succour the
thirsty populations of these regions.

Most of the world's large cities experience average rainfalls
ranging from 20 to 60 inches per annum. Thus New York has
42 inches, Sydney 45 and London 23.4. In these three cities the
rainfall is well distributed throughout the year, whereas
Bombay which has a much higher annual level (72 inches),
experiences 95 per cent of this during the monsoon between the
months of June and September. In Canada the average rainfall is
20 inches per year and in the USA 30 inches with wide
variations from one state to another. In England and Wales in
the 10 years between 1959 and 1969 the mean annual rainfall
fluctuated between 28.9 and 43.2 inches. There are great
regional differences in the UK, some areas in North West
Scotland topping the 200-inch mark, while those in South East
England averaging only 20 inches. In Britain drier areas tend to
have the densest populations and the greatest degree of
industrial development; on the other hand, areas with high
rainfall are usually sparsely populated and much less industrialised.

The rivers and streams of the world are a major source of our
water supply, and hydrologists and civil engineers with a
particular interest in water spend much of their time measuring
their capacity. They generally express their results in terms of
acre feet, this being defined as the volume of water standing one
foot deep in an area of one acre. The acre foot is a difficult
yardstick for the non-specialist to grasp. However, for those
who have visited Edinburgh and have enjoyed swimming in the
newly constructed Royal Commonwealth Pool there the statistic may appear less esoteric when they are reminded that the
pool contains 1.31 acre feet of water!

The term run-off is much used in hydrological parlance and can be conveniently defined as 'the proportion of the precipitation on the land which reaches streams and rivers'. The world's total run-off from surface waters is enormous, being in the neighbourhood of 20,000 million acre feet each year. Of this total some 12,000 million acre feet are contributed by 80 major rivers. In Africa, the main suppliers are the Nile, the Zambezi, the Congo and the Niger. In Asia they include the mightly Yangtze Kiang, the Hwang Ho, the Tigris, the Euphrates, the Indus, the Ganges, the Brahmaputra, the Irrawaddy and the Mekong. In Asiatic Russia the Lena, the Yenisei, the Angara, the Ob and the Syr Darya are rich sources of water, while in Europe the Danube, the Volga, the Dnieper, the Rhine, the Rhone and the Seine hold pride of place. In North America the major river is the Mississippi followed by the Yukon, the Columbia, and the St Lawrence; in Australia the monarch of the waterways is the Murray. Latin America has the world's largest river in the Amazon, but it also has notable contributors in the Plata and the Orinoco.

Groundwater constitutes a further important source of water supplies. It cannot be used directly for recreation, navigation, or the generation of power; however, it is important in maintaining the flow of rivers and it is the source of numerous springs. Groundwater is believed to produce approximately half of the water required by trees and vegetation; its composition remains relatively constant, little if any of it being lost through evaporation. Generally the movement of groundwater is very slow; it seeps lazily in complex channels through porous rocks, and it oozes through fissures and cavities in rocks which are impervious to water. Groundwater completes its part of the hydrological cycle when it is finally discharged onto the earth's surface by springs or when it finds its way into rivers, streams, lakes and oceans.

Aquifers are underground reservoirs of groundwater; some of them are very large indeed. London is surrounded by chalk hills beneath which lie numerous aquifers; as the population of South East England increases by leaps and bounds these sources are being tapped to an ever greater extent. The Great Artesian Basin in Australia is said to be the world's largest aquifer. It covers over 600,000 square miles of dry inland territory; it can yield up to 8 million gallons per hour, and it has been tapped by bores to a depth of 7,000 feet.

Canada has more fresh water lakes and rivers than any comparable area of the world, and its supplies of groundwater are believed to exceed those of surface waters by a factor of 30. In the USA groundwater is in wide use, and, at present, it is estimated that 20 per cent of all water consumption, excluding that used for the generation of power, comes from this source. Two other countries which depend to a major extent on groundwater for their domestic supplies are the Netherlands and Federal Germany. India is depleting its groundwater resources at a disturbing rate in an attempt to grow more food for its burgeoning population. According to the Ehrlichs in their *Population, Resources, Environment*, the Indian government drove 2,000 new tube wells between July 1968 and June 1969; during this time private enterprise drove 76,000 new wells and 246,000 new pumps were installed.

Although, as mentioned previously, the amounts of fresh water participating in the hydrological cycle are enormous in absolute terms, this does not mean that all areas of the earth are equally fortunate in having plentiful water supplies. Indeed a vital point taught to children in their geography classroom is the unevenness of the distribution of water over the earth's surface. Thus many of our great rivers wend their way far from big cities through areas of low population density, and not infrequently the countryside which they traverse is infertile and quite unsuitable for agricultural development. Moreover, the flow of water in many of the world's rivers varies greatly from one year to another. It can be virtually zero under conditions of drought, while after heavy rains serious flooding can pose major problems.

*   *   *

In modern society demands for water are prodigious; furthermore, they are rising steadily year by year; so much so that by 2000 AD the water needs of the world are likely to have quadrupled! The factors responsible have already been touched upon in this essay; they are, of course, the population explosion and the worship by our political mandarins of the juggernaut of raw economic growth. Amongst the developed countries of the world the USA highlights in its most acute form the dilemma of inadequate water supplies, this being observed particularly in the western part of that country. Thus California experiences a perennial water shortage of varying severity, and it is common knowledge that in Greater Los Angeles water consumption is 1,000 times in excess of that precipitated in the rainfall! Southern California is making herculean efforts to draw its water from far afield, and currently supplies are being piped in from the nothern part of the state and even from neighbouring states. So desperate is the plight of California likely to become in future years that plans are already afoot to obtain water supplies from areas as far distant as the North West territories of Canada. Needless to say the cost of such elaborate projects will be enormous.

The production of foodstuffs consumes vast amounts of water. For one egg 225 gallons are required, for a pound of meat between 2,500 and 6,000 gallons, for a pound of dry wheat 60 gallons, for a pound of rice between 200 to 250 gallons, for a quart of milk 1,000 gallons. Even a pint of beer requires 44 gallons of water. A cow in milk needs 30 gallons per day, other cattle 10 gallons. Farmland requires on an average 3 to 4 gallons per day per acre, but in areas of intense dairy farming the daily demand may rise to 7 gallons per acre. Market gardens and glasshouses consume great amounts of water. Throughout the year a large glasshouse will use some 2,500 gallons each day; obviously during periods of rapid plant growth the figure will be much higher.

Industry has an insatiable thirst for water, and some examples will illustrate this point. For the manufacture of a ton of synthetic rubber 616,000 gallons are required, for a ton of steel 650,000 gallons, of artificial silk 150,000 gallons, of aluminium 300,000 gallons. The paper industry hungers incessantly for water. Each ton of paper accounts for 60,000 gallons, and Bugler writing in the *Observer* in May 1971, comments that each copy of his newspaper with its attendant colour supplement will have used 42 gallons, while the whole issue will have accounted for over 35 million gallons! The average office block consumes 25 gallons per head per day. In hotels each occupied room disposes of 300 gallons per day, while laundries utilise 4 gallons per pound of material sent to them. Perhaps the thirstiest organisation of all in Britain is the Central Electricity Generating Board which requires literally mammoth amounts of water in order to cool its generators.

Domestic consumers are also heavy users of water although they rate third after industry and agriculture. The more sophisticated the gadgetry within the establishment, the more water is required. An extra bathroom has its effect; so do elaborate washing machines, garbage grinders and all the other accoutrements associated with the treadmill of materialism. Bugler states that at present in an 'average' city house in Britain each person uses each day 11 gallons of water for washing and bathing, 11 for flushing the toilet, 3 for laundry, 3 for washing up, 2 for the car and the garden and 1 for drinking and cooking. Demands will inevitably rise in ensuing decades.

There are wide international variations in water consumption, a point well brought out by Twort in his *Textbook of Water Supplies.* In Great Britain the average total water consumption in non-industrial areas lies between 35 and 45 gallons per head per day; in industrial towns it rises to 55 gallons or more, while in rural districts it is lower, ranging from 25 to 35 gallons. In the USA rates of water use are much higher than in Britain, and in major cities in that country the demand can be of the order of 200 gallons per head per day. And they are continually increasing for according to Eipper, writing in *Science* in 1970, the per capita utilisation of water in the USA, exclusive of its use in transportation and recreation, is doubling every 40 years! Another country with high rates of water consumption is Australia, Twort quoting figures of 73 gallons per head per day for the cities of Sydney and Melbourne and 94 gallons per head per day for Perth.

*   *   *

Large quantities of rain fall on Britain every year; the Britisher knows this to his cost and the visitor to our country soon learns the fact with chagrin. Nevertheless, in spite of our humid climate, serious shortages of water could occur in the UK and these could be manifest well before the end of the present century.

In 1960 some 2,200 million gallons of water were supplied each day to homes and industrial concerns in England and Wales. By 1969 the figure had risen to 2,900 million gallons; over the next 30 years the demand is expected to double, being not far short of 6,000 million gallons by 2,000 AD. Other parts of the UK will no doubt show a comparable increase in requirements. The South East region of England is the area of highest population density and was recently the subject of a special investigation conducted by the Water Resources Board. The findings, published in 1969, were far from reassuring. The Board concluded that by the end of 1971 additional water resources would have to be developed for this region to the tune of 100 million gallons each day. But the scenario for a much more critical situation has already been written for by 1981 the extra demand is likely to amount to 400 million gallons and by 2000 AD to 1,100 million gallons per day!

There is already strong evidence purporting to show that certain areas of Britain will fare increasingly badly as the century grinds to its close. The North of England is a good example, and unless remedial action is taken in this region, there is likely to be a deficit amounting to 860 million gallons per day by 2000 AD. Another area in which thirst is likely to be endemic is that extending from Northampton in the north through Buckinghamshire and London to Essex. Here a deficit of 650 million gallons per day is predicted for some 30 years from now.

Re-use of water, increased tapping of groundwater resources, transfer of water from one catchment area to another, desalination—these have all been bruited as solutions to the water shortage. But the major weapon in the armamentarium of officialdom will inevitably be the construction of more and more reservoirs. The effects of such construction will undoubtedly be far reaching, for ecological disasters will inevitably ensue, our environment will be placed in jeopardy and the quality of our lives will be even further eroded.

Already in Britain we have a well nigh classical example of the clash of interests which can occur when a proposal is made to construct a reservoir in an area of high scenic attraction. The example concerns Cow Green, an upland valley in Upper Teesdale. The valley was very beautiful; furthermore it contained rare species of Alpine plants which had survived from the Ice Age. Cow Green was generally considered to be sacrosanct and to be shielded in perpetuity from the onward march of technology. But its virginity was short lived for in 1965 the maiden became a candidate for rape when the Tees Valley and Cleveland Water Board proposed to construct a reservoir in that part of the country. That the reservoir would be useful was not in doubt for not only would it provide extra water for the burgeoning population of Teesside but it would also meet the needs of the expansion envisaged by our industrial giant, Imperial Chemical Industries. Conservationists and environmentalists were outraged by the proposal, demanding that Cow Green be spared and that an alternative site be found for the reservoir. However, in these far off days of the mid-1960's the conservationist voice was still faint, having not yet attained the lustiness of the early 1970's when it was a major factor in overturning the recommendation of the Roskill Commission that the Third London Airport should be built at Cublington in Buckinghamshire. As might be expected the Water Board ignored the pleas of the conservationists; it remained intransigent, adhering to its original proposal in its entirety. The whole topic caught the public imagination, and it was hotly debated both in the press and in the parliament of the day. Industrial interests thundered that if the reservoir was not built a water shortage could well develop between 1969 and 1971, and that as a result the employment of 50,000 workers at the Imperial Chemical Industries could be jeopardised. What was the outcome? As might be expected the conservationist cause was defeated and collapsed in disarray. Permission was granted for the reservoir to be built; the Alpine plants vanished never to return; the original Cow Green was violated beyond recognition, and yet again environment and amenity were sacrificed on the altar of short-term expediency.

Let no one imagine that the tragedy of Cow Green is unique.

It is merely the forerunner of what will inevitably happen in Britain as demands for water become ever more clamant. And what can conservationists do in the face of such a potent threat to environment and amenity? At least they can band together, speak with a united voice and oppose such legislation with all the resources at their disposal. For if they do not the captains of industry will have raised the portcullis and stormed the castle before the defending troops can even reach for their weapons.

References

ARVILL, ROBERT (1969). *Man and Environment.* London, Penguin Books.

BROWN, I. C. (1969). *Water.* Edited by NELSON, J. G. and CHAMBERS, M. J. London, Methuen, Ch. 2.

BUGLER, JEREMY (1971). 'Will Britain run dry?'. *Observer Magazine*, 16th May, pp. 11-18.

CASS-BEGGS, D. (1969). *Water.* Edited by NELSON, J. G. and CHAMBERS, M. J. London, Methuen, Ch. 1.

EIPPER, A. W. (1970). 'Pollution Problems, Resource Policy, and the Scientist'. *Science*, **169**, pp. 11-15.

HUBERTY, MARTIN R. and FLOCK, WARREN L. (1959). *Natural Resources.* New York, McGraw-Hill Book Co., Inc.

LAVERTON, SYLVIA (1964). *Irrigation—Its Profitable Use for Agricultural and Horticultural Crops.* London, Oxford University Press.

LAVRISHCHEV, A. (1969). *Economic Geography of the USSR.* Moscow, Progress Publishers.

LINSLEY, RAY K. and FRANZINI, JOSEPH B. (1964). *Water-Resources Engineering.* New York, McGraw-Hill Book Co., Inc.

MINISTRY OF HOUSING AND LOCAL GOVERNMENT (1961). *Pollution of Water by Tipped Refuse*—Report of the Technical Committee on the Experimental Disposal of House Refuse in Wet and Dry Pits, London, HM Stationery Office.

MINISTRY OF HOUSING AND LOCAL GOVERNMENT (Scottish Development Department) (1970). *Disposal of Solid Toxic Wastes.* London, HM Stationery Office.

MCGAUHEY, P. H. (1968). *Engineering Management of Water Quality.* New York, McGraw-Hill Book Co., Inc.

STEELE, F. N. (1971). 'Nor any drop to drink'. *The Ecologist*, **1**, No. 13, pp. 4-9.

TWORT, A. C. (1963). *A Textbook of Water Supply.* London, Edward Arnold (Publishers) Ltd.

VALLENTINE, H. R. (1967). *Water in the Service of Man.* London, Pelican Books.

V

DEVILS IN WATER

Pollution of water, like that of air, is as old as man himself, and ancient civilisations and dynasties recognised the need to keep water clean and uncontaminated. For example, in the Persia of Cyrus and his successors citizens were much concerned with purity of mind and body and laws expressedly forbade the discharge of refuse and filth into rivers. The Assyrian and Babylonian Empires took considerable pride in their hygienic standards, and many of their cities boasted sanitary systems of high efficiency. In Biblical times Moses was a strong upholder of cleanliness and exhorted the Israelites to bury their waste products in the earth rather than pollute rivers and streams.

The Middle Ages were an era of low hygienic standards and ubiquitous pollution. In the thirteenth century St Hildegard wrote that the waters of the Rhine if drunk unboiled would 'produce noxious blue fluids in the body'. In these days sewage disposal was unknown; the streets of all main cities were loaded with excrement, and at certain times of the year particularly in warm weather the stench became intolerable for the inhabitants. In such an environment it is scarcely surprising that epidemics were rife, and that diseases such as cholera, typhus, typhoid and bubonic plague decimated the population.

The Industrial Revolution of the late-eighteenth and early-nineteenth centuries not only caused atmospheric pollution; it was also responsible for massive contamination of streams and rivers. The two main factors operating to produce this state of affairs were the same as for the air—the rapid growth of population and the spread of all types of industrial activity. The time was one of high hope for mercantilists and entrepreneurs; indeed to this section of the community the world was their domain and the possibilities for trade and commerce seemed illimitable. Nowhere did these hopes run higher than in nineteenth century Britain.

The social costs to Britain of the Industrial Revolution were high, and the literature of the last century is replete with accounts of the damage caused to rivers by the new era of technological innovation. Previously our inland waterways had been reasonably clean; fishing was an important industry in some rivers and angling had become a favourite sport amongst certain sections of the populace. Now all was changed. The population grew and became aggregated in large conurbations on the banks of waterways; raw sewage was piped into the latter in mounting quantities. Factories sprouted on all sides and their untreated effluents were discharged into rivers, no thought being given to the consequences of such action. Soon the results were apparent; in many waterways fish and other forms of aquatic life rapidly succumbed, while the rivers themselves groaned and protested and were finally converted into barren stretches of water.

The most affected parts of Great Britain during the Industrial Revolution were Yorkshire, Lancashire, the industrial Midlands and the area around London. A classical case of water pollution was the River Irwell in Lancashire, and during the nineteenth century the scum on that waterway was so solid that birds could walk upon its surface without fear of sinking! Another example was at the Bradford Canal in Yorkshire where in the 1870's it was a favourite occupation to ignite the methane gas produced by industry and to 'see blue flames arise some six feet in height and envelop the barges in their course as they ran like gunpowder a distance of 100 yards along the water'.

The situation in London was especially bad because there had been a huge increase both in population and in industrial activity. Moreover water closets were being used on an increasing scale in the home and untreated excrement was being passed into the Thames in large amounts. Much of this sewage remained undecomposed for long periods of time, and it was carried backwards and forwards throughout the centre of the city on the ebb and flow of the tide. During this era it was not unusual for both Houses of Parliament to have to adjourn their deliberations because of the noxious odours emanating from the

Thames, and in 1855 that renowned diarist, the Reverend Benjamin Armstrong, remarked 'what a pity that this noble river should be made a common sewer'.

Epidemics, particularly of cholera, finally forced the passage of reforming legislation, although traditional attitudes to the disposal of sewage died hard. For example, when in 1854 Edwin Chadwick, that great social reformer and apostle of the creed of Philosophical Radicalism, attempted to improve the sanitary facilities of London the riposte of *The Times* of August 1st was 'we prefer to take our chance of cholera and the rest rather than be bullied into health!'. *The Times* lived to rue its words, for in 1865 a particularly severe outbreak of cholera occurred in London resulting in many deaths. By this time the situation had become a national scandal. There was clamour for action and eventually the Government heeded the popular outcry. It attempted to put pressure on local authorities to provide proper sewers and to arrange for refuse disposal, and it stressed the dangers to health of drinking contaminated water. But these mild forms of persuasion were inadequate, and in 1875 a Public Health Act was passed making it mandatory for local authorities to deal effectively with the disposal and treatment of sewage. In the following year (1876) the renowned Rivers Pollution Prevention Act reached the statute book making it an offence to discharge solid and liquid sewage into a river without first rendering it inoffensive. The Act was a model of its kind; indeed, it remained the linchpin of legislation in this area until the mid-twentieth century.

The Industrial Revolution was no respector of frontiers or national boundaries, and the rivers of other countries were afflicted in a manner similar to those in Britain. Western Europe industrialised itself rapidly and *pari passu* it presented acute problems of river pollution. But the process was to reach its zenith in the North American continent where in the newly independent USA the banner of capitalism had already been unfurled, industrial exploitation was on the march and a fiercely competitive and highly individualistic society was taking shape. Then history provided a further nudge to the whole process for in 1860 the American Civil War broke out. Early victories went to the secessionist states of the South—so

much so that Gladstone in England came near to recognising the
Confederacy as a sovereign nation. But the North had surplus
manpower, and even more important it had heavy industry and
manifold indigenous resources. It geared its economy to a war
footing and after a series of bloody campaigns, it brought the
Confederacy to its knees and preserved the Union. But there
was a reckoning in environmental terms although at the time no
one was in a position to appreciate it. The surge of economic
activity in the North had caused pollution on a scale hitherto
unknown in America and amongst the major sufferers were the
rivers. Indeed the American literature of the latter part of the
nineteenth century provides us with numerous examples of
harassment of rivers by the rapid advance of technology.
Perhaps one of the most vivid—and reputedly not apocryphal—
stories concerns a tributary of the Chicago River which came to
be known as Bubbly Creek. This stream received industrial
effluents and raw human sewage on a truly monumental scale
and soon it became covered with a thick impenetrable scum.
The end result was that the inhabitants of Chicago, like the
birds of the Irwell in Lancashire, could tread the surface of the
river with impunity!

*   *   *

There are three major sources of river pollution—discharge
from industrial enterprises, domestic sewage, and the so-called
'runoff' from farms, especially those in which large quantities
of fertilisers are used. These types of pollution are man made,
but in addition natural forces, especially what are designated
'storm waters', can make a significant contribution.
    A vast array of substances are capable of befouling rivers; in
fact such materials are as diverse as the industrial skills of man
himself. The complexity of the situation is well illustrated by
the scenario of two of our British waterways—the Thames and
the Irwell. The Thames from the borough of Wandsworth to the
mouth of the estuary can expect to receive effluent from some
23 sewage works, from more than a dozen power stations, from
at least one distillery, from sugar and oil refineries, from
factories making a whole host of products including edible oils,

soaps, detergents and chemical fertilisers, from industrial plants producing oil, tar and concrete, and from mills making cardboard and paper; as if this were not enough, there are, in addition, numerous storm water discharges particularly in the upper courses of the river. The course of the Irwell is shorter but no less eventful. Effluents reach it from several sewage works, from firms specialising in bleaching and dyeing, from distilleries, from numerous paper mills, from chemical factories and from many other sources. By the end of its course the Irwell has been well and truly ravished. Indeed, even officials recognise this fact when with typical British understatement they concede that the river, at its confluence with the Mersey is 'very bad' with respect to pollution.

Pollutants, irrespective of their origin, produce some general effects on streams, rivers, estuaries and lakes. One of the most important of these is to interfere with the oxygen content of the water. Dissolved oxygen is the life blood of rivers, reaching them by abstraction from the atmosphere and by photosynthesis from plants. In the disposal and detoxication of river pollutants oxygen is vital. It is the mainspring of what are known as aerobic organisms included in whose numbers are bacteria, fungi and protozoa. Aerobic organisms have as their main function the breakdown of complex organic matter in sewage and industrial discharges to much simpler compounds such as carbon dioxide, water, ammonia and various salts particularly nitrates. These organisms can therefore be regarded as the scavengers of the rivers, purifying organic material and rendering it much less harmful from the point of view of pollution. Aerobic organisms act in conjunction to produce a defence screen. But the screen is not inviolate; indeed it can readily be overwhelmed if the oxygen supplies in the water become inadequate due to an excess of inorganic material. Then there appear the much more sinister anaerobic organisms which do not require oxygen for their nefarious purposes. Putrefaction sets in and foul-smelling gases such as hydrogen sulphide are liberated; noxious bubbles rise to the surface of the water; fungi proliferate, organic pollution has been established, and the river degenerates into a stinking sewer.

A reasonably good assessment of the degree of pollution of a river by organic material is obtained by measuring what is known as its *biochemical oxygen demand* (BOD), this being the amount of oxygen which a given amount of sewage or other pollutants will absorb from the water under standard conditions. The higher the value for the BOD the greater is the degree of organic pollution and the poorer the health of the river. It may not be generally recognised that the ability of organic pollutants to deprive water of oxygen is considerable. For example, some authorities report that the amount of sewage produced by each human being per day gives rise to an oxygen demand of as much as ¼ lb, this representing the total amount of the gas dissolved in over 2,000 gallons of water. Certain industrial wastes have an even greater potential for deoxygenation than does human sewage, and were it not that river water protects itself by abstracting considerable amounts of the gas from the atmosphere, the degree of contamination would be even greater than is currently found.

Apart from its action on oxygen supplies pollution can cause several other general effects which are highly undesirable. Fish and other forms of aquatic life are assailed and not infrequently an early indication that pollution of streams and rivers has taken place is the finding of dead fish floating on the surface of the water. Sometimes the changes due to the pollution take a more subtle form in that the migratory habits of the fish alter as does the composition of the river's fish community. The organisms on which fish normally feed may be eliminated through pollution, and although the animals may retain their ability to spawn, there may well be interference with the hatching of eggs and with the development of larvae. In lakes and estuaries an excess in the water of minerals such as nitrates and phosphates can cause an over-production of minute plants known as phyloplankton. These may damage fish, and in extreme cases the proliferation of phyloplankton may be so dense that the gills of the animals become clogged and they choke to death. Furthermore, certain types of phyloplankton, particularly single-celled organisms known as dinoflagellates, produce a highly virulent nerve toxin which is capable of paralysing and killing large numbers of young and adult fish. Shellfish such as oysters, clams and mussels are especially susceptible to this toxin, and deaths in humans have followed the ingestion of fish contaminated in this way.

Polluted waters have other highly unattractive characteristics. As mentioned earlier, the smell emanating from them can be most unpleasant. Also the water may become discoloured through the presence in it of a variety of pigments, most of these being derived from dye stuffs used, for example, in the manufacture of textiles and in the papermaking, photographic and woollen trades. Laymen place much emphasis on discolouration of water and tend to equate this with the degree of pollution. However, most experts take the view that discolouration *per se* is a rather poor guide to the extent of the contamination. But polluted waters are not only discoloured and malodorous; they are also likely to be cloudy or turbid, and if they emanate from industrial enterprises they are not infrequently overheated as well.

*   *   *

Individual pollutants must now engage our attention. As mentioned already a plethora of such substances exist, and a comprehensive discussion of the effects which they produce is obviously outwith the scope of this book. Several standard works on this topic exist and some of these are listed in the bibliography at the end of the chapter. Here I intend to deal with three main categories of pollutants—*organic, inorganic* and *miscellaneous.* Contamination by radioactive substances is considered separately in Chapter XII.

Organic Pollutants

Included in this group are proteins, carbohydrates (sugars) and fats. Proteins of all types are frequent constituents of the effluents emanating from sewage works and from industrial enterprises such as slaughterhouses, dairies, and tanneries. When exposed to anaerobic bacteria, proteins readily undergo putrefaction forming smaller compounds with highly objectionable odours. Much of the unpleasant smell of untreated sewage is now known to be due to the presence in it of breakdown products derived from proteins, and especially obnoxious in this connection are substances known to the chemist as indole and skatole.

Carbohydrates are very widely distributed throughout the whole of the animal and vegetable kingdoms and important members of this group are substances such as starch, dextrose and cellulose. All are used extensively in a great variety of industrial processes such as papermaking, printing and the manufacture of materials like artificial silk and cotton; it is therefore not surprising that discharges from factories of this type provide a rich source of sugars. Resins exude from plants and trees; they are complex chemical substances which resemble sugars in certain respects. They have many uses in industry, effluents from plants manufacturing textiles, linoleum and paints being especially rich sources. Fatty substances are also important pollutants; they are frequently to be found in large quantities in effluents from sewage works and in trade wastes produced by soap factories, laundries, wool mills and plants for the manufacture of edible oils. Soaps and waxes are closely related to fats in their chemical structure. Soaps are a normal constituent of sewage particularly of the sludge which follows sewage treatment; they are also prominent in trade wastes from laundries and textile mills. In the case of waxes, major contributors are textile factories and paper mills.

One type of organic pollution which merits special attention is that resulting from synthetic detergents. Here the full weight of highly sophisticated modern techniques of advertising and salesmanship has been concentrated on the housewife and not surprisingly, in view of the intensity of the propaganda, her response has been to use such products in the home on an ever increasing scale. The UK provides a good example of the soaring sales of detergents. Between 1963 and 1967 the British population increased by 2½ per cent, but during that time the sale of detergents rose by more than 7 per cent. In 1963 sales of detergents in the UK were estimated to be running at 240,000 tons; by 1969 the corresponding figure was close to 400,000 tons. Synthetic detergents cannot be disguised as pollutants. They rapidly attract attention because of their propensity to produce large quantities of persistent foam, the latter usually being seen to its greatest extent some way below the point at which a sewage works discharges its effluent into a river. Occasionally the foam aggregates into large lumps, is fanned by the wind and makes its appearance in city streets; to such invaders the picturesque term of 'detergent swans' has been given.

Synthetic detergents not only cause aesthetic damage; they also produce serious effects on water. They are powerful deoxygenators, and it is now recognised that as little as 0.1 parts per million of detergent can halve the rate of uptake of oxygen by a river. Detergents are highly lethal to certain species of fish—for example, the rainbow trout will only survive for approximately 10 days at a concentration of detergent of four parts per million. They impart an unpleasant taste to drinking water, and when they pass through sewage works they tend to reduce the efficiency of the filters and thus to interfere with the quality of the effluent produced. Particularly harmful as pollutants are the so-called 'hard' detergents which have branched chain molecules and are very stable. Fortunately in most countries these are now rapidly being replaced by 'soft' or 'biodegradable' varieties the molecules of which have straight chains and are more readily broken down by sewage treatment.

Pollution by oil is a matter for increasing concern. Each year increasing quantities of both crude and refined oil are transported across the world's seas, and in the early 1970's it is reported that the annual load of this commodity carried by tankers is in excess of 700 million tons. Oil pollution affects seas, estuaries, beaches and rivers. At sea tankers are the prime source of the contamination. In rivers tankers and barges are major contributors; however pollution can also occur through spillage from roads and as the result of the activities of innumerable industrial enterprises among which engineering works, metal factories and garages are prominent. Oil pollution is particularly unpleasant because it is readily visible and forms a thin film on the surface of the water. Furthermore, so-called 'soluble' oils have the disagreeable property of producing milky emulsions. Tar, like oil, is another highly distasteful form of pollution. It is produced as a by-product of a myriad of industrial processes outstanding amongst which are the manufacture of chemicals and the destructive distillation of fossil fuels. As with oil, tar is readily visible in waterways where it is often seen floating on the surface of streams and rivers attached to suspended matter.

In recent years the effects of oil on various forms of aquatic life have come under intensive investigation, and one point which has been established is that refined fuel oils cause more severe immediate damage than do crude oils. During acute episodes of oil pollution fish gills become clogged and the respiration of air breathing marine vertebrates such as reptiles, birds and mammals can be impaired. Sea birds, especially divers, are especially susceptible to oiling of their plumage; as a result they cannot fly and eventually they die from drowning or starvation. The birds become almost frantic and make desperate attempts to rid their feathers of the oil; in the process they frequently ingest it with resultant gastroenteritis, degenerative changes in the liver and kidneys and eventually impairment of reproductive performance. Ecological damage also results when, instead of an acute episode of oil pollution as was the case with the *Torrey Canyon*, there is a continuous low level of contamination for long periods of time. Under such circumstances there is an impoverishment of marine life, the latter declining both in variety and in quality.

There is a special hazard when oil and tarry wastes are tipped on to the land. While other forms of solid waste either remain *in situ* or require percolating rain water to carry them downwards into the earth, wastes from oil and tar can travel underground spontaneously. Consequently, they can contaminate groundwater and so deplete our water capital, already under heavy attack in certain areas of the world.

The list of organic pollutants affecting waterways is almost endless. Pesticides such as DDT are important contaminants and they will be considered separately in Chapter VII; other substances within this general grouping include phenols, aerosols, cyanides, benzene, various types of hydrocarbon, alcohol, aldehydes and alkaloids. From small beginnings the science of water pollution has now grown into a towering edifice and assuredly the complexity of the specialty will further increase with the passage of time.

Inorganic Pollutants

Into this category come acids, alkalis, minerals and salts. Numerous industries discharge acid wastes in their effluents, foremost amongst them being iron pickling and the paper-making trade. Many acids are produced—sulphuric, hydro-chloric, phosphoric and nitric being especially prominent. Alkalis, for example ammonia, caustic soda, sodium carbonate and lime, are often present in trade wastes especially in effluents from tanneries, from plants manufacturing wools and cottons and from chemical works. Wastes containing acids and alkalis are highly inimical to waterways. Alkalis can be very toxic to fish and to other forms of aquatic life; acids also possess this property, but in addition they can corrode metal and can cause the liberation of the foul-smelling gas, hydrogen sulphide.

Salts of heavy metals such as lead, iron, copper, zinc, nickel, silver and mercury are important inorganic pollutants. Poisoning by lead can occur through drinking the water of contaminated rivers; this is one of the major sources of lead toxicity, others being the inhalation of polluted air and ingestion in the diet. Iron salts feature in a particularly objectionable type of contamination—that caused by brine water. This is also known as 'mine drainage' or 'pit water' and it is generally found in coal mining areas. Not only functional coal mines show this form of pollution; water draining from abandoned pits can also be similarly affected. Iron salts deoxygenate water, cause putre-faction and kill aquatic life; they also impart a reddish brown or yellow colour to the water which then becomes highly offensive to the eye.

Copper sulphate is frequently used as a weedkiller; it is poisonous to fish, and one of the major difficulties attending its use is to strike a balance between the amount which will control the growth of weeds yet will not harm any form of wildlife. Zinc salts can kill some species of invertebrate animals in concentrations as low as 0.3 parts per million; however, other species are less sensitive and can survive levels as high as 500 parts per million.

Pollution of waterways by mercury has received much publicity in recent years. Japan first highlighted the danger, for in the Minimata Bay region of that country 160 people died between 1953 and 1960 as a result of eating fish the bodies of which were contaminated by a mercury-laden effluent from a plastics factory. Subsequently other countries were affected, and persistent reports of mercury toxicity appeared in newspapers in Sweden, Canada and the USA. Mercury was known to miners as quicksilver and in days gone by it was extensively used in the separation of gold and silver from their ores. Now the main sources of mercury are factories making chlorine and caustic soda by processes utilising mercury electrodes, and the pulp, papermaking and electrical industries. Substantial amounts of the metal are also consumed in agricultural practice in the form of pesticides and seed dressings. It is currently believed that the world production of mercury is about 9,000 metric tons per year.

Mercury is one of the most sinister metals with respect to pollution, for the heavy mercury poured out in industrial wastes does not sink harmlessly to the bottom of the river or estuary. Instead it is acted upon by bacteria and is converted into highly toxic compounds, one of the most important of which is methyl mercury. The latter is highly persistent and can remain in the sediments of lakes and rivers for up to 100 years! Mercury can produce profound effects on all manner of living organisms. Phyloplankton are highly sensitive to it, and very small amounts of the metal can cause a precipitous fall in their photosynthetic rate. Fish can die in large numbers as a result of mercury pollution, and birds of prey can come close to extinction. Japanese cats eating a diet consisting solely of fish derived from Minimata Bay 'went mad', showed highly bizarre behavioural patterns, jumped into the sea and drowned themselves! Symptoms of methyl mercury poisoning in humans can include blindness, deafness, lack of coordination and intellectual deterioration. The disease may be exceedingly difficult to diagnose in man because of its insidious onset and the lack of specificity of its early manifestations.

The fluoride content of water is a subject which in recent times has been associated with bitter controversy, often of a

highly coloured and emotional character. Good evidence now
exists that by adding fluoride to drinking water the incidence of
dental caries in children will be much reduced. However, the
key factor appears to be the concentration of the fluoride in the
water, and the standard set by the World Health Organisation as
the optimum is approximately 1 part of the metal per million.
Various authorities have stated that if the optimum is exceeded
damage to teeth in the form of undue brittleness and an
increasing tendency to decay may ensue. What is now clear is
that the margin between a 'safe' and an 'unsafe' level of fluoride
in drinking water is narrow, and there have been suggestions
that in some parts of the world, particularly in the North
American continent, the amount of fluoride ingested by
individuals is excessive. Pollution of rivers by fluoride undoubtedly poses problems. Many industrial effluents contain it,
especially those from chemical plants and from factories making
plastics and insecticides. Fluoride is toxic to fish; at concentrations between 3 and 6 parts per million it can kill rainbow trout
and its degree of lethality is higher in soft than in hard water.
All drinking water obtained from rivers should now be carefully
monitored for fluoride. If this is not done the community may
face a health hazard due to the ingestion of abnormally high
concentrations of the metal.

There are many other soluble salts in streams and rivers; these
include chlorides, sulphates, nitrates, phosphates and bicarbonates. Small quantities of chloride are harmless; however, if
large amounts are discharged as, for example, in wastes from
salt works, fish and vegetation may suffer. High concentrations
of chlorides can make fresh water brackish, and the latter then
becomes quite unsuitable for irrigation. Excessive quantities of
bicarbonates cause water to become unduly hard, while
sulphates favour the production of sulphuric acid which is of
course highly corrosive. As mentioned previously soluble salts
of iron are especially unpleasant as pollutants because of their
propensity to discolour the water.

Nitrates and phosphates merit special attention. They are
major constituents of fertilisers, and each year millions of tons
of these salts are dumped into the earth in an attempt to
increase food supplies for an expanding world population.

Nitrates and phosphates are washed off the land into rivers and lakes; there they kill fish and stimulate the growth of water weeds or algae. As a consequence the oxygen content of the water diminishes and the ability of the latter to digest raw sewage and industrial effluent is impaired. This whole process is referred to as *eutrophication*; enrichment or overfertilisation would be equally good terms. As will be seen in Chapter VI eutrophication reaches its apogee in the case of Lake Erie, but is by no means confined to that waterway.

Eutrophication is not the only problem posed by nitrates. These substances can also be injurious to human health, particularly to that of young babies. The nitrates are converted in the intestine into other salts known as nitrites; these are absorbed into the blood stream and there they combine with the pigment in the red blood cells which normally carries oxygen. The disease produced goes under the name of methaemoglobinaemia and its main symptoms are a blue coloration of the skin and breathlessness. If not recognised at a sufficiently early stage or if inadequately treated following diagnosis the condition may prove fatal.

Other Forms of Water Pollution

So far the main thrust of this chapter has been towards pollution arising from specific chemical substances. There remain for our consideration three other types of contamina-tion—that caused by material in suspension, that arising from the tipping of toxic wastes and house refuse, and that resulting from overheating.

Water is frequently polluted by suspended matter; the latter can take a multiplicity of forms, such as gravel, sand, silt, clay and coal. Numerous industrial enterprises discharge these materials in their wastes, prominent offenders being sand washing and china clay works and stone quarries. Waste water from coal mines is often a rich source of suspended matter as is domestic sewage. Suspended matter is usually a mixture of inorganic and organic constituents, and its effects on streams, rivers and estuaries are predictable. Oxygen supplies are diminished, the growth of algae is smothered, fish die and the water becomes turbid and opaque. Rivers polluted in this way are quite unfit for any type of recreational activity and are especially unpleasing to the eye.

Groundwater can be contaminated by the tipping of toxic wastes and some of these can penetrate down as far as the aquifers. This type of pollution has frequently been reported from the USA and from certain parts of Europe; in the UK at the time of writing it appears to be relatively infrequent. Typical sources of such contamination are stated to include septic tanks, leaking sewers and flood water. Does the tipping of house refuse pollute groundwater? This is a highly complicated subject which was investigated in detail by an Expert Committee in the UK in the early 1960's. The conclusion of the Committee was that at least in Britain this did not constitute a serious form of contamination.

Thermal pollution results from the discharge of hot industrial wastes into rivers and streams. As mentioned in Chapter IV, industrial processes, especially plants which generate electricity, are avid consumers of water and frequently they return it to waterways in a heated state. Nuclear power plants are particularly culpable in this respect, and their effects will become more and more obvious as the world's stocks of fossil fuels diminish and industry becomes increasingly dependent on nuclear power as a source of energy. Already in the USA there are plans to build a whole host of breeder reactors, and the effects of this decision are likely to be far reaching as far as the ecology of waterways is concerned. Indeed it has been stated that by 1985 it will be necessary to utilise one-quarter of the surface water supply of the USA for purposes of cooling and that by the year 2000 AD the figure may have risen to one-third! Thermal pollution will not only affect rivers and streams; estuaries will also suffer, and at present there is much unease about the decision of the Baltimore Gas and Electric Company to construct a large 1,600,000 kilowatt nuclear reactor in the vicinity of Chesapeake Bay. We are often told that thermal pollution is not a serious matter in Britain. However, this is merely the soothing anodyne of politicians and officials, conditioned to making euphoric statements. For due mainly to our policies of economic growthmanship the writing is on the wall for us as well as for the USA. Already some rivers in our country show thermal pollution, a good example being the Trent where it flows through heavily industrialised areas. One does not have to be clairvoyant to predict that before the turn of the century other rivers will share the fate of the Trent.

The effects produced by thermal pollution resemble those caused by other forms of contamination. Water is deoxygenated, fish die, the toxicity of other poisons is increased and excessive growth of water weeds is encouraged. Various types of treatment for thermal pollution have been devised; these include the building of cooling towers and the construction of artificial lakes. Such approaches have proved to be promising but a number of technical problems remain to be solved.

In addition to thermal pollution there exists a condition known as *thermal stratification.* This is a natural phenomenon occurring in deep lakes and reservoirs, and it depends on the fact that warm water, being lighter than cooler water, tends to float nearer the surface. By spring or early summer a two-tier system has been established with the top layer warm, in continuous circulation and well oxygenated and the lower layer cooler and less well aerated. During the summer months a precipitous fall in the oxygen content of the lower layer can occur as it accumulates organic material with subsequent putrefaction. If now the lake or reservoir discharges water from its lower layer into rivers and streams debouching from it, pollution of the latter is very liable to take place.

Sewage—A Monarch Amongst Water Pollutants

Sewage has been defined as the 'liquid wastes of the community'. Its main sources are domestic, industrial and agricultural; all three are of great importance. Industrial sewage currently accounts for about half the total, but in recent years there has been a marked increase in the component derived from agriculture. The quantities of sewage produced are daunting. Each day in England and Wales some 3,000 million gallons must be got rid of, and this figure is expected to double by the end of the century!

Water makes up 99.9 per cent of sewage while only 0.01 per cent is in the form of solids. Sewage is a cloudy liquid, highly complex in composition. Solid matter is present in numerous forms; sometimes it floats as a suspension; sometimes it is gelatinous. The solid constituents include items such as corks, soaps, food materials, faeces, fats and oil. Detergents are frequently present and these cause much foaming and frothing; they also contribute to the phosphate content. Sewage contains a wealth of organic matter, which in the absence of adequate supplies of dissolved oxygen, rapidly decomposes and putrefies producing foul odours. Sewage is rich in nitrogen and phosphates derived from urine and faeces. Ammonia and its salts are also present in large quantities as is sodium chloride derived from urine and from trade wastes. Organisms of all types thrive in sewage; they include bacteria, viruses, fungi and protozoa. Most of them are quite harmless, but a few are very dangerous and can cause infections such as gastroenteritis, typhoid fever, dysentery and infective hepatitis. In tropical and subtropical countries, where, in general, sanitary conditions are poor, the contamination of water by raw sewage is a major health hazard and is responsible for the spread of cholera, amoebic dysentery, infectious jaundice and hookworm infestations.

As indicated previously human habitations are a major source of sewage, bathrooms, kitchens and sinks being the main suppliers. Growth of population, affluence and increasing mechanisation in the home will inevitably swell the flow of sewage. In the USA the kitchen sink waste disposal unit, commonly referred to as the garbage grinder, has become very fashionable. This gadget can use up to 1½ gallons of water per person per day and has been a significant factor in overloading already inadequate facilities for sewage disposal. Should garbage grinders proliferate to a comparable extent in Britain a similar problem could well arise. The industrial enterprises contributing to sewage production are legion, but prominent amongst them are slaughterhouses, tanning yards, dairies and factories for the production of textiles and fish meal.

Allusion has already been made to the increasing contribution of agricultural wastes to sewage. Fertilisers containing nitrates, potash and phosphates are widely used by farmers, and the runoff of these materials from agricultural land to streams, rivers and lakes is rising each year. A recent study in England was concerned with the Great Ouse River, parts of which are heavily polluted. It had been known for many years that contamination was present, but what came as a blinding revelation to the investigators was the discovery that drainage from fertilised land contributed most of the pollution caused by nitrates, potash, chlorides and sulphates. In the USA manure from farm animals is officially recognised as a waste product. It is a major contributor to sewage; in fact it doubles the amount produced each year. Surely this is a cogent argument for the view that, irrespective of cost, as much manure as possible should be returned to the land for use as a fertiliser.

In addition to domestic, industrial and agricultural components the weather plays a role in sewage production. When it is wet and windy there tend to be accumulations of storm waters which can make sewers overflow; as a consequence untreated sewage passes directly into rivers without the intervention of a sewage works. Storm overflows often originate from agricultural land and frequently they are rich in salt, minerals and various types of vegetation; moreover, they can contain large quantities of suspended matter and are correspondingly turbid. Rivers generally bear the brunt of storm overflows, their situation being especially serious when protracted heavy rain follows a long dry spell, or if a rapid thaw takes place after a period of intense cold.

Standards for sewage effluent discharged into rivers have been laid down and are adhered to in some parts of the world. In the UK the Royal Commission on Sewage Disposal sat for the phenomenally long period of 17 years (1898-1915)! It eventually recommended that sewage effluent should have a solid content no greater than 30 parts per million and that the biochemical oxygen demand (BOD) (see page 67) should not exceed 20 parts per million. This is what is known as the 30/20 effluent, and in establishing the standard the Commission envisaged that the effluent would be diluted eight times with clean river water with a small BOD of some 2 parts per million. The 30/20 standard is still regarded by many as a useful minimum requirement with respect to sewage effluent, and in the UK and elsewhere such a figure is readily attainable provided that modern methods of sewage treatment are used appropriately. However, an upgrading of the standard will undoubtedly become necessary in the future, because, as pointed out in Chapter IV, the pressure on water resources is likely to increase in a dramatic fashion. Re-use of water will become routine; furthermore, it will become mandatory that river water into which sewage plants are discharging is extracted with maximal efficiency. Another aspect which will undoubtedly receive increasing attention is the range of measurements which should be performed on water. Most river authorities now agree that estimations of solid content and BOD alone are inadequate and that whenever feasible monitoring for specific substances such as ammonia, heavy metals, fluoride, phenols and cyanides should be undertaken.

Methods for the treatment of sewage are certain to become of mounting importance. Two techniques are in wide use in sewage plants, both of them depending on oxidation of the sewage by aerobic organisms. The procedures mimic nature and can be likened to the ordinary processes of purification which take place in rivers polluted by organic wastes. The most widely used method employs percolating filters made of clinker or broken stones through which the sewage slowly makes it way. During the time of percolation the filter bed becomes covered with a great number of organisms which act as scavengers and remove much of the organic matter. The other procedure is termed the 'activated sludge process', sludge being the accumulated solids produced during the treatment of sewage. In this technique the raw sewage is run into tanks. To it is added sewage which has already been treated and which contains the appropriate organisms to ensure aeration; the mixture is stirred continuously and eventually the organic material in it is effectively broken down. Two end products result from the process—a clear effluent and a 'sewage sludge' which, after drying, can be used as a fertiliser. Techniques depending on filters and tanks are generally successful in providing effluents of suitable standards for discharge into a water course. If, however, an effluent of especially high quality is required a so-called 'polishing stage' can be incorporated. 'Polishing' sewage is generally expensive and can involve its surface irrigation over grass plots, its retention in lagoons, and its slow filtration through sand. By such devices effluents of a 10/10 rather than a 30/20 standard can readily be prepared.

References

EHRLICH, PAUL R. and EHRLICH, ANNE (1970). *Population, Resources, Environment.* San Francisco, W. H. Freeman & Co.

GEORGE, J. DAVID (1971). 'Can the seas survive? Long term effects of pollution on marine life'. *The Ecologist*, 1, pp. 4-9.

HAMMOND, A. L. (1971). 'Mercury in the environment: Natural and human factors'. *Science*, 171, pp. 788-789.

JONES, DAVID (1970). 'Hazards of enzymes and detergents'. *Your Environment*, No. 2, pp. 55-61.

JONES, J. R. ERICHSEN (1964). *Fish and River Pollution.* London, Butterworth.

KLEIN, LOUIS (1962). *River Pollution II: Causes and Effects.* London, Butterworth.

KLEIN, LOUIS (1966). *River Pollution III: Control.* London, Butterworth.

ROYAL COMMISSION ON ENVIRONMENTAL POLLUTION (1971). London, HM Stationery Office.

TAKEN FOR GRANTED: REPORT OF THE WORKING PARTY ON SEWAGE DISPOSAL (1970). London, HM Stationery Office.

THE PROTECTION OF THE ENVIRONMENT, THE FIGHT AGAINST POLLUTION (1970). London, HM Stationery Office.

UI, JUN and KITAMURA, SHOJI (1971). 'Mercury in the Adriatic'. *Marine Pollution Bulletin*, 2, pp. 56-58.

WATER POLLUTION RESEARCH (1969). London, HM Stationery Office.

VI

TROUBLED WATERS EVERYWHERE

Water pollution knows no national or ideological boundaries. Here we look at some aspects of the world scene beginning with the USA which, as in the case of air pollution, is pre-eminent in this field.

The North American Continent

In 1965 the celebrated American entertainer Tom Lehrer introduced a song which rapidly became a big hit. Its title was *Pollution* and when describing US cities its lyric ran 'don't drink the water and don't breathe the air'. Lehrer was a good diagnostician because in the USA in the late 1960's over 90 million people, the majority of them urban dwellers, are believed to drink water which is either below the standards set by the Federal Government or is of unknown quality. The abnormalities found in such water are numerous, but the major ones are an unduly high content of bacteria and an excess of chemical impurities. Indeed the US Public Health Service has recently stated that the water supplies of some 60 major cities is 'unsatisfactory' or 'capable of producing a potential health hazard'. By 1980 the demand for water throughout the USA will have doubled, making an already perilous situation even worse.

The plight of US rivers has been graphically described in a series of recent articles emanating from that country. The Potomac flowing through the nation's capital, Washington, is typical, and an articulate Congressman, referring to the river during cherry blossom time, described it as 'the best dressed cesspool in America'! The Potomac is dirty and sluggish; its colour is generally brown, but from time to time it changes to bluey green due to the discharge of industrial effluent from a variety of sources. Logs and all forms of debris float on its surface. Swans are much less frequent than in days of yore, while it is now usual for the Potomac seagull to sport a black ring on its abdomen where it dips into the grimy waters in search of food. Slowly but surely fish are disappearing from the Potomac; some species such as the shad and the Atlantic sturgeon are now giving up the unequal struggle, although others including the white perch seem to be tougher and more resistant to the ever increasing load of pollution.

The Mississippi River has been aptly termed the 'colon of mid-America'. Throughout the lower parts of its journey to the Gulf of Mexico its banks are replete with notices forbidding individuals to consume food in its immediate vicinity much less to bathe in its waters! Pollution has already affected the Mississippi by the time it reaches Minneapolis. As it traverses Iowa the degree of contamination becomes really serious, and from St Louis southward the situation gets worse and worse. In 1962 it was said of St Louis 'if river disposal of waste were suddenly denied the city, the city fathers would have to decide what else to do with the daily discharge of 200,000 gallons of urine and 400 tons of solid body wastes, to say nothing of all the industrial wastes'. Since 1962 the population of St Louis has increased and so has its industrial activity. In 1966 a group of conservationists inspected the Mississippi near St Louis. They noted with dismay that 100 pipes were pouring untreated sewage into the river; they also found that samples of the water from the river south of the city were so toxic that, even if they were diluted 10 times with fresh water, they still killed certain species of fish within one minute!

The situation of other US rivers is similar. According to the Federal Water Pollution Control Agency the most polluted waterway in the country is the Ohio which outstrips even the Mississippi and the Potomac in this respect. The Missouri is another badly affected river, and because of its degree of contamination it has been seriously suggested that the Missouri should cease to provide a source of clean water but should merely be used as a large receptable for the removal of sewage! The river Cuyahoga, flowing through Cleveland, is the first area of water in the world to be classified as a fire hazard; this is due to its tendency to burst into flames as a result of pollution, and sometimes the fires which have been generated have come close to burning down the bridges which span the river. Southern areas of the USA have their problems just like the industrial North; textile and carpet mills are relatively frequent here, and the resulting effluents produce a milky white opalescence in rivers. In the River Delaware the favoured colour is black due to the proliferation of oil companies on its banks, while in Clarion County in Pennsylvania an inky blue colour emanating from printing works meets the eye of the beholder.

There is now increasing publicity in the USA with respect to the harmful effects of chemicals discharged into rivers. Nitrates were mentioned in the previous chapter and their ability to produce the blood disease in babies known as methaemoglobinaemia (see page 75) was noted. In certain parts of California especially in the region of St Joaquim valley, rivers are significantly polluted with nitrates, and as a result it is necessary for doctors to recommend that infants under their care be given only pure bottled water. Some time ago a small US town—Elgin in Minnesota—was forced to find a new water supply because the content of nitrate was above 10 parts per million, this being a level decreed by the authorities to be unsafe for human consumption. The wholesale dumping of mercury into rivers could lead to very serious consequences in relation to human health because, as mentioned previously, toxic salts of this metal, in common with pesticides such as DDT, are very stable and could well persist in the sediments of rivers and lakes for up to 100 years. Men and women usually contract mercury poisoning by eating contaminated fish. Recently two states of the Union, Michigan and Vermont, banned all commercial fishing because of the high mercury levels in their river water, and in the autumn of 1970 in the state of Virginia the Health Commissioner imposed a ban on fishing on the north bank of the Holston river because of high concentrations of mercury in fish.

In addition to containing poisonous chemicals, polluted waters in the USA and elsewhere can be the carriers of a wide variety of diseases. A sample recently taken from the Connecticut river showed the presence of numerous organisms;

included amongst them were those responsible for typhoid and paratyphoid fevers, cholera, dysentery, poliomyelitis and tetanus. In addition, numerous viruses were identified together with a variety of worms and flukes. American anglers are facing hard times. A good example is provided by the fate of the River Aroostook in Maine, once the Mecca of the salmon fisher, and formerly providing the Atlantic salmon with more than 70 miles of delectable spawning grounds. Now a mixture of industrial pollution and dam construction has robbed the waterway of this most precious heritage.

Sewage disposal in the USA is a problem of mammoth proportions. At present one-quarter of the towns and cities in that country have no sewage treatment facilities of any kind; in others the facilities which do exist are ineffectual and obsolescent, while in only a very small proportion could standards be regarded as satisfactory. Unfortunately, no immediate amelioration to this situation is likely. Instead things are likely to become much worse unless prodigious amounts of public money are spent. By the year 2000 AD the US could have gained an extra 100 million people, bringing the population to over 300 million. If this occurs the amount of municipal sewage which will have to be dealt with each day could well exceed 30,000 million gallons or approximately 130 gallons for every man, woman and child inhabiting that country!

Lakes in the USA have suffered from pollution to an even greater extent than rivers and streams. The classical example of the damage produced is, of course, Lake Erie, and in the opinion of many authorities the degree of pollution of this lake has reached such a pitch that it is virtually irreversible. Once Lake Erie was an area of public recreation in which boating, swimming and angling were much enjoyed. By 1965 most of these activities had ceased, and it was then necessary to cordon off most of the lake because the water had become unsafe for human beings.

Fish have borne the brunt of the pollution of Lake Erie. In 1937 the catch of blue pike was 20 million lbs; in the early 1960's the corresponding figure was 7,000 lbs! By the mid-1960's the greater part of the western end of the lake was dead from the biological point of view, its foul and deoxygenated water being quite incapable of supporting any form of marine life. The fish which remain in Lake Erie often show abnormally high concentrations of mercury, and for this reason in April 1970 the State of Michigan placed an embargo on the sale of wall eyed pike and perch from areas of the lake under its jurisdiction. Only the sea lamprey has found the toxic waters of Lake Erie to its liking. This predator fish which resembles the eel, has massacred large numbers of trout and other species and has posed a major problem to the fishing industry.

In his *Population Bomb*, Paul Ehrlich vividly describes how in the early 1960's he and a colleague conducted a research project on the habits of water snakes which inhabited the islands of Lake Erie; when they revisited the site some years later the snakes had virtually disappeared as had the fishes on which they fed. In Ehrlich's graphic words 'the once beautiful lake is now a septic tank—a stinking mess'. Others have described Lake Erie as having been 'murdered' or as 'choking to death'. It has also been likened to an 'ecological slum', a 'cesspool extending over 9,000 square miles' and a 'rank muddy sink'.

Many sources contribute to the pollution of Lake Erie. Raw sewage is tipped into it in great quantities from nearby conurbations such as Cleveland and Toledo with the result that every day the lake comes more and more to resemble a sewage lagoon. In addition, Lake Erie is reputed to receive over one ton of industrial chemical per minute from industrial plants, foremost amongst which are the Ford Motor Company and a variety of steel works. A further important source of pollution is the runoff from adjacent farmland which has been heavily fertilised with nitrates and phosphates, and in 1968 a Report of the Federal Water Pollution Commission estimated that the lake was receiving 37,500 tons of nitrogen each year from farmlands in addition to the 45,000 tons of this material pumped into it from municipal sewage. As mentioned in Chapter V nitrates and phosphates are the major culprits in the production of eutrophication, the main feature of which is algal blooming. Such salts also sink to the bottom of the water, and in Lake Erie they produce a layer of filth varying in thickness from 30 to 125 feet. The cost of saving Lake Erie from eutrophication would be prodigious. It might cost the USA as much as $1,400 million and Candada $200 million. Barry Commoner, the noted American biologist, has stated that an amount of money equivalent to the annual budget for the American space programme would be required to salvage the lake.

What of the other Great Lakes? Huron and Superior have so far escaped major pollution; however this cannot be said for Ontario and Michigan. Already Lake Ontario shows evidence of eutrophication, and because of this its recreational potential is dying. As with Lake Erie the major factors contributing to the pollution are untreated human sewage together with industrial effluent from cities such as Toronto, Buffalo, Rochester and Syracuse.

A critical situation is rapidly developing with respect to Lake Michigan. Eutrophication is present, fish are dying and opportunities for recreation are becoming ever more circumscribed; the southern end of the lake is especially badly affected. According to Charlier, writing in 1969, a notable feature of Lake Michigan is that the concentration of the pesticide DDT is higher in its waters than in any other lake in the USA. A prime villain in the case of Lake Michigan is industrial pollution arising mainly from the area of Greater Chicago. The shores of the lake are plagued by overpopulation, there being in excess of five million people in close proximity and a further seven million in Metropolitan Chicago. The demands of these areas on Lake Michigan are staggering. Every day the municipalities surrounding the lake consume over one million gallons of its water and industrial enterprises account for a further 4,000 million gallons. The grand total used each day exceeds 5,000 million gallons, and by the year 2020 AD, if current trends continue, the overall demand for water will have more than trebled! No lake, however sturdy, could ever be expected to withstand an assault of this magnitude.

Estuaries in the USA, like those of other developed countries, are highly polluted especially when they are the site of large conurbations; two of the most outstanding examples are the harbours of Boston and New York City. In both the main culprit is untreated sewage, although industrial effluent comes a close second. In New York Harbour, which as every schoolboy knows, receives the River Hudson, the sewage frequently moves to and fro in the estuary without attaining discharge to the sea; the effects of such a situation on local amenity and hygiene require no elaboration. Outside the estuary in the open sea there is heavy pollution from Sandy Hook in the State of New Jersey right up to the mouth of the Hudson River. The degree of contamination in this area is so great that marine life has vanished and for practical purposes the sea has become dead.

Canada, like the USA, has problems of water pollution; this might be expected in an affluent society with an expanding population. Canadian lakes, other than Erie, are contaminated. In Lake St Clair high concentrations of mercury have been found in fish especially in the wall eyed pike and the perch, and during 1969 the Lake of Two Rivers in Algoquin Park, a residential area some 160 miles from Toronto and much favoured by holidaymakers from that city, had to be closed to swimmers because of pollution.

Even in far off Nova Scotia contamination of waterways is present, while in the Prairie Provinces, rivers have become so poisoned with mercury that fishing has had to be banned. As might be expected rivers which traverse the major centres of population show the highest degree of contamination. A good example is the Don which finally reaches Lake Ontario having run the gauntlet of industrial Toronto. Not long ago the Don was a healthy stream where salmon frisked and anglers disported themselves. Now it is a filthy waterway polluted by industrial effluent and domestic sewage and carrying each day in its waters some 20,000 pounds of suspended solids.

The United Kingdom

Formidable problems with respect to water pollution undoubtedly exist in Britain. The fact that their scale is somewhat less than in the USA should give us no cause for complacency.

Approximately one-third of the public water supplies in England is derived from rivers which receive human sewage and industrial effluent, and many rivers in the vicinity of large conurbations remain dead, foul smelling and totally unfit for recreational use. There have been various surveys of the situation over the years. In 1958 one such survey was conducted by the Ministry of Housing and Local Government; this disclosed that some 5,000 miles of our rivers were polluted to a varying degree. By 1966 some improvement had accrued; in that year samples were taken from 4,000 miles of British rivers, and the conclusion was reached that 80 per cent of our waterways were free from pollution. In 1969 there was a further study—this time by the Ministry of Technology, which following the election of the Conservative Government in 1970, was absorbed into the new Department of Trade and Industry. The survey was based on data obtained between April 1966 and March 1967, and on this occasion approximately one-fifth of the total length of our main rivers—3,661 out of 18,486 miles—was sampled. The conclusion reached was that 11 per cent of the total length was 'badly or grossly polluted' according to accepted standards.

There are some glaring examples of river pollution in the UK, the Irwell in Lancashire being amongst the worst. At its source the Irwell is a pure, clear stream which has been likened to a virgin maid. But the situation changes rapidly, for by the time the river has flowed through industrial Lancashire and has received its complement of domestic sewage and industrial effluent from cities such as Manchester, Salford and Rochdale, its virginity has long since departed, and instead it has become a weary harlot totally resigned to its fate. Indeed as the Irwell reaches the Manchester Ship Canal, a waterway which each day receives some 90 million gallons of sewage and 180 million gallons of trade effluent, its waters bear some resemblance to those of the Mississippi south of St Louis.

After the Severn and the Thames the Trent is Britain's longest river. It is also one of the most heavily polluted as are some of its tributaries; indeed many stretches of the waterway can no longer support fish. One of the worst points is in Buckinghamshire at the junction of the Trent with the grossly contaminated River Tame; however there are also some very bad spots nearer to the sea. The Trent basin houses over 5½ million people. The river is polluted by sewage, detergents, cyanide and heavy metals especially zinc and lead; now thermal pollution is rearing its ugly head. Major polluters include the British Steel Corporation at Stoke and Scunthorpe, the Central

Electricity Board, numerous private factories, and, above all, the sewage authorities at Stoke. In addition to the Trent stretches of other rivers such as the Mersey in the Warrington area, the Don around Sheffield, the Tawe in Wales, the Severn, the Ribble and even Shakespeare's Avon at Stratford are contaminated to a high degree with sewage and industrial effluent. In Tyneside domestic sewage from approximately one million people is discharged directly into the river. In the 1860's the annual catch of salmon in the Tyne was 80,000; now fish of any kind are a rarity in its waters. As compared with other rivers the Great Ouse is relatively clean. However, it traverses heavily fertilised agricultural land, and in 1968 it was reported that its nitrogen content was abnormally high, as much as one-quarter of the fertilisers applied to the land finding their way into the river.

Accidental discharges of substances into rivers sometimes attract attention in the UK, as they do in other parts of the world. For instance, an industrial firm recently released cyanide into the waters of the River Chelmer in Essex; more than 60,000 fish died, and it was necessary to withdraw the river from public water supplies for some days. In August 1968 dead fish were found floating on the surface of the Kennal river near Ponsanooth in Cornwall; a chocolate-brown discharge from a leaking pipe leading from the premises of the South Cornwall Water Board was found to be the culprit. In October of the same year a tanker carrying 4,300 gallons of liquid phenol overturned on the A6 road beside a tributary of the River Petteril in Cumberland; all fish life in the river was destroyed for a distance of 16 miles. The problem of contamination of waterways by detergents, although less acute than previously, is far from being solved. Such materials still abound in many rivers, three characteristic examples being the Trent throughout much of its course, the Mersey below Howley Weir at Warrington and the Calder at Castleford.

One might expect that of all the rivers in the UK the Thames, because of the excess of population crowding its banks, would be amongst the most heavily polluted. Indeed the problem of the Thames is mammoth in its proportions. For example, between Teddington and Southend at least 20 sewage works discharge their effluents directly into the river. Effluents are also received from a myriad of industrial enterprises including some 24 power stations, and the situation is further complicated by the addition of storm waters to the polluting load, particularly in the stretch of the river 10 miles above and 10 miles below London Bridge. But over the past few years the situation of the Thames has not deteriorated; rather has it improved and the river is frequently cited as the classical example of how modern technology can combat water pollution. By the application of technological expertise the quality of both sewage and industrial effluent has been raised, and as a result the degree of contamination of the river has declined. Whereas in the early 1950's fish had vanished from the Thames, in 1970 some 40 species had returned included amongst their number the haddock, the herring, the sprat, the perch and the pike; indeed there was even the suggestion that salmon may reappear, and that as in bygone days, the river might become a favourite hunting ground for anglers. However in October 1970 all the achievements with respect to the Thames over the past decade were placed in jeopardy. This was because of a strike of sewage workers which lasted for some weeks and in the course of which large amounts of raw sewage entered the river. The long term effects of the strike remain to be evaluated.

So far British lakes show no equivalent of Lake Erie or Lake Michigan. However, pollution by the phosphates and nitrates contained in fertilisers does occur, and early signs of eutrophication have been reported from Lough Neagh in Ulster and Loch Leven in Scotland; in the latter there are now suggestions that fishing has been adversely affected by this change. It would indeed be tragic if a situation comparable to that affecting the Great Lakes in North America was allowed to occur in Britain. Only constant vigilance on the part of the authorities will prevent such a development.

Britons can take no pride in their estuaries and tidal waters. Seventy-five per cent of our sewage and industrial effluent is treated with varying efficiency in disposal works and discharged thence into inland rivers; however, the remaining 25 per cent is discharged raw or with only minimal treatment either into estuaries or into the open sea. Accordingly it comes as no

surprise to learn that estuaries in Britain, housing as they
frequently do large centres of population, are grossly polluted,
and are in this respect much inferior to our inland rivers and
canals. The short-sighted policy of caring for rivers and
neglecting estuaries is based on two major fallacies. The first is
that the relatively high salt content of esturial waters has a
specific purifying action. The second is that estuaries, in
contrast to rivers, provide the possibility for almost unlimited
dilution of sewage and trade wastes rendering the latter
relatively harmless. Many people appear to forget that the river
and the estuary do not operate in isolation. Rather are they
mutually dependent, and in areas of high population density it
is not uncommon for there to be a backward movement of
polluting material from the estuary to the river. This is
especially liable to occur at the time of the spring tide and in
the presence of a favourable wind; it is of serious import, for it
can be a major factor in nullifying any attempts which have
previously been made to purify the river itself.

Amongst the most seriously contaminated estuaries in
England are the Mersey, the Tees, the Tyne, the Humber, the
Usk, the Severn and the Ribble. The situation on Tyneside has
already been commented upon, and it is worth noting that in
this waterway bacterial pollution affects not only the estuary
but extends some five miles out into the open sea. The Tees
estuary houses a population of over 400,000 and has been
stated to receive as many as 500 untreated discharges; it is
therefore not surprising that in recent years the oxygen content
of the water has plummeted and that fish have vanished. On the
other hand the Thames estuary, like the river itself, remains in a
reasonably satisfactory state largely due to the herculean
attempts of the Greater London Council to extend facilities for
sewage treatment in that area.

In Scotland some 80 per cent of rivers are relatively
unsullied, but in the central belt of the country—in an area of
high population density—there is pollution of both Clyde and
Forth estuaries. The worst area of the Clyde extends for 12
miles below Glasgow, and here marine life is under constant
attack. In August 1970 pollution of the Firth of Forth in the
Seafield area of Edinburgh received considerable publicity in

the local press. A group of doctors working at the Eastern General Hospital in that city complained that within 100 yards of their wards there lay some 10,000 yards of untreated sewage. They noted that on warm evenings the heavy and highly obnoxious odour of hydrogen sulphide permeated the hospital, nauseating patients and staff alike. They took a long cool look at the social priorities of their city which at very large expense had just acted as hostess to the Ninth Commonwealth Games and which was currently preparing to receive guests for the Twenty-Fourth International Festival. In their opinion Edinburgh had got its values wrong and stood accused of 'having powdered its nose and having neglected to wipe its bottom!'.

Grossly polluted estuaries are both unattractive and squalid. Indeed, they are the Achilles heel of those who utter soothing platitudes about the British situation with respect to environmental contamination. Our esturial waters frequently exude offensive smells; amenity of all kind disappears, and the capacity for recreation is destroyed. If the degree of pollution is severe bathing may become a health hazard and diseases such as typhoid and dysentery have been known to follow such exposure. The angler bemoans esturial pollution, and one of the problems which he faces is that migratory fish such as trout and salmon fail to make their appearance in inland rivers because they find it impossible to pass the barrier of contamination in the estuary. Frequently estuaries contain valuable shell fisheries which are rich in species such as oysters, mussels, clams and cockles. If the estuary becomes polluted the fish become diseased and are no longer suitable for human consumption. A situation of this type is already developing in certain parts of the UK. Oyster fishing has now ceased in the Tamar and Lynher Rivers and has been reduced elsewhere, for example on the Colne and the Roach. At Morecambe, at Lytham and in the estuary of the Wash mussel fisheries are encountering difficulties. The town of Musselburgh is in close geographical proximity to Edinburgh and draws its name from its shellfish; however, in recent years as a result of the pollution of the Firth of Forth from raw sewage, notices have appeared on Musselburgh's beaches indicating that the mussels can no longer be eaten.

What of sewage disposal in the UK? Is it better or worse
than elsewhere? On a comparative basis the record is not too
unsatisfactory, and in 1970 a report issued by the Ministry of
Housing and Local Government stated that 94 per cent of the
population of England and Wales was provided with main
sewage drainage. Nevertheless, over one million dwelling houses
and more than three million people remain unconnected to this
form of drainage and even in this day and age there are still
some 270,000 houses without WC's! Even the most sanguine
official would surely agree that these figures give no cause for
complacency. However, there are three additional factors which
are important. The first is that our population, far from
remaining static or tending to fall, continues to rise, and this will
undoubtedly further tax our resources in relation to sewage
disposal. Secondly, many of the sewers which are currently in
use are defective due to excessive age or to faulty original
design. Finally, the standards used to assess the degree of river
pollution must now be regarded as inadequate, having been laid
down by a Royal Commission which after deliberations
extending over 17 years finally published its recommendations
in 1915 at the height of the First World War!

Amongst the major polluters in the UK local authorities hold
pride of place. From the day of their election our city fathers
are conditioned to the belief that sewage does not bring them
votes; as a result in their political spectrum other activities such
as house building and education generally take precedence over
repairs to inadequate sewerage systems and to the construction
of new plants. Nationalised industries such as the National Coal
Board and the Central Electricity Generating Board are heavy
polluters as is privately owned industry. An increasingly
important source of contamination comes from farms which
each year pump more and more phosphates and nitrates from
fields into rivers. All these organisations carry much weight in
the corridors of power and in this sphere of activity they speak
with a united voice. Who is there to oppose them and to put
forward the conservationist viewpoint?—only our diligent,
efficient but relatively weak River Authorities. The analogy of
David and Goliath does not come amiss!

Europe and the USSR

The countries of Western Europe take pride in their industrialisation and affluence; as a result pollution of their water supplies is occurring on an ever increasing scale. Indeed the River Rhine must now be a contender for the world's most contaminated waterway. The heavy industries of the Ruhr in West Germany pour their effluents into the Rhine and there is also a heavy discharge of untreated sewage. The Dutch, well known for their dedication to the reclaiming of land—a not unreasonable activity in their highly overpopulated country—urgently require diversions from the Rhine's waters in order to flush salt out of areas of land reclaimed from the sea. In recent years this process has become increasingly difficult because the cleansing capacity of the water has been reduced due to the contamination of the river as it traverses France and Federal Germany. In June 1969 pollution of the Rhine became headline news throughout the world. Small quantities of a highly toxic insecticide, endo-sulphan, were loosed from a barge into the stretch of the Rhine which flows through Germany. The river was polluted as far as its outlet to the sea in the Netherlands and large numbers of fish died.

Water pollution is rife in France and many rivers in the vicinity of industrial towns remain heavily contaminated. Sewage disposal in France would appear to be especially unsatisfactory, and an article in the newspaper *Figaro* in September 1969 stated that out of 25 French cities with more than 100,000 inhabitants only six or seven possessed a sewage works! On the Côte d'Azur near Nice and other major cities beaches are polluted with raw sewage and the sea in the vicinity is dying. Lakes in Western Europe are failing rapidly. The once beautiful Lake Constance on the German-Swiss frontier is reported to be accumulating trade wastes and other contaminants at an alarming rate. The beaches of Lake Lugano are befouled; the Lake of Zurich is stated to be virtually devoid of marine life, while northern Italian Lakes with the possible exception of Garda are polluted by sewage, industrial effluent or both. The waters of Lake Geneva are now deoxygenated because of the increasing deposition of pollutants, and unless remedial action is taken quickly eutrophication will be the result. Fish in Lake Geneva are now under attack. Once the perch was free to roam the lake and send the gourmet into transports of delight; now the numbers of this species are diminishing, as it is forced to live in an ever shallower layer of water at the top of the lake.

Sweden is a highly affluent society with a low population density except in its major cities. In recent years it has been plagued by water pollution, and its government has been forced to introduce stringent legislation in an attempt to control it. Contamination by mercury has been serious; there have been widespread deaths amongst bird populations and the fertility of the survivors has been impaired; fish have died in large numbers and at one time fishing had to be banned in some 80 districts in the country. Although industrial enterprises contributed to this form of pollution the main source was the widespread use of seed dressings containing methyl mercury. Sweden is exceedingly rich in lakes; it has over 100,000 which in aggregate occupy some 10 per cent of the land area. Many of them remain grossly polluted—not only with mercury but with all types of industrial contaminant. Good examples are Lake Trümmen near the industrial town of Vaxsö in Central Sweden and Lake Hornborga in the southern part of the country. In the former the major culprits are raw sewage and pulp mill effluent. The latter was once a sanctuary for wild fowl, but now the water is befouled and the birds are departing.

At the commencement of this chapter is was stated that water pollution knew no ideological boundaries. Indeed it is manifest in countries with Marxist regimes just as it is in their capitalistic counterparts. Communist countries place great emphasis on production, and traditionally the government official on whom the accolades are showered is the one who conclusively demonstrates that his efforts have resulted in an increase in economic activity in the area under his jurisdiction. But what of the condition of the waterways in that self same area? Up till now these have featured little in his apologia although in the future they may become a prime concern.

The example of Lake Baikal in Siberia is important. It is believed to be the largest fresh water lake in the world; it has a wealth of scenic beauty; it has been described as an ecological paradise and around its shores rare plants and animals flourish. Now pulp and papermaking plants are in the process of construction in close proximity to the lake; as a result squalid effluents are being discharged into its waters and plants and animal life are being placed in jeopardy. And all this is happening in spite of strong protests from conservationist groups throughout the Soviet Union.

There is at present much anxiety in the USSR with respect to its great inland sea, the Caspian. Kasymov (1970) states that there is now every reason to expect that the Caspian will die, that fish and other animals will no longer be able to inhabit it and that it will become useless from the technological point of view. Each year the Caspian receives approximately one million tons of petroleum and petroleum biproducts, 100,000 tons of asphalt, the same amount of sulphuric acid and 10,000 tons of other industrial materials toxic to aquatic life. The activities of the Caspian Steamship Line and the Caspian tanker fleet cause pollution as does raw sewage emanating especially from the area around the city of Baku. The result has been that the oxygen content of the Caspian's water has decreased, the concentrations of substances such as ammoniacal nitrogen, phosphates and nitrates have markedly risen, marine organisms such as phytoplankton and zooplankton have been markedly reduced in number and fishery reserves have been grossly depleted.

In the last 34 years catches of fish in the Caspian Sea have plummeted from 300 million to 110 million kilogrammes. Species which have suffered preferentially include the sturgeon, the sea pike, the roach and the sild. The sturgeon is the source of 95 per cent of the world's caviare, and in 1960 the catch in the Caspian fell to a record low figure of 11,000 tons. Now the Soviet Government is attempting to restock the Caspian with young sturgeons from hatcheries.

The Third World

Water pollution is rampant throughout the underdeveloped continents of Asia, Africa and Latin America. However, the control of water pollution is low on the list of priorities of governments faced by the appalling problems of over-population, burgeoning urbanisation, illiteracy and the ever present menace of famine. Many rivers in the underdeveloped world are nothing more than open sewers, and the plight of cities straddling their banks is to be seen to be believed.

Egypt is a somewhat special case. It is an underdeveloped country the population of which is likely to double in as little as 25 years; it has a very high population density near the Nile valley; elsewhere it is sparsely settled. During the early 1950's Egypt commenced negotiations with the Western Powers, especially the USA and Britain, to build a dam at Aswan on the Nile. The enterprise was lauded by Egyptian politicians; this would be the dawn of the millennium which would bring untold economic benefits to their country. Then politics intervened. Due mainly to the vacillations of the then US Secretary of State, John Foster Dulles, negotiations with the West were broken off, and this was a major factor in precipitating the Suez Crisis of 1956. Nasser turned to the Soviet bloc and since then the funds for the construction of the dam have been supplied mainly by the USSR. The dam is now virtually complete, and before Nasser's death in late 1970 Alexei Kosygin of the Soviet Union officiated at its ceremonial opening. But major problems are occurring with the dam; indeed there is already evidence that from the ecological point of view its presence may be highly deleterious. In the first place the Egyptian sardine fishing industry centred in the Mediterranean has been severely affected, mainly because the nutrients discharged by the Nile in the form of silt into the Mediterranean Sea are held back by the dam and do not traverse the river. Secondly, the loss of nutrients in the silt has made it necessary to treat the previously fertile lower Nile Valley with fertiliser, the latter being manufactured in factories which have diverted electric power from the dam itself. Thirdly, there are difficulties in relation to the 200-mile long Lake Nasser which is currently forming behind the dam. Evaporation of water from the lake has proved to be much higher than was originally anticipated and may in the long term equal the amount which the Nile was expected to provide for irrigation. Furthermore, the lake could eventually silt up, thus nullifying any temporary advantage which might have been gained by its construction. Another and totally unexpected complication is that the warm and slow moving waters of the irrigation ditches are likely to provide an ideal breeding ground for the snails which are the intermediate hosts of the parasitic worms carrying the serious and crippling disease known as Schistosomiasis. Already this condition is endemic in Egypt, and it would certainly be ironic if its incidence were increased further as a result of the construction of the dam.

The Aswan dam provides a classical example of the perils which are likely to ensue when technological development is undertaken in complete ignorance of the long term effects which may be produced. The facile and short-sighted view of politicians that a country's economic problems will be solved by prestige symbols of this type has been proved to be erroneous on so many occasions that it is indeed surprising to find that such costly projects continue to find favour throughout the underdeveloped world. The final tragedy with respect to the Aswan dam is that, quite apart from the ecological disadvantages which will result from its construction, any beneficial effects which might have accrued are likely to be neutralised immediately by the sheer growth of human numbers since the project was initiated. How much better for the fragile Egyptian economy would it have been if the funds squandered on the dam had been used instead in a sustained effort to limit the soaring population of that country.

Ailing Seas

Traditionally the world's oceans have been regarded as a dumping ground for all manner of products including oil, sewage, chemical effluent, heavy metals, pesticides, radioactive wastes and lethal gases used in warfare. It has only recently been recognised, firstly that the capacity of oceans to absorb such materials is not illimitable, and secondly that the long term biological effects resulting from contamination of the sea by such products are completely unknown and could well be highly inimical to the human race. For instance, what information is currently available on the long term effects to humanity of the 67 tons of lethal nerve gas dumped by the USA in August

1970 in the Atlantic Ocean less than 160 miles from the Bahamas and in an area served by the Gulf Stream? We are forced to admit our total ignorance of the repercussions of this unfortunate act, but we are now only too well aware that the overall pollution of the world's oceans is increasing apace. This fact was high-lighted by the experience of the intrepid Norwegian explorer, Thor Heyerdahl, who navigated the Atlantic during 1969 in his papyrus raft ship called *Ra.* Heyerdahl found that he and his colleagues could not fill their tooth mugs from the ocean because of the filthy condition of the water and stated that much of the mid-Atlantic 'looked like a sewer' due to pollution by oil and solid matter.

Oil pollution by tankers constitutes one of the major threats to the sea and its beaches, and in recent years this type of contamination has received much publicity. Oil pollution is of two types—accidental which arises from human error, and operational which is deliberate, oil being loosed into the sea from tankers as part of an internationally accepted procedure. It is the former type of contamination which generally attracts the newspaper headlines.

To the British people pollution by oil was thrown into sharp relief in March 1967 when the large tanker *Torrey Canyon* ran aground off Cornwall near Lands End. Some 177,000 tons of crude oil were spilled. The sea was powerless to absorb it, and slowly and inexorably the chocolate-coloured slick made its way to the Cornish coast and three weeks later to the coast of Brittany. The British Government mounted an action comparable to a military campaign. The Royal Air Force dropped napalm bombs on the slick and a fleet of warships arrived on the scene armed with detergents which they proceeded to spray wildly and haphazardly in all directions. The pollution of beaches continued, the slaughter of wildlife was pathetic to witness and the tourist traffic to Cornwall went into temporary eclipse in spite of Harold Wilson's reassuring statement that his holiday in that part of the world would not be cancelled.

There have been many other disasters of a similar kind. In January 1969 beaches in the Californian resort of Santa Barbara were polluted by oil believed to emanate from an underground source. In early 1970 in Canada the tanker *Arrow* ran aground at Arichat in Nova Scotia. The oil leaking from the vessel polluted beaches for miles around and there was much destruction of bird life. In May 1970 the Norwegian tanker *Polycommander* caught fire after an explosion; the result was oil pollution of several beaches between Vigo and Bayonne on the North West Atlantic coast of Spain. In November 1970 the Liberian tanker *Marlena* went aground on the coast of Sicily near Syracuse. Fourteen thousand tons of crude oil were spilled, but fortunately damage to beaches by the slick was relatively slight.*

Oil is not the only villain of the seas. Other agents make their contribution, and this is well illustrated by the example of the Baltic where a very serious situation is rapidly developing. The main factors responsible for the pollution of the Baltic are untreated sewage discharged from cities such as Leningrad and Malmö, industrial effluent emanating particularly from the wood pulp industries of Sweden and Finland, and agricultural waste derived from land sated with fertilisers. Sewage with its high content of synthetic detergents has increased the phosphate content of Baltic waters by a factor of 3 in 15 years. The degree of oxygenation is falling, and the DDT content of Baltic seals is reported to be 10 times higher than that of their fellows inhabiting the North Sea. Unless present trends are reversed the Baltic is likely to become an 'oceanic desert' comparable to the Black Sea or Lake Erie. Other areas of sea are now showing symptoms similar to those of the Baltic. Thus marine life is dying in the Oslo Fjord in Norway while, as indicated previously, an area of the Atlantic Ocean in the vicinity of New York City is so heavily polluted with sewage and industrial efflent, that it can no longer cleanse itself and is for all practical purposes dead.

Now there are disturbing reports of upsets of ecological balance in some of our oceans. Taylor in his *Doomsday Book* is pessimistic on this score and calls attention to the great increase in numbers which has recently taken place in the coral-eating star fish known as *Acanthaster Planci.* This fish has already destroyed over 1,000 miles of the Great Barrier Reef off North

---

* The most recent oil spillage took place in Japan in December 1971 when the Liberian tanker, *Juliana*, on charter to Shell, broke in two after hitting a breakwater in the large port of Niigata. There was a leakage of 5,000 tons of oil resulting in marked ecological damage.

East Australia and is now attacking other Pacific islands such as Wake, Guam, the Marshall Islands and Fiji. The situation could prove serious from the economic point of view because most of these islands have a brisk fish trade and the reefs which are currently disappearing contain the lagoons in which the fish are caught. The reason for the proliferation of *A. planci* is not at present known, and it is possible that its presence bears no relationship to the activities of man. On the other hand, as suggested by Taylor, the stimulus to the reproductive bonanza of *A. planci* could be the presence of pollutants particularly DDT in the waters of that area.

In Britain pollution of beaches is commonplace. A major and highly unattractive contaminant is raw sewage, and it was because of its frequency that the Coastal Antipollution League once compared the UK to 'a jewel set in a sea of sewage'. Many of our beaches are highly squalid, being littered with choice items such as faecal material, sanitary towels, dirty toilet paper and contraceptives especially the condom. In the North East of England wastes from collieries constitute a special problem, and each year the National Coal Board dumps some four million tons of colliery wastes on to the beaches of Durham and Northumberland rendering the latter desolate, blackened and scarred and reducing their marine life to exiguous proportions.

The territorial waters surrounding the UK also receive large amounts of untreated sewage. Furthermore, they are the recipients of what is known as sewage sludge, this being the solids accumulated during sewage treatment. Thousands of tons of sewage sludge are dumped into the sea each day, two major sites for this activity being the outer Thames estuary and the vicinity of Liverpool. Sludge has recently been recognised to be an important carrier of synthetic pesticides such as DDT, and it will be stressed in Chapter VII that such substances can be very harmful to many forms of aquatic life. A rich diet of industrial effluents is also being supplied to the waters around our coasts, special offenders in this respect being iron and steel works, paper and pulp mills, distilleries, and factories for the production of fish meal and for food processing. Indeed the assault on British territorial waters is really prodigious and at present it is estimated that along the East and South coasts of England alone there are discharged into the sea each day about five million cubic metres of domestic sewage, three million cubic metres of industrial waste and seven million cubic metres of cooling water from power stations in the vicinity. Eventually our fishing industry must reel from this onslaught and our highly lucrative shrimp and salmon fisheries would appear to be especially vulnerable in this respect. Polluted beaches and seas give rise to health hazards when bathing, and sooner or later we are likely to see increases in the incidence of diseases such as typhoid fever, dysentery, hepatitis and various types of gastroenteritis. The position of seas and beaches in the UK with respect to pollution must be regarded as highly unsatisfactory. Only governmental intervention tied to increasing public expenditure is likely to improve matters.

Control of Water Pollution

Mechanisms for the control of water pollution vary greatly in different countries. However, in general, they are highly complicated and cumbersome as the example of the UK will illustrate with considerable clarity.

In Britain the water which we drink from the tap is supplied to us by the courtesy of our Water Boards. Local councils supply the drains which remove the water from our houses and from factories; they also operate our sewage works and take responsibility for the quality of the sewage effluent which is discharged. Although Water Boards and local authorities are important in the general scheme of water resources pride of place in caring for our rivers goes to our so-called River Authorities. These organisations came into being in 1948; there are 29 such bodies in England and Wales and 9 in Scotland where they are termed River Purification Boards. The jurisdiction of the River Authorities extends from the source of the river to the mouth of its estuary, and they are the only body to which the river in its entirety is important. In theory they should be very powerful; in practice they are weak and, as has been noted previously, they are frequently over-ruled by other public bodies notably local councils and nationalised industries.

An analogy from political life is apposite to the present

situation of our River Authorities and a former Prime Minister, Stanley Baldwin supplies it. Baldwin had been harried mercilessly for months by the press lords, Rothermere and Beaverbrook. Finally in March 1931 at a meeting chaired by Duff Cooper he erupted, and in one of his most famous phrases he described his tormentors as seeking 'power without responsibility, the prerogative of the harlot throughout the ages'. At present the position of our River Authorities is precisely the reverse of that of our former press barons because to them is vouchsafed responsibility in the absence of real power.

Lord Kennet, writing just prior to the defeat of the Labour Government in June 1970, stressed that river pollution in the UK did not stop with River Authorities, local authorities and Water Boards. Several Ministers of the Crown are also implicated. Thus if there is a possible hazard to fresh water fish the Minister of Agriculture must be consulted and he, together with the Minister of Housing, must approve any bye-laws passed by the River Authorities. If materials dangerous to the public are being carried in rivers the responsibility becomes that of the Minister of Transport, while in Scotland and Wales, the respective Secretaries of State would expect to be consulted on such matters.

What of other countries? In the USA a landmark in the control of river pollution was the passage by the Congress in 1965 of the Water Quality Act which directed the individual states of the Union to establish appropriate standards for their water supplies. The Federal Government provides financial support to combat water pollution, but at the time of writing, many of the schemes which have been put forward have foundered because of lack of money. During 1969 President Nixon established under his own chairmanship an Environmental Quality Council; this subdivides into numerous sub-committees one of which deals with water pollution. The efficacy of this type of administrative structure remains to be established. Sweden has shown great interest in the control of environmental pollution, and recently the Swedish Government set up a single organisation known as the National Conservancy Board which is expected to assume responsibility for all forms of pollution including that involving water. Time will tell whether a unitary organisation of this kind will prove to be more efficient than the highly diffuse types of administrative structure which have grown up piecemeal in most other countries.

The control of sea pollution, like that of rivers, is a highly complicated topic, and again the UK provides a good example of the tangled administrative web which has grown up with the passage of years. The Board of Trade* is responsible for the prevention of oil pollution of the seas, and the same body regulates the transport of dangerous goods by sea. If oil escapes from submarines or from pipelines the responsibility formerly lay with the Ministry of Technology; now presumably it will be vested in the new Department of Trade and Industry. Should the oil pollute our beaches the local authorities, working in collaboration with the Minister of Housing and Local Government,† must ensure its removal. Eleven sea fisheries in England and Wales make their own bye-laws regarding the pollution of territorial waters, and such bye-laws must be approved by the Ministry of Agriculture and Fisheries. At present no statutory control exists with respect to the discharge of sewage into the sea, but there is a strong likelihood that this situation will alter in the future.

Pollution of the open sea as distinct from territorial waters is a matter of even greater complexity. In this field there exists a body known as the Inter-Governmental Maritime Consultative Organisation (IMCO) within the framework of which a number of international conventions have been negotiated. In recent years the organisation has been increasingly concerned by the dangers which are likely to be posed as a result of the discharge of oil from tankers, and episodes such as those of the *Torrey Canyon,* and *Arrow* and the *Polycommander* have emphasised the importance of this aspect of its work. Problems involving international relationships are generally very difficult to solve. Pollution of the sea is no exception, and rapid progress in this area cannot be anticipated.

In the overcrowded and contaminated world of the 1970's

* Now merged into the Department of Trade and Industry.
† Now incorporated in the Department of the Environment.

penalties for water pollution have usually been grossly inadequate. For example, the British firm which recently released cyanide into an Essex river was taken to court and convicted; a fine of £25 was imposed! Similarly a Derbyshire firm of bleachers and dyers was convicted of four offences of discharging effluent into a river and polluting it. The firm was fined £10 for each offence, the total being £40! In the USA the inability to 'make the polluter pay' has been largely responsible for much of the sad saga recounted earlier in this chapter. However, the situation in North America now appears to be changing rapidly, and there are recent press reports that fines of as much as $10,000 per day are being levied on industrial enterprises which fail to conform to recognised standards with respect to the quality of their effluent. As in so many other areas of modern life the laws in relation to water pollution are antiquated and anachronistic, based as they are on a world scene totally at variance with that encountered in the early 1970's. There is no question that the laws require to be changed. Will our legislators grasp the nettle and act before it is too late? Or will they employ what C. P. Snow has so aptly termed the 'technique of the intricate defensive' obstinately preserving the status quo by an endless stream of highly sophisticated rhetoric justifying the reasons for inaction?

References

ARTHUR, DON R. (1969). *Survival: Man and his Environment.* London, English University Press Ltd., Ch. 11.
BALTIC BECOMING DEAD SEA (1970). *The Times,* 6th March.
BUGLER, JEREMY (1970). 'Can industry afford to come clean?'. *Observer,* 1st February.
CHARLIER, ROGER H. (1969). 'Crisis year for the Great Lakes'. *New Scientist,* 18th December.
EHRLICH, PAUL R. (1968). *The Population Bomb.* New York, Ballantine Books Inc.
GOLDMAN MARSHALL, J. (1970). 'Russian roulette—Environmental disruption in the Soviet Union'. *The Ecologist,* 1, pp. 18-23.
HOGBERG, GENE H. (1970). *Europe confronts environmental crisis.* Pasadena, California, Ambassador College Press.
HORNING, ROBERTA and WELSH, JAMES (1970). 'A World in danger—The Environment: Is it Problem No. 1?'. *Washington Star,* 11th January to 18th January.

HUBERTY, MARTIN R. and FLOCK, WARREN L. (1959). *Natural Resources.* New York, McGraw-Hill Book Co. Inc., Ch. 2.

KASYMOV, A. G. (1970). 'Industry and the productivity of the Caspian Sea'. *Marine Pollution Bulletin*, 1, pp. 100-103.

KENNET, LORD (1970). *Controlling our environment.* London, Fabian Research Series 283, February.

LEACH, GERALD (1970). 'New Pollution scare in US–Mercury Poisoning'. *Observer,* 2nd August.

MARX, WESLEY (1970). *The Frail Ocean.* New York, Ballantine Books Inc.

O'MALLEY, MARTIN (1970). 'Pollution casts grim shadows'. *The Times,* 23rd February.

OUR POLLUTED PLANET (1970). Pasadena, California, Ambassador College Press.

PACKER, EDWIN (1970). 'Our filthy rivers—here are the guilty men'. *Medical News Tribune.*

TAKEN FOR GRANTED: REPORT OF THE WORKING PARTY ON SEWAGE DISPOSAL (1970). London, HM Stationery Office.

TAYLOR, G. R. (1970). *The Doomsday Book.* London, Thames and Hudson.

THE POLLUTERS–COAL BOARD PLAYS HAVOC WITH DURHAM'S BEACHES (1970). A News Team Enquiry, *The Times*, 25th March.

WHALE, JOHN (1969). 'River cleaners'. *Your Environment*, No. 1, pp. 22-25.

WHEELER, ALWYNE (1970). 'The fish that came back'. *Your Environment*, No. 2, pp. 62-63.

VII

ALL-PERVASIVE PESTICIDES

If you poison us, do we not die?

The Merchant of Venice

There are many definitions of the term pesticide. One which is convenient and which has been widely favoured is to define it as 'a chemical agent used by man in order to kill or to control living organisms'. The meaning of the word is broad, including as it does substances such as insecticides, weedkillers (herbicides) and compounds which are lethal to recognised pests such as fungi, worms and mice.

Pesticides are very numerous; moreover, their numbers are rapidly increasing. They are of great interest to many sections of the community including scientists, agriculturalists, veterinarians, doctors, industrialists and conservationists. Furthermore, they are a matter of intense concern to the lay public who on the one hand fear them because of the ill effects which they may eventually produce in mankind, yet on the other hand, recognise and appreciate the benefits which may accrue from their use in terms of the prevention of disease and increase in crop yields.

Where does the truth lie in relation to pesticides? Are they the friend of *homo sapiens* or are they his deadly foe? The overall situation is exceedingly complex, and the ultimate conclusions are far from clear. I shall begin by discussing the insecticides, concentrating particularly on DDT.

Two main chemical groups of compounds are currently used as insecticides. The first and more important comprises the *chlorinated hydrocarbons* or *organochlorine compounds.* Foremost in this category is DDT together with its breakdown products, DDD and DDE; also included are substances such as dieldrin, endrin, aldrin, isodrin, heptachlor and toxaphene. The second group, the *organophosphates,* includes important compounds such as parathion, malathion, Menazon and Azodrin. Of all these materials DDT has been by far the most widely used, and Rudd, in his *Pesticides and the Living Landscape,* estimated that in 1964 the total world production of DDT was in the region of 225 million lbs; since then the figure has undoubtedly increased to a considerable extent. In 1964 a report from the World Health Organisation stated that 50,000 metric tons of insecticides, the major component of which was DDT, were being used each year in projects aimed to eradicate malaria. Taylor in his *Doomsday Book* of 1970 states that the amount of DDT distributed on the earth's surface is of the order of one million metric tons.

The Saga of DDT

Research workers first succeeded in synthesising DDT towards the end of the nineteenth century. For over six decades its insecticidal properties remained unrecognised, and the compound was relegated to an inconspicuous place on the laboratory shelf. The First World War came and went without the use of DDT. In this conflict louse-borne diseases such as typhus, trench fever and relapsing fever ran rampant and caused high mortality rates amongst the troops. Such infections were prevalent in almost every theatre of war; they were present on the Western Front, while in 1916 during the ill-fated operation at Gallipoli, they caused much distress and suffering. Their incidence was especially high in Eastern Europe where the armies of Tsarist Russia were opposing those of Imperial Germany and Austria-Hungary; indeed in these theatres of war there was scarcely a soldier who did not harbour lice.

The picture in the Second World War was entirely different. Even in 1939 when the hostilities began, effective insecticides had already become available. One of these was a compound known as pyrethrum; it was prepared from flowers such as chrysanthemums and it had a reasonably good record when used against the mosquito. About this time DDT was introduced, and there can be little doubt that it altered the course of history. The effects produced by the compound were notable in two major ways. Firstly, it controlled the spread of louse-born typhus, and as a result the epidemics of this disease so characteristic of the First World War failed to make their appearance in the Allied armies; on the other hand, in German occupied territories where DDT either was not used at all or was employed to a very limited extent, serious epidemics of this disease occurred and exacted a heavy toll. Secondly, the effect of DDT on the mosquito appeared to be nothing short of miraculous. When swamps were sprayed with relatively small amounts of the compound they were rapidly freed from these insects, and as a result of the use of DDT a decisive step had been taken in eliminating malaria from our planet.

The Allied Powers had every reason to be thankful to DDT because, together with the atomic bomb dropped on the Japanese cities of Hiroshima and Nagasaki in 1945, it was a major factor in winning the war for their cause. The widespread use of the insecticide enabled successful campaigns to be undertaken in tropical countries where previously military operations would have been either difficult or impossible; as a result victory against the Japanese forces was notably hastened. Like the antibiotics penicillin and streptomycin, DDT took its place amongst the 'wonder drugs' of the twentieth century; indeed it was hailed as one of the major 'saviours of mankind'. Assuredly its record at that time was most impressive. It had proved a vital factor in military operations; it was saving countless civilian lives from diseases which had hitherto proved fatal; it was protecting crops at reasonable cost, and as a result it was increasing agricultural production in areas where, since time immemorial, famine had been endemic. Obviously the stage was set for a period of euphoria.

The euphoria lasted well into the 1950's. Then disturbing reports began to appear. In the course of campaigns against malaria fish were seen to be dying in large numbers in streams and rivers treated with DDT. Whole populations of birds in countries such as the UK and the USA were either dying or failing to reproduce, and when examined under laboratory conditions, were found to contain large amounts of DDT in their muscles and fatty tissue. There were widespread and persistent rumours that pests were becoming increasingly resistant to DDT and that such resistance was liable to continue even when ever increasing amounts of the insecticide were used.

Then in 1962 *Silent Spring* was published. Written by the

biologist Rachel Carson the book was addressed to a general rather than to a specialist audience; it became an immediate best seller. *Silent Spring* was the work of a scientist holding deep convictions, and it took the form of an impassioned plea for a more rational approach to the use of pesticides throughout the world. The book concentrated particularly on the deleterious effects produced by DDT and other insecticides on birds and other forms of wildlife, but, in addition, concern was expressed regarding the possible long term effects of ingestion of such pesticides in man himself. As might have been anticipated the book came under violent attack from powerful economic and business interests in the USA, such organisations being determined to continue with the manufacture and use of pesticides irrespective of the consequences. Seldom did the dialogue between the conservationist and industrial viewpoints reach such a pitch of acrimony. All manner of pejorative comments were made about *Silent Spring* by those to whom the views expressed were anathema. Thus the book was claimed to be unscientific, uncritical and even wilfully misleading; the integrity of the author was assailed together with her objectivity. Now in the somewhat calmer atmosphere of the early 1970's what appraisal can be made of *Silent Spring*? It can now be said that Rachel Carson's warnings, far from being alarmist as they were initially portrayed, held much validity. Indeed no greater vindication of her views is available than the fact that politicians in several countries have finally reacted to public clamour either by an outright ban on the use of DDT as in Sweden, Norway, Denmark and Canada, or by an attenuation of its use as in the UK and the USA.

Some Examples of the Misuse of Insecticides

The pesticide literature is replete with horror stories which relate mainly to the malign effects produced by these compounds on wildlife. Birds of all types have been especially vulnerable to pesticide toxicity and as a result have suffered severely. The list of birds which have been affected is almost endless and includes robins, quails, turkeys, Bermuda petrels, ospreys, pheasants, partridges, chaffinches, ducks, falcons, eagles and seagulls. Fish also have been singled out for attack, foremost amongst them being the trout and the salmon. Mammals have not been immune to poisoning by pesticides, and there are reports of adverse effects in mice, rats, opossums, badgers and foxes. Here I cite some examples of the type of damage which has been produced, drawing illustrations from the USA, the UK and Latin America.

The classical US example of pollution by an insecticide remains that of Clear Lake in California, and data in relation to this episode have now been carefully and critically documented. Clear Lake is a renowned beauty spot much beloved by anglers and noted for the recreational facilities which it provides for water-skiers and holidaymakers of all kinds. However, the lake had one major disadvantage, namely that at certain times of the year it tended to become infested with midges or so-called gnats, the larvae of which lived in its waters. Vacationers became increasingly irritated by the presence of such gnats, and eventually in the late 1940's it was decided to spray the lake with an insecticide. Some consideration was given by the authorities to the substance which should be used and eventually a decision was made in favour of DDD. As mentioned earlier, this is a breakdown product of DDT; it is a close chemical relative of the parent compound but was considered to be less lethal to fish and other forms of aquatic life than DDT itself. The lake was first sprayed in 1949 at which time the calculation was made that, had the insecticide been dispersed evenly throughout the water, the very low concentration of 0.015 parts per million would have resulted. The spraying of 1949 was hailed as an unqualified success and this seemed a valid conclusion. Almost all the gnats had been eliminated; lethality to fish had not been demonstrated, and vacationers and officials were jubilant. In 1950 no further spraying was undertaken; during the year the gnats returned in small numbers but were not unduly troublesome. However, over the next two years the population of gnats again increased, and because of this two further sprayings with DDD were undertaken, one in 1954 and the other in 1957.

Two main types of ecological damage ensued. The first was increasing resistance to the pesticide; this was evidenced by the fact that by 1951 not only had certain strains of the typical Clear Lake gnat become resistant to DDD but an additional 150 species of insects and other pests also showed this property in varying degree. The second and much more sinister effect was the damage wrought by the insecticide to birds known as the Western Grebes. The latter resemble ducks, are noted for their skill in diving and feed mainly on small fishes and other forms of aquatic life. Prior to the first spraying some 1,000 pairs of grebes were known to be nesting in the vicinity of Clear Lake; however, by as early as 1950 there was definite evidence that the breeding habits of the birds had been disturbed. In 1954 after the second spraying large numbers of dead grebes were found; dead birds were also present in 1955 and 1956, and their numbers increased markedly after the final spraying in 1957. But in addition to killing the birds the pesticide gravely interfered with the reproductive capacity of the survivors. Thus no young were produced between 1950 and 1961, and it was only in the latter part of the decade of the 'sixties that some semblance of normal fertility was restored.

The story of Clear Lake provides an excellent example of how a pesticide is concentrated as it ascends the various component parts of the food chain. It has already been mentioned that the amount of DDD added to the water in 1949 produced a low overall level of less than 0.02 parts per million. However, rapid concentration of the pesticide subsequently occurred. The plants growing in the water concentrated it some 250 times to reach a figure of approximately 5 parts per million. Small fish eating the water weeds boosted the concentration to 10 parts per million, and predatory fish living on the small fish increased it further to some 200 parts per million. But the grebes were at the end of the food chain; they ate the predatory fish and as a result concentrated the DDD even more to levels ranging from 700 to 1600 parts per million. No doubt remained as to the cause of the high mortality rate amongst the grebes in Clear Lake; the villain of the piece was undoubtedly DDD.

The second example of the consequence of misuse of pesticides concerns Dutch elm disease. This is a condition caused by a fungus and carried by a bark beetle. The disease was first recognised in America in the early 1930's. Its incidence gradually increased over the years, and as a result elms—often planted as shade trees especially in surburban areas—came under increasing attack. From the mid 1950's onwards elms in various parts of the USA were sprayed repeatedly with large amounts of DDT. The beetles died as a result, but unfortunately so did many birds, one species preferentially affected being the American robin. There followed much research designed to elucidate the reasons for the high mortality rate amongst the robins; the conclusion was eventually reached that the birds had died both from direct poisoning due to the insecticide and from the ingestion of worms and caterpillars which had become contaminated with DDT. Even now the problem of the eradication of Dutch elm disease by pesticides has not been solved in the USA and elsewhere. Indeed as late as 1968 the newly formed Environmental Defense Association filed a suit against the Michigan Department of Agriculture and against numerous municipalities which were continuing to use the chlorinated hydrocarbons, DDT and dieldrin, in an attempt to control the condition.

Other illustrations of the misuse of pesticides in the North American continent abound. For example, when in Pennsylvania an attack was launched on the gypsy moth by spraying DDT on to the land with the aim on attaining a level of 1 lb per acre, anglers noted with dismay that fish were dying in large numbers in local streams. Similarly when during the 1950's the forests of northern New Brunswick in Canada were sprayed with DDT in an attempt to control an epidemic of spruce budworm, high lethality amongst fish, particularly salmon, was a major consequence. The sad story of what has been termed the 'Mississippi fish kill' is ably recounted by Frank Graham, Jr in his book *Disaster by Default*. The massacre took place in the early 1960's; endrin was the main culprit, the compound seeping into the river from agricultural land so treated and also being discharged from a manufacturing plant in Memphis, Tennessee. As a result of the contamination of the Mississippi between 10 and 15 million fish died over a period of three years. In addition to fish, numerous instances have been reported from the USA of other aquatic organisms, particularly fresh water molluscs, suffering at the hands of insecticides. Such animals are especially susceptible to this form of poisoning because they obtain their oxygen supplies from the water, and in order to 'breathe' adequately must pass very large amounts of water through their bodies.

Mention must be made of the tragic saga of the fire ant, for it represents a classical example of the chain of events likely to ensue when a highly complex problem is approached in a headlong and uncritical manner. One of the major points of controversy with respect to the fire ant was that considerable doubt existed in the minds of many as to whether the animal really constituted a crop pest. Nevertheless, in spite of the conflicting nature of the evidence the US Department of Agriculture was adamant and in 1957 embarked on a large spraying programme in nine States of the Union in an attempt to eradicate the fire ant. The pesticides employed in this enterprise were two in number—dieldrin and heptachlor—and they were applied in dosages as high as 2 lbs per acre of land. Effects on wildlife were catastrophic and in some areas bird populations were reduced by as much as 80 per cent. Harlem County in Texas was once famous for its quail; since 1957 the quail has been a rarity and in the words of the US Conservation Foundation the species was 'literally massacred' by the application of the pesticides. The final irony lay in the fact that the spraying programme was a total failure. It cost $15 million; however, it did not eradicate the fire ant which has now 'reinfested' most of the areas originally treated.

Although the USA has been the country in which the grossest examples of pesticide misuse have occurred, we in Britain have no cause for complacency in this respect. All types of wildlife have been affected in our country, and some of the most careful and painstaking work relating DDT and other insecticides to reproductive failure in birds has been published in the UK. The British experience with respect to the spider mite has been ably recounted by Mellanby in his *Pesticides and Pollution* and furnishes an interesting example of the disturbance in ecological balance which can ensue when an insecticide such as DDT is applied in excessive quantities. In Britain and throughout much of Western Europe it has been the custom to spray orchards with insecticides at frequent intervals in order to eliminate recognised pests such as the codling moth, the winter moth and various types of aphid, notably greenfly and black fly. As a result of such treatment the red spider mite which was known to inhabit outdoor fruit trees but which had previously not been troublesome, gradually altered its status to that of a pest. The reason for the excessive reproduction of this species soon became clear; it resulted from the ability of DDT to reduce the numbers of predatory insects the main function of which was to keep the population of spider mites within bounds.

Examples of resistance of various types of organism to DDT are numerous and Britain like other countries has had its troubles in this sphere. Our literature is already replete with reports purporting to show that initial applications of insecticides eliminate troublesome organisms such as house flies, cockroaches and bed bugs. However, later articles are often forced to admit that as the treatment continues, larger and larger dosages of the pesticide are required in order to keep the pest at bay. An analogy from the practice of medicine comes to mind here because the situation bears some resemblance to that of the heroin or morphine addict who requires ever increasing dosages of the drug in order to avoid the unpleasant sequelae associated with deprivation.

Our example from Latin America comes from the Cañete Valley in Peru. The details were provided by the Californian entomologist, R. F. Smith, and the story has been graphically recounted by the Ehrlichs in their *Population, Resources, Environment.* The aim of the exercise was to increase the valley's cotton yield by the elimination of pests such as aphids, the tobacco leaf worm and the boll weevil. The insecticides used initially were all chlorinated hydrocarbons and included DDT, benzene hexachloride (BHC) and toxaphene. The pattern of events was familiar but they had a dramatic quality seldom observed elsewhere. In the first few years from 1949 onwards the results of the spraying were highly gratifying, yields of cotton rising from 400 lbs per acre in 1950 to 648 lbs per acre by 1954. The cotton farmers were exultant, and it was decided that in view of the success the amounts of insecticides used should be increased. Draconian measures followed, in the course of which aeroplanes were used to spread insecticides 'like a blanket over the valley'. Trees were felled indiscriminately, bird life vanished from the area and insect predators were eliminated. The reckoning followed swiftly. In 1952 aphids became resistant to BHC; by 1954 toxaphene was failing to curb the spread of the tobacco leaf worm. By 1955 the boll weevil was back in large numbers and was causing major damage to crops. Furthermore, other old pests were reactivated, the most prominent of these being the larvae of the moth *Heliothis virescens* which showed a high degree of resistance to DDT. But even worse was to come. It was soon obvious that six completely new pests had made their appearance; these were unique to the Cañete Valley not being encountered in areas in which the insecticides had not been used. Soon the situation became desperate. Chlorinated hydrocarbon insecticides were abandoned and synthetic organophosphates were substituted; the sprayings became even more frequent. What was the end result? It was a disaster for the Valley for the yield of cotton in 1955 and 1956 decreased by some 300 lbs per acre.

Some General Effects of Pesticides on Ecosystems

There are many such effects. They include high toxicity, a tendency to affect predator animals rather than their prey, the ability to produce resistance in living organisms, a considerable degree of persistence, and wide dissemination throughout our planet. Many admirable reviews on these topics exist in the literature, those by Rudd, Moore and Mellanby being especially recommended.

The first point to stress is that pesticides have profound effects on ecosystems. The latter have been termed the 'web of life'; they are the environmental systems provided by nature and when undisturbed they form a functional whole. Chemically pesticides are frequently rather simple compounds. However, on the other hand, ecosystems are of very great complexity, and even now after a great deal of fundamental research much of their workings remain shrouded in mystery. Basically ecosystems consist of myriads of plants, animals and bacteria; also contained in them are organisms which man has at various times designated as pests. The relationships normally existing between the various components of the ecosystem are delicate and subtle, and because of this it is possible for the individual constituents of the system to live together harmoniously in a state of equilibrium to which the term ecological balance is generally given. In their natural state ecosystems possess great stability, and this characteristic is mainly due to the complicated network of reciprocal relationships which operate to maintain the *status quo*. A good example of a highly complex ecosystem is a wood or a forest, and an illustration of the checks and balances which occur within it is provided by the series of events which take place when a predator animal such as the fox is eliminated from its natural environment either by disease or by the intervention of man. Under such circumstances it might be expected that the animals on which the fox preys, mainly rats, mice and rabbits, would increase in numbers. However, this does not generally happen because other predators substitute for the fox and so maintain the ecological balance.

Pesticides produce their effects by their inherent toxicity and because of this property they have radical effects on ecosystems. Generally their action is both crude and non-specific and could be likened to the heavy blow of the axe rather than to the delicate thrust of the rapier. The overall result of pesticide treatment is to simplify the ecosystem and so to destroy its innate diversity of flora and fauna. A simplified ecosystem becomes much less stable; it tends to disintegrate rapidly, and examples of the type of disorganisation which may take place have been provided earlier in this chapter. Prominent victims when an ecosystem becomes simplified by pesticide treatment are the meat-eating animals or carnivores. In their natural state carnivores are essential for the preservation of the ecological balance, and one of the main reasons for the all-too-frequent failure of pesticide treatment is the virtual elimination of such species from the ecosystem.

There are many examples in the literature of predator animals being exterminated by pesticides with resultant proliferation of their prey. Good illustrations are the rise in the population of sparrows in the UK and elsewhere due to the deaths of hawks and ospreys, and the plague of aphids in Norfolk following the large scale destruction of ladybirds which normally kept them under control. Because of the misuse of pesticides it has now been found necessary to re-introduce predators in various parts of the world. Thus in Poland otters have had to be loosed in rivers in order to control a population explosion amongst fish, while in certain areas of Spain birds are being used to counteract a similar explosion amongst insects. The predilection of pesticides for predatory animals occurs irrespective of whether the ecosystem exists in a terrestrial, fresh water or marine environment. The world scene in terms of predators has recently been critically assessed by Moore. He states that everywhere such animals are decreasing in numbers and that the decline has been particularly marked during the last decade. Moore believes that a major factor in the production of this state of affairs is the increasing use of pesticides.

Pesticides promote resistance in their target animals and with the passage of time this is proving to be a problem of increasing magnitude. Examples of resistance to pesticides are legion, those of the fire ant in the USA and the proliferation of pests in the Cañete Valley being particularly blatant. Resistance to pesticides is especially likely to occur in plant-eating animals or herbivores, this group including such well known pests as leaf worms, beetles and boll weevils.

The precise genetic factors which cause herbivores to develop resistance to pesticides remain unclear. However, a major cause of the phenomenon is undoubtedly the high reproductive rate of insect pests which lay huge numbers of eggs and which, in contrast to mammals, are capable of producing many generations within one year. The majority of the insects may initially be susceptible to the pesticide; however, resistant strains soon develop and multiply at an accelerating rate. Two main mechanisms of resistance to pesticides in insects have been described. In the first the insecticide is prevented from damaging the insect because the latter produces an enzyme which detoxicates it. In the second the behavioural pattern of the insect alters and as a result contact with lethal amounts of the insecticide is reduced.

Experience has shown that if an insect becomes resistant to a particular pesticide it will almost certainly become equally resistant to another compound of a similar chemical composition. Thus if resistance has been demonstrated to the chlorinated hydrocarbon, DDT, it is unlikely that the use of structurally related compounds such as dieldrin and endrin will be attended with success. On the other hand, if a change is made to a compound with a completely different chemical structure, such as an organophosphate, the outcome may be more satisfactory.

The finding of strains of insect which are resistant to a variety of insecticides is not infrequent. Under such circumstances a rather unedifying contest is liable to develop. On the one side there is the chemist in his laboratory desperately attempting to synthesise and introduce new insecticides. Placed against him is the pest, which full of insouciance, is rapidly developing resistance to one substance after another. Moreover, as mentioned previously—and illustrated by the saga of the red spider mite and by the events in the Cañete Valley—pesticide spraying may cause the emergence of completely new pests or may advance into the category of pests insects which previously were not troublesome.

Resistance to pesticides is especially prevalent in herbivores, a fact which has been mentioned before. Do other forms of wildlife such as birds, mammals and fish also develop resistance? Almost certainly they show this property and the literature of today contains a number of documented cases of such resistance. However, it must be emphasised that because of their much lower reproductive potential, resistance in these groups of animals is much less common than is the case with insects.

Another major characteristic of many pesticides is their high degree of persistence. This is especially so in the case of the chlorinated hydrocarbons such as DDT which break down very slowly in ecosystems and may persist in soils for several decades. This quality of persistence allows the pesticides to be passed from one animal to another and if, as is the case with DDT and similar compounds, storage in body fat occurs, concentration in food chains of the type previously described becomes inevitable.

The quality of persistence of pesticides has been highlighted by the American workers, Kennedy and Hessel. They stated that at present our environment contains about 1,000 million pounds of DDT and its derivatives. However, even if we stopped using these compounds today our environment in 1979 would still contain 500 million pounds of pesticides and by 1989 there would still remain some 250 million pounds.

Intimately linked to the persistent nature of chlorinated hydrocarbon insecticides is their widespread dissemination throughout the planet. Chapters V and VII commented on the contamination of waterways by these compounds, and later in this chapter the point will be made that most human beings carry DDT residues in their body fat. Organochlorine insecticides have been demonstrated in the world's most remote areas. Thus they have been found in the fat deposits of Eskimos, in plants in the far North Western territories of Canada and even in Antarctica where skuas, Adelie penguins and Weddell seals contain such residues in their bodies. Admittedly, the degree of contamination in these cases is relatively small, but the fact that it is present at all is obviously a matter of some consequence. Another potentially serious effect of pesticides is their action of phyloplankton, which are the small green plants inhabiting the world's oceans and inland waterways. Like other green plants a major function of phyloplankton is to conduct photosynthesis, and recently disturbing evidence has come to light suggesting that chlorinated hydrocarbon insecticides, particularly DDT, can reduce their photosynthetic rate even if they are present in miniscule concentrations. Cole, the distinguished ecologist from Cornell University in the USA, is one who takes a serious view of the effect of insecticides on phyloplankton because he fears that in this way a depletion of the world's oxygen supplies may eventually occur. Other authorities have also expressed anxiety on this score, and some have gone so far as to predict a future ecological disaster if pollution of oceans with chlorinated hydrocarbons continues at its present rate.

Pesticides and Wildlife

Examples have previously been given of the deleterious effects produced by insecticides on wildlife. This is an important topic and it is now necessary to consider it in rather more detail.

The first point to emphasise is that all pesticides, including insecticides, produce their effects as a result of their inherent toxicity. They are applied because they kill living organisms, and if they did not possess this property, they would not be used. Much has been written on the mechanisms whereby pesticides cause death, and much research still remains to be performed in this important area. However, the currently accepted view is that insecticides produce their primary and potentially lethal effect on the nervous system of the animal and that they do this by inhibiting the action of an enzyme known as cholinesterase, the latter being present in such tissue in relatively large quantities. Although death is by far the most dramatic result of pesticide application, other effects are also conspicuous. These include a failure in reproductive performance and a change in the pattern of behaviour.

Much of our knowledge on the injurious effects of insecticides on wildlife comes from studies in predatory birds, such investigations having been conducted mainly in the UK and the USA. As Moore and others have emphasised studies of this type present formidable difficulties largely because, at present, reliable data on spontaneous fluctuations occurring in bird populations throughout the world are either meagre or completely non-existent. Nevertheless, bearing in mind the limitations and constraints imposed by work of this kind, there is now incontrovertible evidence that DDT and other chlorinated hydrocarbons can interfere to a marked extent with reproductive processes. Indeed one of the major effects produced in raptorial birds is to decrease the thickness of the egg shell; as a result the eggs become unduly brittle and are likely to be crushed by the weight of the nesting parents. The process of nesting itself may be impaired by the ingestion of DDT, and, in addition, there is an increased tendency for the birds to smash and even to eat their own eggs.

How do DDT and related compounds produce their anti-fertility effects in birds? The subject is still controversial although one of the major actions is undoubtedly to interfere with the ability of the birds to handle calcium, a mineral vital to the formation of egg shells. The precise mechanism whereby the interference with calcium metabolism is produced is unknown. However, one suggestion which has been offered is that the main effect might be mediated through the female sex hormone, oestrogen, a substance known to be important in the handling of calcium by birds and which in the presence of relatively high concentrations of DDT, tends to be broken down at an unduly rapid rate by enzymes produced by the bird's liver. Not only female birds are affected by pesticides. The fertility of male birds is also impaired there being a reduction in the number of sperm produced by the testis, a finding especially conspicuous in fowls.

In Britain the species of predatory birds studied in most detail have been the peregrine falcon, the sparrowhawk and the golden eagle. The peregrine falcon has been described by the naturalist G. H. Thayer as 'the embodiment of noble rapacity and lovely freedom'. In the latter part of the 1960's it became apparent that the population of peregrine falcons had dropped considerably as compared with that of the early 1950's. Moreover, there was good evidence to indicate that the reproductive activity of the birds which remained had been impaired. For some years there was speculation regarding the cause of the decline in numbers of the peregrine falcon. Eventually it was shown that the content of chlorinated hydrocarbon insecticides in the fatty tissues and organs of the birds was abnormally high, and there was no escaping the conclusion that in many of the cases the quantities present must have been large enough to cause death from poisoning.

The history of the British sparrowhawk is similar to that of the peregrine falcon. In previous decades this was a bird which was seen throughout the length and breadth of the country. Now it is a rarity, being confined to the more remote parts of our islands. Its reproductive performance has been notably impaired and again the causative factor has been the ingestion of excessive quantities of DDT and related compounds. Ratcliffe and his colleagues made a careful study of eggshell thickness in peregrine falcons and sparrowhawks in the UK for some 20 years starting in 1940. Their findings were striking, the major point of interest being the marked reduction in eggshell thickness in both types of bird following the introduction of DDT in the late 1940's.

A notable characteristic of peregrine falcons and sparrow-hawks is that both species eat a relatively high level in the food chain. Therefore they frequently kill other birds which are contaminated with pesticides and consequently suffer the same fate as their lower orders. The situation is different with other types of predatory bird such as tawny owls and kestrels; their eating habits are more varied and furthermore, their predilec-tion is for insect herbivores. As a result the numbers of tawny owls and kestrels in the UK has not been significantly reduced by the widespread application of pesticides. The heron eats mainly fish but, at least in Britain, does not appear to have suffered at the hands of insecticides; this could well be due to the high degree of resistance of this species to pesticide toxicity.

Good evidence now exists that reproductive function amongst golden eagles in the UK has been adversely affected by pesticides. During the 1960's numbers of these birds declined precipitously particularly in the Western Highlands of Scotland. When chemical analyses were performed on the unhatched eggs of the survivors relatively large amounts of chlorinated hydro-carbon insecticides were found. A major constituent of the diet of golden eagles is sheep carrion. This was subsequently shown to contain large amounts of dieldrin, the latter being an important constituent of some sheep dips. The source of the poisoning was no longer in doubt.

In the USA the situation with respect to predatory birds has been similar to that of the UK. Again birds which eat at high levels in the food chain have been the main sufferers, those eating at lower levels being much less affected. The example of the quail has already been cited (page 115), and it will be recalled that this species was decimated in the course of the witch hunt for the fire ant initiated by the US Department of Agriculture. Another American bird which has been much damaged by pesticides is the bald eagle, and nesting failures of this particular species in Florida and elsewhere have recently threatened its survival. The structure of the egg shells of predatory birds has also been studied in the USA, and thinning of such shells has been found to coincide with the widespread introduction of DDT as an insecticide.

Fish and mammals as well as birds have been gravely damaged by insecticides. Fish are especially susceptible to this form of poisoning, and certain species along with other aquatic organisms such as molluscs and crustaceans are likely to be killed when exposed to concentrations of dieldrin as low as 0.005 parts per million. Insecticides not only kill fish by direct toxicity. They also reduce reproductive performance, this being evidenced by the fact that a concentration of DDT of some 5 parts per million in trout eggs can markedly interfere with the hatching of the young fish from the eggs. Tadpoles are also affected by pesticides, and it has recently been reported that saline containing 0.05 parts per million of DDT drives them into a frantic tail lashing state which may reduce their chance of survival by making them more conspicuous to predatory newts.

The effects produced by pesticides on animal behaviour are especially prominent in mammalian species, and symptoms of overdosage which have been described include increased activity, tremors, lack of co-ordination, visual difficulties and alterations in personality. A good example of the sequence of events is produced by the behaviour of foxes in some of the eastern countries of England during the winter of 1959/60. In these areas approximately 1,300 dead foxes were found, and prior to their death it had been noted that the animals had exhibited a variety of symptoms including convulsions, transient blindness and coma. Moreover, the foxes had apparently lost their fear of man, became unduly thirsty and sought water on all possible occasions. For some time there was considerable doubt regarding the cause of the high mortality in the foxes. However, it was eventually shown that the fatty tissue and organs of the majority of the animals contained high residues of the organochlorine insecticide, dieldrin. The source of the dieldrin was next investigated and a seed dressing was found to be the culprit. This material had been ingested in large quantities by various birds; they had concentrated it in their tissues and the foxes in preying on the birds had received a lethal dose of the compound. In 1969 a similar situation developed in British badgers. Again a high mortality was noted in association with symptoms such as excessive thirst, staggering due to muscular inco-ordination and defective vision. High pesticide residues, especially of dieldrin, were discovered in the bodies of the animals and it was concluded that a causative relationship existed between such residues and the symptoms produced.

The precise significance of pesticide residues in the corpses of birds and other forms of wildlife has been carefully reviewed by Mellanby, who has rightly emphasised the great difficulties involved in drawing meaningful conclusions in this highly complex field. Chemical methods for the detection of pesticides have improved markedly in recent years; they now employ techniques depending on gas-liquid chromatography and possess exquisite sensitivity, thus enabling very small quantities to be detected in various types of tissue. These advances in method-ology have proved of great value, but the fundamental question remains regarding the level at which contamination by the residue will actually prove harmful or fatal to the animal. Here it must be stressed that widespread variations among animals are known to exist, a relatively high residue in one individual causing little or no effect, while a small residue in another affecting reproductive performance and even proving lethal. Criteria in this general field have been put forward by Mellanby. He suggests that harmful effects to wildlife following the ingestion of DDT are likely to arise when the tissue concen-tration of the compound exceeds 30 parts per million. In the case of dieldrin, the safety limit is much lower, reproductive performance being impaired at concentrations as low as 2 parts per million and other harmful effects including death occurring when residues rise to 10 parts per million. Mellanby emphasises that figures for toxicity and lethality with DDT and dieldrin are based on data obtained under relatively acute experimental conditions. Accordingly, there remains a strong possibility that had the birds been exposed to the pesticides for longer periods of time extending over months or years, damage would have been produced at much smaller concentrations.

Pesticide residues in wildlife have been estimated in various parts of the body including brain, liver, chest muscles and fatty tissues. The favoured sites have generally been liver and fatty tissue, the latter having the advantage that very low levels can be detected.

*   *   *

Before leaving the subject of agents which are widely disseminated throughout the world and are harmful to wildlife, mention must be made of the group of compounds known as polychlorinated biphenyls (PCB's). These are not pesticides; instead they are used widely in industrial processes, being important constituents of paints, varnishes and lubricating oils. They are released into the environment in several ways. Thus they pollute the air over big cities, being emitted from factory chimneys and from motor tyres as they wear down. They are also released into streams, rivers, lakes and oceans as a constituent of industrial effluent. PCB's in concentrations ranging from 2 to almost 100 parts per million have been detected in many types of wildlife in widely separated areas of the world. For example, they have been noted in Swedish pike, in Baltic and Scottish seals, in predatory birds in various parts of the USA and even in animals living beyond the Arctic Circle. A careful and detailed study of the distribution of PCB's in the USA has been conducted by Robert W. Riseborough, a zoologist at the University of California. His conclusion was that ecosystems throughout North America were significantly contaminated by such compounds.

What are the biological effects of PCB's? There now appears little question that such compounds are harmful to wildlife; furthermore, their actions are similar to pesticides in that small concentrations impair reproductive performance, while larger amounts can cause fatalities. In humans PCB's have been found in measurable quantities in mother's milk; their presence has also been detected in human hair. Long term effects of PCB's in man remain to be elucidated. However, Riseborough expresses concern with respect to possible toxic effects which are likely to ensue when such substances are inhaled in the form of vapour. He is also uneasy regarding the contamination of human food supplies with this type of compound.

Pesticides and Human Health

This is a controversial and highly complex topic and, like the issue of fluoridation of water supplies, it has strong emotive overtones. On the one hand there are those, who, while admitting that DDT and related substances are widely distributed throughout the planet, consider that the risks to humanity as a result of their ingestion are negligible. Proponents of this viewpoint emphasise the lack of reliable evidence that DDT has actually killed anyone, and stress the fact that the compound has saved millions of lives in campaigns designed to eradicate malaria and other infectious diseases. The diametrically opposed opinion is represented by those who believe that DDT and related compounds are cumulative poisons which in the long term are likely to militate against the survival of the human race.

Can the findings in animals aid us in this all important area? As has been noted earlier incontrovertible evidence now exists that DDT, dieldrin and other chlorinated hydrocarbon insecticides can impair the fertility of fish, birds and mammals, and can cause their death if ingested in sufficiently large quantities. Effects in animals studied in the laboratory under experimental conditions also give cause for some disquiet. Thus, in certain susceptible strains of mice DDT can increase the incidence of cancer of the liver and possibly also of the lungs and the lymph glands. Whether this finding has any relevance to the human situation is not known. Furthermore, in the livers of birds and of several mammalian species, DDT and related substances can raise the content of certain enzymes and in this way have the potentiality for altering the breakdown in the body of both male and female sex hormones; again the significance of this finding as far as man is concerned is quite obscure. DDT has also been claimed to stimulate the production of the female sex hormone, oestrogen, in a number of animal species, but it is not yet known with certainty whether this action is in any way related to the impairment of fertility so notable in various types of wildlife.

At this stage mention must be made of the well recognised difficulties of extrapolating data obtained from experimental animals to man. The author of this book, whose basic training is in the medical speciality of endocrinology, is particularly aware of this fact because his literature contains a classical example of the type of situation which can develop. The example concerns a compound known as clomiphene which has received a certain amount of publicity in recent years as a so-called 'fertility pill'. The substance was thoroughly tested in a variety of animal species, and on the basis of the findings observed, it was introduced into human medicine as a contraceptive agent which was reputed to be active when given by mouth. Ironically enough its action in the human female was precisely the opposite of that predicted by the animal experiments. Far from acting as a contraceptive clomiphene stimulated the female ovary causing the egg to be shed, and the compound has found its place in modern medicine as a means of treating female infertility. To my knowledge no clearer example exists of the dangers implicit in equating results obtained in experimental animals with those in man.

*   *   *

Mention has already been made of the wide distribution of DDT throughout the planet and indeed most of the citizens inhabiting our universe contain it in their body fat. The highest concentraion of DDT anywhere (26.0 parts per million) has been found in Indians residing in the vicinity of New Delhi; why such individuals are singled out for this distinction is not known, but the wide use made of the pesticide in the preservation of food may have played some part. Another country in which the DDT content of body fat is high is Israel, the average figure obtained in a survey there in the 1960's being 19.2 parts per million; probably the very intensive agricultural programmes of that country together with the widespread use of pesticides in the home account for this high figure. Yet another region in which DDT residues in human fat tend to be rather high is Eastern Europe, and in Hungary during 1960 the average concentration was reported to exceed 12 parts per million.

Concentrations of DDT in the fat of US citizens appear to vary greatly, average figures for the country ranging from 7 to 12 parts per million depending on the district. It should, however, be noted that the concentrations appear to have been levelling off and have not risen appreciably since the early 1960's. The pesticide load carried by US citizens is far from negligible, and it has been estimated that the fat of an obese American business tycoon may contain as much as 100 milligrammes of DDT and its breakdown products. In Britain concentrations of DDT in body fat are considerably lower than those of the USA, being generally less than 4 parts per million. On the other hand, concentrations of dieldrin in tissue are higher in the UK than the USA, although it has been stated that the levels found are unlikely to cause damage in adults. During the 1960's pesticide residues in British subjects tended to fall.

Reliable evidence now exists that contamination with chlorinated hydrocarbon insecticides commences very early in life; indeed it appears likely that the fertilised egg from the very start of its existence is exposed to it. Moreover recent studies, one of the more carefully documented of which is that of O'Leary and his associates in Miami, Florida, have indicated that DDT and DDE can pass the barrier interposed between mother and child by the afterbirth or placenta. As a result insecticide residues have been demonstrated in foetal blood, in the fluid which surrounds the foetus in its sac and in the so-called vernix caseosa, this being the greasy substance covering the foetal skin. O'Leary was also able to detect DDT and DDE in maternal blood, levels being in the same range as those encountered in non-pregnant subjects of similar age and geographical location.

In a study conducted by Selby and his colleagues in New Orleans blood samples from pregnant women and from placentae were analysed for chlorinated hydrocarbon pesticides. A number of such compounds were demonstrated, these including DDT, DDE, DDD, dieldrin, aldrin and heptachlor. The amounts detected were very small indeed, ranging from 0.13 to

24.07 parts per *billion*. Curley and co-workers in Atlanta, Georgia, examined the organs of stillborn babies and of babies dying soon after birth for contamination with chlorinated hydrocarbon insecticides. They were able to detect DDT and its breakdown products together with dieldrin and heptachlor. The quantities present were variable, those for DDT ranging from 0.15 parts per million in the liver to 7.6 parts per million in the kidney, and thus being similar to the amounts present in the general adult population of the USA. No correlation could be demonstrated between the age of the foetus and the degree of the contamination. Furthermore, it appeared to make little or no difference to the pesticide residues whether the foetus was born dead or died immediately after birth.

Information is also available regarding the content of chlorinated hydrocarbon insecticide residues in mother's milk, and studies of this type have been reported from a number of countries including the USA, the UK, the Soviet Union, Hungary, Sweden and Italy. The amounts found have generally varied between 0.05 and 0.26 parts per million, although Damaskin from the USSR claims to have detected concentrations as high as 4.88 parts per million. According to the Swedish National Institute of Public Health the average DDT content of mother's milk in that country is approximately 0.12 parts per million, and it is considered that this level is some 70 per cent higher than would be regarded as acceptable. Breast-fed babies in the UK and USA are reported to consume 10 times more dieldrin than the maximum acceptable dose, while in Western Australia where the amounts of dieldrin used are relatively large, the figure rises to 30 times the acceptable dose.

Important studies on the effects of DDT in adults are those of Hayes and co-workers published in 1956 and of Laws and associates reported in 1967. In the first of these investigations DDT in amounts considerably higher than those to which the general population of the USA are routinely exposed, was administered daily to convicts for up to 18 months. The volunteers stored the DDT in their fatty tissue in amounts which were roughly proportional to the dosage administered. After approximately one year maximum storage of the insecticide had been attained, and thereafter the amount in the tissue did not rise in spite of continued administration. An important feature of the study was that none of the volunteers complained of any symptoms or showed any signs of illness which could be directly attributed to the ingestion of DDT.

The researches of Laws and his associates were conducted in 35 men who had been exposed to DDT for periods of time ranging from 11 to 19 years as a result of their occupation in a chemical plant in Atlanta. As might have been anticipated, such individuals had a high rate of storage of the pesticide and its breakdown products in their fatty tissues, the figures ranging from 38 to 647 parts per million, as compared with an average of 8 parts per million in the general population. However, no ill effects attributable to exposure to the insecticide could be found on the basis of routine clinical and laboratory examinations.

What conclusions can be drawn from this morass of apparently conflicting evidence? The data available are at best equivocal, and in the present state of our knowledge it would be unjustifiable to assert dogmatically that the long term ingestion of DDT and other chlorinated hydrocarbon insecticides is injurious to human health. The situation in this respect is somewhat analogous to that encountered with the oral contraceptive pill, a compound to which human subjects can also be exposed for relatively long periods of their lives. Undoubtedly the Pill has side effects; however, the majority of these are trivial, and there is as yet no evidence to suggest that the long term administration of oral contraceptives is associated with the development of really serious diseases such as cancer. Furthermore, the social effects of the Pill in preventing pregnancies in a greatly overpopulated world must be regarded as very beneficial, and at the time of writing there can be no question that the overall advantages of this form of medication far outweigh any disadvantages which may accrue from its use. As indicated earlier chlorinated hydrocarbon pesticides have been shown to affect the fertility of a number of animal species. It could therefore be postulated that a similar effect might occur in human subjects and that the first sign of DDT toxicity might be an increase in the incidence of sterility in the population with a consequent fall in the birth rate. However, when one surveys the world scene one is forced to conclude that as yet no secure evidence exists linking DDT levels in body fat with reproductive failure in humans. Indeed in India and in Israel, where the DDT content in the body fat of the populace is higher than anywhere else on earth, birth rates remain high, the figure for India in 1971 being 42 per 1,000 and for Israel 26 per 1,000. Moreover the fact cannot be dismissed that such birth rates are considerably higher than those encountered in countries such as the UK and Federal Germany where the average pesticide load carried by the population is considerably lower.

The ultimate consequences of exposure to DDT and related compounds are a matter for speculation. Again the question must be posed—are these substances harmless contaminants or are they lethal poisons? The situation remains enigmatic and our present state of knowledge does not permit a definite conclusion to be drawn. Undoubtedly, however, writers of the twenty-first century will have the answer.

Some Observations on Herbicides

The extensive use of weedkillers is a feature of present day life; indeed their rate of increase in recent years outstrips that of insecticides such as DDT. Man employs herbicides for a variety of reasons. He is especially prolific with them in agricultural practice where he expects them to prevent the growth of weeds without damaging crops. Orchards, gardens and forests are frequently sprayed with herbicides in order to counteract the proliferation of weeds, the latter being unsightly and uneconomic. Herbicides have also been used to regulate the growth of weeds on roadsides and alongside railway tracks; in children's playgrounds they are employed as a means of preventing weeds from appearing through the asphalt. Aquatic as well as terrestrial environments are often treated by weedkillers. These include swimming pools rendered unusable because of waterweeds, canals choked by plant growth, and irrigation schemes functioning inadequately for the same reason. A very special use of herbicides which merits more detailed consideration is their widespread application as defoliants by the US Armed Forces in Vietnam (see page 137).

As with the insecticides numerous types of herbicide exist. Arsenical compounds, one of the more popular of which is a substance known as sodium arsenite, came into use many years ago and until quite recently were extensively applied in the UK and elsewhere. It was soon apparent that such compounds were highly toxic not only to wildlife but also to man himself, and cases of arsenical poisoning in human subjects as a result of their excessive application are anything but rare. Furthermore, such herbicides have the serious disadvantage that their residues in soil remain poisonous for long periods of time, and many areas of Britain are still contaminated by them. Fortunately, because of their high toxicity and persistence in ecosystems, the usage of arsenical compounds as weedkillers has greatly decreased in recent years.

In the 1930's another important class of weedkillers came into use. These were the so-called dinitro compounds, two of the more important of which, DNOC and Dinoseb, rapidly found favour in agricultural practice. Indeed it has been claimed that during the Second World War DNOC played a vital role in increasing food yields in the UK and was thus instrumental in circumventing Nazi Germany's blockade of these islands. Like the arsenicals, DNOC and related compounds are highly poisonous and have caused much damage to all types of wildlife including insects, birds and mammals. Neither is man immune to their toxicity, and it has been pointed out that the amount of the DNOC normally applied to one acre of land is sufficient to cause fatal poisoning in 1,000 human beings! With the introduction of newer herbicides the use of DNOC has greatly diminished.

So-called 'hormone weedkillers' are widely used today. This category includes compounds such as MCPA, 2,4-D, 2,4,5-T and picloram; they are derivatives of phenoxyacetic acid and, like the chlorinated hydrocarbon insecticides, can be prepared synthetically. They have certain properties in common with the naturally occurring plant hormones or auxins and are chemically related to a substance in plants which regulates growth and which is known as indoleacetic acid. When sprayed in relatively high concentrations the main effect of hormone weedkillers is to cause weeds to grow. However, the growth is of a highly abnormal character. The root does not elongate, the growth being mainly confined to the basal stem; young leaves fail to expand and also lose their chlorophyll. As a result of these changes the plant dies. Herbicides of this type are reasonably selective in their action, and because of this cereal crops and grasses are little affected by their application. Hormone weedkillers have the great advantage over arsenical compounds and substances such as DNOC that they are much less poisonous. Indeed in the UK where MCPA is widely used, a human death as a result of poisoning by this substance has yet to be reported; in addition, damage to wildlife producd by MCPA has been slight. Unlike DDT and related substances, compounds such as MCPA and 2,4-D are relatively non-persistent, being broken down by soil bacteria within weeks or months of application. However, other hormone weedkillers notably 2,4,5-T and possibly also picloram, are likely to remain active in soil for longer periods of time.

Herbicides such as Simazine and Monuron can also be prepared synthetically and are now being used on an increasing scale; however the mode of action of such substances is quite different to that of MCPA and related compounds. Neither Simazine nor Monuron promotes abnormal growth of weeds; instead they interfere with photosynthesis as a result of which the plant is starved of nutrients and rapidly dies. Unlike the hormone weedkillers Simazine and Monuron have rather prolonged effects on ecosystems and can prevent the re-growth of weeds for up to one year. On the other hand, another synthetic herbicide known as Dalapon, which has recently found much favour in the control of weed growth on the banks or rivers and canals, persists for only six to eight weeks. One of the most rapidly inactivated of all the synthetic herbicides is the substance Paraquat which looses its effect within a few hours. This is indeed fortunate because if ingested by humans, Paraquat can be very toxic affecting particularly the function of liver, kidneys and lungs.

Herbicides and Ecosystems

Information regarding the effects of herbicides on ecosystems is much more meagre than is the case for chlorinated hydrocarbon insecticides, and this is an area in which the need for further research is clamant. In general it may be stated that since herbicides are less persistent than insecticides, their effects on ecosystems are less likely to be profound. However, this is not to say that such actions are negligible.

Damage inflicted by herbicides on soil organisms or on animals such as larvae and earthworms inhabiting the soil appears to be small or nonexistent. Phenoxyacetic acid derivatives such as MCPA are rather rapidly degraded by soil organisms and persist in soil for only two to four weeks; accordingly, they are unlikely to contaminate supplies of groundwater. The primary effect of a herbicide is to eradicate plant populations. Consequently it will also effect herbivorous animals, particularly those which, because of their specialised eating habits, feed on one type of plant or on a small number of different plants.

If herbicides are ingested in sufficiently large quantities by mammals ill effects are likely to ensue. A good example of this is provided by the experience of reindeer in Lapland, the story being recounted by Jones in the periodical *Your Environment.* A high mortality amongst a herd of reindeer was noted; of the 600 animals 250 died, and in the survivors there was definite impairment of reproductive function, this being indicated by a high incidence of abortions and of premature deliveries. Eventually the deaths were traced to the fact that the animals had eaten leaves from trees which had been sprayed with the defoliants, 2,4-D and 2,4,5-T. The compounds had apparently been quite persistent, for when the leaves were examined some nine months after the spraying they were still found to contain 25 parts per million of the former and 10 parts per million of the latter compound.

At present, information regarding the effect of herbicides on aquatic life and particularly on marine algae or diatoms is very rudimentary. However, there now appears to be a distinct possibility that the ever increasing run off of herbicides from agricultural land into lakes, rivers and streams will notably exacerbate the problem of water pollution.

Although many of the actions of herbicides on ecosystems remain obscure one effect is now certain, namely that the long term use of these substances will inevitably lead to the condition known as *laterisation*. This term is derived from the Latin word, *later,* meaning a brick, and denotes the conversion of the land into a rock-like substance known as laterite. Tropical areas to which weedkillers such as picloram have been applied in large quantities have so far been mainly affected by this process. Characteristically, tropical soils are of poor quality; they lack essential nutrients such as calcium, phosphorus and potassium, these being found mainly in the vegetation. When such vegetation is destroyed by herbicides, and in particular if a definite programme of defoliation of trees is undertaken, whatever nutritional value the soil initially possessed is rapidly destroyed. The soil gives up the unequal struggle, dies and is converted into laterite. At present laterisation is quite extensive in the Amazon basin in Brazil, where defoliation of trees has been undertaken on a wide scale as part of government policy. Laterisation will undoubtedly follow the rape of Vietnam by American forces, and elsewhere it will become increasingly widespread as attempts to feed the Third World's starving millions become more and more desperate.

Herbicides in Vietnam

Mention of herbicides inevitably leads to a discussion of the use made of these substances by the American forces in Vietnam. As the US involvement in that country deepened a number of reports appeared in the world literature describing the ecological effects which such compounds were producing. One of the most authoritative of these and the one on which much of the ensuing discussion is based, emanates from the Biology Study Group in Stanford University, California.

The relevant military operations formed part of what was euphemistically termed a 'resource-denial programme' designed to deprive the North Vietnamese forces of necessary food supplies and thus to hasten the end of the war. The operations had two main features. The first was the defoliation of large areas of vegetation throughout the country; in the course of this action great numbers of trees were destroyed. The second was the elimination of crops in territory occupied by the Vietcong.

Three main herbicides were employed—*Agent Orange* being a mixture of 2,4-D and 2,4,5-T, *Agent White* consisting mainly of picloram, and *Agent Blue* in which the content of arsenic in the form of cocodylic acid was high. In general, the herbicides were sprayed over the land by aeroplanes. The rate of application was very high indeed being on the average some 13 times greater than that recommended by the US Department of Agriculture for domestic use.

The area of territory sprayed by defoliants rose dramatically during the decade of the 1960's; in 1962 it stood at 17,000 acres, but by 1968 it had risen to more than one million acres. Jones, writing recently in *Your Environment,* puts the figure even higher and states that in all some 4 million acres of South Vietnam amounting to more than 10 per cent of the total land mass of that country and roughly equivalent to the area of Wales, have been sprayed with defoliants.*

The ecological effects of this form of warfare have been profound. Crop damage in Vietnam has been especially severe. In 1959 South Vietnam exported some 246,000 tons of rice; by 1968 850,000 tons had to be *imported* mainly from the USA. In addition to rice, other crops notably pineapples, sugar cane, manioc, sweet potatoes and mango have suffered. The end result of the spraying has been that the overall agricultural production of South Vietnam has been reduced by some 30 per cent.

The report from the Stanford Campus also made clear that the rubber industry, traditionally an important source of foreign capital for Vietnam, has been grievously affected, mainly due to the defoliation of trees in rubber plantations. Thus between 1960 and 1967 yields of rubber per acre of land dropped some 25 per cent. In 1960 the total production of dry rubber in Vietnam was 77,500 tons, this yielding $48 million in exports; by 1967 the figures had plummeted to 42,150 tons and the export value of the crop had shrunk to $13 million. More recently plantations in neighbouring Cambodia have felt the

* A recent report (*Observer,* 5th December 1971) states that although spraying of Vietnamese crops by herbicides appears to have decreased largely as a result of public agitation, other forms of destruction including large bull-dozers and 'superbombs' are still in use. One authority states that by this means 1,000 acres of Vietnamese land is being destroyed each day.

impact of the war, and during 1969 rubber production in that country decreased markedly.

Without any exaggeration Vietnam can now be described as an ecological disaster, and long after the departure of the US troops from that unfortunate country, the effect of their military presence will remain. As mentioned earlier, Agent Blue contains a relatively high proportion of arsenic, and this will leave poisonous residues in the soil for months or years. Even more serious is the fact that the massive and uncontrolled application of herbicides on an unprecedented scale has already wrecked and will irretrievably damage the delicate ecological balance existing in the tropical forests and soils of Vietnam. One of the results will be that plant nutrients such as nitrates, phosphates, calcium, potassium, magnesium and sulphur will be lost into rivers and streams. Any fertility which the soil initially possessed will quickly disappear, and as a consequence, pest species of plant, for example the giant bamboo which is notoriously resistant to defoliants, will rapidly fill the breech. Such plants will soon form impenetrable thickets in the Vietnamese countryside and will aid in the destruction of the latter's already meagre agricultural potential. Vietnamese rivers too have been war casualties, and in particular the natural processes of delta formation have been significantly inhibited. Fish have suffered at the hands of the US forces, their habitats having been destroyed and their reproductive processes impaired.

Laterisation is inevitable as a result of herbicide application and this will be a permanent memorial to the American intervention in Vietnam. Eventually, just as in the Amazon basin in South America, large areas of the countryside will be transformed into solid rock. Once laterisation has taken place the damage produced is irreversible. The permanence of the process is well illustrated by the fact that in neighbouring Cambodia there exist the renowned Khmer ruins in the vicinity of Angkor Wat. These ruins consist of sandstone and laterite, and they are the remains of cities and temples constructed between 800 and 1,000 years ago long before Christopher Columbus discovered the North American continent!

The ecological effects produced by herbicides in Vietnam form only one part of the tragedy, for in addition, there is evidence suggesting that these substances may constitute a hazard to human health. The danger arises from the property of herbicides, if ingested in large enough quantities, to cause harmful effects to the unborn child. These are known as teratogenic actions and they have been reported following the administration of large amounts of 2,4,5-T to pregnant rats, mice and hamsters; the abnormalities found in the offspring of these animals have been numerous and have included lack of eyes, cysts in the kidneys, cleft palates and enlarged livers. Can similar effects be produced in humans? We do not know for certain but in 1967, following a two-year period during which herbicides were very widely applied to the countryside of Vietnam, newspapers in Saigon carried headlines describing a novel type of birth defect which was termed the 'egg bundle-like foetus'.

The South Vietnamese press reports caused a furore in the USA. Some authorities stated that the foetal defects had nothing to do with the spraying. Others averred that a definite relationship existed, but again controversy erupted regarding the causative agent. Some blamed the compound 2,4,5-T directly, while others were convinced that a contaminant present in commercial preparations of the herbicide and known as dioxin was the *enfant terrible*. Further research was undertaken and showed that, although dioxin appeared to have a marked tendency to be teratogenic in a variety of animal species, pure 2,4,3-T also had such an effect. Moreover, it was demonstrated that even if the spraying was undertaken with 2,4,5-T in the complete absence of dioxin, the latter would still be formed when 2,4,5-T and 2,4-D were heated. Accordingly, the combusion of timber and other materials exposed to the defoliants could well liberate large amounts of dioxin into the air, with injurious effects to the foetus if pregnant women inhaled it.

*   *   *

The transcendent theme of this chapter has been the poisoning of the land by insecticides and herbicides. But the land has suffered at the hands of man in a variety of other ways. It will be the purpose of the next three chapters to discuss some of these.

References

BRITISH MEDICAL JOURNAL (1970). 'Pesticides and preventive medicine', iv, pp. 189-190.

CARSON, RACHEL (1962). *Silent Spring*. Boston, Houghton-Miffin.

COLE, LAMONTE C (1968). 'Man and the Air'. *Population Bulletin,* 24, No. 5, pp. 103-113.

CURLEY, AUGUST and KIMBROUGH, RENATE (1969). 'Chlorinated hydrocarbon insecticides in plasma and milk of pregnant and lactating women'. *Arch. Environ. Health,* 18, pp. 156-164.

CURLEY, AUGUST, COPELAND, FRANK and KIMBROUGH, RENATE (1969). 'Chlorinated hydrocarbon insecticides in organs of the stillborn and blood of newborn babies'. *Arch. Environ. Health,* 19, pp. 628-632.

ECOLOGIST (1970). 'Science: redefine or abolish it?', 1, No. 5, p. 3.

EHRLICH, PAUL R. (1968). 'The Population Bomb'. New York, Ballantine Books Inc.

EHRLICH, PAUL R. and EHRLICH, ANNE (1970). *Population, Resources, Environment.* San Francisco, W. H. Freeman and Co.

GRAHAM, FRANK JR. (1966). *Disaster by Default—Politics and Water Pollution.* New York, M. Evans and Co. Inc.

GRAHAM, FRANK JR. (1970). *Since Silent Spring.* London, Hamish Hamilton.

HAYES, WAYLAND J., DURHAM, WILLIAM F. and CUETO, CIPRIANO JR. (1956). 'The effect of known repeated oral doses of chlorophenothane (DDT) in man'. *JAMA,* 162, No. 9, p. 890.

JONES, DAVID (1970). 'The Defoliant Story: A Cautionary Tale'. *Your Environment,* No. 4, pp. 118-123.

KENNEDY, DONALD and HESSEL, JOHN (1971). 'The Biology of Pesticides'. In *Global Ecology.* Edited by HOLDREN, JOHN P. and EHRLICH, PAUL R. New York, Chicago, San Francisco, Atlanta, Harcourt Brace Jovanovich Inc.

LAWS, EDWARD R., CURLEY, AUGUST and BIRDS, FRANK J. (1967). 'Men with intensive occupational exposure to DDT—a clinical and chemical study'. *Arch. Environ. Health,* 15, pp. 766-775.

LOCKIE, J. D., RATCLIFFE, D. A. and BALHARRY, R. (1969). 'Breeding success and organochlorine residues in Golden Eagles in West Scotland'. *J. App. Ecol.,* 6, pp. 381-389.

MELLANBY, KENNETH (1969). *Pesticides and Pollution.* London, Fontana.

MOORE, N. W. (1967). 'A synopsis of the pesticide problem'. *Advances in Ecological Research,* 4, Edited by CRAGG, J. B. New York and London, Academic Press, pp. 75-129.

NOBLE, JOHN and ROTHMAN, HARRY (1970). 'PCB'. *The Ecologist,* 1, pp. 12-14.

O'LEARY, JAMES A., DAVIES, JOHN E., EDMUNDSON, WALTER F. and REICH, GEORGE A. (1970). 'Transplacental passage of pesticides'. *Amer. J. Obstet. Gynec.,* 107, pp. 65-68.

PEARALL, D. B. (1967). 'Pesticide induced enzyme breakdown of steroids in birds'. *Nature,* **216,** pp. 505-506.

PRESTT, IAN, JEFFERIES, D. J. and MOORE, N. W. (1970). 'Polychlorinated biphenyls in wild birds in Britain and their avian toxicity'. *Environmental Pollution,* **1,** pp. 3-26.

READ, SHEILA T. and MCKINLEY, W. P. (1961). 'DDT and DDE content of human fat'. *Arch. Environ. Health,* **3,** pp. 91-95.

RUDD, ROBERT L. (1966). *Pesticides and the Living Landscape.* Madison, Milwaukee, London, The University of Wisconsin Press.

SELBY, LLOYD A., NEWELL, KENNETH W., HAUSER, GEORGE A. and JUNKER, GLADYS (1969). 'Comparison of chlorinated hydrocarbon pesticides in maternal blood and placental tissues. *Environ. Res.,* **2,** p. 247-255.

SHEA, KEVIN P. (1971). 'Pollution by Pesticides'. In *Can Britain Survive?* Edited by GOLDSMITH, EDWARD. London, Tom Stacey, pp. 164-174.

SLADER, WILLIAM J. L., MENZIE, C. M. and REICHEL, W. L. (1966). 'DDT residues in Adelie Penguins and a Crabeater Seal from Antarctica'. *Nature,* **210,** pp. 670-673.

TAYLOR, G. R. (1970). *The Doomsday Book.* London, Thames and Hudson.

THE DESTRUCTION OF INDO-CHINA—A Legacy of our presence (1970). Stanford Biology Group, Stanford University.

ZAVON, M. R., TYE, R. and LATORRE, L. (1969). 'Chlorinated hydrocarbon insecticide content of the neonate'. *Annals of the New York Academy of Sciences,* **160,** pp. 196-200.

VIII

THE PILLAGE OF MINERAL RESOURCES

The adequacy of resources stands with peace and population control among the crucial problems of our time and the future. It places constraints both on the ultimate sizes of populations and on the level of living that populations of any density may enjoy.

Frederick Seitz, President,
National Academy of Sciences, 1968

Pollution by pesticides is by no means the only way in which man has damaged his most precious heritage, the land. He has also depleted it of the rich mineral resources which occupy the earth's crust; furthermore, the pace of destruction of these reserves both as regards metals and sources of industrial energy is increasing year by year. Two major and closely interlocking factors are contributing to resource depletion. The first is the economic structure of Western society which is characterised by high production and high consumption; the second is the explosive growth of world population particularly within the past three decades. Economic factors and overpopulation receive consideration elsewhere in this book. The present chapter is devoted to a discussion of the earth's resources of metals and of fossil fuels, the most important materials in the latter group being coal, oil and natural gas. The subject of nuclear energy derived either from atomic fission or fusion is not reviewed here; nor is the vital question as to whether such a source of power is in the long term likely to replace that currently generated for industrial purposes by fossil fuels. A survey of these topics is provided in Chapter XII.

The Earth's Metals

One of the major factors responsible for the Industrial Revolution of the late eighteenth and nineteenth centuries was the discovery of metals in the earth's crust. It was of course true that metals had been mined before—indeed this had happened almost since the dawn of history. Now, however, the scale of these operations increased enormously. The Industrial Revolution was a time of high optimism; entrepreneurial activity proliferated, and it was generally assumed that the earth's resources were virtually illimitable. Now after the plunder of that era and the ravages of the more modern cult of economic growth we face the inevitable reckoning. Our credit is diminishing fast and soon this will be manifest in a world hunger for metals.

Basic facts regarding the distribution of metals throughout Spaceship Earth are well established and have been reviewed in recent years by recognised authorities such as the Americans Lovering, Cloud and Skinner. A point of considerable importance is that the total amount of workable mineral deposits represents a very small portion of the earth's crust, amounting to not more than 1 per cent. Moreover, such deposits must always be mined where they exist, and frequently their site of location is far from the centres in which they will eventually be consumed. Finally, one must face up to the relentless truth that even in spite of new and exciting discoveries in various parts of our planet, such resources are finite and will eventually be exhausted. No second crop will appear and once the metal has vanished it will not return. The situation is therefore precisely analogous to that pertaining in the case of wildlife. Thus when a rare species of animal is eliminated from our planet either by man's activities or from natural causes, an irreversible act has been committed.

Metals vary greatly in their distribution and quantity. Some such as aluminium, iron and magnesium are present in relative abundance. Others such as copper, lead, zinc and vanadium are much less plentiful, while yet others including mercury, silver, tin, tantalum and platinum are now quite scarce. It is in the last category of elements that shortages are soon likely to become apparent. Indeed, in the case of some of these metals experts predict that available reserves will be exhausted well before the end of the present century.

The appetite of industry for metals is voracious. Iron is much the most widely used; fortunately, the earth is so liberally endowed with this element that even at current rates of consumption shortages are unlikely to occur for some hundreds of years. However, with respect to other metals widely used in industry, for example lead, copper and zinc, depletion of existing resources is a much more pressing problem. The same comment applies to the so-called 'mineral vitamins' such as tantalum and tungsten which, although required in relatively small quantities by industry, are crucial to the operation of a number of its processes which in their absence would be unable to continue.

Where are these important metals to be found? As mentioned previously they have a wide and erratic distribution throughout our planet; moreover, they are no respectors either of ideology or of politics. Major sources of supply have altered out of all recognition with the passage of time. Thus 3,000 years ago, the Middle East was an area rich in iron, and mining of this metal was an important industry for the civilization of that time; today such an activity is little seen, oil rather than iron being the major mineral resource of this region. Classical Greece was fortunate in its plentiful deposits of lead and silver and for many years she exploited these as important economic assets. In the Europe of the Middle Ages, large amounts of lead, zinc and silver were mined in Germany, while nineteenth century Britain owed a not inconsiderable part of her greatness to her rich indigenous metallic deposits. Thus between 1700 and 1849 approximately 50 per cent of the world's lead was mined in the British Isles; between 1829 and 1840 she provided some 45 per cent of the world's copper, and in 1890 her iron production was half that of the entire planet. Soon afterwards the ores of many of her metals became exhausted, and no doubt this has been a factor contributing to the diminution of her stature as a world power.

What are the locations of the world's main metallic resources today? As might be imagined the overall pattern changes constantly as new ores are discovered and others become exhausted from excessive mining. Iron remains widely distributed. There are numerous deposits in the USA, a particularly rich area still being the so-called 'iron ranges' in the state of Minnesota; especially well endowed with iron is the Soviet Union, and the ores of Krivoi Rog in the Ukraine are world famous. Plentiful iron deposits are present in northern Sweden and in Labrador in Canada. In addition, the soils of many tropical countries are rich in this metal and herein lies a vast potential source for the future.

The Soviet Union is the largest producer of manganese, but India, Brazil, Ghana and South Africa also have plentiful resources of this element. Eighty per cent of the world's chromium is supplied by four countries—the Soviet Union, South Africa, Turkey and the Philippines. With respect to copper the USA still leads the world production, followed by the Soviet Union, Chile and Zambia. There are rich deposits of tin in Malaysia, Bolivia and Thailand, the first mentioned country taking pride of place. The major producers of lead and zinc are the Soviet Union, Australia, Canada and the USA, while for mercury the renowned Almadén mine in Spain which has now been operating for over 2,000 years, remains the predominant source. Deposits of silver, a metal the stores of which are being rapidly depleted, stretch throughout the Americas from Alaska to Tierra del Fuego, the major producing countries being Mexico, Canada, Peru and the USA. The Rand mines in South Africa constitute the main source of the world's gold, but there are also important reserves of this precious metal in the Soviet Union, Canada, the USA and Australia.

A striking feature of the contemporary scene is the richness of the Soviet Union in mineral resources. In the late 1960's she held first place for the world production of chrome, iron, lead, manganese, magnesium and phosphate rock. She was runner up with respect to asbestos, gold, nickel and copper, and occupied third place in the case of mercury and bauxite. Other industrialised nations fared much less well than the USSR. For example, Japan, a country which possesses one of the highest economic growth rates in the world, is poor in indigenous resources, completely lacking many metals and producing relatively small quantities of most others.

The USA regards itself as the world's greatest industrial nation. It houses only six per cent of the planet's population; yet it is reputed to consume 40 per cent of the output of its raw materials. Indeed, between 1930 and 1960 the USA alone accounted for more mineral products than all the previous peoples of the world had collectively used since history began. And the American rate of consumption is increasing steadily year by year; so much so that by 1980 it may reach 80 per cent of the total world production of raw materials.

A number of American authorities have recently commented on their country's situation with respect to metallic resources. For instance, Ian MacGregor, Chairman of the American Metal Climax Inc., noted with some dismay that over the past 20 years the consumption of aluminium per head of population had risen from 12 to 45 lbs. The US Bureau of Mines has endeavoured to project the needs of the nation in terms of metals for the year 2000 AD, assuming that the present rate of industrial expansion continues unabated. The figures make sobering reading, for the forecast is that the demand for aluminium will rise from 4.4 million to nearly 35 million short tons per year, for copper from 2 to 6.5 million, for pig iron including ferroalloys from 114 to 171 million and for lead from 1.3 to 1.8 million.

American officials are becoming increasingly haunted by the realisation that, for the foreseeable future, the USA will be increasingly dependent on sources outside its own territory for supplies of the majority of its mineral resources. Certainly, there is no doubt that the era of US self-sufficiency is drawing to its close and that the age of dependence is dawning. A feature which must cause especial anxiety to the White House, State Department and Pentagon is that many of these vital resources are located in areas of the world which to them appear to be politically unstable, or alternatively are ruled by governments who make no secret of their hostility to the whole system of Western capitalism and free enterprise. Data collected by the UN strongly support the contention that the period of US hegemony in metals is fading. Thus in 1967 she led the world only in the production of copper, molybdenum, vanadium and uranium, was in second place with respect to iron and was well down the list in the case of many other metals.

The noted geologist, Preston Cloud, addressing the American Association for the Advancement of Science in 1969, spoke eloquently of his country's predicament. He noted that at present the US imported the greater part of its chrome, cobalt, tin and bauxite. He admitted that she still had resources of lead, zinc, copper and tungsten; but these were no longer adequate for her needs, and consequently she was relying more and more on foreign sources for supplies. That US self-sufficiency still extended to bulk non-metallic materials such as stone, sand, cement, gravel and phosphate was granted by Cloud. However, in his opinion, such a happy state of affairs was unlikely to continue indefinitely because of the demands made on these resources by society. As long ago as 1957, Brown, Bonnar and Weir in *The Next Hundred Years* pinpointed the dilemma. Even then there had to be dug from the earth's surface 3½ tons of stone and gravel for each US citizen each year, and each year every American was using directly or indirectly more than 500 lbs of cement, 400 lbs of clay, 200 lbs of common salt and 100 lbs of phosphate rock. Since *The Next Hundred Years* was written the US population has increased markedly and her consumption per head has soared. Obviously no country, however richly endowed, can withstand indefinitely such an onslaught on its natural resources.

*   *   *

If the US situation for the latter part of the twentieth century is unsatisfactory that of Britain is much more perilous. Once the UK was relatively rich in mineral deposits, and as has been noted earlier, this was a contributory factor to her world leadership at the time of the Industrial Revolution. Now all is changed; our credit in this area was exhausted long ago and in comparison with many other nations we are exceedingly poor in natural resources. True—and this will be mentioned again later—large supplies of coal remain in our islands, these probably being adequate for our needs for several centuries. However, our coal must now be regarded as an asset of declining importance for its usage in industrial practice is steadily diminishing; indeed coal mining in our country is in the throes of a depression and its work force is being progressively reduced. Apart from coal Britain has some tin and iron ores, and in the late 1960's we occupied 12th and 16th places respectively in the list of nations producing these metals. Copper ores have been located in Snowdonia in Wales and recently the Government, in the teeth of opposition from conservationist forces, has given the Rio Tinto-Zinc Corporation authority to mine them.* However, in world terms, such deposits are likely to be small and moreover, their mining is almost certain to result in severe environmental damage to an area of high scenic beauty. The recent strikes of natural gas and of oil in the North Sea are most welcome, but it would be naïve to assume that such discoveries will be adequate to satisfy completely the growing needs of our industry for power and energy.

The unpalatable fact must be faced that now and for the foreseeable future, Britain is dependent for its minerals, its raw materials and its sources of industrial energy on goods imported from other parts of the world. Herein lies one of the major reasons why politicians incessantly exhort us to increase our exports. These, they proclaim, are the life blood of our economy, enabling us to pay for imports from overseas, which in turn make it possible for us to operate our industries and so to maintain our standard of living. Given this state of affairs it is hardly surprising that our economy is poised as on a razor edge, being exquisitively sensitive to conditions, political, economic and otherwise, prevailing in other parts of the globe. Admittedly in recent years the terms of world trade have favoured nations such as ours which live by the production of manufactured goods. However, should these terms turn in favour of the countries which are the primary producers of raw materials, or alternatively should such countries develop the resources to manufacture these goods themselves, our international trading position would be significantly weakened.

* * *

One is forced to conclude from the evidence that the metallic resources of the USA and particularly of the UK give no cause for complacency. But what of the general world scene?

* The director of exploration for Rio Tinto-Zinc is Lord Byers a former chairman of the Liberal Party. Stoutly defending the activities of his company in Snowdonia and the Mawddach estuary he is reported to have said 'we are conservationists; we are also miners'! The laconic comment of *Your Environment* (1971 Vol. II, p. 25) was 'with friends like this . . .'.

An accepted fact of modern life is that, irrespective of religion, ideology and politics, our planet is divided into two groups of nations. Many designations have been applied to these two categories; thus they have been termed the developed and the underdeveloped, the rich and the poor, the 'haves' and the 'have-nots'. Almost for as long as one can remember the rhetoric of politicians, government officials and economists has been directed to the prime necessity of 'developing' the poorer countries of the world by a programme of massive industrialisation. The moral background of such rhetoric has been impeccable. Thus it embodies the belief that modern technological expertise will 'drag such nations into the twentieth century', will transform their sluggish agriculturally orientated economies into that of a modern industrial state and, as a consequence, will dramatically raise the living standards of their peoples. As a direct result of the pursuance of these policies the economic gap which currently exists between the rich and the poor countries will be progressively narrowed and a better life will be enjoyed by all.

But the dream on which such idealism is based is fast fading. A major factor in eroding it has been the population explosion of the Third World; another has been the sheer lack of availability of the resources which are critical for the industrialisation of the poorer countries. In such calculations metals bulk largely, and estimates have been made of the series of events which would be necessary in order to raise the living standards of all the peoples of our planet to that at present being enjoyed by the citizens of the USA. The Ehrlichs in their *Population, Resources, Environment* provide such calculations and they are formidable indeed. Thus in order to achieve such an overall standard of living there would have to be wrested from the earth's crust almost 30,000 million tons of iron, more than 500 million tons of copper and lead, more than 300 million tons of zinc and over 50 million tons of tin. The attainment of such theoretical figures would mean that the extraction of iron each year would have to increase 75 fold, that of copper 100 fold, of lead 200 fold, of zinc 75 fold and of tin 250 fold.

Is there any possibility whatsoever that the earth could be capable of yielding such resources? As mentioned previously, our planet is richly endowed with iron ore; reserves of this metal particularly in tropical soils remain unexploited, and it is conceivable, given a surge of innovative skill, that a figure of the magnitude quoted could be attained. However, in the case of the other metals—always barring the twin possibilities, firstly that there will be really revolutionary changes in technology, and secondly that reserves so far undreamt of will be discovered—such extraction figures are manifestly unattainable because of the exhaustion of available ores. Moreover, the data quoted by the Ehrlichs almost certainly understate the case. They are based on the present world population of some 3,600 million and they take no cognizance of the fact that numbers will rise steeply for the remainder of this century, reaching a figure not far short of 7,000 million by 2000 AD. In addition, the figures presume that current rates of economic consumption will continue, and this is a premise which is simply not supportable in an era in which worship of a rising Gross National Product has become a national fetish.

The very difficult task of predicting the lifespan of world resources of certain metals has been attempted by Cloud. Although implicit in such calculations are inaccuracies associated with a rising population and increasing rates of consumption, some indication of future trends does emerge. Cloud's conclusions are depressing. He forecasts that by the end of the present century world supplies of tin, zinc, gold, silver and platinum could well be exhausted. He considers that supplies of metals such as copper and tungsten might last into the twenty-first century, but he states that by the year 2100 AD, some 130 years from now, only reserves of iron, manganese, cobalt, chromium and aluminium will be present in reasonable quantities.

*   *   *

In the presence of Cloud's conclusions how can there be anything but pessimism vis-à-vis the earth's supplies of metallic resources? Surprisingly enough, euphoria continues to reign in most official quarters. The argument runs that technology will solve all problems, that metallic deposits hitherto unknown will be discovered, that more metals will be recycled and that more abundant metals will be substituted for those which are becoming scarce.

Economists have always been in the vanguard of those who claim that the earth's metallic resources are virtually inexhaustible. They state that the exhaustion of current reserves will merely necessitate the removal of mining operations to other sites. It is admitted that ores of inferior quality may have to be mined, but this will be compensated for by the fact that the latter will be present in ever more abundant quantities. To support this postulate economists cite the principle initially enunciated by the geologist S. G. Lasky and embodied in what is termed the arithmetic/geometric (A/G) ratio, this relating the grade of metal mined to the tonnage produced. Lasky was careful in his initial conclusions, but his paper did include the statement that 'in many mineral deposits in which there is a gradation from relatively rich to relatively lean material, the tonnage increases at a constant geometric rate as the grade decreases'. However, it is important to stress that Lasky was not speaking of all mineral resources. On the contrary his remarks referred exclusively to pophyry copper, and only to some deposits of that metal. He was not concerned with ores of other metals such as mercury, lead, zinc, gold and antimony; his remarks were therefore of a specific rather than of a general nature. The restricted significance of the A/G ratio has subsequently been emphasised by many geologists. Indeed Lovering has bluntly stated that the index 'should not be used in estimating the unfound reserves of a region or a nation'.

The economics of mineral resources is a highly complex topic. However, it appears reasonable to assume that as supplies of metals diminish costs will ultimately rise. Up till recently technological innovation in mining appeared to be holding its own against rising labour and capital costs. Now the situation seems to be changing, and Lovering, speaking mainly of the USA, states that in spite of technological wizardry, extraction costs are rising. But much worse may well be in store, for a number of authorities now predict a 10-fold increase in the cost of some basic metals within the next decade.

A somewhat facile suggestion frequently aired is that because of improvements in methodology, metals will eventually be extracted from common rock rather than from conventional ores. Professional geologists are sceptical regarding the feasibility of this development, emphasising the formidable scientific problems which would first have to be solved. Others amongst whom economists of the cornucopean school are especially prominent, see in the seas and oceans of the world the answer to the problem of our fast vanishing mineral resources. But what are the prospects for such a solution? There is little doubt that such materials, possibly in large quantities, can be obtained from the sea; the glittering prize is almost certainly there, but unfortunately its attainment will be both arduous and expensive. Cloud has written an admirable monograph on this subject in the course of which he has dealt at length with the mineral resources which might eventually be wrested from our oceans. What are his conclusions? He agrees that efforts in this direction might be attended by a modicum of success. However, at the same time he emphasises that such success is only likely to be the result of 'persistent, imaginative research, inspired invention, bold and skilful experiment and intelligent application and management'.

Our Vanishing Fossil Fuels

The petroleum family of fossil fuels, so vital to our everyday existence, has three main categories—*gaseous* of which by far the most important is the natural gas of industry and commerce, *liquid* of which crude oil is the main member, and *solid* which embraces various types of tar together with a substance known as kerogen found in oil shales. Finally, there is *natural gas liquid*, a material intermediate between natural gas and crude oil.

To geologists the sweep of time is all important. They are concerned with changes occurring on the earth's surface over millions of years; they measure centuries as we ordinary mortals measure seconds. When the geologist places the era of fossil fuel usage in the broad context of history two major facts immediately impress him. The first is the extreme brevity of the time during which such fuels have been exploited as a source of the world's energy. Thus one-half of the coal produced in the last 800 years has been mined in the past 30 years, while half of the total world production of the petroleum family of fossil fuels occurred between 1950 and 1968. The second point which is crystal clear to the geologist but which is greeted by officialdom with an embarrassed silence, is that at current rates of production and consumption the earth's resources of fossil fuels will be rapidly exhausted. The era of the use of these fuels is short and ephemeral; in terms of geology these materials are literally 'here today and gone tomorrow'. In *Tam O'Shanter* the Scottish bard, Robert Burns, wrote:

> *But pleasures are like poppies spread—*
> *You seize the flow'r, its bloom is shed;*
> *Or like the snow falls in the river—*
> *A moment white—then melts for ever.*

These lines are peculiarly apposite to the epoch of utilisation of fossil fuels.

Coal is first for consideration and on the subject of its distribution on earth valuable information has been provided by the US geologist Paul Averitt. The use of modern geological techniques enabled Averitt to arrive at an estimate of the total resources of coal originally present in our planet. His overall figure was 16,830 billion* short tons, this having been calculated by adding together (a) resources already known to exist, and (b) probable additional resources in areas so far unmapped and unexplored. One of the features of Averitt's data was their clear illustration of the highly erratic manner in which coal is distributed. North America, Europe and Asia were well endowed, their combined total amounting to 97 per cent of the world's reserves. The richest areas of all lay in the European part of the Soviet Union, which together with Asian deposits accounted for 65 per cent of the total. Twenty-seven per cent of the earth's coal deposits were located in North America, while Western Europe including the UK contributed some 5 per cent.

Until the beginning of the twentieth century by far the

* Throughout this chapter the US designation billion = 1,000 million is used.

greatest amount of energy for industrial purposes was generated by coal. Since then the position has altered radically; the relative importance of coal has declined, its supremacy having been increasingly challenged by oil and natural gas. The trend is self-evident in the figures. Thus in 1900 the overall contribution of coal to industrial energy was just under 90 per cent; by 1965 it had fallen to some 30 per cent. In the same period the contributions of oil and natural gas had risen from 8 to almost 70 per cent. How did other sources of industrial energy fare during this time? The main point to note is that in relative terms their contribution remained very low. Thus between 1900 and 1965 the rise in energy derived from water power was only marginal (from 3.2 to 4.1 per cent of the total), while, even in 1968, the amount furnished by nuclear energy was quite insignificant being approximately 0.1 per cent.

Prior to the nineteenth century the total world production of coal and of the closely allied substance, lignite, was exiguous by modern standards. By 1880 it was still less than 500 million metric tons per year; however almost a century later in the early 1970's it had climbed to a figure of over 2.5 billion metric tons. The US production of coal and lignite in 1900 AD was some 200 million short tons; by the 1920's, following the rapid industrialisation associated with the First World War and the period of boom which succeeded it, the figure had risen to over 500 million short tons per year. Output fell during the Great Economic Depression of the thirties, but following the New Deal programme introduced by the Roosevelt administration in 1932 and the spur to industry provided by the Second World War, production began to rise steadily, reaching an all time peak of over 600 million short tons during the fifties. Thereafter the tendency has been for the American rate of production of coal and lignite to diminish as oil and natural gas have become of increasing importance in industrial practice.

Figures issued by the UN in the late 1960's indicate that the US still leads the world in coal production. Huge quantities of this fuel are also produced by countries of the Communist bloc, notably the Soviet Union, the People's Republic of China and Poland. The UK with a figure of approximately 175 million metric tons per year was also a major producer, occupying fourth place in the world list of nations.

As with other fuels, resources of coal are not inexhaustible. Is it possible to estimate what period of time must elapse before they have entirely vanished from the earth's crust? Obviously prognostications of this type cannot be precise because of the large number of variable factors involved. Nevertheless, approximations can be made on the basis of evidence currently available and the renowned American geologist M. K. Hubbert is one who has attempted to make such a prediction. Hubbert's forecast is that if coal is used as a source of industrial energy at approximately its present rate of consumption the greater part of the world's reserves will be used up in between 300 and 400 years. On the other hand, if for any reason such as exhaustion of supplies of oil and natural gas, coal again became the predominant fuel of industry, its lifespan would be much shorter. Under such circumstances it is doubtful whether available reserves would last for more than 200 years, and there is a strong possibility that they would be approaching exhaustion well before the end of the twenty-first century.

                          *   *   *

In 1967 W. P. Ryman of the Standard Oil Company of New Jersey provided data on the quantities of crude oil which, utilising techniques available at that time, could ultimately be recovered from the earth. He expressed his figures in billions of US barrels and he divided the earth into a number of geographical regions. For each region the total which he quoted represented the sums of (a) present cumulative production, (b) that of proved reserves, (c) that of probable reserves and (d) that which was likely to accrue as a result of future discoveries. Hubbert made a careful analysis of Ryman's data, and although he recognises their obvious limitations, he nevertheless considers them to be the most accurate relative assessment of the world's crude oil resources which exist at the present time.

Ryman's total for the ultimate recovery of crude oil from the earth was 2,090 billions of US barrels. As in the case of coal and metallic reserves marked geographical variations in distribution were apparent. Thus the oil-rich countries of the Middle East made up some 30 per cent of the total. The USA, including quantities obtained in the recent strikes in Alaska, accounted for approximately 10 per cent as did the Far East, Latin America and Africa. Most of the remaining 30 per cent was located in states of the Communist bloc, particularly in the Soviet Union, Rumania and possibly in China, although Ryman was careful to stress that accurate figures for the last mentioned country were difficult to obtain.

In the late 1960's the USA still led the world in the production of crude petroleum; not far behind were the Soviet Union and Venezuela. Fourth, fifth and sixth places were held respectively by Saudi Arabia, Iran and Kuwait; Libya, on which Britain is becoming increasingly dependent for her oil supplies, occupied seventh place, while another important UK supplier, Nigeria, held sixteenth place. Recent evidence indicates that the governments of countries which act as primary producers of oil, particularly those of the Middle East as well as Libya, are becoming increasingly aware of the indispensability of their product to the highly complex and exceedingly vulnerable technological societies which characterise the Western world. This point of view was much in evidence at a meeting held in Teheran in February, 1971, in the course of which the primary producing countries extracted significant price rises from the international oil companies. These negotiations compelled Britain in common with other Western countries to pay more for their oil supplies; the chronically ailing British economy, at present showing a curious admixture of inflation and high unemployment, is unlikely to benefit from these manoeuvres.

Reliable figures for the world's resources of natural gas and natural gas liquids are much more difficult to obtain than is the case for coal and crude oil. This is mainly because, until recently, accurate statistics were simply not kept, much of the gas which was produced being either wasted and not used by industry. Furthermore, geological techniques for the mapping of sources of natural gas are still less refined than are those for other fossil fuels. However, in spite of constraints imposed by currently used methods it is still possible to arrive at approximate estimates. Hubbert has made such calculations and quotes a figure for the ultimate world production of natural gas of 12,000 trillion cubic feet and of natural gas liquids of 420 billion US barrels.

How long will it be before our planet is denuded of resources of the petroleum family of fossil fuels? Again as in the case of coal and metals predictions must of necessity lack precision. Nevertheless, the general trend is not in doubt, and the overall conclusions can only be described as profoundly disquieting. Whereas in the case of coal it might be anticipated that supplies would endure for as long as two or three centuries, a much shorter lifetime is vouchsafed to oil, natural gas and natural gas liquids. For example Cloud doubts whether at present rates of consumption oil supplies will last much beyond the early years of the 21st century, while he considers that reserves of natural gas will be exhausted by the 1990's.*

It is tempting to postulate that, even at this relatively early stage, the countries which act as the primary producers of oil see the writing on the wall. Was this the real reason behind their recent successful demands for higher oil prices? Is this why a country such as Libya under its young and energetic leader Colonel Gadaffi is currently adopting such a militant posture on the international stage? Shortages of oil and natural gas in the absence of an alternative source of power such as nuclear energy, will undoubtedly play havoc with the complex technological societies which have been built up in Western countries. We in Britain shall be severely affected by such shortages. Indeed we may already have had a foretaste of the future when in December 1970 nation wide power cuts were imposed as a result of a 'work to rule' amongst employees in the electricity industry. The public was rightly incensed by the inconvenience caused, and it appears probable that their reaction was a major factor in bringing the strike to an end. However, future

* A recent article in the *Daily Telegraph Magazine* (3rd December, 1971) ably summarises the position with respect to the world's diminishing resources. It also points to the draconian measures which developed countries are likely to take when their mineral supplies can no longer be assured. Under such conditions military action against the country controlling such materials would become a strong possibility, and the Anglo-French landings in Suez in 1956 in an attempt to safeguard the flow of oil supplies might well be regarded as a portent for the future.

generations inhabiting these islands and faced with a mounting world scarcity of energy resources are unlikely to be so fortunate and could well conclude that people of our time had little of which to complain!

For undoubtedly the world faces a grim future with respect to supplies of fossil fuels. What will happen when eventually such resources are exhausted? Few people appear to give much thought to this matter, either considering that it is irrelevant because it may not affect them during their lifetime, or naïvely assuming that the march of technological innovation will provide all embracing solutions. It is true that alternative sources of industrial energy are being sought, and that the pace of research in this area has quickened in recent years. Thus attempts are being made to harness the sun's energy and to utilise on a growing scale the sources of power and energy resident in water and tides. Above all—and herein probably lies the greatest hope for mankind—strenuous efforts are being made to develop nuclear power as the prime source of industrial energy. But, as with most human enterprises in which a radical change of policy has become necessary, this course of action will be attended by major difficulties. Some of these difficulties receive consideration in Chapter XII.

References

AVERITT, PAUL (1969). 'Coal resources of the US—1st January 1967'. *US Geological Survey Bulletin*, p. 1275.

BROWN, HARRISON, BONNER, JAMES and WEIR, JOHN (1957). *The Next 100 Years*. New York, Viking Press.

CLOUD, PRESTON (1969). *Resources, population and quality of life*. Address Annual Meeting, American Association for the Advance of Science, December.

CLOUD, PRESTON (1969). 'Mineral Resources from the Sea'. In *Resources and Man*. San Francisco, W. H. Freeman and Co., pp. 135-155.

CLOUD, PRESTON (1971). 'Minerals'. In *Can Britain Survive*? Edited by GOLDSMITH, EDWARD. London, Tom Stacey, pp. 121-127.

EHRLICH, PAUL R. and EHRLICH, ANN (1970). *Population, Resources, Environment*. San Francisco, W. H. Freeman and Co.

FULLARD, HAROLD F. (1970). *Geographical Digest.* London, George Philip and Son.

HAWKES, NIGEL (1971). 'Living beyond our Resources'. *Daily Telegraph Magazine,* 3rd December.

HENSMAN, C. R. (1971). *Rich against Poor: The Reality of Aid.* London, Allen Lane, The Penguin Press.

HUBBERT, M. KING (1969). 'Energy Resources'. In *Resources and Man.* Edited by CLOUD, PRESTON. San Francisco, W. H. Freeman and Co., pp. 157-242.

LASKY, S. G. (1950). 'How tonnage-grade relations help predict ore reserves'. *Eng. Mining J.,* **151,** (4), pp. 81-85.

LOVERING, THOMAS S. (1969). 'Mineral Resources from the Land'. In *Resources and Man.* Edited by CLOUD, PRESTON. San Francisco, W. H. Freeman and Co., pp. 109-134.

LOVERING, THOMAS S. (1971). 'Non-Fuel Mineral Resources in the Next Century'. In *Global Ecology.* Edited by HOLDREN, JOHN S. and EHRLICH, PAUL R. New York, Chicago, San Francisco, Atlanta, Harcourt Brace Jovanovich Inc., pp. 39-55.

OGBURN, CHARLTON J. R. (1970). 'Why the global income gap grows wider?'. *Population Bulletin,* **26,** pp. 3-36.

SKINNER, BRIAN J. (1969). *Earth Resources.* Foundations of Earth Science Sources.

U.S. BUREAU OF MINES (1965). *Metals and minerals—Minerals Yearbook.* Washington D.C., **1.**

IX

BOUNDLESS CITIES

Hell is a city much like London—
A populous and smoky city.

> Shelley. *Peter Bell the Third,* pt. 3. *Hell,*i.

'I for my part can only call this a disease of the soul.'

> Procopius of Caesarea, on mob-violence in the cities
> of the East Roman Empire, AD 532. (History of the
> Wars, I. xxiv. 6.)

One of the major social changes which has characterised the second half of the twentieth century has been the movement and in certain areas of the world, the veritable stampede of population from countryside to cities. This trend can be observed throughout our planet, and although it is seen in its most acute form in the underdeveloped nations of Asia, Africa and Latin America, it is by no means confined to these continents. Urbanisation has no ideological, political or religious frontiers, occurring irrespective of whether the regime currently in power is capitalist and Catholic as in the majority of the Latin American states, nominally socialist as in some Middle Eastern and African countries and Marxist as in the USSR, in the People's Republic of China and more recently in Chile.

It is a matter of considerable difficulty to obtain accurate statistics with respect to the degree of urbanisation. This arises partly from the rapidly changing scene particularly in under-developed countries, and also because of the relative infre-quency and sometimes doubtful reliability of population censuses. In addition, problems with respect to definition are formidable. Thus to some the terms urbanisation and growth of cities are synonymous, whilst to others including professional demographers such as Kingsley Davis of the USA, urbanisation has a more precise meaning connoting the proportion of the total population concentrated in urban as opposed to rural settlements. And there are further complications. Thus the delineation of what constitutes an 'urban area' is notoriously difficult in practice and may vary from one country to another. International bodies are worried by such confusion, and in an attempt to facilitate nomenclature in this field, the UN authorities have recommended the use of the term 'urban agglomeration', defining this as 'the city proper and also the surburban fringe or thickly settled territory lying outside of or adjacent to the city boundaries'.

Some figures from the world scene illustrate the magnitude of the current problem of urbanisation and indicate what may be expected in the future. Arvill, in his *Man and Environment* states that in 1800 AD the world possessed a mere 50 cities with populations of over 100,000; just over 150 years later in the 1960's, the corresponding figure exceeded 900. Taylor in his *Doomsday Book* comments that in 1970 there are some 300 cities in the world with a population exceeding half a million. Lavrishchev, talking of the Soviet Union, states that in that country alone between 1926 and 1967 the number of towns with a population greater than half a million rose from three to 31, while the Athenian, Doxiades, looking into the future, forecasts that by the middle of the twenty-first century, 90 per cent of mankind will inhabit cities and only five per cent will be found in rural areas.

In the 40 years between 1920 and 1960 the world's urban population trebled while its country dwellers increased by only one-third. In 1920 countrymen outnumbered city dwellers by 6.4 to 1; by 1960 the ratio had fallen to 3 to 1; by 2000 AD it will be negative, town dwellers outnumbering those in rural areas. Davis states that at present some 38 per cent of the total world population live in large towns and cities and over 20 per cent reside in conurbations containing 100,000 inhabitants or more. His predictions for the remainder of the century are pessimistic. He forecasts that if the degree of urbanisation characteristic of the 1950's continues unabated, then by 1984, the year made famous in George Orwell's satirical books, more than half of the world's population will be city dwellers. An even grimmer outlook is vouchsafed for the twenty-first century. By 2020 AD Davis postulates that the vast majority of the earth's population will be existing in cities of one million inhabitants or more, while by 2044 virtually 'everyone' will be living in cities of that size. What will be the effects of this change? They will inevitably be far reaching. New York City is claimed to be virtually ungovernable now; Los Angeles, Chicago and other US cities do not lag far behind. As will be emphasised later pitiful conditions already exist in great numbers of towns and cities throughout the underdeveloped world. If the prophecies of Davis come to fruition—and there appears no reason to believe that they will not—the lot of future generations inhabiting this planet will indeed be unenviable.

My aim so far has been to indicate that urbanisation is spreading throughout our universe like a cancerous disease of high malignancy. I shall now proceed to examine its effects in various parts of the world.

The British and American Scenes

Within the term United Kingdom are included England, Wales, Scotland and Northern Ireland; this is one of the most thickly settled and heavily urbanised areas of the world. The population density of the UK is 228 persons per square kilometre and, if one excludes small islands and city states, the figure ranks eighth in the world's list of nations. The population density of England and Wales is even higher—323 persons per square kilometre—and in world terms this is exceeded only by one other country namely Formosa (Taiwan). Even the thickly settled nations of the European Common Market—Belgium, the Netherlands and Federal Germany—are not so unfavourably placed because their population densities are somewhat lower than that of England and Wales. In Great Britain in the 1970's there is only just over one acre of land per person; in the case of England and Wales the corresponding figure drops to 0.79 acres.

The 'high noon' of urbanisation in the UK occurred at the peak of the Industrial Revolution, the swiftest rise in town dwellers taking place between 1811 and 1851. Subsequently the process continued albeit at a somewhat slower tempo. Nevertheless the drift from land to cities remained quite considerable, and by 1961 the proportion of the total population living in cities of over 100,000 inhabitants was not far short of 80 per cent. The number of males engaged in agriculture in Britain was at its maximum in 1851 when 1.8 million were so employed; by 1961 the figure had fallen to some 0.5 million and it continued to decrease throughout the remainder of the decade.

A recent report by Edwards and Wibberley provides important information on the distribution of land in the UK. The total area of the country amounts to 59.5 million acres. Of this some 48.5 million acres are used for agriculture; crops and grass account for 30.6 million acres and rough grazing for 17.8 million; approximately 4.5 million acres are covered by forest and woodland, while just over five million acres are urbanised or semi-urbanised. Since the end of the Second World War transfers of land from agriculture to urban growth have averaged about 40,000 acres per year in England and Wales. In Scotland for which comparable information exists only for the decade of the 1960's losses have averaged 6,000 acres per year, while in Northern Ireland the corresponding figure is some 2,000 acres per year.

These figures show that Britain is urbanising at a moderate tempo; our population is also rising, fortunately at a relatively slow rate as compared with that of other parts of the world. Because of these not unfavourable trends it might be anticipated that our housing situation would be in reasonable balance. However, everyone in Britain recognises that this is far from being so. Even with our modest rate of population increase, we must still attempt to build 100,000 new houses each year. Furthermore, we must make herculean efforts to replace accommodation which has already become obsolescent or is grossly substandard. The housing record of a city such as Glasgow in my native Scotland is nothing short of shameful. Thus of the total stock of 320,000 dwellings some 43,000 have been condemned or categorised as substandard, while another 50,000 will require to be replaced within the next 10 years.

Russell, writing in *The Ecologist* in 1971, has stressed that housing is one of Britain's key resources. He comments that our population outstripped our housing resources in the early nineteenth century in the heyday of the Industrial Revolution. Since then the deficit has never been made good nor is it in his opinion ever likely to be met in spite of the ceaseless rhetoric of party politicians.

The scarcity of houses and land has undoubtedly been an important factor in producing a steep rise in costs, and this process has notably intensified during the past two decades. Thus according to Russell the cost of land for building in the London area increased some 7-fold between 1951 and 1963. Between 1960 and 1970 the price of a new house, including the cost of land more than doubled, and between 1969 and 1970 the average cost of a new house shot up by as much as £300.

Leaving aside the question of our housing shortage—which many would regard as insuperable without a dramatic decrease in our population—does Britain face other dangers because of its progressive urbanisation? Views on this subject are notably divergent and are frequently clouded by emotive overtones. Some authorities are very pessimistic. For example, Watts bemoans the fact that by the end of the century some 2.5 million acres of farmland, an area equivalent to that of the counties of Cornwall and Devon, will be the victim of urban encroachment. The Conservative Member of Parliament, Sir David Renton, in correspondence with the former Prime Minister Harold Wilson reported in *New Horizon* during 1967, expressed acute anxiety about the amount of Britain's farmland being urbanised and stated that such a situation was fraught with peril to a country which was forced to import almost half of its foodstuffs. Renton recommended that the tempo of urban development be slowed and declared that if this were not done an area the size of Leicestershire would be 'converted to tarmacadam, concrete or bricks and mortar' between 1967 and 1977. Others apart from Renton are worried about the proliferation of new towns of which some 25 are currently reported to be under construction. However, Best believes that the dangers accruing from the building of new towns have been exaggerated and considers that the latter are more conservative in their demands for land than is new development around existing towns.

The reason behind the construction of new towns is readily discernable. Each day in Britain births exceed deaths by approximately 700 and accordingly cities the size of Notting-ham and Bradford are required every year only to house our new citizens! Milton Keynes in Buckinghamshire and Livingston in West Lothian are good examples of new towns. The former, which is sited in the heart of a rural area and which is expected to accommodate 250,000 people by 2000 AD, will destroy over 22,000 acres of farmland. The building of Livingston, which by 2000 AD planners confidently expect to house a population of 100,000, will lose to Central Scotland over 6,000 acres of fine agricultural land.

But the construction of new towns by no means gives the complete picture. Progressive destruction of amenity is con-stantly occurring, and Arvill has written eloquently of the damage produced to the heathlands of Southern England by population growth and the proliferation of dwelling houses. In the early part of the nineteenth century the Dorset heathland had an area of approximately 75,000 acres; by 1960 the figure had shrunk by two-thirds to 25,000 acres. However, this was not the only complication. Not only had the overall area of the heathland been reduced by urban development, but the land which remained had been broken up into a series of small tracts, the value of which was very limited indeed. Thus they were virtually useless for recreational activity; they failed to provide any sense of open country, and their flora and fauna had either been markedly reduced or completely eliminated.

*   *   *

A somewhat more optimistic view of the overall British situation, at least as far as the present century is concerned, is provided by the careful and painstaking investigations of Best, Edwards, Wibberley and their associates at Wye College in Kent. Writing in the periodical *New Society* during 1970, Best stated that in the early 1960's urban development occupied only 11 per cent of the total land mass of England and Wales; the corresponding figure for the whole of the UK was even less at 8.5 per cent. On the other hand, approximately 80 per cent of the land was in agricultural use, while forest and woodland accounted for just under 8 per cent. Best did not deny that the tempo of urbanisation in Britain had been rapid; indeed during the first 60 years of this century the area converted from countryside to town actually doubled. He did however make the interesting point that, contrary to popular belief, the peak period with respect to conversion of rural to urban land did not occur following the Second World War; instead it took place during the Great Economic Depression of the 1930's when agriculture was in the doldrums and land could be purchased cheaply. Since the Second World War the acquisition of rural areas by towns has certainly continued; however, as compared with the 1930's, the pace has slackened largely due to the fact that successive governments, both Labour and Conservative, have been unwavering in their partiality for high-density housing, the latter reaching its apogee in the construction of high rise flats or tower blocks. Surprisingly enough, it now seems that afforestation rather than urbanisation is the main villain of the piece as the chief absorber of farmland, and according to Edwards and Wibberley the amount of land in the UK covered by forest and woodland will increase from 7.8 per cent in 1965 to 10.9 per cent by 2000 AD. How does the figure of 8.5 per cent urbanised land for the UK compare with that of other industrialised nations in Europe? According to Best it is in no way exceptional. Thus in two countries of the European Economic Community—the Netherlands and Federal Germany— the comparable figures are very similar, being 7 and 10 per cent respectively.

What is the possibility that urban encroachment of arable land will produce serious food shortages in the UK? Edwards and Wibberley, talking of the years intervening between now and 2000 AD, see little if any immediate danger. Their prophecy is that British agriculture, with its high standards of efficiency and technological expertise, will be able to accommodate the degree of urbanisation and afforestation envisaged, and in spite of such encroachments will still be able to make an even greater contribution to feeding the population of these islands than it did in the 1960's.

But all is not golden, for looking beyond 2000 AD and

peering into the mists of the twenty-first century Best is much less sanguine. He notes that increased mechanisation and intensification of farming will progressively damage the rural scene. Even more ominously he predicts that if present trends continue, almost one-quarter of the whole of the land surface of England and Wales will be urbanised by the latter third of the next century. He fears the psychological tensions and neurotic manifestations which will undoubtedly appear when great numbers of people are herded together in confined spaces; he bemoans the destruction of amenity, the steady growth of traffic and the ever-increasing pollution of air, water and land. To Best as to many of us who view the future with concern the underlying malady is overpopulation. Indeed there seems little doubt that unless we restrain our proclivity for reproduction our descendants will literally crowd themselves off our island.

*   *   *

In the USA urban encroachment on rural reserves is proceeding apace and is proving to be a baneful influence. However, in contrast to crowded European nations such as the UK, the Netherlands, Belgium and Federal Germany, the US must still be regarded as a country relatively rich in land resources. After all, its overall population density is only 22 persons per square kilometre and there are some 12 acres of land per head of population.

But will this enviable situation last? In view of current trends the answer must be in the negative. For example, in 1968 alone it was estimated that one million acres of land, admittedly of variable quality with respect to agricultural potential, were lost to urban development. The US Soil Conservation Service is one of the organisations which gives a dismal prognosis for the future. In 1969 it reported that between 1958 and 1967 the amount of privately owned rural land in the USA decreased by almost 15 million acres; moreover, it produced firm evidence to support the contention that the major factor producing this depletion was the rapid growth of cities. In June 1969 one of the country's leading authorities on urbanisation, testifying to a Senate Subcommittee, stated that by the year 2000 AD, 75 per cent of the US population would be crowded into no more than 2 per cent of the area of the country. Already the predilection of American citizens for city life is obvious, two out of every three people opting to reside in metropolitan areas.

The US decennial census of 1970 disclosed important information. One interesting point to emerge was the precipitous drop by as much as one-third in farm population. As a result this section of the community now amounted to only 10 million or less than 5 per cent of the total population of the country. Above all, however, the census highlighted the geographical shift of people from central cities to suburbs. Indeed some two-thirds of the population growth in the USA was found to have taken place in the suburbs, the residents of which for the first time in history outnumbered those of central cities. And this trend will undoubtedly continue—so much so that George H. Brown, Director of the American Bureau of Census, predicts that by 1985 half of the total population of the country will be residing in suburban enclaves.

The movement of population from central cities to suburbs has important sociological connotations particularly with regard to the racial scene. This is because the main migration outwards from cities has been on the part of the white citizens; on the other hand, the negro population has tended to move into the city centres, and indeed some three-quarters of the growth of the black population in the USA since 1960 has occurred in such areas. The flow of black immigration is unlikely to be staunched; by 1985 Brown estimates that one-third of the residents of central cities will be black as compared with only one-fifth in 1970. The opportunities for racial conflict provided by such movements of population are too obvious to require elaboration.

To the visitor to the USA in the 1960's and 1970's one of the outstanding impressions is of the continuous erection of huge masses of bricks and mortar. The eastern seaboard of the country vividly illustrates this point, for in that region an almost uninterrupted succession of urban dwellings now meets the eye of the beholder from Boston in Massachusetts to Washington DC. American journalists are noted for their pithy statements, and for this so-called 'development' the scarcely euphonious but highly descriptive term of 'Boswash' has been coined. Desecration of the once beautiful state of California has proceeded apace in recent decades. In 1850 the population of California was some 80,000; just over 100 years later in 1966 it was 19 million and if present trends continue it could well be 1500 million 100 years from now! The state that once was golden has now been tarnished irrevocably and foremost amongst the factors producing this unhappy situation has been excessive urbanisation. The growth of cities in California has been mainly in the coastal belt, and at present 15 out of every 20 people live along the 530 miles of coastline between Oakland in the north and San Diego in the south.

The plight of the major US cities has been referred to earlier. In the census of 1967 the population of Greater Los Angeles was in the region of 7 million, and since then numbers have continued to rise because of the continuing migration of people to the western United States. Los Angeles is the quintessence of urban sprawl. Its boundaries slide indeterminately into the surrounding countryside, and it possesses a highly characteristic combination of slum and suburb which spreads outwards from the centre in a serpignious manner. The city is a microcosm of the maladies of our modern technological society. It vies with and possibly outstrips New York and Tokyo for the accolade of the world's capital of atmospheric pollution; its rates of criminality, delinquency and violence are high and it has a racial problem of formidable proportions.

In New York City buildings do not sprawl outwards as in Los Angeles; rather do they sprout upwards producing huge skyscrapers. In the 1967 census the urban agglomeration of New York City contained just over 11½ million people and even then it was bursting at the seams. In recent times large numbers of Puerto Ricans and coloured immigrants from the Deep South of the USA have migrated to New York, have swelled its population and have produced enormous social and economic problems. This, to the outsider, is the ungovernable city par excellence, and it is small wonder that in journalistic parlance its mayoralty has been described as 'the worst job in the world'.

The Agony of the Third World

The grimmest features of excessive urbanisation are to be found not in developed countries such as Britain and the USA but in the underdeveloped continents of Asia, Africa and Latin America. It is here that the flight of humanity from countryside to city is most evident, and indeed between 1960 and 1970 it was estimated that some 200 million people—close to the current population of the USA—left the land and became town dwellers.

Cities in Africa, Asia and Latin America are under continuous siege by hordes of impoverished peasants lacking any skill, yet desperate for work and shelter. Space is at a premium; overcrowding is intense; burgeoning slums result, while street sleeping and squatting are accepted ways of life. Here talk of the 'dignity of man', a phrase which trips so lightly from the lips of politicians and officials, has a shallow ring. Instead there are privation, deficient sanitation, ubiquitous disease, social disintegration and poverty on a massive scale.

Of all areas of the world Latin America is the one in which the population is rising most rapidly. Throughout that continent slums are endemic, their names varying with the region involved. Thus in Rio de Janiero and other Brazilian cities they are called *favelas*, in Caracas *ranchos*, in Lima *barriadas* and in Columbia *tugurios*. Brazil and Venezuela mirror accurately the situation in many Latin American countries and will serve us as examples.

Brazil has been described as a prodigy of growth. It is the seventh most heavily populated country of the world and is the most populous nation of the Latin American continent. It has a problem of urbanisation which is amongst the most acute and intractable in the world. What are the facts?

The cities of Brazil are currently growing at a rate of 5.4 per cent per annum. In 1965 Brazil had only two state capitals—Rio de Janiero and São Paulo—with a population of over 1 million people; by the beginning of the decade of the 1970's there will be five—Recife, Porto Alegre and Belo Horizonte having been added to the list. Shortly afterwards another two cities, Fortaleza and Salvador, are expected to pass the million mark. In the ten years between 1950 and 1960 urban growth in Brazil proceeded at a rate almost double that of the country as a whole. In 1950 cities with more than 100,000 people represented 13.1 per cent of the population; by 1960 the corresponding figure was 18.8 per cent. The metropolitan areas of Rio de Janiero and São Paulo grew by more than 6 per cent per annum between 1940 and 1960, and during this period both cities were doubling their population every 12 years. In 1950 only 31 per cent of the Brazilian population was urbanised; by 1960 the figure had risen to 40 per cent and by 1980 it is expected to be in the neighbourhood of 55 per cent. In 1960 Rio de Janiero and São Paulo shared 22 per cent of the total urban population of Brazil; between 1960 and 1970 São Paulo alone is expected to gain 2.7 million in-habitants.

The effects of rapid urbanisation are observed most clearly in the *favelas* which cluster on the edges of many Brazilian cities especially Rio de Janiero and São Paulo. It is estimated that in Rio de Janiero 30 per cent of the total population occupy such slums. Many of the inhabitants are permanently unemployed or can only find work for brief periods of time; even if they succeed in securing employment their wage earning capacity is low. All types of deprivation abound in the *favelas*. Many of the shacks lack utilities of any kind, and sewerage systems are generally primitive or non-existent. Of the 630,000 domiciles registered in Rio de Janiero in 1960 fewer than half had water connections and an even smaller proportion were connected to sewers. The simple matter of disposing of human excrement remains a formidable problem in the *favelas* as it does in slums all over the world. It is often necessary to discharge the excre-ment into ditches shared with large numbers of people; alternatively it may simply be left to rot and decompose between the slum dwellings. Who can wonder that under such conditions diseases such as gastroenteritis, infective hepatitis, dysentery, typhoid fever and various types of parasitic condition abound? And the situation is becoming

worse rather than better because in Brazil as in other underdeveloped countries urbanisation is rapidly outstripping
industrialisation.

The problems of Venezuela are similar to those of Brazil;
indeed in some respects they are even worse. Abrams in his
Housing in the Modern World states that the proportion of
rural and urban squatters in Venezuela exceeds 65 per cent
of the total population. In Caracas, the capital, 35 per cent
of the people come into this category while in Maracaibo
the figure is even higher being close to 50 per cent.

In Brazil it was the *favelas*; in Venezuela the shanty
towns are termed *ranchos*. In Caracas they dominate the
view, perched as they are on the surrounding mountain
ranges; however, they also infiltrate into the city proper and
some are situated quite close to the main shopping streets.
The *ranchos*, which usually consist of only one storey, are
fashioned from all types of material including earth, cardboard, old boxes, tin, scrap metal and brick tile. Their
sanitation is either primitive or non-existent; public services
are quite unable to keep pace with the mounting population, and in the rainy season a veritable cascade of human
excrement descends from the *ranchos* on to the roads
beneath. The outlook for the future is most unpromising
because the population of Caracas, like that of most other
Latin American cities, continues to soar. Thus in 1950 it
housed 694,000 inhabitants; by 1961 the total had climbed
to 1.3 million, and in the population census conducted
during 1967 the figure quoted for the 'urban agglomeration'
of Caracas was close to 2 million.

*   *   *

Everywhere throughout the underdeveloped world the
story is the same. Thus in Turkey squatters are reported to
make up 45 per cent of the population of Ankara, 21 per
cent of Istanbul and 18 per cent of Izmir. In Karachi in
West Pakistan which at the time of the 1968 census had a
population close to 3 million, one-third of the inhabitants
are squatters; and Philippine capital of Manila has a squatter

rate of 20 per cent. In Singapore it is 15 per cent and in Kingston, Jamaica, 12 per cent. In Algiers the 'tin can' towns or *bidonvilles* can be observed close to the centre of cities; in Tunisia and Southern Spain squatters must live in caves hewn from hillsides, while in Johannesburg the squatter colonies seen on the periphery of the city and inhabited mainly by negroes, constitute a national disgrace.

In Panama the pressure of population is so acute that sleeping must be done in relays. In 1960 in Ghana the average occupancy of a single house was 19.3 persons. In the villages of Egypt crowding is intense; housing is primitive, and in the early 1960's 27.5 per cent of the houses did not even possess a roof. In Hong Kong the population density can be as high as 2,000 per acre, people living herded together in huts lacking water and deprived of even the most basic forms of sanitation.

India has been termed the 'cradle of overpopulation' and the designation is well merited. Thus in Bombay in 1963 it was officially stated that 1 in every 66 persons was homeless, while a further 77,000 people lived under stairways, on landings, in cattlesheds and in other highly unsalubrious surroundings. In New Delhi it is reported that the number of squatters exceeds 150,000 and that the majority of those live on public land.

Calcutta has been called the 'capital of overpopulation' or the 'world's worst city'. In the 1968 census the population of Greater Calcutta was estimated to be 5.1 million. Forecasts for the population of the city in the future vary greatly, but all agree that a massive increase of numbers will take place. Some authorities state that the population will 'more than double' by 1986; others are much more gloomy and aver that by the year 2000 AD Greater Calcutta will house 66 million people, 10 million more than the present population of the UK and over 13 times the city's present numbers!

Street sleeping in Calcutta is a recognised mode of life, and Abrams puts its current incidence as high as 600,000 each night. The influx of agricultural workers into the city from the surrounding countryside is on the increase, and even ten years ago was estimated to be running at 100,000 per annum. The vast majority of the inhabitants of Calcutta inhabit overcrowded tenements or slums popularly known as bustees; approximately 60 per cent of multimember families have only one room in which to live and each member is fortunate if he possesses 30 square feet of space. Three quarters of the population dwell in decaying shacks without tap water and sanitation; open sewers are conspicuous, and it is quite frequent for one water tap to be used by 30 persons and one latrine by 20. Public services are rudimentary or non-existent, and as a result garbage is piled high in the streets and remains uncollected. During the monsoon season the already bad conditions rapidly deteriorate. At that time much of the populace literally wades through its own excreta, and diseases such as cholera and yellow fever stalk the city. But these are not the only miseries for, in addition, the traffic situation in Calcutta is appalling. Each day some 500,000 pedestrians and over 30,000 vehicles struggle to cross the Howrath Bridge in the centre of the city. As a consequence jams at both ends of the bridge are a constant feature, progress being slowed by rickshaws, oxen-drawn carts, water buffaloes and the never-ending surge of humanity.

The picture of present day Calcutta is horrendous. Indeed one wonders how long the city can survive before its social fabric is shattered beyond repair. Will Calcutta eventually be the catalyst for a world holocaust precipitated by over-population? Only time will provide the answer to this fateful question.

Hazards of City Life

In bygone days the concept of the city was indissolubly linked in the mind of man with freedom and with his dreams and aspirations for the future. Frequently man equated the city with his idea of heaven as phrases such as the 'Celestial City', the 'Holy City' and the 'New Jerusalem' have indicated. Such dreams have seldom been fulfilled although for some, even in the last third of the twentieth century, a certain richness still attaches to life in cities. Unfortunately such riches are in danger of turning to ashes under the continued assaults of the motor car, racial conflict, environmental pollution and the physical and psychological effects attributable to overcrowding.

The term 'New Jerusalem' to describe a city has a particularly ironic ring in the world of the early 1970's. Jerusalem was unified and incorporated in the Israeli state following the Six Day War of 1967. This was a time of great patriotic rejoicing in Israel, and the highlight of the victory was the occasion upon which Israeli leaders, including their prestigious Secretary for Defence Moshe Dayan, made their obeisances at the Wailing Wall. But what are the prospects for the New Jerusalem? They are bleak indeed because of a vast increase in numbers. The present population of the city is not unduly large at 270,000. However, by 1985 it is expected to rise to 600,000 and by 2010 AD to 900,000! Since the city was unified Israeli town planners have been hard at work and have now proposed that the answer to Jerusalem's population explosion is the construction of a 'commuting belt' stretching from Ramallah in the north to Bethlehem in the south. The effect of such a development on the Holy Places can be left to the reader's imagination.

The Athenian, Doxiades, has written eloquently of city life both now and in the future. He considers that life in modern cities is inhumane even for those who are not impoverished. In support of his view he cites the lack of mobility of the individual within the boundaries of the conurbation, the ever-increasing pollution of air and water and, above all, the baneful influence of the motor car. In his hard hitting monograph *The Costs of Economic Growth*, E. J. Mishan, the London economist, is scathing in his condemnation of the trappings of modern urban life. In a memorable sentence he provides his assessment of the present scene—'lorries, motor cycles and taxis belching fumes, filth and stench, snarling engines and unabating visual disturbance have compounded to make movement through a city an ordeal for the pedestrian at the same time as the mutual strangulation of traffic makes it a purgatory for motorists'. Mishan talks of cities having been converted into 'roaring workshops' and pours scorn on the hapless local authorities who are impotent to deal with the fundamental causes of the problem and can only recommend a series of palliative measures such as road widening, bridging and patching.

The great American statesman Adlai Stevenson once described our era as one of 'rising expectations' and foremost among such expectations is the possession of a motor car. Indeed, just as the sculptor perceives an angel imprisoned in the block of marble, so does the aspirant politician see in the promise of automobile ownership a ticket to his election and continuing popularity. In the serried phalanx of political clichés the phrase the 'democratisation of the motor car' occupies a high position, ranking, for example, with classical exhortations such as those bidding us to think of our 'children's children' and to have 'pride in our past and confidence in our future'. But what has been the effect of this much published democratisation of the motor car in our overcrowded island? The result is only too plain in a traffic problem of monumental proportions. The relevant figures have been made available by our Road Research Laboratory and they make sombre reading. Thus in 1970 the total number of vehicles on the roads of Great Britain was in the neighbourhood of 16 million. But much worse is in store. By 1980 the total will have risen to 25 million, by 1990 to 30 million, by 2000 AD to 34 million and by 2010 to 38 million!* However, the harsh realities of existence will almost certainly prevent the attainment of such figures, for the Road Research Laboratory points out that the so-called 'saturation level' of 0.45 cars per person is likely to be reached as early as the mid-1980's.

*   *   *

In recent years a number of authorities have written with force and passion on the social evils which accrue when great numbers of people are herded together in the overcrowded and insanitary slums which are now so characteristic of many of the

---

* Such figures will, of course, depend on the continuing availability of oil, a highly questionable factor (see Chapter VIII). With a world-wide shortage of oil pending the recent decision by the British Department of the Environment to build 1,000 miles of motorways by the 1980's would seem to be inappropriate.

world's large conurbations. A recent and important convert to this cause is apparently Pope Paul who in his Apostolic Letter of May 1971 entitled '*Rerum Novarum*' stressed that excessive urbanisation was imperilling society and could jeopardise the basic framework of existence; unfortunately Catholic dogma prevented him from citing overpopulation as the major factor in producing this malaise! Certainly there should be universal concern about our planet's big cities because within them a host of social problems abound. Thus there are abnormally high rates of juvenile delinquency, violent behaviour and outright criminality; illiteracy is rife, drug addiction and alcoholism are widespread, and neurotic illness with or without complete disintegration of the personality is commonplace.

Within the past decade psychologists and psychiatrists have been giving increasing attention to the effects of overcrowding on mental health. Work in this area has been notably stimulated by animal experimentation and especially by the finding that in a variety of species including apes, cats, rats and hens, overcrowding produces symptoms of acute stress and may cause marked behavioural derangements. Carstairs, in a thoughtful article published in 1969, pointed out that one of the major factors which correlates well with the incidence of attempted suicide in humans is overcrowding in large cities. Under such circumstances the weaker citizens become harassed beyond endurance; they despair for their future, and this is a major factor in their attempt to take their own life. Another important point made by Carstairs was that the very act of migration to a city from the countryside has almost certainly raised hopes in the heart of the individual that his living standards will immediately rise. When this does not happen and when there is a perpetuation of the same grinding poverty which he experienced as a rural dweller, disappointment and frustration become even more intense. Cohn in his perceptive monograph, *The Pursuit of the Millennium*, has identified a number of situations which are likely to demoralise the population and seriously affect their mental health and stability. These include movement from an unskilled occupation to a much more complicated type of work, massive and protracted unemployment, widely contrasting living standards between rich and poor, weakening of traditional moral and religious backgrounds and the breakdown of civic authority. Many of these factors are operative in varying degree in the crowded slums of most large cities, and it is therefore not surprising that in such areas mental illness abounds.

But there is another most important factor. The under-privileged masses of today have a window on the world denied to their progenitors. This is, of course, through the mass media of communication especially through television. By this medium the impoverished citizens of the underdeveloped world can readily observe the material benefits enjoyed by their more fortunate brethren in the developed and materialistically orien-tated countries of the West. Such a contrast in living standards is bound to intensify emotions such as envy and frustration, thus further exacerbating social tensions. The late Achmed Sukarno, President of Indonesia from the time that country gained its independence from the Dutch until the mid-1960's and still to many of his countrymen the idol, the magician and the near-God, once said 'a refrigerator can be a revolutionary symbol—to a people who have no refrigerators. A motor car owned by a worker in one country can be a symbol of revolt to a people deprived of the necessities of life'. In our turbulent world of today, time would not be wasted in musing on the relevance of these prophetic words.

*   *   *

Obliterate slums, rehouse the populace! These are the aims of all right thinking people. In political manifestos issued at the time of local or general elections housing programmes occupy a prominent place, and in democratic societies opposing parties vie with one another in their promises to build more and yet more homes. The benefits of slum clearance are plain for all to see. Indeed to those in positions of authority it is nothing short of axiomatic that the house in the new estate or the flat in the tower block must be infinitely preferable to the sordid, if convivial, slum. But have the effects of such an uprooting on the mental and physical health of individuals been adequately studied? Evidence is now accumulating to indicate that they have not, as three examples from the British literature will illustrate.

A publication by Martin and his colleagues in 1957 was concerned with a housing estate built by the London County Council in Hertfordshire. It stressed the relatively high incidence of psychological disorders in the inhabitants of the estate and ascribed this state of affairs to the dislocating effect of the rehousing process together with the acute sense of loneliness and social isolation generated by the new environment. In 1966 a general practitioner called Beatson Hird investigated the mental health of a community residing in a housing estate in the English Midlands. He commented on the frequency of neurotic illness as compared with that found in the general population, and he noted that such illness appeared to be especially prevalent in families living in flats containing two or more storeys. In Beatson Hird's mind there was little doubt as to the precipitating causes of the psychoneurotic manifestations in his patients. He cited such factors as the frictions generated in the community by the inadequate space available for children to play, the excessive noise produced by children running up and down communal stairways, and, in the early days of the estate, the complete absence of services such as shops, buses and even a local pub.

One of the most careful investigations in this field is that of Fanning published in the *British Medical Journal* during 1967. This doctor was concerned with the health of families of members of the British armed forces stationed in Federal Germany. Two groups of families were compared, one living in modern flats consisting of 3 or 4 storey blocks, and the other in houses similar to those found in any modern local authority estate. The most striking finding to emerge from Fanning's study was that the rate of illness in the flat dwellers exceeded that of the house residents by well over 50 per cent. In particular, respiratory infections in young women and children and psychoneurotic disorders in women were shown to be especially frequent in the former group. Fanning considered that a major factor contributing to the increased incidence of respiratory infections was the relatively small amount of space available in a flat as compared with a house. With respect to neurotic illnesses he made the important observation that these become more frequent the higher up the flat the individual lived. Contributory factors to the neuroses were many but included the general monotony and boredom of existence and the feeling of social isolation generated by living in such surroundings.

If such psychological tensions are so prevalent in flats of only 3 or 4 storeys are they not likely to be even more common in high rise flats containing in some cases as many as 30 storeys? The answer is almost certainly in the affirmative. In Britain high rise flats were once regarded as the answer to our housing problem and, as was noted earlier in this chapter, successive governments, both Labour and Conservative, strongly favoured policies designed to increase environmental densities by this form of construction. Now disenchantment with high rise building appears to be on the increase. Thus the city of Liverpool abandoned it in September 1967, while the Greater London Council states that when its present building pro-gramme is completed 5 or 6 years from now no further tower blocks will be constructed. It would be a matter of considerable satisfaction to be able to report that care for the environment and realisation of possible psychological traumata to the inhabitants were the mainsprings for discontinuing the erection of high rise flats. Unfortunately, this does not appear to have been the case, the decision having apparently been taken mainly on economic grounds.

For psychoneurotic disturbances will undoubtedly show an increased incidence in those destined to spend a significant part of their lives in high rise flats. Those of a brittle and dependent personality will suffer most; the strong and self-reliant will be less affected. Feelings of loneliness and isolation will be prominent; many will feel a sense of insecurity and will complain that they are isolated from the mainstream of life. Children will be handicapped because of restricted play facilities, and on the basis of a recent report from the National Society for the Prevention of Cruelty to Children there is already mounting evidence that such deprivation may be the cause of behavioural disturbances later in life. But adults will also be affected and to those of a sensitive disposition the stress of internal noise produced, for example, by lifts and other types of machinery may ultimately prove to be intolerable. One can predict with confidence that the medical and sociological literature of the 1970's and beyond will be replete with reports which dissect in the minutest detail the deleterious effects of flat dwelling on the human personality. Unfortunately in such publications it is likely that the root cause of the malady, namely overpopulation, will receive but passing comment.

References

ABRAMS, CHARLES (1966). *Housing in the Modern World.* London, Faber and Faber.

ARVILL, ROBERT (1969). *Man and Environment.* London, Pelican Books.

BEATSON HIRD, J. F. (1966). 'Planning for a New Community'. *J. Coll. Gen. Practitioners,* **12,** Supplement 1, pp. 33-41.

BEST, ROBIN (1970). 'Laying the land-use myths'. *New Society,* 2nd April, pp. 556-558.

BEST, ROBIN (1968). 'Extent of urban growth and agricultural displacement in post-war Britain. *Urban Studies,* **5,** pp. 1-23.

BEST, ROBIN and CHAMPION, A. G. (1970). *Regional conversions of agricultural land to urban use in England and Wales, 1945-1967.* The Institute of British Geographers, Transactions and Papers, Publication No. 49, pp. 15-32.

BOSE, NIRMAL KUMAR (1965). 'Calcutta: a premature metropolis'. *Sci. Amer.,* **213,** pp. 91-102.

BROWN, GEORGE H. (1970). *1985. Population Reference Bureau,* Selection No. 34, November.

CARSTAIRS, G. M. (1969). *The Story of Violence in America.* Edited by GRAHAM, H. D. and GUNN, T. R. New York, Prodger, Ch. 21, pp. 751-764—also in Paperback, Bantam Books.

CHRISTIAN, GARTH (1966). *Tomorrow's Countryside.* London, John Murray.

COHN, H. (1957). *The Pursuit of the Millennium.* London, Secker and Warburg.

COLE, LAMONTE C. (1968). 'Man and the Air'. *Population Bulletin,* **26,** pp. 103-113.

DAVIS, KINGSLEY (1965). 'The urbanization of the human population'. *Sci. Amer.,* **213,** pp. 41-53.

DOXIADIS, C. A. (1967). *The Inhuman City: In Health of Mankind.* Ciba Foundation 100th Symposium, pp. 178-195.

EDWARDS, A. M. and WIBBERLEY, G. P. (1971). *An Agricultural Land*

Budget for Britain 1965-2000. Ashford, Kent, Wye College, School of Rural Studies and Related Studies.

FANNING, D. M. (1967). 'Families in Flats'. *Brit. med. J.,* 2, pp. 383-386.

KENNET, LORD (1971). 'When we run out of England'. *New Scientist,* 21st January.

LAVRISHCHEV, A. (1969). *Economic Geography of the USSR.* Moscow, Progress Publishers, Translated by MYSHNE, DAVID.

MARTIN, F. M., BROTHERSTON, J. H. F. and CHAVE, S. P. W. (1957). 'Incidence of Neurotics in a New Housing Estate'. *Brit. J. prev. soc. med.,* 11, pp. 196-202.

MISHAN, E. J. (1967). *The Costs of Economic Growth.* London, Staples Press.

MOORHOUSE, GEOFFREY (1971). *Calcutta.* London, Weidenfeld and Nicolson.

POPULATION BULLETIN (1969). 'Brazil: a prodigy of growth'. 25, No. 4, September.

RENTON, SIR DAVID (1967). 'The Population Problem'. *The New Horizon,* No. 264, January, p. 5.

RUSSELL, W. M. S. (1971). 'Population and Inflation'. *The Ecologist,* 1, No. 8, pp. 4-8.

STAMP, SIR DUDLEY (1969). *Nature Conservation in Britain.* London and Glasgow, Collins.

TAYLOR, G. R. (1970). *The Doomsday Book.* London, Thames and Hudson.

UNITED NATIONS (1969). *Demographic Year Book.* New York.

WATTS, M. (1968). *Britain's Population Problem.* Conservation Society: Collected Reprints, 1, (w) 1-16.

X

OTHER ASSAULTS ON THE LAND

In the preceding three chapters our topics were pesticides, the plunder of mineral resources and urbanisation. However, these are by no means the only ways in which man has damaged his most precious heritage the land. Other forms of trauma have been inflicted and this chapter discusses three of them. The first two—soil erosion and deforestation—are as old as history itself, while the third, the proliferation of litter, is a phenomenon highly characteristic of Spaceship Earth in the latter part of the twentieth century.

The Creeping Palsy of Soil Erosion

Soil is by far the most important constituent of the land. It takes the form of a relatively thin layer the depth of which varies from 25 to 100 inches. Its most productive part is the topsoil which throughout the whole of our planet is little more than 10 inches in thickness.

In Chapter VII we have already seen that soil in its natural state provides a classical example of a complex ecosystem. The composition of soil is constantly changing; it contains a myriad of chemical substances and living organisms, harmoniously existing together as a result of a series of delicate and highly sophisticated interrelationships. With loving care nature has built up her productive soil over thousands of years; on it plants feed and the whole basis of life ultimately depends. Man has made little attempt to cherish the soil and foremost among his deleterious activities has been erosion.

Erosion literally means a wearing away, and in the process there are two main components. The first is a loosening and detachment of particles of soil from its main body, the second the removal of these particles from their original site to another position. The term *geological erosion* is given to a natural process which bears no relationship to man's activities. Its principal aim is to bring the earth's surface to a uniform level. It is gentle and exceedingly gradual in pace occurring over millennia; frequently it is self-repairing in that the removal of the soil from the land's surface is matched by new soil formation. Although geological erosion proceeds very slowly it must not be thought that the process lacks an inherent dynamic. This it most certainly possesses, the point being well illustrated by the fact that the Appalachian Mountains in the USA are now believed by American geologists to be approximately one-half of their original height!

Soil erosion dictated by man is a very different affair. It is much less sophisticated, proceeds at a relatively rapid pace and destroys the soil much too rapidly for nature to renew it. The profit motive has been the major force behind man-made soil erosion, his desire being to gain the maximum monetary advantage in the minimum of time. As a result erosion has been associated with a number of other activities. Foremost amongst these have been deforestation, overcultivation and overgrazing pastures. In the last mentioned sphere sheep and goats, quaintly termed 'nature's lawnmowers', have been the main culprits, and in certain areas of the world, notably Spain and North Africa, these animals have succeeded in reducing large tracts of initially fertile land to nothing more than desert.

Many agents can produce soil erosion, but water and wind are of particular importance. Water erosion is often associated with gullying and it tends to be especially severe when steep slopes are ploughed. Rapidly running water carries with it relatively large quantities of soil; on the other hand, slowly moving water seldom causes a high degree of erosion. As will be seen later parts of the world subject to torrential rains, for example the humid tropics of Africa and Asia, frequently show water erosion. In such regions the soil cannot absorb the rain as rapidly .as it falls; as a consequence the soil becomes dislodged and runs off. Other areas prone to soil erosion are those with heavy rainfall but with a mild climate so that the soil is not frozen for lengthy periods of time throughout the year.

When soil is eroded by wind it is blown around in all directions and frequently in large quantities. Wind erosion is at its maximum in areas in which the soil is unprotected or is only sparsely covered with vegetation; it is especially damaging in regions with a lower than average rainfall. Soil blowing markedly reduces the fertility of the land and can cause severe injury to crops. In a short time the soil can pile up against buildings, fences and other structures; when really severe soil blowing can even obstruct the movement of traffic on highways.

Civilisations and dynasties have toppled as a result of soil erosion. A good example is the ancient Babylonian Empire which was at the height of its power some 2,000 years before the birth of Christ. The Empire is reputed to have harvested two crops per year and to have grazed sheep on the land between the crops. Overgrazing and overcultivation took their inexorable toll. Barely one-fifth of modern Iraq where the Babylonian Empire once proudly stood is now cultivable, and the landscape of that country is strewn with old irrigation wells filled with silt, the latter being the end product of soil erosion. Once Ur was a flourishing seaport; now it is 150 miles inland, with its historic buildings largely forgotten and buried in silt.

The Babylonians were by no means alone in succumbing to soil erosion. The Great Persian Empire of Darius I which reached its zenith in the sixth century BC crumbled from the same cause. Classical Greece is said to have had well forested hills, plentiful water supplies and good productive soils; the land was overcultivated, overgrazed and denuded of trees; soil erosion became extensive and the end result was both melancholy and predictable. Once Ancient Egypt was the granary of the Roman Empire; it had extensive irrigation schemes and could grow crops for seven months each year. Now much of the land in that area of the world is completely infertile and useless for agricultural purposes. Throughout China and India and in various parts of Africa and Latin America, ancient irrigation schemes stand derelict, abandoned and filled with silt. In the India of today it is stated that one-half of the country's farmland is inadequately protected from soil erosion. British rule in India may have enhanced our imperial glory and greatly increased our trade and commerce. However, comparable benefits were not conferred on the land mass of that country to which we bequeathed a legacy of widespread soil erosion and silt formation. Population pressures were undoubtedly a major factor in the India of the Raj. When the British assumed the reins of power numbers stood at approximately 60 million; however by the time of independence the figure had risen almost six-fold and stood at 350 million. The hungry mouths of the subcontinent's ever growing numbers had to be filled, and accordingly the British authorities permitted excessive ploughing, overgrazing and deforestation on a hitherto unprecedented scale.

In modern times the most florid example of soil erosion by wind is undoubtedly the American Dust Bowl. This affected predominantly the Middle West of the country, the brunt of the calamity falling on states such as Oklahoma, Kansas, Colorado and Texas. A number of factors contributed to the final tragedy. There had been overgrazing and overcultivation in the earlier part of the twentieth century, and there had been a succession of dry years. However, the ultimate indignity was the introduction in the 1920's of mechanised farming in the form of the tractor. The soil could stand no more; it protested and rebelled, became impoverished and was whirled away by the wind in the form of dust clouds.

Soil erosion in the American Middle West produced human problems of a most poignant character, and these are nowhere better described than in John Steinbeck's best selling novel, *The Grapes of Wrath*. This is an angry and indignant book yet with a curiously moving quality. It centres around the activities of the Joad family, dispossessed of their small area of Oklahoma farmland by the advent of modernisation and mechanisation. Their odyssey to the promised land of California in search of work is a major theme, and a graphic account is given of the miseries and frustrations which they encountered in the course of their journey and upon arrival. Early passages of the book vividly portray the condition to which the once rich farmland of Oklahoma had been reduced. Let Steinbeck himself speak, for his language is without peer, 'every moving thing lifted the dust into the air; a walking man lifted a thin layer as high as his waist, and a wagon lifted the dust as high as the fence tops, and an automobile boiled a cloud behind it. The dust was long in settling back again'.

Of the nations of the world which pride themselves upon their agricultural efficiency the USA has been a major sufferer from soil erosion. In that country water erosion is seen in its most acute form as a result of the activities of the Mississippi river which is said to carry over 700 million tons of soil each year into the Gulf of Mexico. Millar, Turk and Foth in their *Fundamentals of Soil Science* state that up till now erosion has mortally injured or has ruined for agricultural use some 282 million acres of land; moreover, a much larger area amounting to as much as 750 million acres has suffered significant damage in terms of its topsoil. But even this is not the whole story. Of US land currently being used for the production of crops the fertility of 50 million acres has been seriously impaired by erosion and a further 100 million acres, although still cultivable, are gradually becoming impoverished.

Apart from North America other continents are being slowly crippled as a result of soil erosion. Africa is a good example. In the humid tropical lands of that continent the torrential downpours of rain constitute a powerful erosive force especially in areas which are no longer covered by vegetation. Throughout Africa both overgrazing and overstocking by animals are prevalent. The animals eat the vegetation and trample the soil; the latter becomes exposed and erosion ultimately develops. African countries with major problems in relation to soil erosion are numerous and include Nigeria, Sierra Leone, the Republic of South Africa, Zambia, Malawi and Rhodesia. But it would be false to imagine that the malady is confined to the more southerly parts of the continent. It also exists in the north, and, for example, it has been stated that Algeria loses some 250 acres of land each day as a result of soil erosion.

Asia, like Africa, is afflicted with soil erosion. Regions subject to monsoons are especially affected, and the condition has already reached serious proportions in areas such as the Northern Deccan of India, Sumatra and Korea. The People's Republic of China is also a major sufferer and indeed parts of that country have had a history of deforestation and over-grazing extending over many centuries. In North Western China and in Turkestan high winds are frequent at certain times of the year; in these areas wind erosion has wrought much damage and has markedly impaired the general fertility of the land. The other major communist power, the Soviet Union, has its share of soil erosion. In European Russia it is widespread in the southern steppe lands of the Ukraine where it is frequently associated with gullying and crop damage. In the far east of the country, known to geographers as the Pacific Region, there has been extensive deforestation with resultant soil erosion. In 1954 the Soviet authorities commenced their attempts to develop the agricultural potentialities of the south west region of Siberia. This was the famed 'Virgin Lands' enterprise of the Krushchev era, undertaken in order to provide extra food for their rapidly growing population. Huge areas of wild steppe were subjected to the plough and by 1960 more than 100 million acres had been sown with grain. Formidable problems arose on every side. One of the major difficulties was the occurrence of soil erosion, and at one time it appeared probable that conditions reminiscent of the American Dust Bowl of the 1920's might make their appearance.

We have ranged the globe in quest of soil erosion and have found the condition to be widely disseminated. What of our own country Britain? Both wind and water erosion certainly occur in our islands. Wind erosion has been observed in the peat fens of Cambridgeshire, in the Isle of Ely and in the eastern half of Fifeshire. Water erosion has been noted in areas of high rainfall such as Glengarry in Inverness, while in the Spey valley in Scotland and elsewhere deforestation has been followed by a reduction in the surrounding level of the soil. Neither wind nor soil erosion presents an immediate problem in the UK, and at the time of writing draconian measures to deal with them are not required. However, this is not to say that the situation will remain static, for unless there is constant vigilance combined with good agricultural husbandry a rapid deterioration could well occur as a consequence of the widespread destruction of hedges, hedgerows, copses and thickets.

Although soil erosion may not yet cause our agriculturalists sleepless nights they have little justification for resting easily on their beds. For there are other problems in relation to the land which may prove much less tractable. Into this category comes the fate of our trees and hedges to which we must now turn our attention.

The Destruction of Trees and Hedges

Joyce Kilmer (1888-1918) wrote

> *I think that I shall never see*
> *A poem lovely as a tree.*
> *Poems are made by fools like me,*
> *But only God can make a tree.*

Poets and poetesses have traditionally waxed lyrical, over trees. However, the harsh truth must be faced that man has not heeded his bards and for century upon century he has been profligate in the expenditure of his woodlands. Trees have been felled indiscriminately for a whole host of reasons—for the building of dwelling houses, for fuel, for industrial purposes, for shipbuilding and for the construction of other forms of transport. During times of war the slaughter of trees has been especially severe and this tendency has persisted even into modern times. For example, in the Second World War the 'scorched earth' policy adopted by retreating armies caused wholesale destruction of forests in Europe and in other parts of the world. The damage done was great and will not be repaired for several generations. Nowhere in our planet has the pillage of timber resources been more profound than in our own country Britain, as a brief consideration of her history will clearly show.

When the Romans invaded Britain before the birth of Christ they found the country lushly forested; the woodland was mainly deciduous in type, the predominant tree being the oak. The Romans had little interest in trees; their desires were to build cities, to erect fortifications and to open up arteries of communication. Such aims necessitated the widespread levelling of forests, a process which was continued by later settlers. Thus Angles, Saxons and Danes all cleared large tracts of land for human habitation; they built their ships of timber and they used them in the wars which played such a major role during that period of history. As year succeeded year and century succeeded century the lumbering industry prospered and the plunder of our woodlands continued. The tempo of destruction attained such momentum that even in Tudor times during the reign of Queen Elizabeth I (1558-1603) official statements claimed that Britain's forests had been 'utterly destroyed' and that the damage inflicted was wellnigh irreparable. But still no action was taken and the conservationist voice remained muted. Such a state of affairs persisted until the late eighteenth century when, following the abortive Jacobite rebellion of 1745, a small number of Scottish landlords encouraged the planting of trees in some remote areas of the Highlands. About the same time in England the conscience of the land-owning classes was stirred, and it became fashionable to plant imported species of trees in parklands and in clumps.

The Industrial Revolution of the late eighteenth and nineteenth centuries took its inevitable toll of woodland. Lumbering was an integral part of the drive towards industrial supremacy, and by the beginning of the twentieth century it was plain for all to see that Britain was a country exceedingly poor in natural resources of timber. This fact was highlighted in the First World War during which the necessity to import large quantities of wood pulp threw a major strain on our shipping resources, already much depleted by the German submarine campaign. In 1919, following the cessation of hostilities, Lloyd George's coalition government finally took action. The Forestry Commission was established. Its major aim was clear—man's mistakes of the past were to be redeemed by a vigorous programme of afforestation.

Like most human activities, afforestation poses manifold problems. Chief amongst these is the fact that the process is essentially long term; accordingly, the rewards are reaped not by those currently inhabiting the planet but by future generations. Even with trees which are relatively fast growing such as poplars and certain types of conifers, thirty years may have to elapse between sowing the seed and harvesting the crop. In the case of the more slowly growing conifers, mature timber may not be available for from 60 to 80 years, while oaks are unlikely to attain their full maturity for a century or more.

Britain has always had the tradition of accepting trees from foreign sources. Thus it is reported that we received the sweet chestnut from the shores of the Mediterranean in Roman times and the sycamore from Central Europe in the fifteenth century. The majority of the planting undertaken by the Forestry Commission has been of conifers from overseas. These have included spruces from North America and Norway, larches from Japan and various continental varieties of the Scottish pine. How successful have the Commission's activities been? Some relevant statistics are quoted by Stamp in his *Nature Conservancy in Britain*. Thus in 1913/14 the area of Great Britain under forest and woodland amounted only to 2,736,188 acres; by 1962 this figure has risen to 4,205,000 acres representing an increase of almost 100 per cent. Christian in his *Tomorrow's Countryside* states that the woodlands under the control of the Forestry Commission are expanding by almost 45,000 acres per year and that by the early 1970's forests should cover more than 4,500,000 acres of our land surface.

Such figures may seem impressive but they certainly give no cause for complacency. Only 8 per cent of our total land space is being devoted to trees; we are now and have been for some time one of the most sparsely wooded nations of Europe. We must import some 90 per cent of our timber, and it has been estimated that each day £1,250,000 worth of wood and timber products enter British ports. Obviously our all-too-fragile balance of payments situation cannot benefit from this state of affairs, and it is therefore not surprising that an increase in the tempo of afforestation is planned for the remainder of this century and beyond.

Many other European countries apart from Britain have extensive afforestation schemes. Those in Austria and Switzerland date back for over 100 years and have aided considerably in the prevention of soil erosion in the Alps. The USA is taking an increasing interest in afforestation and in recent years millions of acres in that country have been planted with trees. One especially extensive area stretches for over 100 miles through Nebraska and Kansas into Northern Texas. The lesson of the earlier part of the century has apparently been learned by the American authorities; the conditions characteristic of the Dust Bowl of the 1920's are not to be allowed to return, and the true value of trees in preventing soil erosion is finally being appreciated. The Democratic Administration of Lyndon Johnson could not solve the riddle of the Vietnam war. However, it was notable for its prosecution of conservationist policies, and in 1966 the President, no doubt recalling the tragic errors of the past, averred 'we cannot restore—once it is lost—the majesty of a forest whose trees soared upwards 2,000 years ago'.

Are campaigns for afforestation being successful on an international level? It must never be forgotten that the demands of modern industry for timber are prodigious. The manufacture of paper alone consumes huge areas of woodland, and a telling fact in this connection is that each Sunday issue of the *New York Times*—a compilation containing more words than the whole of the Bible—accounts for an amount of timber equivalent to that produced by 150 acres of land! An appraisal of the international scene with respect to timber resources has been given by Arvill in his *Man and Environment.* He quotes a US report of the late 1950's, which pointed out that, although afforestation was on the increase in that country, the quality of trees being planted was diminishing. Moreover, the demands of industry for timber were rising steeply, and were likely to continue to do so for the foreseeable future. He also cites a UN publication of 1964 which discussed the European scene. One of the conclusions reached in the document was that by the year 2,000 AD a yawning chasm would exist between Europe's consumption of timber and the quantities which could be produced from its own woods and forests.

The situation with respect to timber is therefore precisely analogous to that obtaining with certain metals and with fuels such as oil and gas, serious shortages of which are likely to become apparent in the not too distant future (see Chapter VIII). The twin factors of rising economic growth rates and expanding population have depleted the world's resources of timber to such an extent that however diligently schemes of afforestation are prosecuted, it appears unlikely that the wolfish appetite of industry for this commodity will be satisfied. But, as optimists are wont to cry, will not the limitless tropical forests of Latin America, Africa and South East Asia meet all our expectations and solve all our problems? A number of authorities do not believe that such a solution is possible because of factors such as the inaccessibility of the timber, its distance from foreign markets and its unsuitability for many of the purposes for which it would be required. However in spite of these disadvantages, there seems little doubt that as the world situation with respect to timber supplies progressively worsens these forests will be sacrificed. Furthermore, when the decision is taken to destroy them in order to assuage the thirst of the industrial markets of the West, ecological factors will count for little, and the conservationist viewpoint stressing the permanent damage likely to be inflicted on these areas of the planet by such a course of action, will carry little weight.

Too late it has been recognised that the tree is not the foe of man; rather is it his trusty friend and ally. Trees conserve the soil; they protect it from the ravages of weather, prevent its erosion and may even increase its fertility. When forests are cleared to satisfy man's lust for power and profit climatic aberrations especially floods and avalanches are more likely to occur. As noted in Chapter VII forests contain innumerable species of flora and fauna. When trees are felled the delicate ecological balance so important for the preservation of our environment is destroyed with repercussions undreamt of by those who so cheerfully wield the axe. Trees are also vital to the spiritual aspects of human life*. Throughout the world great numbers of people enjoy walking in woods and forests, there to enjoy tranquillity and to observe wildlife in its natural state. Will this be yet another pleasure which we must forfeit in order to feed our planet's industrial colossus?

Let the last word go to the poet William Wordsworth

> *Books! 'tis a dull and endless strife:*
> *Come, hear the woodland linnet,*
> *How sweet his music! on my life,*
> *There's more of wisdom in it.*

Children inhabiting the planet today may well come to look on verses such as these with acute nostalgia.

* A few architects, some of a bygone age, have recognized this poet. For example, the Edinburgh architect, William Stark, in his paper of 1814, entitled *Report . . . on the Plans for laying out the Grounds for Buildings between Edinburgh and Leith* stated 'trees enrich and give interest to the whole surrounding scene'.

As with trees so has it been with hedges and hedgerows. At least in England where our story is mainly set.

The Open Field system of agriculture which in many ways resembled the Canadian prairies of today, was characteristic of the England of the Middle Ages and before. Gradually, however, and despite the heavy fines levelled on landowners by reigning monarchs especially in the fifteenth and sixteenth centuries, the process of enclosure of fields by hedges went ahead. Eventually the attitude of officialdom became more tolerant. Thus during the interregnum of Oliver Cromwell (1649-1660) few restrictions were placed on enclosures, while following the Restoration and throughout the reign of Charles II (1660-1685) many writers emphasised the benefits of such a system and urged its increasing adoption.

But on the whole progress remained slow. Then suddenly during the eighteenth century there was a burst of activity, and the 'high noon' of enclosures was reached during the reigns of the early Hanoverian monarchs and in the era of that great statesman Pitt the Elder. At the start of the century there was no evidence that such a trend would take place. For example, between 1710 and 1720 only 8 Enclosure Acts were passed through Parliament. However, the tempo of enclosures rapidly accelerated and in the decade 1790-1800 the number of Acts topped the 500 mark. Historians recount that the golden era for enclosures were the 30 years between 1750 and 1780. During that period the whole face of rural England was profoundly altered, and there came into being the countryside as we know it today, a countryside of small farms, patterned with fields and crisscrossed by hedges.

The process of enclosure continued during the nineteenth century. However, by now the dynamiç had lessened, and one of the main reasons for the construction of hedges was to subdivide large fields. Frequently the subdivision was associated with a change from grazing to arable farming, the latter receiving much impetus as a result of the technological discoveries associated with the Industrial Revolution. Taken as a whole the enclosures of the eighteenth and nineteenth centuries represented a major undertaking, and Christian in his *Tomorrow's Countryside* states that during this period more than 180,000 miles of hedges were planted in England alone. In 1962 it was estimated that there were 616,000 miles of hedge in Great Britain, occupying some 448,000 acres. By 1966 the mileage figure had fallen to just over half a million.

In 1967 Moore, Hooper and Davies of the Nature Conservancy wrote an admirable article for the *Journal of Applied Ecology*; in it they defined a hedge as a living fence. In Britain hawthorn hedges take pride of place, although mixed types containing hawthorn, beech and Scots pine are also quite common. Hedges subserve many functions, but in particular, they are rich repositories of flora and fauna. Thus according to Hooper some 250 species of plants occur with such regularity in hedges that they can be classified as hedgerow plants. Hedgerows are a most important habitat for insect species, and although reliable figures for the lodgement of such species are difficult to obtain, Moore suggests that in Britain the number of adult butterflies residing in hedgerows may exceed 250 million.

Song birds such as thrushes, chaffinches and blackbirds greatly favour hedges for their nesting as do game birds especially the partridge. It has been estimated that in Britain hedges support, on average, one pair of birds per 100 yards and that as many as 10 million birds may breed in hedges and hedgerows. Studies from the USA have indicated the important relationships which exist between birds and hedgerows, and in an investigation conducted in the state of Wisconsin between 1930 and 1950 and involving over 4,000 acres of land, loss of hedgerow cover was shown to be directly related to the reduction in the population of the bobwhite quail. Thus when there was one mile of hedgerow cover for every 450 acres of land the numbers of this species averaged 23 per mile; when the ratio fell to one mile of hedgerow for every 650 acres of land the population of quails fell to zero.

Another important function traditionally accredited to hedgerows is the shelter from the elements which they provide for crops and more especially for livestock. Although in recent years their key role in this respect has not been stressed as much as in the past, many experts still regard the provision of shelter as one of their major uses. In certain regions of Northern Europe hedges have been shown to reduce the evaporation of moisture from the soil, to raise its fertility and to increase crop yields; they may also be useful in preventing soil erosion, a fact mentioned earlier in this chapter. Hedges furnish the habitat for many predator species of animal, the function of which is to control insect pests, and which have recently tended to be killed off in unduly large numbers due to the overenthusiastic application of DDT and other organochlorine insecticides (see Chapter VII).

Hedges and hedgerows provide plentiful and exceedingly valuable resources of timber, and this point was emphasised in a series of reports published by the British Forestry Commission in the early 1950's. At that time it was estimated that there were some 73 million trees in parks and hedgerows, these amounting to approximately one third of Britain's hardwood timber reserves. Indeed hedges were found to contain no less than one fifth of the nation's stocks of trees such as the oak, ash, elm, beech and sycamore. The ratio of saplings to mature trees was also investigated by the Forestry Commission, and it was noted that some 30 per cent of the total consisted of the former group. Since then it is believed that the relative proportion of saplings to mature trees has decreased significantly.

There is general agreement that there are fewer hedges in Britain now than there were in former times. It is also recognised that the loss of hedges is a nationwide phenomenon not being confined to any particular region of the country. However, at this point the consensus of opinion ends, because there is much divergence of view as to the precise rate of hedge removal. Here estimates are very variable indeed ranging from a lower level of 1,000 miles per year to an upper limit of 14,000 miles per year. However, irrespective of the rapidity of the process, many authorities express unease about the present situation. One points out that if the true rate of hedge removal in Britain is approximately 7,000 miles per annum the country will be completely denuded of hedges by the middle of the twenty-first century. Another states that in the county of Huntingdonshire, where careful records have been kept over long periods of time, the number of hedges present in 1965 was similar to that found in 1364! The whole subject of hedge removal in Britain was discussed in detail in 1968 at a meeting held under the auspices of the Nature Conservancy. A number of experts commented upon the variability of existing estimates. A lively discussion ensued and eventually it was agreed that the most realistic figure for hedge removal, at least between the years 1949 and 1962, was in the neighbourhood of 4,500 miles per annum.

Why are hedges disappearing from our countryside at such an alarming rate? Undoubtedly creeping urbanization has played a role; this has been especially so in the south east region of England where the sprawl of cities has occurred mainly at the expense of hedged fields. However, the major factor has unquestionably been the increasing mechanisation of agriculture this being associated with the change from grassland to arable farming. Indeed the tractor may prove to be as formidable a foe to the English hedge of the 1970's as it was to the small farmer of the American Middle West in the 1920's. Economic factors are paramount in modern agricultural practice. Cost-effectiveness is the telling phrase, and undoubtedly crops are very profitable indeed as compared with pasture. A hedge is expensive in terms of upkeep—one estimate puts the cost of one mile of hedge at £40 per annum—and therefore it must disappear. If any form of enclosure is required a wire fence rather than a hedge is the barrier of choice.

It is of interest that demolition of hedges and hedgerows is by no means universal. Indeed in other parts of the world, notably in the USA, the Netherlands and Federal Germany, millions of acres have been planted with hedges in recent years. In the Netherlands this activity has been especially marked in farms created in land reclaimed from the sea, and it is obvious that the agricultural authorities in that country view hedges with considerable approbation. In Britain the accelerating tempo of destruction of hedges and hedgerows can only be deplored. It will alter irrevocably the unique character of the English countryside, detract from amenity, cause impoverishment of wildlife and further reduce our country's already meagre timber resources. Yet another of life's aesthetic enjoyments will vanish, for history will not repeat itself and there will be no further crop of enclosures. For the pleasures of our woodlands we quoted Wordsworth. In the case of hedges let us turn to Keats who passionately loved the English countryside and who wrote in his poem *On the Grasshopper and Cricket*

> *The poetry of earth is never dead:*
> *When all the birds are faint with the hot sun,*
> *And hide in cooling trees, a voice will run*
> *From hedge to hedge about the new mown mead.*

It is to be much regretted that future generations of Englishmen will not have the opportunity of savouring such delights.

A Plague of Litter

A recent article by Roberta Hornig and James Welsh of the staff of the *Washington Star* was headed *Garbage piles up, and up, and up.* And this is certainly no exaggeration for we, earth's occupants, are fouling the once fair face of our planet at a prodigious rate. Such littering goes under the designation of 'solid wastes', and along with air and water pollution it constitutes the third member of the unholy trinity of major types of environmental contamination.

The quintessence of pollution by solid wastes is seen in the capitalist societies of the Western world with their pursuance of high economic growth rates and with their economic structure geared to ever increasing production and consumption. However, not only do such countries manufacture and consume goods at breathtaking speed. They also discard them with equal alacrity, thus meriting the journalistic description that their economies are of the 'throw away' type. It will be no surprise to learn that the USA takes pride of place with respect to litter pollution, for implicit in the so-called American dream is the promise of high affluence, unlimited prosperity and ever increasing living standards. That the dream is no longer operative and that it is being replaced by a nightmare of solid waste pollution is gradually being recognised by an increasing proportion of its citizenry.

The US statistics make formidable reading. Each year the country discards 3,600 million tons of solid waste, one ton for every inhabitant on earth in the early 1970's. Each day each US citizen generates 5.3 lbs of garbage; but in 10 years time as production and consumption increase exponentially this figure will have almost doubled, thus far outstripping the country's present rate of population growth. In 1969 Americans threw away 50,000 million cans and 30,000 million bottles and jars. Four million tons of plastics, the pride of modern industrial practice, were got rid of, much of this material being virtually indestructible by methods currently available. Eight million television sets were discarded together with seven million cars and trucks. Ten million tons of iron and steel were scrapped quite apart from the quantities of these materials used in the automobile industry, and huge amounts of slag, ash and waste rock were unceremoniously dumped wherever a place could be found to accommodate them.

As was noted in the preceding chapter the current plight of US cities is especially acute, and it has been estimated that the total amount of urban waste collected annually is in excess of 100 million tons. In Los Angeles 12 million cubic yards of refuse are dumped each year into tips or what are euphemistically known as landfills. Litter disposal in New York City has become an issue charged with strong emotive overtones. All public services in that complex and grossly overcrowded megalopolis are exceedingly vulnerable, none more so than that involving refuse collection. New Yorkers know to their cost the chaos which follows when a strike or a 'work-to-rule' on the part of the city's garbage collectors takes place. At such times they can merely writhe in their impotence as litter piles high in the streets and as the dangers of serious health hazards become daily more acute.

Only the most optimistic would take the view that the malady of solid waste pollution in the USA can ever be adequately treated. A solution to the problem would involve the expenditure of vast amounts of public money, and there is at present no evidence to indicate that any administration, whether it be Republican or Democratic in composition, would be prepared to authorise funding of this magnitude. Accordingly, short term expediency must be the order of the day. Admittedly there is some recycling and re-use of garbage especially with regard to waste paper. Overall, however, such forms of salvage are still operative on a relatively small scale. At present approximately 10 per cent of the country's refuse is incinerated, but this mode of disposal is now losing favour because of the very real dangers of air pollution (see Chapters I and II). The great majority of the garbage continues to be deposited in city dumps; here it poses hazards largely because it can contaminate the land and pollute water supplies. Some municipalities in the USA favour the use of so-called 'sanitary landfills' in which the garbage is buried under a layer of earth; at present some 5 per cent of solid wastes are disposed of in this way. Landfills have obvious disadvantages. They are capable of polluting the precious groundwater referred to in Chapter IV, and, moreover, they are greedy for territorial aggrandisement constantly engulfing areas of land which could be utilised to much better purpose.

The United Kingdom does not lag far behind the USA in the sphere of solid waste pollution. Britons who had been unaware of this fact were rudely awakened to it by the events which ensued when our municipal workers struck for more pay in late 1970. During what came to be known as the 'dirty jobs strike' litter was piled high in the streets of our main cities, our rivers became grossly polluted, fish disappeared from the Thames, and we were extremely fortunate that epidemics of diseases such as dysentery, typhoid fever and infective hepatitis did not make their appearance.

All of us in the UK—whether it be man, woman or child—contributes 5 lbs of garbage each day; this amounts to 35 lbs per week or 0.81 tons per year. With our total population in excess of 55 million the overall production of solid wastes in our country reaches the quite remarkable total of 45 million tons. Some examples illustrate the magnitude of the problem. Thus each year we throw away 350,000 tons of packages made of plastics and other synthetic polymers; these constitute a special hazard because, as mentioned earlier, they are notoriously resistant to destruction. In the New Forest near London some 800 tons of litter must be removed each year. At Bank Holiday weekends it takes approximately a million man hours to clear up the 10,000 tons of litter which accumulate, while after the

World Cup Final in Wembley in 1966 it took 170 men and eight lorries one full day to deal with the mess! A. P. de Boer, Chairman of the Keep Britain Tidy Group, informs us that during the summer season local authorities in the seaside resort of Southend must clear 10 tons of litter each weekend from the beaches, while in another favourite holiday centre, Blackpool, the cost of street clearing approximates to £90,000 per annum.

Throughout our country beauty spots and recreational areas are under constant siege from the spread of refuse. This is especially so during the summer months when on each weekend seething masses of humanity debouch from our major cities into the countryside. Ownership of motor cars is relatively high in the UK, and this combined with the so-called 'leisure boom' produces effects on the environment which are highly inimical. It is a matter of regret that many of our tourists and sightseers lack self-discipline and are inconsiderate of others; moreover, few of them have ever been taught to care for much less to cherish the countryside as a precious and non-renewable heritage. As a consequence great quantities of litter accumulate everywhere, amenity is destroyed, pollution becomes rife and wildlife is placed in peril.

And what will be the future of our islands? We are forced to the melancholy but inevitable conclusion that our green and pleasant land of England is destined to become much less green and considerably less pleasant. To this deterioration in our quality of life many factors will have contributed, but amongst them pollution by pesticides, urban sprawl, deforestation, removal of hedgerows and the proliferation of litter will all have played their distinctive and highly individualistic roles.

References

ALLABY, MICHAEL (1971). 'Disappearing Hedgerows'. In *Can Britain Survive?* Edited by GOLDSMITH, E. London, Tom Stacey, pp. 93-97.

ARVILL, ROBERT (1969). *Man and Environment*. London, Penguin Books.

BARBER, DEREK, editor (1970). *Farming and Wildlife*. Wisbech and London, Balding and Mansell.

EHRLICH, PAUL R. and EHRLICH, ANNE (1970). *Population, Resources, Environment*. San Francisco, W. H. Freeman and Co.

CHRISTIAN, GARTH (1966). *Tomorrow's Countryside*. London, John Murray.

HOOPER, MAX (1970). 'Hedges and History'. *New Scientist*, 31st December, pp. 598-600.

HOOPER, M. D. and HOLDGATE, M. W. (1968). *Hedges and Hedgerow Trees*. Monks Wood Symposium No. 4, Part 1, The Nature Conservancy.

HORNIG, ROBERTA and WELSH, JAMES (1970). 'Garbage piles up, and up, and up'. *Washington Star*, 11th January to 18th January.

HOWE, G. MELVYN (1968). *The Soviet Union*. London, Macdonald and Evans.

JARRETT, H. R. (1970). *Africa*. London, Macdonald and Evans.

LORAINE, J. A. (1970). *Sex and the Population Crisis*. London, Heinemann Medical Books.

MILLAR, C. E., TURK, L. M. and FOTH, H. D. (1965). *Fundamentals of Soil Science*. New York, John Wiley and Sons, Ch. 16.

MOORE, N. W., HOOPER, M. D. and DAVIS, B. N. K. (1967). 'Hedges: Introduction and Reconnaissance Studies'. *J. App. Ecology*, **4**, pp. 201-220.

ROBINSON, H. (1966). *Monsoon Asia*. London, Macdonald and Evans.

STAMP, SIR DUDLEY (1969). *Nature Conservation in Britain*. London and Glasgow, Collins.

STEINBECK, JOHN (1939). *The Grapes of Wrath*. London, William Heinemann Ltd.

XI

CACOPHONY UNLIMITED

They fell asleep, but not for long . . .
The axle creaking under the wagons wakes the man who has his
house beside the highway.

Callimachus, *fragment* 260. 3rd century BC

'*What iron nerves or deadened ears you must have, if your mind*
can endure so many noises, so various and discordant.'

Seneca, *Epistulae Morales,* 56.3. 1st century AD

Pollution by noise is very much a feature of recent times particularly of the last two decades. For most of us noise pollution is inextricably linked with the ever-increasing use which modern society makes of transport.

Noise has been defined as 'unwanted sound' and as 'sound undesired by the receipient'. Both definitions betray the intrinsic difficulty associated with noise pollution, namely that it can only be a highly subjective form of nuisance. Just as beauty is in the eye of the beholder, so noise is in the ear of the listener and as a result it means very different things to different people. For example, the roar of the highly tuned sports car or motor cycle can be the acme of perfection to the young enthusiast but can drive to distraction those of us who live adjacent to a motorway; the high-pitched scream of a jet airliner may excite the imagination of the youthful adventurer dreaming of far away places, but it can also produce insomnia and psychoneurotic manifestations in people unfortunate enough to reside close to a modern airport. Indeed it is probable that on our planet there are just as many people who like noise as there are who detest it. However, leaving aside such subjective questions, the inescapable fact emerges that living conditions are becoming progressively noisier, and that with the passage of time it is becoming a matter of increasing difficulty to discover a place where one can be quiet and at peace. This chapter will attempt to review the noise problem, to assess as far as possible the real or potential harm which it poses to human health and amenity, and to discuss methods which can be used to control it.

Noise must be measured quantitatively; this is especially difficult because it possesses more than one attribute. Thus as well as simple loudness, there are marked variations in pitch. The pitch may have a high frequency as, for example, a whistle or the scream of a jet engine; on the other hand the frequency may be low as with a ship's siren or a diesel engine. Furthermore, some noises may be much more irritating than others and because of this property they are perceived more readily. Noise occurs as a result of the liberation of energy, and the greater the amount of energy made available the louder is the noise. Noise is generally measured in 'decibels', the number of these providing a measure of sound intensity. Some examples of the intensity of various noises are shown in the following table:

Sound source	Noise levels in decibels	Possible effects on humans
Normal threshold of human ear	1	
Normal breathing	10	
Leaves rustling in wind	20	
Whisper/watch tick	30	
Quiet office	40	
Quiet restaurant	50	May interfere with sleep
Conversation	60	
Motor car	70	
Food mixer	80	Ear damage can occur
Diesel lorries	90	
Niagara Falls (at the base)	90	
Jet aircraft overhead	100	
Circular saw	110	
Jet aircraft taking off	120	Threshold of pain
Machine gun at close range	120	
Riveting steel plates	130	

The decibel scale is now in universal use. However, it must not be forgotten that the scale is logarithmic rather than linear in character. Accordingly, a 10-fold increase in the sound strength adds 10 units to the decibel scale, a 100-fold increase 20, a 1,000-fold increase 30 and so on. Thus a diesel lorry creates approximately 10,000 times more noise than is found in a quiet restaurant, and a jet aircraft during take off makes roughly a thousand times more noise than a lorry. Distance from a noise source must always be taken into account, and it is now generally accepted that halving or doubling the distance multiplies or divides the sound intensity by a factor of four.

Like other organs in the body the human ear is not without its deficiencies, and one of these is that it cannot perceive sound in direct relationship to the energy of the noise created. For example, it is now known that the addition of 10 decibels to the noise load usually produces only a doubling of the noise which the ear can perceive. Thus a jet aircraft, flying overhead and creating 10 times more sound than a lorry, sounds only twice as noisy to the human ear.

Sources of Noise

Transport is the main culprit whether it be the conveyance of people in motor cars, buses and aeroplanes, or the haulage of goods and commodities in lorries. Railways have steadily diminished in stature as noise polluters, the main reasons being firstly that the overall volume of rail traffic has tended to decrease, and secondly that the newer diesel and electric locomotives are quieter than the steam engines of bygone days. Furthermore, it has been argued that many of the population have grown up since childhood with noisy trains and that because of its familiarity such a sound produces little or no distress.

Attempts to control noise in Britain are not new. Indeed as far back as 1934 the Ministry of Transport set up a committee to investigate the control of noise, and when the Second World War broke out legislation in this field was being prepared. Few then could have foreseen the huge increase in automobile ownership and the proliferation of lorries which the post war years would bring. The situation was still tolerable in the 1940's; it worsened greatly during the 1950's and 1960's, and in 1963 the Buchanan report disclosed that traffic noise had assumed the stature of a major nuisance which was destroying the amenity of dwellings and was proving prejudicial to the enjoyment of life in cities. In 1968 the Ministry of Transport reported that noise caused by traffic in city streets was increasing at the rate of one decibel every year, and in a more recent governmental survey traffic noise was claimed to affect one-third of people in their homes and was branded as by far the most irritating facet of modern existence.

A frustrating feature of the current scene is that the technical expertise to control traffic noise exists; what is lacking is the proper legislative machinery to enforce it. Every year the situation deteriorates, and one of the major reasons for this is the current trend towards the construction of bigger and heavier lorries. These so-called 'juggernauts' of the road are capable of registering 100 decibels in built up areas; furthermore, because of their immense power they can weaken the structure of buildings situated close to the highway. Fortunately juggernauts have so far been banned in Britain; however, they are in general use throughout the countries of the Common Market and if, as now seems inevitable, Britain joins this organisation she will be compelled to authorise them. Indeed even now there is evidence that foreign operators working in association with our long-distance haulage firms are putting pressure on the Government to increase the maximum permissible weight of lorries and so to allow the 'juggernauts' to roam without impediment on British roads. Although so far the British Government has shown good sense in refusing hospitality to the juggernauts, a similar sense of urgency has not prevailed with respect to large diesel lorries. These are inveterate noise makers; the sound produced by one of them is equivalent to that of 10 cars on a motorway, and even a slight increase in the gradient of a road will cause the noise level of lorries to rise sharply.

Manufacturers of motor cars show little restraint in the field of noise pollution; indeed the louder the noise produced, particularly by sports cars, the better are likely to be the sales. Although the Motor Industry Research Association in Britain states that research on noise abatement is constantly being prosecuted, there is little doubt that such work has a low priority, coming a poor third after safety precautions and air pollution. Furthermore, much of the research which is performed is devoted to noise generated within the vehicle and therefore has no relevance to the external noise affecting the pedestrian or the householder living near to an urban motorway.

*   *   *

Fewer of us are directly influenced by aircraft noise than by noise from motorways. But for those of us who are, the predicament is infinitely worse because the level of the sound is so much greater and there is little or no respite through the night.

London Airport at Heathrow is the busiest international airport in the world in terms of numbers of international passengers handled; furthermore, like a huge octopus, it is continuously extending its tentacles into the surrounding countryside. In 1960 there were some 130,000 'aircraft movements' at Heathrow, 15 per cent of them by jet airliners; by 1970 the number had risen to over 270,000; jets were now accounting for two-thirds of them and in that year almost 16 million passengers were passed through the airport. From the economic point of view Heathrow is a national asset handling £1,000 million worth of cargo each year and supporting directly or indirectly nearly a quarter of a million people. Indeed the Wilson Report on noise clearly recognised this fact when it stated that a substantial reduction of the air services at Heathrow would have grave effects on the British economy.

The noise in the vicinity of Heathrow is appalling, and because of this there have been repeated attempts by bodies such as the British Association for the Control of Aircraft Noise to reduce the din particularly at night. Appeals of this type are generally countered in highly emotive terms by the airlines themselves and by the British Airport Authority. Both these organisations put forward the traditional viewpoint that stricter control would merely drive foreign airliners from Heathrow to other airports with less stringent legislation, and they cite specifically the benefits which would accrue to Orly Airport in Paris which handles some 9 million passengers per year and is the second busiest airport in Europe after Heathrow. John Barr in his *Assaults on our Senses* has challenged this judgment. In his view the ticket-holding passenger rather than the airline decides the place of destination. Accordingly, if more people wish to fly to London than to Paris foreign airliners will fly them there irrespective of restrictions. If they failed to do so competitors would step in and a lucrative market would be lost.

Noise limits exist at Heathrow, Gatwick and many other British airports; the limit set is 110 decibels for take off by day and 102 decibels for night flying. These figures may not appear unreasonable until one recollects that the upper limit is roughly the same as that produced by heavy gunfire! The minimum altitude of flight over central London has now been raised from 2,000 to 3,000 feet; however, even at this level the noise emission can reach 95 decibels.

The siting of Heathrow has proved to be disastrous because of the high population density in the immediate vicinity of the airport. Currently it is estimated that the noise from aeroplanes overhead at intervals of only 100 seconds severely disturbs 65,000 people in the immediate vicinity; furthermore, millions of other individuals living or working beneath the flight paths and 'stacking areas' where incoming aircraft queue to await their turn to land, are also inconvenienced.

The post-war boom in air traffic has totally outstripped the predictions of even the most optimistic planners. This together with the delay in the siting of the Third London Airport has tended to make Heathrow a unique example of the malevolent effects of modern technology on human affairs. Nevertheless in spite of the example afforded by Heathrow the tendency in Britain and elsewhere has been to site airports within easy reach of urban agglomerations; it is therefore not surprising that virtually all airports in the UK present a noise problem of varying intensity. Thus difficulties are now occurring at Gatwick which handles two million passengers per year, at

Glasgow and Manchester each of which handles more than one-and-a-half million, and at Belfast and Jersey where the annual figure exceeds one million.

What compensation is paid to those unfortunate people condemned to live in the vicinity of Heathrow? In recent years the Government has instituted a scheme whereby the British Airport Authority is required to pay 50 per cent of the cost of sound proofing buildings within a central area around the airport. Unfortunately the amounts provided are totally inadequate, the maximum allowed to each householder being of the order of £100. Obviously such a meagre sum has made little difference, and the plight of those living near Heathrow remains pitiful in the extreme.

Into this imbroglio there may soon be injected supersonic aircraft such as the Anglo-French Concorde.* These machines will certainly be a good deal noisier than the present day subsonic aircraft such as the VC10 and Boeings 707, 727 and 747, which are creating such havoc for those living close to airports. But in addition to being noisy the Concorde and its ilk will almost certainly produce a sonic boom along the whole length of their flight-path. In the presence of such cacophony our country could eventually come to resemble a veritable inferno of noise from which escape is almost impossible.

*   *   *

Noise is not the sole prerogative of transport; it presents problems in industry and has done so since the early days of the Industrial Revolution. Barr states that 'someone early on took hold of the notion that noise is proof of progress—the deplorable correlation between noise making and wealth making persists today'. Noise is energy, and the more energy utilised the more noise is generated. Modern industry with its emphasis on high production and high consumption is noisier than ever before. So much so that noise levels in many factories

* On December 10th, 1971 the Minister for Trade and Industry, Mr John Davies, flew in Concorde and described it as a 'fabulous aircraft'. Full governmental backing for the project can now be expected.

frequently exceed the 80-85 decibel range at which physical damage to the human ear can result.

In Britain recent studies have shown that 25 per cent of loom workers in cotton mills are on the verge of requiring hearing aids. Riveters working where noise levels were in the region of 115-128 decibels had a loss of hearing amounting to 15.7 per cent after one year's work and 38.6 per cent after five years. All these men were under the age of 40; yet their hearing was comparable to that normally found in much older men. At the University of Southampton research workers have shown that as many as 100,000 workers in Britain would be entitled to compensation for occupational hearing loss were this disability included within the framework of industrial benefit.

A recent noise survey conducted in the USA showed that between 5 and 14 million industrial workers suffer some damage to their hearing as a result of their occupations. This is a matter of no surprise in view of the fact that some 8 million American workers are believed to be exposed to noise levels in excess of 95 decibels for periods of time greater than 5 hours each day. Office noise is a potent cause of inefficiency in the USA, and it has been estimated that industry and commerce lose $4 million per day on account of it.

Apart from transport and industry many other types of noise nuisance exist. Good examples are the din emanating from construction and demolition sites, the ubiquitous transistor radio, the circular saw, and the powered lawnmower in the private garden. There are some who argue that, with a few notable exceptions, noise in various forms is something with which we have always lived and that we have no alternative but to continue to do so. Certainly in some situations noise can prove stimulating and exhilarating. Thus sound intensities of 110 decibels have been recorded in roars from football crowds, and the noise of pop music inside the confined spaces of modern discothèques is said to be of the order of 120 decibels. The contention put forward with respect to the inevitability of noise could well be valid if at the same time it could be demonstrated that noise levels were not increasing. However, this is certainly not the case and indeed the evidence is very much to the contrary. For example, a survey carried out in

Britain in 1948 showed that only 23 per cent of people were disturbed at home by noises outside, while 50 per cent 'did not notice noise'. In 1961 a survey of a similar type was conducted and the results were totally different. It was demonstrated that 50 per cent of people were disturbed by noise, only 9 per cent claiming to be unaware of it. A survey conducted in 1972 would almost certainly underline even further this dramatic shift in public opinion. Furthermore, it would probably indicate that complaints about noise straddle the whole spectrum of society and are not confined, as at one time, to a small minority of the upper and middle classes.

The Effects of Noise on Health

The World Health Organisation defines 'health' as 'a state of complete physical, mental and social well-being and not merely an absence of disease and infirmity'. Certainly there is no doubt that present-day noise is a menace to health both in relation to well-being and because of its propensity to cause infirmity.

Excessive noise undoubtedly produces deafness, and reference to 'gunfire deafness' can be found as long ago as 1591. In 1782, 80 broadsides from the battleship HMS Formidable are said to have rendered Admiral Rodney almost entirely deaf for a period of 14 days. Even in the pre-industrial era various occupations are listed as giving rise to deafness, one of these being the hammering of copper by boilermakers and black-smiths. In 1830 the *Lancet* carried an article on deafness amongst blacksmiths, and at about that time the term 'boiler-makers ear' was added to the medical literature.

Noise of fairly low intensity can damage ears. Unfortunately, the individual is unaware of the early effects, and it is possible for irreversible damage to have been caused before the listener can detect any impairment of hearing in conversation with his fellow men. Dr D. E. Broadbent of the Medical Research Council Applied Psychology Unit in Cambridge has found that a major effect of excessive noise is to render the hearing mechanism less sensitive. Initially the disability is temporary; however, with repeated exposure, injurious effects build up with the result that permanent deafness can be produced without the victim realising what is happening. Susceptibility to noise varies considerably with the individual concerned; however, most sufferers do not complain of deafness until they have a permanent hearing loss of more than 30 decibels.

Modern man is certainly deafer than his ancestors, and it appears likely that because of occupational noise we age rather rapidly in terms of our hearing. This point was well brought out by the researches by Dr P. H. Beales on a primitive Sudanese tribe known as the Mabaan. To the tribe items such as roads, guns, drums and motors were completely unknown. Beales' investigation showed that Mabaan tribesmen in their eighth decade of life had a hearing corresponding to that of American men in their fourth decade notwithstanding the fact that most of the latter had never been exposed to excessive noise.

Undue noise in factories impairs efficiency and performance so reducing the accuracy of the work and increasing the liability to error. For example, a survey in an English electronics factory demonstrated that noisy conditions caused 110 assembly workers to make 60 mistakes in 24 hours; when the background noise was significantly reduced only 7 mistakes were made in the same time. Noise has important effects on mental health, and the treatment of mental illness cannot proceed satisfactorily under noisy conditions. Noise above a level of 50-60 decibels interferes with patterns of sleep and can produce irritability and other psychoneurotic manifestations. Some countries take this very seriously, and in 1968 the National Research Council of Canada warned that if a change in sleep patterns due to noise continued for more than 10 days in a given individual profound personality changes could ensue.

The Wilson Report of 1963 concluded that the general effects of noise on health are mainly psychological in nature and that with the exception of deafness, moderate noise does not produce any measurable effects on the 'average' person. Professor William Burns of Charing Cross Hospital, London, is one who believes that, as yet, no evidence exists that noise causes any specific physical disease. These conclusions may well be valid at present; however in the future they may become less tenable for all the indications are that overall noise levels will markedly increase. Suggestions have been made in the literature that excessive noise can impair the circulation, alter the secretion and composition of gastric juice, increase the secretion of the adrenal glands and cause an unduly high incidence of heart disease in workers. At the time of writing, none of these suggestions has been validated.

The Control of Noise

No dazzling feat of innovative technology is required to control noise, for silencers and muffles are available and these are capable of reducing the sound intensity of most offensive noises. Furthermore, with the possible exception of noise produced by aircraft, adequate silencing procedures are not particularly expensive. The control of noise pollution therefore rests with governments which must legislate to enforce the use of adequate silencing procedures or alternatively must restrict the occasions on which a given noise may be heard. The remainder of this chapter discusses some of the measures adopted throughout the world to reduce unwanted noise.

The British Government has been slow to act on noise pollution, and any legislation which has been enacted has been strongly criticised as being completely ineffectual. However, the recent report by the Royal Commission on Environmental Pollution remarked that reduction of noise should be given priority by the Government, and it is therefore possible that the situation will eventually improve. At present individuals pestered by noise can invoke the Noise Abatement Act of 1960; alternatively they can attempt to obtain satisfaction by means of local bye-laws and through Common Law. Legislation of this type is sometimes successful in controlling intermittent noise, although the bureaucratic machinery which must be set in motion is formidable. For example, under the terms of the Noise Abatement Act a local authority, following a complaint, must first serve a statutory notice; then, after the time allowed in the notice has expired, the authority must secure a hearing in the local magistrates' court in order to obtain a nuisance order. After such a long delay it is more than likely that the noise will have ceased spontaneously. However, even if it has not, the fines imposed under the Noise Abatement Act (£5 initially and £2 per day thereafter), are so miniscule that they would be received by most commercial concerns with derisive laughter!

In the industrial field Britain is failing to keep abreast of other countries in controlling the degree of noise by means of adequate legislation. For example in the UK deafness is not yet even considered a significant cause for financial compensation, while in most European countries and in many states of the USA schemes have been introduced enabling compensation to be paid for occupational deafness. Britons place little emphasis on noise control in industry. However, in factories in Austria noisy machinery must be isolated, while the Scandinavian countries insist that if harmful factory noise cannot be dealt with satisfactorily then the process concerned must be interrupted. Power stations in Helsinki are operated under stringent noise limitations; indeed the Finns are so noise conscious they have recently invented the most silent toilet in the world! Czechoslovakia forbids the import of machinery unless it conforms to strict noise limits, while in Brazil industrial noise in excess of 80 decibels is considered hazardous and justifies the payment of 'danger money' to workers.

While industrial noise levels are rightly causing concern, even more important is that produced by modern transport. Legislation to guard against traffic noise has been on the drawing board for over 30 years, but still no effective controls have been developed. In 1968 Britain became the first country in the world to institute roadside noise checks; however, the technical problems arising from actually measuring the noise of vehicles moving on roads or motorways have proved to be very considerable, and as a result the number of offenders prosecuted since such checks were instituted has been very small indeed. During 1970 noise limits were imposed on all new vehicles, this applying to lorries and buses as well as to motor cars. However, the limit did not affect vehicles already on the road and therefore the value of the legislation was very restricted.

The Noise Abatement Society in Britain is active and militant. However, faced with an explosion of vehicular traffic and with the sure knowledge that in the next decade the situation will become much worse, society members must feel as though they were assaulting a heavily fortified castle with a catapult. Recently the Society has perfected a cheap portable noise meter which can be held in the hand and which, when pointed at a moving vehicle, indicates by means of a red light whether or not the vehicle is exceeding a given noise limit; increasing use of such meters should be greatly encouraged by local authorities. An urgent aim of the Noise Abatement Society and one which deserves strong public support, is the establishment of noise testing centres throughout the country which will provide a service similar to that given by garages which assess the roadworthiness of vehicles.

Some countries have imposed tougher and more enforcible controls on vehicle noise than exist in Britain. France puts a limit of 83 decibels on car noise, a figure lower than that in the UK. In Paris the use of motor horns has been banned for some years, and the type of legislation enacted by the government entitles the French police to confiscate the cars of repeated offenders. Japanese cities have designated zones of silence, and anyone making a noise in such areas is prosecuted. The Swiss law imposes a noise limit as low as 70 decibels on traffic arteries during the day and this falls to 60 decibels during the hours of darkness.

Legislation designed to produce a reduction of noise around airports has so far been singularly ineffective. This is mainly because aircraft engines as currently designed are excessively noisy pieces of machinery. Improvements in design are certainly possible, and the introduction of the turbofan engine has perceptibly reduced the noise levels of the new Jumbo Jet airliners. Unhappily all international airports handle more and more traffic each year with the result that overall noise levels will undoubtedly rise rather than fall.

In 1966 an international conference was held in the USA in an attempt to ensure that aircraft flying over the large cities of the future would be no noisier than those in operation at that time. A major decision of the conference was that all new aircraft should be issued with a noise certificate. This was before the days of supersonic machines, and there is no question that under the regulations proposed by the conference aeroplanes such as the Anglo-French Concorde would fail to obtain a certificate. However, even the issue of noise certificates is merely a palliative and has no potential for cure. The correct decision would of course be to build no more international airports, but in the present climate of opinion such a resolve would meet the strongest of opposition.

In early 1971 the British Government opted to site the Third London Airport at Foulness rather than at the two inland sites previously proposed, namely at Cublington in Buckinghamshire and at Stansted in Essex. This decision is certainly to be welcomed although a much better course of action would have been to dispense with the airport altogether. Nevertheless, at least it can be said that in siting the airport at Foulness, the British Government eventually appears to have accepted the all too obvious fact that airports and people make bad bedfellows.

The one great exception to the localised damage produced by aircraft noise is the sonic boom. Every supersonic aircraft from the moment at which it breaks the sound barrier until it ceases to fly faster than sound emits such a boom which can be heard along its total flightpath at a width varying from 50 to 80 miles. The British and US governments have conducted what they have termed feasibility studies in order to test public reaction to this form of noise pollution. Although in Britain all the tests were followed by a spate of complaints as well as by claims for financial compensation for damage (including a successful claim by one gentleman who was awarded £10,000 because the foundations of his home had been cracked by a sonic boom), there still appears to be some disagreement about the desirability of supersonic flights over land. The USA conducted a series of sonic boom tests in the state of Oklahoma during 1964 in the course of which the inhabitants were subjected to 8 booms per day for six months during daylight hours. There were varying views on the tests, but the consensus of opinion was that Oklahomans could learn to live with the booms for reasons of national prestige!

In 1971 it would appear that attitudes in the USA to noise pollution have altered, and this is indicated by the recent decision of the Congress to discontinue the development of supersonic aircraft in that country. However, on our side of the Atlantic such an enlightened policy has not so far prevailed with the result that at the time of writing work on the Anglo-French Concorde is continuing apace with a view to introducing the aircraft into commercial use. Concorde will be bad enough; but future generations of supersonic aircraft will almost certainly be even noisier. If such machines are allowed to monopolise the skies then an era will dawn when there will be no peace and quiet for anyone from one end of the earth to the other.

References

BARR, JOHN (1970). 'Noise'. *Your Environment*, 2, pp. 36-40.
BARR, JOHN (1970). *The Assaults on our Senses*. London, Methuen, Ch. 4 and 5.
BEALES, PHILIP H. (1965). *Noise, Hearing and Deafness*. London, Michael Joseph.
BELL, ALAN (1966). *Noise: An Occupational Hazard and Public Nuisance*. Geneva, World Health Organisation.
BROADBENT, D. E. (1963). 'Differences and Interactions between Stresses'. *Quart. J. Exp. Psychol.*, 15, pp. 205-211.
BURNS, WILLIAM (1968). *Noise and Man*. London, John Murray.
FERGUSSON, ADAM (1970). 'Controlling the mounting roar of Britain's traffic'. *The Times*, 17th March.
FERGUSSON, ADAM (1970). 'Never out of earshot of an aircraft'. *The Times*, 18th March.
FERGUSSON, ADAM (1970). 'The danger to health of excessive noise'. *The Times*, 19th March.
H.M. STATIONERY OFFICE (1963). *Noise–Wilson Report*. London.
NOISE ABATEMENT SOCIETY (1969). *The Law on Noise*. London.
RODDA, MICHAEL (1967). *Noise and Society*. London, Oliver and Boyd.
TAYLOR, RUPERT (1970). *Noise*. London, Pelican Books.
THE ECOLOGIST (1971). 'The relief of Heathrow', 1, No. 10, p. 3.

XII

THE MENACE OF RADIOACTIVITY

The main thrust of this chapter concerns the perils to which mankind will be exposed as a result of pollution by radioactivity. However, before describing such dangers in detail it is essential to recognise why this type of contamination will become increasingly important in the decades which lie immediately ahead. To find the reason one must return to the points made in Chapter VIII. There it was emphasised that the earth's resources of fossil fuels were finite and were vanishing rapidly. Thus at present rates of consumption coal supplies would probably be exhausted in from two to three hundred years, while in the case of crude oil and natural gas the situation was much more serious, available stocks being at risk even before the end of the present century.

These dismal facts make it a matter of prime urgency to discover at the earliest possible opportunity a substitute for fossil fuels as the major source of industrial energy. However, some would have us believe that there is no cause for alarm and that the fears of the doomwatchers are groundless. According to this school of thought the ideal solution has already been found in the form of nuclear power which possesses major advantages over fossil fuels and which, it is claimed, will smoothly replace the latter throughout the whole spectrum of industrial practice.

Is this optimistic viewpoint realistic or is it yet another mirage conjured up by those whose belief in the magic of technology is unbounded? Let us proceed to examine the facts as they currently present themselves.

*   *   *

The whole topic of nuclear energy is intimately bound up with the radioactive metallic element uranium. The latter as it occurs naturally in ores consists of three isotopes, designated respectively uranium-234, uranium-235 and uranium-238. Of these uranium-235 is of paramount importance because it is the material on which the reaction of atomic fission is totally dependent, at least in its early stages. Unfortunately, the content of uranium-235 in ores is relatively small, representing less than 1 per cent of the total naturally occurring metal. Of the two non-fissionable isotopes uranium-234 occurs in amounts so small as to be almost negligible, while uranium-238 is present in relatively large quantities, constituting more than 99 per cent of the total.

What is the world situation with respect to uranium resources? The metal, like others discussed in Chapter VIII, is distributed throughout our planet in a highly irregular fashion. Since the end of the Second World War, uranium has been the focus of especial interest, and during the 1950's and 1960's it received the most intensive geological investigation ever accorded to a metal. These studies disappointed many, for they led to the overall conclusion that the earth's supplies of uranium were not particularly plentiful and did not appear to be as large as had originally been anticipated. In 1967 the USA led the world in the production of the metal; other major producers were Canada, South Africa and France. Australia is a country in which rich uranium deposits have recently been discovered and in 1967 she produced more than 300,000 metric tons of the element.

The basis for the supply of atomic power for industrial purposes is the nuclear reactor. All such plants utilise the reaction of atomic fission and they are of three main types—*burners, converters* and *breeders.*

The commercial reactors of the 1970's are mainly burners. They employ light rather than heavy water and they rely exclusively on uranium-235 for the generation of their energy. Such dependence produces two major drawbacks, the first arising from the fact that the isotope accounts for less than 1 per cent of the total amount of naturally occurring uranium, and the second from the realisation that, just as in the case of other metals, world supplies of uranium ore are finite and will eventually be exhausted. At present rates of industrial consumption, future shortages of the metal are inevitable, and some experts consider that they may become apparent well before the end of the present century. An early symptom of such a deficiency will be a rise in the price of uranium in world markets, and this will have the effect of rendering energy derived from atomic power economically non-competitive as compared with that generated by fossil fuels.

Trends in the development of nuclear reactors are now becoming apparent. Thus with the passage of time burners will become obsolescent and will be replaced by converters and more particularly by breeders. The new types of reactors have the immeasurable advantage over their predecessors in that they can change non-fissionable material into isotopes which can then be used in the fission reaction. Foremost among such elements are uranium-238, the major component of the naturally occurring ore, and thorium-232. Because of their propensity to be converted into fissionable material uranium-238 and thorium-232 are designated fertile compounds. The conversion itself is performed by bombarding them with neutrons, and the whole process of transforming fertile into fissile material is termed conversion, or under certain circumstances, breeding. In a converter reactor only a fraction of the fertile material can be converted into fissile substances before the latter are completely exhausted. However, in a breeder reactor the situation is more favourable, with the result that the amount of fissile material produced is greater than that consumed. Consequently it is theoretically possible for a breeder reactor to utilise the entire supply of fertile material available with a corresponding increase in the amount of energy obtained.

Writing in the monograph *Resources and Man* the US geologist M. K. Hubbert has provided us with a masterly survey of current and future trends *à propos* the use of nuclear energy in industrial practice. Most of the conclusions which he reaches are ominous. Hubbert considers that the lifespan of nuclear reactors of the burner type will be short. As noted earlier they are totally dependent on uranium-235; soon readily accessible supplies of this element will be exhausted, and when this happens costs will rise dramatically. At that stage nuclear power

generated by burners will be quite unable to compete economically with energy derived from water and from fossil fuels.
Hubbert takes the view that when this point is reached the only
possible solution will be greatly to increase the number of
breeder reactors, thus making it possible to use for the fission
reaction low grade ores of uranium and of thorium which at
present cannot be employed for this purpose. A whole new vista
would then open up with respect to the generation of power.
For instance, it has been estimated that the energy obtainable
by breeder reactors from rocks occurring at mineable depth in
the USA could well be hundreds or even thousands of times
larger than that of all the fossil fuels combined! Hubbert
exhorts mankind to change with utmost speed from burner to
breeder reactors. He comments that 'failure to make this
transition would constitute one of the major disasters in human
history'.

From the point of view of industry and commerce few would
deny that the large-scale introduction of breeder reactors should
have high priority. However, technical problems in this area
have by no means been solved, and some of the difficulties
which are likely to arise have been highlighted in a recent review
by Ogburn. Plants of this type are exceedingly complex and the
cost of their construction will undoubtedly be high; moreover,
the danger of a nuclear explosion resulting from their operation
cannot be completely eliminated. The opinion of Glenn T.
Seaborg, Chairman of the American Atomic Energy Commission—a body not generally renowned for its pessimistic
outlook—is of interest in this context. In a speech in 1969
devoted to future developments in the field of nuclear reactors,
Seaborg stated that it was unlikely that large safe commercial
breeders would be available on a significant scale in the USA
until well into the 1980's. Other countries including Britain will
almost certainly lag behind the USA in this development.

If breeder reactors finally come into universal use their
ecological effects will be profound and could well be irreversible. Mention has already been made of some of these in
Chapter V. The major danger which such plants will pose is that
of thermal pollution of waterways, and it is certain that this
form of contamination will be much more severe than that

produced by the burner reactors of today which are already causing overheating in some US rivers and estuaries. Predictions with respect to the effect of breeder reactors on environmental systems by the end of the present century strike notes of gloom and foreboding. Thus it has been stated that if the degree of proliferation of such reactors currently envisaged for North America for the year 2000 AD actually takes place, it will then be necessary for as much as one-third of the fresh water supplies of that continent to flow through these plants for purposes of cooling! The flora and fauna of American waterways are unlikely to benefit from a diversion of this type.

* * *

If nuclear fission is beset by such grievous problems can we hope for an amelioration of our lot by the use of nuclear fusion? Theoretically the answer must be in the affirmative. However, it must at once be stressed that the utilisation of nuclear fusion as a basic source of energy for industrial purposes is at present a dream rather than a reality.* The basic scientific problems in this field remain to be elucidated, just as they do in the case of killing diseases such as cancer and arteriosclerosis, and the unpalatable fact must be faced that the difficulties encountered may be too formidable for human ingenuity and originality to solve. With atomic fission the linchpin of the process was the metal uranium; with fusion it is the gas hydrogen. There are three isotopic forms of the latter— *hydrogen* itself, *deuterium* and *tritium.* The process of nuclear fusion is inextricably linked with deuterium and essentially consists of fusing two atoms of this isotope to produce the substance, helium, this being the next higher element in the atomic scale.

Fusion can be controlled or uncontrolled, and it is the former which would be mandatory as a source of industrial energy. Uncontrolled fusion has already been accomplished, and the

---

* In Britain research on nuclear fusion was reduced some four years ago. At that time the then Minister of Technology, Mr Anthony Wedgwood Benn, is reported to have stated that the possibility of success was remote and that, anyway, the solution would be provided by fast breeder reactors (see *Daily Telegraph Magazine* December 3rd, 1971).

outcome of this experiment has an eerie familiarity to all of us. Some years ago scientists succeeded in fusing two atoms of deuterium to produce helium, and as a result of their endeavours the hydrogen bomb was detonated. The world was changed beyond recognition; it entered the era of the 'balance of terror', and a weapon with a unique potentiality for the annihilation of the human race thrust itself into the forefront of our consciousness.

Undoubtedly a glittering prize awaits those who solve the fundamental problems associated with controlled nuclear fusion. For success in this field would constitute one of the major scientific advances of all time and would place at the disposal of mankind an amount of energy which has been stated to be equivalent to 500 Pacific Oceans of high grade fuel oil! Such supplies of power, even at the high current rates of industrial consumption, could last not for centuries but for millennia; *homo sapiens* would have been rescued from his immediate predicament and could breathe again. And there would be other notable advantages because in all probability plants operated by nuclear fusion would produce less environmental damage and less emission of radioactive biproducts than reactors utilising conventional methods of atomic fission. Who will win the race? Will it be the atomic scientist in his laboratory or will a combination of overpopulation and high economic consumption frustrate his efforts before he can succeed in solving his basic research problems? Perhaps on the result of this awesome contest the ultimate future of humanity will depend.

*   *   *

Willy-nilly our civilisation is becoming more and more involved with radioactivity. First it was through the horror of a nuclear holocaust; now and in the future it will be as a result of the peaceful uses of nuclear energy in the generation of electrical power and in the diagnosis and treatment of human disease. The dangers inherent in the explosion of nuclear devices were self evident, and when it became apparent that the whole of the planet was being increasingly poisoned by radioactive fall-out, the public outcry was intense. The tumult knew no ideological boundaries. Marxism and capitalism joined hands; the clamour was as shrill on the eastern as on the western side of the Iron Curtain. The uproar had the desired effect; it culminated in the Treaty of Moscow in 1963—commonly known as the 'Test Ban treaty'—which forbade the testing of nuclear weapons in the air or at sea. The Treaty was signed by the majority of nations and three of the nuclear powers—the USA, the USSR and the UK—appended their signatures. However there were notable absentees from the conference table, two of them—France and the People's Republic of China—being members of the nuclear club.

In the world of the 1970's the threat of nuclear war has perhaps receded and certainly nuclear testing has become exiguous by the standards of previous decades. Yet, our environment is being contaminated to an ever increasing extent through the peaceful uses of the atom. Alas, few people recognise this fact and even fewer have any appreciation of the inherent nature of radioactivity.

Radioactivity goes completely undetected by the human senses since it is colourless, odourless and invisible. Yet it has the potential of threatening and even destroying man's most precious patrimony, his genetic complement. The correct term for radioactivity is 'ionising radiation', and in order to detect such radiation highly sophisticated electronic equipment must be employed. Ionising radiations are emitted from atoms which give off energy when they disintegrate spontaneously. In this way lighter atoms are formed and they themselves may undergo spontaneous disintegration. Each disintegration, or as it is termed 'decay', is different from its predecessor and eventually an inert substance not containing radioactivity is produced. The time taken for half the atoms in a given radioactive element to decay is designated the 'half-life', a term much used by specialists in this field. Half-lives are exceedingly variable; they can be as short as a thousandth of a second or they can extend over thousands of years. Radioactive elements with long half-lives are the major niggers in the woodpile. Indeed radioactive wastes from nuclear power plants contain substances which can pose health hazards for as long as half a million years.

The effects of ionising radiations on living cells are generally damaging, and when a large dosage is administered the cell dies. Very small amounts may produce no noticeable change but are capable of causing subtle effects within the cell which may eventually prove harmful and even lethal. Radioactivity is measured in a variety of units and one of the most popular of these is the 'rad' which gives an indication of the amount of radiation reaching living tissues. In humans a dose of 1,000 rads is lethal, while dosages as low as 50 rads can produce cancerous growths, kill the embryo in the mother's womb and cause permanent sterility if it affects the ovaries or the testes.

Sources of Radioactive Pollution

It is noteworthy that man's *natural* environment, as distinct from the environment which he has carved out for himself, is by no means free of radioactivity. Indeed it contains by far the greatest amount of radiation to which the vast majority of the citizens of Spaceship Earth will be exposed. The source of this radiation is threefold. The first—and by far the largest amounting to about one-half of the total natural radiation—comes from rocks present in the earth's crust. The activity of these rocks varies considerably but tends to be at its maximum over deposits of uranium and thorium. Areas of the world in which levels of this so-called 'background' radiation are high include the Indian state of Kerala and the region of Guarapary in Brazil. The second source of natural radiation is cosmic rays which reach the earth from outer space, and were it not for the ability of the envelope of air which surrounds our planet to absorb most of these rays, mankind would die as a result of exposure to this form of radiation. Cosmic radiation becomes more intense the higher one ventures above sea level; it is a real danger for the astronaut, and it could well be a hazard for those utilising supersonic air travel in, for example, the Anglo-French Concorde. The remaining source of natural radiation is man himself, for a tiny fraction of the elements contained in his body is radioactive, the most important of these being an isotope of potassium. The estimated dosages per individual from each of these natural sources are shown in the table on p. 227.

Amongst man-made forms of radioactive pollution pride of place must, of course, go to the fall-out associated with the testing of nuclear weapons. The 'golden years' of nuclear testing were from 1945 to 1962, and the earth will continue to bear the radioactive burden imposed on it during this period for thousands of years. The Test Ban Treaty of 1963 improved the situation; however it did not cure it, for as mentioned earlier two major members of the nuclear club did not sign, and since then China has exploded a number of hydrogen bombs. Also, from time to time there are disturbing press reports that other countries which did not sign the Treaty—Israel is a good example—maybe developing a 'nuclear deterrent'. Therefore, although the world's radioactive load may have decreased somewhat in recent years, the threat of environmental contamination from this source is far from having been eliminated.

Source of radiation	Approximate annual dose in millirads per year
Terrestrial radiation from minerals in the earth's crust	50.0
Cosmic radiation	28.7
Within the body (mainly from potassium-40)	21.3

Nuclear explosions are followed by intense radiation and by the dissemination of radioactive gases and particles throughout the atmosphere. The fall-out of such particles is not evenly distributed; the temperature zones of the northern hemisphere of the planet, including Britain, the USA and Western Europe, are affected disproportionately. A variety of substances produced in radioactive fall-out have profound effects on man. Strontium-89 and strontium-90 pass into the human system through milk and are deposited in bones; caesium-137 becomes concentrated in all soft tissues and so irradiates the whole body; carbon-14 can rapidly be assimilated into all biological material and so can cause a very complete form of whole body irradiation; iodine-131 is concentrated to a marked degree by the thyroid gland in the neck. Fortunately the half-lives of iodine-131 (8 days) and of strontium-89 (51 days) are short;

therefore the effects produced by these isotopes on mankind as a result of nuclear explosions of the past can now safely be ignored. But it is a very different matter with strontium-90, caesium-137 and carbon-14. The half-lives of these isotopes are respectively 28, 30 and 4,760 years, and so their effects will remain with us long after a nuclear blast.

Nuclear weaponry, that ultimate in destructive capacity, has had at least one useful 'spin-off'; it has enabled twentieth century man to harness the atom to produce electrical power. Future developments in this field have already been sketched in this chapter. Amongst them are included the rapidly escalating demand for nuclear power, the gradual replacement of burner by breeder reactors, the dangers of thermal pollution of waterways and the eventual necessity of replacing the process of nuclear fission by controlled nuclear fusion.

But what of environmental pollution arising from nuclear reactors in current use? Such contamination is far from negligible, and this combined with the possibility that an accident may occur during the operation of the plant, has been the main reason for siting nuclear reactors far from centres of population and frequently on the sea coast. An adequate and plentiful supply of water is essential for the satisfactory operation of all nuclear power stations. Even so all the radioactivity cannot be removed from the effluent, and in addition some radiation inevitably escapes into the atmosphere especially when waste products are being processed. Officials as well as the public are acutely aware of the dangers of radioactive contamination, and as a result possible pollutants are continuously monitored and rigorously controlled. A good example of the care taken is provided by the experience at the atomic plant at Windscale in Cumberland. Here it is known that the effluent from the plant is concentrated by seaweed, which is processed by the local inhabitants and is made into what is known as 'laver bread'. Yet the control of the radioactive effluent at Windscale is so strict that even if the individual consumed a diet consisting entirely of laver bread he would still not be exposed to more than the permitted level of radiation.

Accidents do happen at nuclear power stations; fortunately these have so far been rare. The most notorious accident occured at Windscale in 1957 when as much radioactive waste escaped into the atmosphere as was loosed over Hiroshima in 1945! The local inhabitants were lucky in that weather conditions were favourable; the lethal radioactive cloud was carried out by the wind over the Irish Sea and was there rendered harmless through dilution. Nevertheless, there was some radioactive fall-out locally, and it was necessary to prohibit the sale of all milk produced by cows grazing in the vicinity of the plant. Similar incidents have occurred elsewhere. For example in 1967/68 there was trouble at the Enrico Fermi breeder reactor in Michigan in the USA, and this caused the authorities to fear for the safety of the $1\frac{1}{2}$ million inhabitants of Detroit.

The transcendent problem created by the present generation of nuclear power stations is their accumulation of vast quantities of waste which is highly radioactive. No means have been found of treating such residues to render them harmless, and therefore they have to be stored in enormous concrete tanks lined with steel. There are nine such tanks at Windscale which acts as our national purification plant. Each tank is capable of holding 10 cubic metres of waste; each has to be constantly cooled lest it boil from the energy of its own radiations, and each will have to be tended for from 500 to 1,000 years. Walter Patterson, writing recently in *Your Environment,* has calculated that the total radioactivity contained in the tanks at Windscale is already equivalent to 0.1 per cent of that present in all the oceans of the world.

Hanford in Washington State houses the US equivalent of Windscale. Unfortunately it was constructed over a geographical fault and should an earthquake supervene, unpleasant complications might ensue. There has recently been much thought in the USA as to how radioactive wastes might be better stored. One suggestion which has been made is that disused salt mines might be employed; if this were done the radioactive liquid wastes would first have to be partially solidified by a process known as glassification in the course of which the concentrated wastes are sealed into ceramic brick. Much hope is placed on the fact that the breeder reactors of the future will probably generate fewer waste products than the burner reactors of today. However, as mentioned previously, breeders are unlikely to come into general use until the 1980's at the earliest, and even then burner reactors will still be called upon to provide a relatively large component of our electricity supply.

The very nature of ionising radiations makes them especially difficult to dispose of. Thus there is no antidote; the radiations cannot be altered and so rendered harmless; instead they must be stored until they decay, a process which may take thousands of years. The handling of such wastes is very dangerous, and this is especially so if, as often happens, they have to be transported by lorries or trucks over considerable distances from power stations to processing plants. Such transportation will significantly increase; indeed by 2000 AD it has been estimated that in the USA alone at any given moment of time there will be 5,000 lorries on the roads engaged in this activity! The possibilities of human error and of a resultant accident do not require to be stressed.

Radioactivity and Health

The relationship between ionising radiations and disease is a topic which engenders much controversy, and it is likely that in the future arguments in this sphere will be characterised by an increasing degree of acerbity. That radioactivity can and does damage health is not questioned; the discord arises *à propos* the level of absorbed radiation which may reasonably be considered safe for human subjects in the light of the mounting radioactive pollution known to be occurring throughout the planet. There are two schools of thought and their views are poles apart. On the one side are ranged the scientists and administrators employed by various Atomic Energy Commissions in the Western world. These are the people who actually use the nuclear power. They eulogise the benefits of their specialty to mankind and they are optimistic about the future. Their contention is that the present safety standards for ionising radiations are much too strict and that they hamper the production of electrical energy from nuclear fission by necessitating the installation of costly anti-pollution devices. Ranged against such officials are a growing number of scientists, who aver that any relaxation of existing safety standards could be exceedingly dangerous and could result in a greatly increased incidence of various forms of malignant disease. Two outspoken and highly articulate protagonists of the latter viewpoint are the Americans Gofman and Tamplin who have recently stated that were everyone to receive the statutory permissible dosage of radiation, there would be a further 16,000 cases of cancer and leukaemia per year in the United States! Gofman and Tamplin believe that the perils to humanity of ionising radiations have been grossly underestimated, and they have gone so far as to propose that the statutory maximal allowable dose should be reduced by a factor of 10.

In July 1909 David Lloyd George made one of the most celebrated speeches of his tempestuous political career. He went to Limehouse in the East End of London and there in sweltering heat addressed a working class audience of more than four thousand people. With the brilliant flourish of invective and the provocative irony of which he alone was capable he inveighed against the English landowners; they were the villains of the piece, and everyone in the country from the richest merchant to the humblest labourer was held in their thrall. His speech horrified the Establishment; the Conservative opposition erupted and even King Edward VII was forced to intervene. Yet the trenchant criticisms made by Lloyd George about the land-owning aristocracy of England could be regarded as almost flattering when compared with the strictures levelled by scientists such as Gofman and Tamplin on the activities of those who set international guidelines for permissible radiation dosage.

In view of the many imponderables it is scarcely surprising that a major scientific controversy has arisen in the field of ionising radiations. In the first place the study of radiation-induced disease is a relatively youthful medical specialty dating only from 1945, which was the year when human beings were first subjected *en masse* to this form of contamination. Secondly, malignant diseases usually have long latent periods; in other words a considerable period of time must elapse between the exposure to the radioactivity and the emergence of the clinical symptoms. Finally, the precise role of natural terrestrial radiation remains enigmatic and, in particular, reliable information does not yet exist as to how mankind will be affected by the summation of the various forms of radiation including (i) terrestrial, (ii) that emanating from nuclear power stations, (iii) that associated with diagnostic radiology, and (iv) that arising as a result of the explosion of nuclear devices. Two questions in this general field are of overriding importance. Firstly, will ionising radiations cause various types of illness, and secondly, will they produce genetic damage?

Radiation and Disease

Evidence for the deleterious effects of radioactivity on health has been culled over the years from observations in three main areas—from the occurrence of different disease states in the inhabitants of Nagasaki and Hiroshima following the two nuclear bomb explosions of 1945, from occupational hazards associated with radiation, and from the appearance of various types of illness in patients who have been treated by radiation for cancer and other conditions.

Individuals who survived the detonation of the atomic bomb over Nagasaki and Hiroshima were subsequently estimated to have received a dose of anything up to 500 rads. In the years following the explosion this population was carefully observed by the Atomic Bomb Casualty Commission, a body established in Japan by the US government. Between 1947 and 1954 an important finding emerged, namely that the incidence of the blood disease leukaemia was over four times greater in those exposed to the bomb than in the general population of Japan. Since 1954 further studies on victims of the bomb have demonstrated an increase in the incidence of other forms of malignant disease. Thus lung cancer has risen by a factor of two; thyroid cancer in adults has increased at a rate proportional to the dose of radiation absorbed by the individual, and in children the rise in the levels of this form of malignancy has been quite spectacular. It has been stated that the incidence of breast cancer has also risen as a result of the nuclear explosions; however, this claim must be accepted with some reserve as it is based on a relatively small series of cases. But the reckoning has not only been in terms of malignant disease, for it has also been noted that the growth of children exposed to the bomb has been retarded as compared with that of subjects who did not suffer the exposure.

People whose occupations bring them into contact with radioactivity have been shown to be more susceptible to certain types of cancer than the general population. Thus hospital radiologists are especially prone to cancer of the skin and to damage of the bone marrow leading to leukaemia and other diseases of the blood; indeed the rise in the incidence of these conditions in radiologists was initially detected by scrutiny of the obituary notices in the Journal of the American Medical Association. The painters of clock and watch faces use luminous paints containing radium and thorium; it has been recognised for some time that these individuals are unduly susceptible to bone cancer. A condition known as 'mountain sickness' was once prevalent in workers in the pitch-blende mines of Joachimsthal and Schneeberg in the eastern part of Germany. This is believed to be a form of lung cancer brought about by exposure to the radioactive gas, radon, the latter being present in relatively high concentrations in the mines.

One of the classical contributions to this field was made by members of the British Medical Research Council who, beginning in 1955, carried out a series of studies in a group of patients who had been treated by X-rays for the painful and crippling disease of the spine known as ankylosing spondylitis. More than 14,000 patients were involved in a retrospective investigation, and the main conclusions reached were striking. They were that such individuals were 9 times more likely to develop leukaemia and 26 times more likely to develop a serious disease of the bone marrow known as aplastic anaemia than were members of the general population. Other forms of cancer were also more frequent in the irradiated group, and it appeared that the degree of risk was directly proportional to the amount of radiation administered.

There are numerous studies in animals which lend support to the data reported by the Medical Research Council in humans. In the course of such experiments it has been possible to determine a so-called doubling dose, this being the amount required to raise the incidence of malignant disease by a factor of two. In the case of leukaemia in man the doubling dose is stated to range from 30 to 60 rads. Considerable controversy still exists as to the ability of low radiation dosages to produce malignant disease in human subjects. The Americans, Gofman and Tamplin, together with the British workers Court-Brown and Doll, postulate the existence of a relationship between the incidence of leukaemia and radiation dosage even after exposure to very small amounts of ionising radiations. However, a number of nuclear physicists, some of them of considerable eminence, hold a contrary opinion, believing that the induction of leukaemia is a threshold event in that the disease will not be produced below a certain level of radiation. Over the years the controversy has ebbed and flowed; unfortunately views have now tended to become polarised, and agreement amongst the scientific fraternity appears to be as far off as ever.

Genetic Effects of Radiation

The origin of man and all other animals is from a single living cell formed by the union of two cells, one from each parent. The parent cells contain long threadlike structures known as chromosomes, the latter being the repository of the genetic information. The new cell, with its equal complement of genetic material derived from each parent, multiplies and proliferates until sufficient cells have been produced to form all the different organs and tissues of the body. Each individual passes on to its progeny the chromosomes inherited from his parents. Rarely changes occur spontaneously in a chromosome, and in this way the genetic information with which it is endowed is altered; this process is known as mutation. Normally mutations are eliminated by the process known as natural selection as a result of which damaging characteristics are removed. A major effect of ionising radiations—and one of the most serious—is their ability to increase the rate at which spontaneous mutations occur.

Certain hereditary conditions are thought to be caused by mutants; these include a malady of the bones known as achondroplasia, the bleeding disease haemophilia and a metabolic abnormality designated phenylketonuria. If a doubling of the mutation rate took place due, for instance, to a rise in amounts of background radiation, it has been estimated that cases of achondroplasia would increase two fold in one generation, that the number of patients with haemophilia would double in six generations, and that the incidence of phenyl-ketonuria would be augmented by one-half in 50 genera-tions. Furthermore, according to a Medical Research Council report entitled *Hazards of Nuclear and Allied Radiations*, a doubling of the mutation rate could raise the incidence of mental deficiency in the population at large by some 3 per cent.

What dosage of radioactivity would be required to increase the mutation rate in humans by 100 per cent? An unequivocal answer to this important question still cannot be given. However, certain estimates have been made, and in the opinion of the British Medical Research Council such a change might be anticipated at a level of exposure of from 20 to 80 rads per individual. Is there any concrete evidence that exposure to current levels of radiation has produced a significant rise in the incidence of heritable diseases? At the time of writing the answer must be in the negative. However, we cannot predict the pattern of future events, and it would be the quintessence of irresponsibility to adopt a complacent attitude. Perhaps an observation which merits attention in this general context is the small but significant shift in the sex ratio in favour of the female which has taken place in children born in Nagasaki and Hiroshima in the years after 1945. This might be interpreted as indicating some degree of genetic damage.

Risks of Radioactivity

How dangerous are the present environmental levels of radio-activity and, if the health of the community is being placed in jeopardy because of them, are there any indications that the incidence of specific disease states is now on the increase? Before considering these controversial topics account must be taken of the actual levels of radiation to which the ordinary citizen is exposed. These are shown in the following table.

Source of radiation	Approximate dose as a percentage of total natural background*
Natural background	100
Diagnostic radiology (x-rays)	14 (UK) 10 (Australia) 50-70(USA)
Occupational exposure, industry, hospital radiology and Atomic Energy Authorities	0.1-1.6
'Fall-out' from nuclear bomb tests	1.0
Luminous watches and clocks	1.0
Television sets	Very much less than 1.0
X-ray fluroscopy for shoe fitting	0.1
Disposal of radioactive wastes	0.003

* Based on a survey conducted by the British Ministry of Health in 1957.

The most impressive feature of the table is the pre-eminent position accorded to diagnostic radiology as the major source of radiation. This is especially so in countries which possess sophisticated medical services, and in such parts of the world contributions from other sources are so tiny as to be almost negligible. Two further points must be made for they are not brought out in the table. The first is that the effect of an accident at a nuclear power station could be disastrous, while the second is that the small proportion of the world's citizenry who happen to live in close proximity to such atomic reactors receive considerably larger dosages of radiation than are indicated.

The table is concerned with very low levels of radioactivity. Do they contribute to the causation of leukaemia and other types of malignant disease in man? As mentioned previously this is one of the most contentious questions of the 1970's; it is also highly emotive and as a result its discussion at scientific meetings is apt to generate more heat than light. If it could be established beyond reasonable doubt that the induction of disease by radiation was not a threshold phenomenon, then a persuasive case could be made for restricting the use of radiology in the diagnosis of disease. However, in the absence of equivocal evidence in one direction or the other, the whole matter must still remain *sub judice.*

Control of Radiation Levels

Roentgen discovered x-rays in 1905. They were soon shown to be highly dangerous to man, and many of the early radiologists suffered severe and irreversible injury because of exposure to them. In 1915 a German Radiological Congress was held in Berlin, at which it was stressed that legal measures would be necessary to protect the public from the effects of x-rays.

Prior to the Second World War few countries were sufficiently concerned about the dangers of ionising radiations to enact the appropriate legislation. However, this state of affairs has altered radically and now most nations have placed such laws on their statute books. Countries such as the Soviet Union and Switzerland favour very detailed legislation, while others such as Canada and Norway are more flexible, laying down general laws but leaving room for voluntary codes of practice. In Britain responsibility for radiation protection rests with the central government, but in the USA there is responsibility at federal, state, city and even lower levels.

Atomic Energy Authorities in most countries employing nuclear power as a source of industrial energy accept the advice of the International Commission on Radiological Protection (ICRP). This body recommends maximum levels of radiation dosage above which damage to health may ensue. At present the statutory level is set at 0.17 rads per year in the case of whole body irradiation. It should however be stressed that the levels of radiation recommended by the ICRP are specifically intended for those whose occupations bring them into direct contact with radioactivity, for example, radiologists and personnel employed in nuclear power stations. In Britain and elsewhere the vast majority of workers who come in contact with ionising radiations in the course of their occupation do not receive anything approaching the maximum permissible dose and are therefore not at risk from leukaemia and allied diseases.

In spite of the vast amount of research which has been devoted to ionising radiations, one cannot but be concerned about the lack of any really reliable evidence concerning the effects of these rays on the genetic make up of whole populations. The present position was well enunciated by Professor Brian MacMahon of Harvard University when he wrote in 1969 'while a great deal more is known now than was known 20 years ago, it must be admitted that we still do not have most of the data that would be required for an informed judgment on the maximum limits of exposure advisable for individuals or populations'. Certainly the genetic hazard to man from ionising radiations is a very real one, and the stakes in terms of his ultimate survival are high. As the highly respected American geneticist J. V. Neel once remarked 'man's most precious possession is his genetic endowment. Each generation holds it in trust for subsequent generations'. In the field of ionising radiations our generation has undoubtedly grasped what Trotsky once called the 'iron broom of history'. What will be the opinion of posterity on our activities? Will it bless us for our percipience or will it curse us for nursing into life a serpent with the capacity to sting mankind to death?

References

BOFFEY, PHILIP M (1971). 'Radiation Standards: Are the right people making the decisions?'. *Science*, **171**, pp. 780-783.

BRIDGES, BRYN (1971). 'Environmental genetic hazards—the impossible problem'. *The Ecologist*, **1**, No. 12, pp. 19-21.

BRYANT, PAMELA M. (1969). 'Radioactive Wastes'. In *Technological Injury*. Edited by ROSE, J. London, Gordon and Breach Science Publishers, pp. 65-77.

BUNYARD, PETER (1971). 'Pollution by Radioactivity'. In *Can Britain Survive*? Edited by GOLDSMITH, EDWARD. London, Tom Stacey, pp. 155-163.

COURT-BROWN, W. M. and DOLL, R. (1957). *Leukaemia and Aplastic Anaemia in Patients Irradiated for Ankylosing Spondylitis*. Medical Research Council Special Report Series No. 295. London, HM Stationery Office.

COURT-BROWN, W. M. and DOLL, R. (1965). 'Mortality from cancer and other causes after radiotherapy for Ankylosing Spondylitis. *Brit. med. J.*, **2**, pp. 1327-1332.

GOFMAN, JOHN W. and TAMPLIN, ARTHUR R. (1971). 'Low Dose Radiation and Cancer'. In *Global Ecology*. Edited by EHRLICH, PAUL R. and HOLDREN, JOHN S. New York, Chicago, San Francisco, Atlanta, Harcourt Brace, Jovanovich Inc., pp. 103-114.

HAWKES, NIGEL (1971). 'Living beyond our Resources'. *Daily Telegraph Magazine*, December 3rd.

HUBBERT, M. K. (1969). 'Energy Resources'. In *Resources and Man*. Edited by CLOUD, PRESTON. San Francisco, W. H. Freeman and Co., pp. 157-242.

INTERNATIONAL COMMISSION OF RADIOLOGICAL PROTECTION (1970). *Radiation Protection—Protection against ionising radiation from external sources*. I.C.R.P. Publication 15, Oxford, Pergamon Press.

INTERNATIONAL COMMISSION ON RADIOLOGICAL PROTECTION (1970). *Radiation Protection—Protection of the Patient in X-ray diagnosis*. ICRP Publication 16, Oxford, Pergamon Press.

JOINT COMMITTEE ON ATOMIC ENERGY, CONGRESS OF THE UNITED STATES (1969). *Environmental Effects of Producing Electric Power*. Washington, US Government Printing Office, Part 1.

LOVINGER, LEE (1971). 'State's rights in radiation control'. *Science*, **171**, pp. 790-793.

MEDICAL RESEARCH COUNCIL (1956). *The Hazards to Man of Nuclear and Allied Radiations*. London, HM Stationery Office, cmd. 9780.

MELLANBY, KENNETH (1967). *Pesticides and Pollution*. London, Fontana, pp. 58-69.

MINISTRY OF HEALTH (1960). *Committee on Radiological Hazards to Patients—Second Report*. London, HM Stationery Office.

XIII

ECONOMIC INTERLUDE

Growth is a process of creative destruction.

Joseph A. Schumpeter, *Capitalism, Socialism and Democracy,*
Part III, Chapter 7

Can we afford to be rich?

Title of leading article, *The Times*, 20th November, 1971

*The practice of economic growthmanship in the world of the
1970's could be likened to planting flowers on the slopes of a
volcano.*

Economics, like overpopulation, impinges on every aspect of
contemporary living. Modern politicians liken a high economic
growth rate to Sir Galahad's holy grail and to the pot of gold
over the rainbow; for them it is the acme of perfection, the
repository of dreams, the goal to which all efforts should be
directed. Such a reaction is by no means surprising, for in the
political vocabulary of today, a rising growth rate is synonymous with the 'good life', with rising prosperity and with
increased living standards for constituents. And on what more
beguiling grounds could the electorate be wooed in an era in
which materialistic considerations are paramount?

Economic factors bulk largely during election campaigns, and
with the passage of years such issues have become more and
more dominant. Irrespective of party allegiance politicians
continuously stress the benefits which will undoubtedly accrue
from increasing production and consumption and from further
augmenting the pace of technological innovation. The British
scene over the past 12 years illustrates this trend with
considerable clarity. Thus in 1959 the Conservative Party under
Harold Macmillan won an election under the materialistic slogan
'you've never had it so good'. In 1964 the Labour Party led by
Harold Wilson took office, having been elected by a very small
majority. The promise was to 'get Britain moving again' and in
this process the 'white heat of technology' was to assume a
major role. In 1966 the Labour Party was re-elected, this time

with a greatly increased majority. Now the slogan was different; it was 'you know, Labour Government works', and the basis for the claim was mainly the economic performance of the Government during the preceding 18 months. By 1970 inflation was rampant in the UK; the cost of living was increasing at an alarming rate, and a new figure 'Mr. Rising-Price' was becoming a favourite amongst cartoonists. In the election of that year the Conservative Party under Edward Heath was swept to power in the belief that it could cure inflation or would at least be able to attenuate this most intractable of modern economic problems. Then during 1971 the issue of the Common Market moved into the centre of the stage. Never had the voice of growthmanship been louder, pro-Marketeers in particular eulogising the past economic performance of the Six and trumpeting forth the manifold advantages to Britain of being part of a 'domestic market' of 300 million people.*

Without any exaggeration, economics can be said to affect the destinies of us all. With the possible exception of sex, no topic is more widely discussed and none raises greater controversy. The science of economics is central to the main themes of this essay. How did it start, who are its great personalties, what were their contributions, and whither are the modern economic prophets now leading us? To these important questions we must now direct our attention.

*   *   *

Britain was the country in which economics first blossomed, and the founder of the subject as we now know it is generally considered to be Adam Smith (1723-1790). In 1776, which incidentally was also the year of the American Declaration of Independence, Smith published his now classical book *The Wealth of Nations.* This was a highly discursive treatise which painted eighteenth century life on a broad canvas. It spoke of aggregate wealth and of its distribution. It stressed the poverty of the vast majority of people inhabiting the planet, and it evinced little hope that a more equitable sharing of resources would

* Such views were well reflected in the jingoistic slogan 'you've got to get in to get on'.

242 THE DEATH OF TOMORROW

occur between landlords, merchants and industrialists on the one hand and the toiling masses of the populace on the other. *The Wealth of Nations* enunciated a variety of new and revolutionary concepts. One was that of the 'Invisible Hand', the basis of which was the postulate that each individual in pursuing his own personal and selfish ends was driven as if by an invisible force to achieve the best situation for the community as a whole. From this assumption it followed logically that any interference with the free competition of the market by governments and through legislation would be highly injurious to the economy. This came to be known as the doctrine of *laissez-faire*; it had profound effects on Victorian England and its effects persisted well into the twentieth century. One of its main intellectual products was that of Philosophical Radicalism, also known as 'Benthamism' after its founder Jeremy Bentham. The essential aim of Benthamism was to provide 'the greatest happiness of the greatest number'. Throughout the nineteenth century the doctrine was modified and refined by intellectuals of the highest calibre including James Mill, his son John Stuart Mill, and Edwin Chadwick. Eventually Philosophical Radicalism, far from being a remote and academic discipline ensconsed in its ivory tower, became a powerful and dynamic force dedicated to social, economic and political reform.

Another direct result of Smith's treatise was the formation of what eventually came to be known as the 'free trade movement' in England. With this movement were associated some of the most illustrious names of Victorian England, including Cobden, Bright, Peel and Gladstone. The movement towards free trade started mildly enough in the 1820's with legislation designed to decrease import duties on a variety of goods. During the 1830's and '40's it received a great impetus and much publicity as a result of agitation against the Corn Laws. Soon it blossomed into a formidable force devoted to the concepts of political liberalism and free competitive enterprise.

The two great figures to follow Adam Smith were contemporaries. They were David Ricardo (1772-1823) and Thomas Robert Malthus (1766-1834). Ricardo was a stockbroker, a self-made millionaire and later a Member of Parliament. Malthus combined the vocations of economist and clergyman. Both Ricardo and Malthus showed an extreme form of pessimism with respect to the future of mankind. They could envisage no alternative to the continuing impoverishment of the masses and to the fact that wages would always tend to approach the bare minimum for subsistence. Moreover, the situation was immutable; it had existed in the past; it was present now and so it would continue. Had Ricardo and Malthus been writing in the 1970's they would inevitably have been classified as doomwatchers. Their statements had a profound effect on contemporary thought, and it was mainly because of their gloomy predictions that Thomas Carlyle, writing of economics in the mid-nineteenth century, described it as the 'dismal science'.

Malthus is best known for his famous *Essay on the Principles of Overpopulation* published in 1798. The essay made two major points. The first was that 'the power of population is infinitely greater than the power of the earth to produce subsistence for man'. The second was that 'population when unchecked increases in a geometrical ratio while subsistence only increases in an arithmetical ratio'. Thus population grows exponentially just like compound interest (1, 2, 4, 8, 16, 32), while food increases in the much slower arithmetic manner (1, 2, 3, 4, 5, 6). The inevitable result was an imbalance between food supplies and population. According to Malthus this situation would bring in its wake 'positive checks' of a most unpleasant character, namely war, famine and disease. The checks would operate by killing vast numbers of people and eventually the appropriate level of subsistence would again be reached. In the meantime 'misery and vice' would stalk the land.

As mentioned previously Malthus could see no alternative to mass poverty; nor did he attempt to produce any remedy for the situation. He took the view that Nature in her infinite wisdom had decreed that there should be a struggle for existence and that, in a way, this was not unwelcome because it prevented poor people from becoming slothful and unduly dependent on state aid for their support. His opinions carried with them a highly political charge, and in Victorian England this was manifested in two major ways. The first was the belief that destitution was in reality a personal failing arising from indolence and general incompetence. From this assumption it followed naturally that unemployment should be made as uncomfortable as possible. The second was the view that the slowly emerging trade union movement would be powerless to improve the lot of working people because the latter would merely procreate until the subsistence level of all concerned fell.

The effect of David Ricardo on economic thought was even greater than that of Malthus. His *Principles of Political Economy and Taxation* was first published in 1817, six years before his death; it has remained a classical work up to the present day. Ricardo had many professional interests, a major one being the investigation of the manner in which the different classes of society shared in the products of the economy. He wrote much about the land, regarding this as an increasingly scarce commodity and predicting that those who owned it would obtain an ever growing financial reward. Landlords he regarded as the recipients of great good fortune; they had been born with silver spoons in their mouths and their luck would be passed on to their descendants. Ricardo was much preoccupied with the rents collected by landlords, the profits accruing to capitalists and the wages of the labouring classes. He strongly favoured investment by businessmen in equipment and machinery, and he was adamant in his belief that a direct conflict between profits and wages was inevitable, a rise in the former being associated with a fall in the latter and vice versa.

Ricardo was responsible for the famous 'iron law' of wages which stated that 'the natural price of labour is that price which is necessary to enable the labourers, one with another, to subsist and perpetuate their race without either increase or decrease'. In Ricardo's view the law was immutable and inexorable. It therefore followed that wages should be regulated by the 'fair and free competition of the market'. State interference was definitely contraindicated and could only be deleterious. Gross inequalities in terms of wealth existed in society and these would undoubtedly be perpetuated. Had Ricardo lived some decades later he would certainly have had no misgivings over the fact that in 1883 Mrs K. Vanderbilt of the USA was able to stage a ball the cost of which was $250,000 or that in 1900 the Scottish-born American industrialist Andrew Carnegie was reputed to have a tax free annual income of $23 million. If Ricardo had been alive in the twentieth century his voice would not have been raised in protest against the extremes of wealth of those such as the Aga Khan or the Greek shipping magnates, Onassis and Niarchos; nor would he have frowned on the flamboyance of a Lady Docker. The world as seen through his eyes was grim, harsh and non-compassionate. Poverty was the natural fate of the majority of mankind, and the only hope for the future lay in the slow and steady accretion of wealth.

Another basic tenet of Ricardian philosophy which came into considerable prominence during the Great Economic Depression, was embodied in the law originally enunciated in the eighteenth century by the well known French economist, J. B. Say. The fundamental tenet of this law was that in the economic system as a whole demand must always equal supply, the latter term referring to labour as well as to the many other factors entering into the process of production. According to Say's law the whole economic system was essentially self-regulatory in nature. It operated by a series of delicate adjustments rather in the manner by which the temperature of a room is kept constant by means of a thermostat. The law proclaimed that any action taken to stimulate demand was unnecessary and even harmful because of the distortion which it would inevitably produce to the smooth and well oiled operation of the economic machine. Moreover, the system was so carefully adjusted and delicately poised that general unemployment over any length of time was a physical impossibility. The Ricardian philosophy became so deeply embedded in the minds of men that it attained the stature of a religious dogma; indeed to deny it was regarded as apostasy. Keynes, that illustrious iconoclast, put the matter succinctly when he commented 'Ricardo conquered England as the Holy Inquisition conquered Spain'.

Closely following on the heels of Malthus and Ricardo was Karl Marx (1818-1883). Marx began as a student of Hegelian philosophy. He drew widely on the works of Smith, Ricardo and Malthus, and he must rank as one of the greatest polemical writers of all time. However, his aims differed from those of his predecessors. Marx abhorred the *status quo* and the doctrine of *laissez-faire* economics with its implicit understanding that the masses would forever live in poverty. Above all he wished to promote change and with this object in view he launched a devastating attack on the whole edifice of capitalism. In 1848 together with Friedrich Engels he issued the Communist manifesto which included the famous lines 'workers of the world unite! You have nothing to lose but your chains'. In 1867 *Das Kapital* was published, this being followed by two posthumous volumes.

One of the topics to which Marx gave extensive consideration was the so-called 'trade cycle', known in America as the 'business cycle'. The main feature of the process, the total duration of which was generally from 8 to 10 years, was an inherent rhythmicity. There was a phase of upswing during which wages, profits and prices would rise and unemployment would drop. This would automatically be followed by a downswing characterised by falling wages, profits and prices and rising unemployment. In other words, just as summer would follow winter so would 'good times' follow 'bad times'. But Marx did not believe that such a state of affairs would continue indefinitely. He saw trade cycles as one of the basic 'inner contradictions' of the capitalist system, and he predicted that the periods of recession would lengthen while those of boom would become progressively shorter. In the 1930's at the time of the Great Depression the economy of most of the world was obstinately stuck at the bottom of the trade cycle and there was massive unemployment. To many at that time it appeared all too clear that, after all, Marx had been an accurate diagnostician and that capitalism was doomed. As a result of the depression the communist cause throughout the world gained large numbers of new adherents, many of the converts emanating from the more intellectual strata of society.

Marx had strong views on population. He did not deny Malthus' basic tenet that population tended to increase at a greater rate than foodstuffs. But to Marx this was merely an artefact of capitalist society which required 'enormous reserves of proletarians' in order to operate its odious system. Under a communist hegemony the situation would be quite different; unemployment would be banished forever and the problem of overpopulation would cease to exist.

We have already noted that Marx fervently desired to promote change. But he also wished to gain converts to his ideological beliefs, and in this sphere he was outstandingly successful, his achievement being on a par with those of Christ and Mahomet. The start was slow. During the latter part of the nineteenth century, although the 'scientific socialism' of Marx and Engels received much attention from intellectuals such as Plekhanov, Martov, Lenin and Trotsky, effective political action did not take place. The great moment came in 1917, when, following the rout of the armies of Tsarist Russia by Imperial Germany in the First World War, the Bolshevik Party led by Lenin seized the reins of government; as a result the world's first communist state came into existence. Had Marx been alive he would undoubtedly have been somewhat surprised at the site of the revolution. He had always predicted that communism would come to power by the overthrow of a blatantly capitalist system, and it was therefore in a way ironic that semi-feudal Russia was the first state to establish this form of rule. Lenin and his colleagues confidently anticipated that the whole of the capitalist world would rapidly crumble and that the communist millennium was about to dawn. However, such a diagnosis proved to be incorrect. Capitalism survived; Lenin died in 1924 and soon after his acolyte Stalin who by now had become the General Secretary of the Communist Party and was the leading figure in the Politburo, proclaimed the doctrine of 'socialism in one country'. So was born the era of the so-called 'Soviet sixth' with defiant Russia, self-sufficient and secure in her own revolution, facing a hostile world.

There were to be no further adherents to the 'socialist camp' until the late 1940's when, after the defeat of Hitlerite Germany in the Second World War, communist governments were established in the Eastern European countries of Poland, Czechoslovakia, Hungary, Rumania, Bulgaria, Yugoslavia and Albania; the Russian zone of Germany, later to become the German Democratic Republic, adopted a similar type of regime. In 1948 the communists under Mao Tse-tung seized power in Mainland China; this followed a protracted civil war at the end of which the Nationalist forces led by Chiang Kai-shek were routed and had to seek asylum in Formosa. Not long after the end of the Second World War a Marxist state was set up in North Korea, and in the mid-1950's, following the conclusion of the Geneva agreements, a similar type of regime was established in North Vietnam under the nationalist leader Ho Chi Minh. The next opening was in Latin America. In 1958 Fidel Castro in Cuba began a victorious campaign against the military regime of Fulgencio Batista. By the early 1960's Cuba was a member of the 'socialist camp' and was receiving military and economic aid from the Soviet Union. Finally in late 1970 a Marxist government under Salvador Allende was elected in Chile on the basis of a free vote. In 1971 the number of people living under Marxist regimes exceeded 1,100 million, this figure being only slightly less than one-third of the earth's total population. Marxists had now overtaken Catholics, those of the latter faith numbering only some 600 million.

*   *   *

Marx did not possess prescience; nor was this quality vouchsafed to Ricardo or Malthus. None of them could foresee the huge technical advances which would accompany the Industrial Revolution and which would enable the world not only to support numbers of people undreamt of in the eighteenth and nineteenth centuries, but also to provide the majority of them with living standards well above a level of mere subsistence. Thus Marx's prognostication that under capitalism 'the rich will become richer and the poor will become poorer' was not borne out by subsequent events. Indeed the reverse was the case, living standards of workers in capitalist countries tending to rise over the years. For example, in Britain even in 1932 at the height of the Great Economic Depression, the real *per capita* income of the worker was more than double that enjoyed when *Das Kapital* was published.

Another rubric of Marxism that proved to be fallacious was that overpopulation was merely a symptom of the overriding disease of capitalism and that it would automatically vanish with the establishment of the communist form of Utopia. He was not in a position to predict the huge rise in numbers in the underdeveloped world, and, could he glimpse the planet of today, he would no doubt be surprised to note that over-population apparently bore no relationship to the type of regime currently in power. Thus this 'strange disease of modern life' has proved to be no respector of political dogma and has obtruded itself in every type of society, whether capitalist as in the greater part of Latin America, nominally socialist as in India or Egypt, militaristic as in Pakistan or Indonesia and communist as in the People's Republic of China. Marx might also be baffled by the different population profiles presented by the world's two major communist powers, the Soviet Union and China. Thus in the USSR—a country of relatively rich resources and still with vast areas which are virtually uninhabited—his classical teaching might still be seen to apply. Certainly the current rulers of the Soviet Union still subscribe to his views, and in the forum of the United Nations the USSR has consistently opposed intervention by that body in the field of world population. On the other hand, a crisis of numbers undoubtedly exists in the People's Republic of China whose present population of over 750 million is expected to double in under 40 years.

Was the crystal ball of Malthus any more reliable than that of Marx? In some respects the answer is definitely in the affirmative. Malthus predicted an imbalance between population and food supplies with widespread famines as one of his 'positive checks'. The immediate course of history appeared to prove him wrong. Massive famines were not a feature of the nineteenth century; nor have they so far been unduly prominent in the twentieth. Indeed until the late 1940's the general world situation with respect to food supplies was gradually improving mainly due to the great advances in agricultural techniques which had followed the Industrial Revolution. But the improvement was not destined to last. In the 1950's and 1960's, following major advances in the practice of medicine which eliminated from large areas of the planet lethal diseases such as malaria, the death rate in the underdeveloped world fell dramatically while at the same time birth rates continued to soar. An imbalance was thus created with population growth far outstripping food supplies. This maladjustment was not to be temporary; instead it has persisted up to the present day, and it has done so in spite of the much acclaimed 'green revolution' in the course of which high yielding strains of wheat and rice have been introduced into the underdeveloped world. Malthus rather than Marx must therefore be credited with the better diagnostic acumen. Could the former be granted a return to earth for a fleeting moment where would his eyes alight?—probably on the slums of Calcutta and Rio de Janeiro or on an average Indian or Latin American village. A wry smile might cross his countenance at his prophetic skill.

*   *   *

Of the economists whose impact was on the twentieth century pride of place must go to John Maynard Keynes (1883-1946). Keynes was a brilliant academic scholar, endowed with a highly original turn of mind. He will be most remembered for the remedies which he proposed to cure the Great Economic Depression, and these he embodied in his classical treatise entitled *The General Theory of Unemployment, Interest and Money* which was published in 1936. But long before this date Keynes had made his mark on contemporary society. In 1919 his best selling tract *The Economic Consequences of the Peace* greatly embarrassed the Whitehall establishment. In this polemic he roundly attacked the decision incorporated in the Treaty of Versailles to extract enormous financial payments in the form of reparations from defeated Germany. Keynes considered such a policy to be both a political crime and an economic blunder of the first magnitude; subsequent events culminating in the rise to power of Adolf Hitler went far to prove the validity of his assumptions. Then in 1925 his essay *The Economic Consequences of Mr Churchill* attracted much attention. In this he attacked the decision of the Government to return to the gold standard at its pre-war parity; again, as the crash of 1931 showed, the verdict of history was in Keynes' favour. The general election of 1929 saw Keynes supporting the Liberal Party under Lloyd George and giving his approval to a policy document entitled *We can Conquer Unemployment*, this recommending amongst other measures, large-scale government investment in public works including roads and housebuilding.

Original thought unfettered by conventional dogma came readily to Keynes. Nowhere were his talents shown to better advantage than during the economic depression of the 1930's. However, in order adequately to appreciate his contributions a short historical digression is first necessary.

The worldwide slump started in 1929 following the Wall Street crash. It continued in an acute form until 1933, but was still manifest in most industrial countries at the beginning of the Second World War. Its most prominent symptom was mass unemployment on a scale never seen before or since. Indeed in 1931, which was described by Arnold Toynbee in his *Survey of International Affairs* as the *annus terribilis*, it was estimated that the total number of unemployed throughout the world exceeded 20 million. Industrialised nations were most affected, 10½ million workers being workless in the USA, 6 million in Germany and over 2½ million in Great Britain. The extent of human misery and degradation was profound and has been graphically described in writings of that period. Moreover, there appeared to be no hope; the situation was rapidly deteriorating and to many it seemed that unemployment had become a permanent feature of the capitalist world.

Dramatic political developments ensued in countries afflicted by high unemployment rates. In the USA the Republican President Herbert Hoover, termed the Great Engineer because of his previous achievements in the economic field, had been elected by a landslide majority in 1928. He was a popular choice and to many he must have appeared a pleasing contrast to his predecessors Harding and Coolidge, whose occupancies of the White House had been far from distinguished. However, Hoover showed himself to be singularly ill-equipped to deal with the slump. He was fixated with the concept of the balanced budget and with the necessity to trim public expenditure in order to achieve this end. In retrospect it would be difficult to imagine any policy more likely to exacerbate rather than to alleviate the existing suffering. The results were predictable; the popularity of the President rapidly declined and by the early 1930's in the wake of a deepening economic crisis he had become a figure of ridicule and detestation. All the ills of the depression were attributed to his administration and to his personal handling of affairs. His name was immortalised in a manner which to him must have been anathema. For on the outskirts of large American cities and also in rural areas there sprang up what came to be known as 'Hoovervilles', these being clusters of nomadic slums housing the unemployed. Here human degradation knew no bounds, and the resemblance of the 'Hoovervilles' to the shanty towns of modern Latin American cities such as Rio de Janeiro, São Paulo, Lima and Caracas is striking indeed.

In Britain a direct result of the slump was the fall of Ramsay MacDonald's Labour Government in 1931. This was succeeded by a National Government headed by MacDonald and Baldwin and dedicated to a defence of the currency. However, such a policy was not to prove successful; mounting pressure on sterling continued and in September of that year Britain went off the gold standard, this time for good. In Germany the repercussions were even more far reaching. Unemployment remained at very high levels, and the deflationary policies pursued by the Chancellor Heinrich Brüning merely exacerbated the situation. In 1932 Brüning resigned, the Weimar republic collapsed and not long afterwards Adolf Hitler was installed in the Reich Chancellary.

How did statesmen, bankers, financiers and businessmen react to the Great Depression? They were completely bewildered by the magnitude and persistence of the slump and particularly by the degree of unemployment which it engendered.* To them the whole process was a nightmare of staggering proportions. After all, had not they been trained in the *laissez-faire* economic doctrines of Adam Smith and particularly of Ricardo? Their minds were closed as if by a straitjacket. The dogma had taught them that supply must equal demand, that the market must be free to operate without state intervention and that budgets must be balanced. Moreover, the whole process was inexorably ruled by the trade cycle. So although times were undoubtedly bad at present, the upswing of the cycle would inevitably occur bringing with it a rise in business activity and a fall in unemployment. All that was necessary was to have patience and to wait. State intervention

* This was the era when the Governor of the Bank of England, Montagu Norman, said of British unemployment 'We have done nothing. There is nothing we can do'.

should be at a minimum except for the necessity of assuring a balanced budget by deflationary policies aimed at a reduction of government expenditure. Indeed as the depression deepened, the cries for balanced national budgets became ever more strident, and in the early 1930's President Hoover went so far as to term it 'the most essential factor to economic recovery'.

However, no improvement was discernable. The economies of industrial nations throughout the world remained obstinately stuck at the bottom of the trade cycle. The promised upswing towards prosperity did not materialise; the incidence of unemployment soared, and as this happened the dichotomy between traditional economic theory on the one hand and the actual pattern of events on the other became ever more glaring. In *The Great Slump* Rees has described the mood of statesmen and officials in these years as one of psychopathic paralysis. And amongst those bearing the brunt of the depression disillusionment and frustration were rife and Marxism profited accordingly.

Keynes had previously proposed remedies to cure the high rate of unemployment in Britain which had been endemic in that country since the end of the First World War. With the advent of the worldwide slump he spearheaded the attack on the traditional belief that depressions were self-correcting. He trumpeted forth the view that mass unemployment was not necessarily a transitory affair which would fall with the upsurge of the trade cycle. On the contrary, it might continue indefinitely and, therefore, positive action by governments was essential in order to stimulate the economy. To Keynes the diagnosis was crystal clear—the immediate cause of the depression was the fall in what he termed effective demand, this being defined as demand backed by money or actual expenditure. But if the cause was clear to him so also was the remedy. The Government should act by increasing the total productive capacity of the economy by stimulating consumption and by raising the level of public investment. In other words, far from adopting policies of *laissez-faire*, governments, through the manipulation of aggregate demand, should actively involve themselves in their countries' economic affairs. If in the course of this process deficit financing occurred and the budget was not balanced this was a matter of little consequence. Full employment was there for the taking, said Keynes, but this could only be achieved provided a sufficient degree of effective demand existed in the economy.

The first major application of the Keynesian philosophy of economics was made by the Roosevelt administration in the USA. This formed an important part of the New Deal programme, and the operation was strikingly successful. There was an immediate fall in unemployment, the detested 'Hoovervilles', symbol of the previous Republican administration, rapidly disappeared, the small businessman was protected from bankruptcy and the disquiet in the agricultural sector of the economy soon faded. Then came the Second World War bringing with it the paramount necessity of maintaining production at the highest possible level. Unemployment vanished from the world's main industrial countries, and Keynes' theories were further vindicated.

In the years following the Second World War virtually all Western countries have practised Keynesian economics either in their original or in a slightly modified form. As a result unemployment has receded and until quite recently a recurrence of the conditions characteristic of the Great Economic Depression seemed unlikely.* The noted American economist Milton Friedman said some years ago 'we are all Keynesians now', and this was not an idle statement. The promise together with the practice of Keynesian economics have until now been seen to be vote catchers for political parties at times of elections. Thus in Britain the 'go' component of the 'stop-go' economic cycle, so familiar to all of us since the end of the Second World War, generally embodies the exercise of Keynesian economics. In the USA in 1964 the Democratic party under Lyndon Johnson proclaimed higher spending as a major item of government policy and won a landslide victory at the polls. In January 1971 the Republican administration of Richard Nixon, anxious for re-election in 1972 and sensing a loss of popular support at the Mid-term Congressional elections, discarded its previous policies of tight money and financial restraint. The President freely admitted that the Federal budget

* At the time of writing unemployment is again high in a number of developed countries including the UK, the USA and Sweden.

would remain in deficit and unashamedly pronounced himself to be a convert to 'Keynesianism'.

The major contribution of Keynes was to demonstrate how the existing resources of a country could be put to their full use. His place in history is undoubtedly that of the successful therapist of economic depressions. Following the Second World War the problems of our planet are different. Until recently unemployment had receded; instead we have had the spectre of inflation which stalks the whole of the Western world and which brings in its train misery and privation especially for those unfortunate enough to have to exist on fixed incomes. Perhaps in an overpopulated world there is and can be no permanent cure for inflation. However, someone of the intellectual calibre of Keynes is urgently required to grapple with the problem. At the time of writing no such figure has appeared on the horizon.

To Keynes production was all important in order to stimulate a flagging economy. Today attention has shifted to the manner in which the economic resources of a nation can be increased. This is the subject of economic growth on which we must now focus our attention.

*   *   *

Economic growth is undoubtedly the catchword of the political vocabulary of the 1970's. Virtually everyone is held in its thrall, politicians, economists, businessmen, scientists, technocrats and trade union officials being especially vociferous advocates of growthmanship. The benefits of economic growth are proclaimed from political platforms throughout the land, and glowing and adulatory references are made to it in party manifestos. In the British general election of 1970 all shades of political opinion—Conservative, Labour, Liberal, Communist and Scottish and Welsh nationalist—were ostentatiously 'for growth'; indeed on this theme the degree of unanimity was striking. Criticisms of growthmanship were not heard during the election campaign; had the voice of dissent been raised it would have been immediately dismissed as a form of eccentricity bordering on subversion. To British politicians seeking re-election in 1970 the definitions had never been more clear. Thus a 'good year' was one in which the growth rate was high, a 'very good year' was one in which it was even higher, while a 'bad year' was one when the rate increased slowly, remained static or, worst of all, tended to fall. Economic growth was seldom out of the news during 1971 for by now the Common Market issue was capturing the headlines. All were for growth— pro-Marketeers and anti-Marketeers alike. Indeed, one of the major reasons why the political dialogue on the issue remained so sterile was the lack of argument on this all-important theme. No anti-growth party had yet emerged in Britain—nor was any such organisation in the offing. Accordingly, much of the rhetoric of party politics was vested with an aura of artificiality.

For is the situation as simple as the conventional wisdom of contemporary politicians would have us believe? Is a high economic growth rate the panacea for the host of social evils which beset us in the latter part of the twentieth century? Is a policy of growthmanship entirely beneficial or can it bring in its train consequences which may be unfortunate and ultimately disastrous for Britain as well as for the rest of the world? Indeed, is the term growthmanship appropriate at all and would not growthmania be a better substitute? These are questions which require to be discussed, but first it is necessary to examine how economic growth rates are measured.

The Gross National Product (GNP) is generally accepted as the best indicator of a nation's growth rate. Samuelson in his textbook *Economics*, defines it as the sum of three main components—the expenditure of individuals on goods and services, the expenditure of governments on goods and services, and the total expenditure on investment. A whole new terminology has recently grown up around the GNP. Thus such terms as 'progress', 'modernisation', 'efficiency', and 'development' are associated in people's minds with a rapidly rising GNP. On the other hand, nations which have 'failed' or are 'losing the race to prosperity' are those in which expansion of the GNP has either been slow or is virtually absent. In current political parlance contemporary Britain falls into the latter category because since the Second World War our economic growth rate has been less rapid than that of other industrialised nations such as the USA, Sweden, Federal Germany, France, Canada and Japan. As a consequence our population has over the past two decades been subjected to a continuous barrage of

political propaganda designed to boost the GNP. Thus successive governments, whether Labour or Conservative, have
exhorted us to work harder, to produce more, to increase our
exports, to be better salesmen and thereby to be truly
'competitive' in the modern world. The oratory has been
impressive from the quantitative point of view, and in the
course of it the barrel of political slogans and clichés has been
drained to the dregs. The effect has been surprisingly small; the
larynx is a poor ally in such a situation, and the British growth
rate has remained obstinately lower than that of most other
Western nations.

The GNP can be related to population; then it becomes the
per capita GNP, and this statistic has been much used by
economists and officials to compare living standards in one
country with those in another. What is the world situation with
respect to *per capita* GNP? The following data, expressed in US
dollars, are based on information provided by the Population
Reference Bureau during 1971.

It is a matter of no surprise to record that the world leader
was the USA with a figure of $3,980. Next came Kuwait
($3,540) where oil revenues presumably boosted the index;
third was Sweden ($2,620) and fourth Switzerland ($2,490).
The Common Market countries boasted high figures for *per
capita* GNP, these ranging from $1,230 in the case of Italy to
$2,170 for Luxembourg; the Scandinavian countries were also
high on the list. The UK's figure was $1,790—14th in world
terms, this being a matter of great chagrin to our politicians. In
the Eastern bloc indices were lower than in the capitalist
countries of the West. The range was from $400 in under-
developed Albania to $1,430 in the much more heavily
industrialised society of the German Democratic Republic. The
USSR had a figure of $1,100, this representing a rise of over
$100 from that quoted by the Bureau in 1970; nevertheless, the
country ranked only 25th in the world list.

Throughout the Third World levels of *per capita* GNP remain
low, and this is one of the major reasons given why such
countries must industrialise themselves with maximum speed.
For instance, in Africa figures ranged from $50 in the case of
Upper Volta and Burundi to $1,020 for Libya, where, as in the
case of Kuwait, much of the national revenue depends on oil. In

Latin America with the notable exceptions of Argentina, Venezuela and Puerto Rico where the index exceeded $800, figures were in the same range as in Africa. In passing it should be noted that the *per capita* GNP in Marxist Cuba ($310) was not dissimilar to that of its capitalist neighbours.

Throughout most of Asia the indices did not differ much from those in Africa and Latin America. The population giants of Asia—China and India—fared badly with respect to *per capita* GNP, the figures being $90 and $100 respectively; the levels for Pakistan and Indonesia were similar. Three Asian countries— Kuwait ($3,540), Israel ($1,360) and Japan ($1,190)—were much more favourably placed than the remainder of the continent, this reflecting their higher degree of industrialisation.

How sensitive an indicator is the GNP, expressed either in gross terms or *per capita*, of the 'progress' or 'achievement' of a nation? It could be cogently argued that it is both rough and imprecise, largely because the statistic sees the world through materialistic eyes and takes little or no cognizance of the aggregate of factors which make up what has been termed the 'quality of life'. For example the GNP gives no indication of the degree of environmental pollution of air, water and land, the ugliness of urban sprawl, the insidious progress of soil erosion, the depletion of the world's finite resources of metals, fossil fuels, timber and water, and the destruction of the earth's ecosystems. But even more important the health of a society, both medical and psychological, has no place in the calculation of the GNP; nor do important spiritual aspects of existence such as satisfaction with one's work, freedom from the fear of starvation or war and the capacity to enjoy leisure. The British economist, E. J. Mishan, is one for whom the GNP holds no magic, and he recently wrote a hard-hitting article in *The Ecologist* in which he stated that the three letters could equally well stand for 'Gross National Pollution'. Mishan discussed in some detail a series of factors all of which are inimical to the quality of life but which nevertheless may contribute to a rise in the GNP. These include the carnage on the roads brought about by the automobile, the decimation of the population by the cigarette—both factors giving rise to increased business for undertakers—creeping urbanisation with destruction of the countryside, the pillage of historic buildings and the construction in their place of ring roads and supermarkets, the felling of trees and whole forests with resultant ecological damage, and the huge proliferation in air travel which with its attendant cacophony is making life almost intolerable for those unfortunate enough to reside near airports.

Other inaccuracies manifest themselves when the GNP is used as the sole determinant of a nation's progress. For example, a comparison of *per capita* figures of the USA and the Soviet Union might lead one to the conclusion that a huge gap in living standards exists between these two countries. This might be so in purely materialistic terms, but there are other factors which must be taken into consideration. One of these is that for almost four decades—in fact ever since Stalin became the dominant figure in the Politburo in the late 1920's—economic development and industrialisation have proceeded apace in the Soviet Union. The harvest became apparent in due course, for in 1957 the first Sputnik was launched, and in late 1970 the Soviet vehicle Lunokhod I was placed on the surface of the moon. These were major landmarks in the space race; they indicated that the technology of the Soviet Union was amongst the most sophisticated on earth. Surely to characterise such a nation on the basis of its *per capita* GNP as 'twenty-fifth on the road to prosperity' would be an egregious fallacy.

An even more serious criticism of the *per capita* GNP is that it provides no indication whatsoever of the ecological damage which citizens of various nations are likely to inflict on Spaceship Earth. Here the major culprits are those inhabiting the developed countries. Thus the index makes no allowance for the fact that the 'average' American will traumatise the planet 100 times more than the average Burmese and that a US citizen will cause a degree of pollution anything between 30 and 300 times greater than that of an Indian.

As mentioned previously virtually all politicians and the great majority of economists vehemently support economic growth. Even governmental ministers charged with responsibility for the environment expound the doctrine, and one of the most ardent advocates of growth in the British political spectrum is Anthony Crosland, who in the latter years of the Labour Government of

1964-1970 held such a position. Writing in his Fabian pamphlet *A Social Democratic Britain* Crosland rejects the case that an increase in economic growth can only lead to a rise in environmental deterioration; he takes this view because he considers that the quality and composition of the growth can be accurately controlled. That such control is feasible has yet to be demonstrated, and certainly the examples of countries such as the USA and Japan in which the quality of life has been seriously eroded by policies of growthmanship do not lend support to Crosland's contention.

The advantages of economic growth have been so loudly trumpeted in recent years that it would be superfluous to discuss them in detail in this essay. High production and high consumption—the grass roots of growthmanship—combine to provide the concept of cornucopean economics in which the veritable horn of plenty is proferred to the world's citizenry in a great variety of forms. All types of luxury goods; shops bursting at the seams with merchandise; gadgets of ever-increasing complexity—these are the stock-in-trade of the last third of the twentieth century. And the propaganda expended by industrial and commercial interests on advertising the 'good life' is nothing short of phenomenal. Indeed it would take a brave man to suggest that existence on our planet would be tolerable without a colour television set in every home, without ever faster, larger and more ornate motor cars, without ubiquitous pesticides and antibiotics to eliminate disease, without educational facilities for all irrespective of their genetic endowment with intelligence, and without the welcoming aircraft ready to whisk the holidaymaker on his annual pilgrimage to warm and exotic lands.

But materialism is only part of the story. Other reasons for promoting economic growth have been adduced and cogently argued. For example, it has been stated that a society is 'happier'—whatever that may mean—in the presence of a surfeit of material goods and that it is unhappy when it is stagnating or is beset by protectionist doctrines. To my knowledge no objective evidence has been produced to substantiate such claims, and the high incidence of criminality, vandalism, psychoneurotic disorders, alcoholism, drug taking and suicide in many developed countries fixated with the dogma of growth-manship might militate against an uncritical acceptance of such a hypothesis.* Political advantages have also been claimed to accrue from high economic growth rates. Thus, throughout the West, growthmanship has been regarded as a means of countering the communist challenge, and of impressing the Third World of the manifold benefits provided by the capitalist system.

*   *   *

The previous discussion might lead one to the conclusion that the attitude of economists to growth is monolithic. This is not entirely true, for there are a few dissenters, two of the most articulate of whom are Galbraith in the USA and Mishan in Great Britain.

John Kenneth Galbraith, at one time the US ambassador to India, is a legendary figure in the economic arena. His *Affluent Society* was a best selling book; it is witty, persuasive and throughout its pages the torch of original thought is held high. To all concerned with contemporary problems of economic growth, inflation and unemployment its perusal is mandatory.

Early in *The Affluent Society* Galbraith enunciated one of his basic tenets, namely that increased production was 'not the final test of social achievement, the solvent of all social ills'. Galbraith was once a Keynesian; now he has become dis-enchanted with the doctrine. He went on to challenge the whole basis of the economics practised since the Second World War. To him modern economists are confined within a straitjacket just as were their predecessors during the Great Economic Depression of the 1930's. Then the straitjacket was the *laissez-faire* tradition of the classical economic school; now it is the new orthodoxy of Keynesianism. Galbraith is profoundly critical of the arts of modern advertising and salesmanship, which in his view are openly and unashamedly conducting a form of brainwashing, and by the endless repetition of the same

* As I pen this chapter it has been announced that the number of murders in the USA during 1970 totalled 15,811.

catch phrase are dulling the critical capacity of the individual and so compelling him to consume more and more. Speaking mainly of the American scene—although his remarks would also be applicable to many other Western countries—Galbraith talked of an atmosphere of 'private opulence and public squalor', contrasting on the one hand the private sector of the economy with its rich gadgetry and manifold appurtenances of a materialist existence, and on the other the public sector with its polluted and festering cities, its grossly undermanned police forces, its ubiquitous litter and its inability to provide adequate educational facilities for its ever-growing numbers of children.

But Galbraith took the argument a stage further. He challenged what is generally known as the *theory of consumer demand* which, by most economists, is accepted as an article of dogmatic faith. Broadly the theory has two main tenets. The first is that the urgency of wants does not diminish appreciably as more and more are satisfied. The second is that the economist is not permitted to question demands which originate in the mind of the consumer; rather must he seek to satisfy these wants irrespective of their nature. To draw an analogy from the practice of medicine the position of the economist is precisely similar to that of the radiologist or of the clinical biochemist in a hospital who, at the request of the medical officer, however junior, is obliged to take the x-ray or to make the appropriate chemical determination. Like the economist, he 'provides a service' and therefore he cannot argue. Indeed he would be most reluctant to do so because frequently the reputation of his department is linked to the number of x-rays which he takes or to the total of biochemical estimations completed within the year.

The economist therefore recognises no categories of need. For him it is just as justifiable to produce a Rolls Royce car for a millionaire as to provide food for the world's starving millions. However, not all economists have subscribed to this viewpoint, and Galbraith was not the first to criticise it. As we have already seen Keynes was always an original thinker unshackled by convention, and in one of his *Essays in Persuasion* written as early as 1931, he stated that human needs might fall into two groups—those such as food and shelter which were absolute and essential to life on this planet, and those which were relative to one's satisfaction and were often requested in order to make one feel superior to others. In Keynes' opinion the latter type of demand might well prove insatiable, and events of the past few decades certainly give resounding support to this conclusion.

Mishan's *Costs of Economic Growth* is a polemical essay written with clarity and élan. Its major aim is to stress the 'diseconomies' or 'social costs' associated with high economic growth rates. Such diseconomies obtrude on every side in the world of the 1970's and include excessive noise, smoke-filled cities, polluted rivers, estuaries and seas, failing amenity, vanishing wildlife and increasingly stressful interpersonal relationships. In a memorable sentence criticising his fellow economists for their preoccupation with expanding the range of goods open to the public, Mishan talks of 'the carpet being unrolled before us by the foot and simultaneously rolled up behind us by the yard'. To Mishan the motor car is an unmitigated disaster; it has wrought tremendous damage in the past and shows no sign of being tamed in the future. Likewise he holds no brief for international air travel on its present scale, and has been a vociferous critic of the decision to build a Third London Airport in any site.

Neither Galbraith nor Mishan hold any brief for the GNP as an index of a nation's health. Nevertheless they recognise that in the present climate of opinion it would be impracticable to bring economic growth to a complete halt. The main thrusts of their argument are that in Western countries much less emphasis should be placed on the production of consumer goods, that the pillage of the earth for non-renewable minerals and metals should markedly decrease, that the desecration of the planet in terms of its environment should cease, and that highly expensive projects undertaken mainly for reasons of prestige and including, for example, the placing of a man on the moon or on Mars and the development of supersonic aircraft such as the Anglo-French Concorde, should immediately be jettisoned. Instead there should occur a marked acceleration of governmental spending and investment on facilities and services specifically designed to improve the aesthetic and spiritual

quality of life on this planet. These would include the control
of pollution, better educational services for all and encouragement of the arts and other forms of recreation. And if in the
course of this reallocation of resources people had to work
slightly less hard and because of this the cherished 40-hour
week—so dear to those of the Protestant ethic—became out-
dated would the heavens really fall? Indeed, would there not be
the strong possibility that by diminishing consumption life
might become more rather than less pleasurable for all?

Galbraith and Mishan do not stand alone. The US economist
Kenneth Boulding has expressed somewhat similar views. In a
classical paper entitled *The Economics of Coming Spaceship
Earth* he picturesquely describes the current scene as being
characteristic of a 'cowboy economy'. Just as the cowboy of
bygone days conjures up a nostalgic vision of the boundless
plains of the American Middle West so our economy of today is
completely open; like the hero of innumerable Western films its
behaviour is 'reckless, exploitative, romantic and violent';
production and consumption are its gods; in its wake come
pollution and resource depletion. But Boulding is convinced
that the cowboy economy cannot last because sooner or later
the constraints imposed by a finite planet will make their
appearance. The successor will be the so-called 'spaceman
economy'. This will be closed; it will discourage production and
consumption, and it will have as a major axiom that the
throughput of the economic system must be minimised rather
than maximised. To modern economists the concept of the
spaceman economy will be revolutionary indeed, just as
unfamiliar as was the doctrine of Keynes to those brought up to
hallow Say's law and bow to Ricardian theory.

The views of Galbraith, Mishan and Boulding appear to
be persuasive because of the overriding consideration that, like
population growth, economic expansion at its current rate
simply cannot continue indefinitely. Just as the horsemen of
the apocalypse will inevitably intervene to stop the population
explosion, so similar constraints will operate in the case of
economic growth. At present growthmanship is assuming an
exponential pattern; in other words it is increasing like
compound interest. What will happen eventually? A good
example is provided by a country such as the USA in which

each year the GNP is increasing by roughly 4 per cent. If present trends continue the American GNP will double six times in a century. Two hundred years from now the figure will be $2,500 trillion (million, million, million) or some 2,500 times the current GNP. The situation will indeed be glorious, for every citizen of that country will then be a millionaire. But the glory will never be attained, for long before that time the earth will have been denuded of its raw materials, its sources of energy will have vanished and its environment will lie in ruins. The cowboy economy will have wrecked the planet, and the pursuit of unlimited growthmanship will have been seen to have produced an insidious yet ultimately fatal disease.*

*   *   *

Economics and population are inextricably intertwined. What is the reaction of economists to the growth of human numbers?

We have noted earlier that the classical exponents of economic theory had strong views on population. Thus Malthus stressed the imbalance which would inevitably occur between population growth and food supplies, and predicted that as a result of this disequilibrium a series of 'positive checks' would operate. Ricardo talked of the inevitable impoverishment of the masses and of the necessity for the vast majority of the population to live on the edge of starvation. Marx ranted against the evils of capitalism, claimed that overpopulation was merely an artefact of that system and stated that it would inevitably disappear once communism held sway.

What of Keynes? Keynesian economics is often associated in the public mind with an expanding population. A typical comment is that of the *Economist* of April 1969 to the effect that 'any good Keynesian should believe that, by and large, more hands mean more prosperity'. But almost certainly the ghost of Keynes would flinch could it read that particular article. For Keynes in his views on population as in so many other respects, was years if not decades ahead of his contemporaries. Thus in 1925 addressing the Liberal Summer

* Some authorities e.g. Forrester (1971) basing his conclusions on computerised data, consider that industrialisation is a greater threat to the planet even than overpopulation (see also Meadows, 1971).

School in his beloved Cambridge, he proclaimed the heretical doctrine that the state should concern itself with the size of the population just as much as with the size of the army and the amount of the budget. It is evident that Keynes' words have fallen on deaf ears, for 47 years later we are still as far as ever from a population policy in Britain in spite of the fact that our numbers have increased dramatically and that the quality of our lives is being constantly eroded as a result of population pressures.

The vast majority of economists of the 1970's hold pro-natalist sentiments; they favour growth of numbers just as they favour a rising GNP. To them the size of the market is all important, because large markets tend to lower the costs of production and thus to increase 'efficiency'. The current British scene in relation to the Common Market represents a well nigh classical example of this approach.

Sheer numbers of people dedicated to production and consumption have undoubtedly played a major part in the British Government's decision to join the Six. Indeed the prospect of belonging to a domestic market of 300 million people has proved irresistible and was the linchpin of the Government's economic case to seek such an association. Small wonder then that in 1971 British growthmen have 'never had it so good'; indeed the influence exerted by growthmanship on British politicians during that year was nothing short of hypnotic. The pro-Marketeers were the most ardent expositors of the dogma. Association with Europe was right for Britain; it would rescue us from our slough of economic despond and although there might be teething troubles before and immediately after our accession to the Market in 1973, these would soon disappear and the vision of the 'good life' would be opened up to everyone in these islands. So economic factors held the stage. But unfortunately it was Boulding's cowboy and not his spaceman economy that was being sought. Therefore, there was no dialogue on the possibility that pollution and environmental degradation might increase and, above all, that the enlarged community—the Europe of the Ten, the 'European Europe' so beloved by Georges Pompidou of France—might by its avowed policies of growthmanship exacerbate the worldwide problem of resource depletion.

But even before the issue of the EEC arose in an acute form there was ample evidence of the reaction of officialdom in Britain to questions of population and economics. A good example is provided in the correspondence between Sir David Renton and the former Prime Minister, Harold Wilson, already referred to in Chapter IX. Renton was attempting to bring pressure on the Government of the day to initiate a population policy for Britain. Wilson rejected his proposals and in so doing fell back on the classical economic concept that, in the UK as elsewhere, more people were required to produce more goods which in turn would be consumed by an even greater number of people! This type of reaction reaches its culmination in strident calls by politicians and economists for more workers to man the labour force. In 1965 such a call was issued in Britain. It was delivered by George Brown (now Lord George-Brown), that archetypal economic expansionist, and it occurred when he was leading the now defunct Department of Economic Affairs. It was Brown's responsibility to introduce the Labour Party's much heralded National Plan; not unexpectedly the latter was strongly orientated towards economic growth and it predicted that by the year 1970 the country would require an additional 100,000 workers!

Economists, like politicians, are therefore pro-people—at least as far as numbers go. But fortunately there are now some faint indications of a split in the monolith, and a notable contribution to this viewpoint is that of Samuelson in his classical and thoroughly admirable textbook *Economics*. Like most of his fellow economists Samuelson is orientated towards growthmanship. He favours big markets and believes that the major reason why the USA and the EEC are so prosperous is that they consist of large free trade areas. But Samuelson has his doubts about current economic policies in relation to population. He cites the famous economic law of 'diminishing returns' which asserts that *after a given point*, the more of one factor of production which is applied to another factor of production, the smaller is the additional output. Malthus was probably the first to invoke this law when he stated that world population would grow faster than food supplies. Samuelson reflects as to whether in developed countries the high level of population is not now threatening societies with diminishing returns, these manifesting themselves by the all-too-familiar features of pollution, destruction of amenity and abolition of privacy. Samuelson did not cite the underdeveloped countries of the Third World as examples of the malign effects of over-population but it would certainly have been appropriate for him to do so. For these are the regions of our planet in which rampant population growth and particularly the huge proliferation of children under the age of 15 years, absorb precious capital and resources and thus prevent their utilisation in raising the living standards of the inhabitants. Indeed the world has moved far from the days of the Industrial Revolution when an increasing population had a tonic effect on the economy. Now the effect is quite different and could perhaps be more accurately described as one of debilitation.

In recent years a few economists, most of them Americans, have espoused opinions more radical than those of Samuelson. Thus Spengler of North Carolina has attacked the well established concept that in developed societies expansion of population is necessary as a means of maintaining a continuously rising GNP. In a memorable aphorism he has warned businessmen that they should 'cease to look on the stork as a bird of good omen'. Wells from Denver, writing in the periodical *Zero Population Growth* during 1971, is a strong advocate of a static rather than a rising population for the USA. He considers the present US market of just over 200 million people to be sufficiently large already, and like Samuelson and Spengler he muses on the disadvantages to the community which will result from population increase. His major tenet is that expanding numbers will inevitably cause land values to soar. But there will be other disadvantages; for example an increasing population with attendant urbanisation and loss to agriculture of arable land, will almost certainly lead to a rise in food prices and will so exacerbate the worldwide problem of inflation.

And so to inflation; like chronic bronchitis, this has been labelled the British disease; certainly it is now rampant in these islands. The cost of living in Britain has been rising throughout the whole of the twentieth century; in 1970 it was six times higher than in 1913 and four times higher than in 1938. But recently the situation has deteriorated rapidly for during 1970 and 1971 the value of money decreased sharply; during this time costs were rising proportionately, those for housing, transport and food being especially affected. Economists unanimously condemn inflation particularly if it is rapid; on the other hand most of them favour an expanding population. Can they have it both ways? One who thinks they cannot is W. M. S. Russell writing in *The Ecologist* during 1971. Russell's article is broad in its historical perspective and international in its compass. One of his main tenets is that a close correlation frequently exists between increasing numbers and the price index, and his overall conclusion is that the growth of population can act as a potent spur to inflation. To economists accustomed to lauding procreative activity Russell's paper will seem heretical and will no doubt be read with scepticism amounting to disbelief.

* * *

I have already commented that as a consequence of the predictions of Malthus and Ricardo economics in the nineteenth century was labelled the 'dismal science'. On the other hand most economists of the twentieth century would have us believe that their subject is basically a cheerful one, being concerned to a large extent with economic growth and with raising the living standards of all peoples. But is this latter view justified and might not the gloomy prophecies of economists of previous generations yet prove to be correct? Indeed could the policies of growthmanship so ardently advocated today be just as deleterious in the long term as were those of *laissez-faire* and balanced budgets which were proclaimed with equal fervour just one generation ago? Only the sweep of history will provide an answer to this question; meanwhile there is already sufficient evidence to merit acute concern.

References

BERLE, A. A., JR. (1968). 'What GNP Doesn't Tell Us'. *Saturday Review,* 31st August.

BOULDING, KENNETH E. (1966). 'The Economics of Coming Spaceship Earth'. In *Environmental Quality in a Growing Economy.* Edited by JARRETT, H. Baltimore, Johns Hopkins Press.

CAIRNCROSS, FRANCIS (1970). 'Galbraith "The goal in this world is not consumption but the use and enjoyment of life" '. *Observer Review*, 22nd November.

CROSSLAND, ANTHONY (1971). *A Social Democratic Britain*. London, Fabian Society.

EHRLICH, PAUL R. and EHRLICH, ANNE (1970). *Population, Resources, Environment*. San Francisco, W. H. Freeman and Co.

FORRESTER, JAY W. (1971). *World Dynamics*. Cambridge, Massachusetts, Wright-Allen Press Inc.

GALBRAITH, JOHN KENNETH (1958). *The Affluent Society*. London, Pelican Books.

H.M. STATIONERY OFFICE (1971). *The United Kingdom and the European Communities*. London.

HARROD, R. F. (1951). *The Life of John Maynard Keynes*. London, Macmillan.

JOHNSON, BRIAN (1971). 'Common Market v. Environment'. *The Ecologist*, 1, No. 11, pp. 10-14.

KEYNES, J. M. (1931). *Essays in Persuasion—Economic Possibilities for our Grandchildren*. London, Macmillan, pp. 365-366.

MILES, RUFUS E., JR. (1970). 'Whose baby is the population problem?'. *Population Bulletin*, 26, No. 1.

MISHAN, E. J. (1967). *The Costs of Economic Growth*. London, Staples Press.

MISHAN, E. J. (1971). 'The economics of hope'. *The Ecologist*, 1, No. 7, pp. 4-7.

ORGANISATION FOR ECONOMIC COOPERATION AND DEVELOPMENT (1971). *Science, Growth and Society—a new perspective*. Paris OECD Publications.

POPULATION REFERENCE BUREAU (1967). 'Soviet Population Theory from Marx to Kosygin'. *Population Bulletin*, 23, No. 4.

POPULATION REFERENCE BUREAU (1971). *World Population Data Sheet*. June.

REES, GORONWY (1970). *The Great Slump—Capitalism in Crisis 1929-1933*. London, Weidenfeld and Nicolson.

RUSSELL, W. M. S. (1971). 'Population and Inflation'. *The Ecologist*, 1, No. 8, pp. 4-8.

SAMUELSON, PAUL A. (1967). *Economics—An Introductory Analysis* (seventh ed.). New York, McGraw-Hill Book Co., Inc.

SPENGLER, JOSEPH J. (1960). 'Population and World economic development'. *Science*, 131, pp. 1497-1502.

STEWART, MICHAEL (1967). *Keynes and after*. London, Pelican Books.

THE ECOLOGIST (1972). 'A Blueprint for Survival', 2, pp. 1-22.

WAGAR, J. ALAN (1970). 'Growth versus the Quality of Life'. *Science*, 168, pp. 1179-1184.

WELLS, JOHN G. (1970). 'The economy doesn't need more people'. *Zero Population Growth*, 2, No. 5.

XIV

THE GLOBAL SPECTRE OF OVERPOPULATION

Sex and the Population Crisis was about human sexuality, birth control and overpopulation. I make no apology for returning to the last mentioned theme for to me it is the supreme dilemma of our time outranking even that posed by the threat of a nuclear holocaust. Overpopulation has dogged our footsteps throughout this book. We have seen it contributing to the pall of pollution over big cities, to the contamination of rivers, lakes and seas, and to the littering of the earth's surface with all manner of debris. We have seen its important role in the depletion of precious and non-renewable resources such as water, metals and fossil fuels, and we have commented upon the fact that the surge of human numbers may be a potent factor in the production of monetary inflation. We have seen the baneful environmental influence exerted by burgeoning automobile ownership, and we have described some of the human tragedies which flow directly from excessive urbanisation. Elsewhere—and there are now numerous texts available—we could read of the likelihood of global famines following the lodestar of overpopulation and of the indiscriminate slaughter of wildlife at the hands of man. And probably most serious of all, we can speculate about the likelihood that overpopulation will be a major factor in producing social conditions conducive to war, particularly in grossly overcrowded areas of the Third World such as India and East Pakistan. Indeed overpopulation, that strange malady of modern life, haunts our every activity. No aspect of human existence remains unsullied by it; there is no escape from it throughout the length and breadth of Spaceship Earth.

The population explosion with its manifold ramifications constitutes the most tangled crisis which our planet has ever faced. And it has certain distinctive features which suggest that, if a solution to the problem is ultimately found, it will be apocalyptic rather than rational in nature. Foremost amongst such features is the fact that questions of population, like those of economic growth, come within the purlieu of politicians who in most parts of the world must stand for re-election every few years. Politicians are singularly ill-equipped to deal with overpopulation. They fear it as an electoral issue; their knowledge of the subject is often meagre; they are captives of a past which insists that more rather than fewer people are required; their preoccupation is with short term policies and they eschew long term planning. As a result there is throughout the world great apathy in the executive branch of government about overpopulation.

How have we arrived at our present predicament? How is it that in a world crammed with technological innovation and in which lunar landings are so commonplace that they generate little but ennui, man is now locked in a titanic struggle with his reproductive processes? What is the origin of our current plague of people? How did it all start?

* * *

Estimations of world population in ancient times must of necessity be very inaccurate. However, it would seem that around 8000 BC the number of people inhabiting the earth was exiguous, probably not exceeding five million. In these far off days man was little more than a predatory animal. He was a nomad wandering ceaselessly; he gathered wild fruits, leaves and roots; he hunted and slaughtered all types of animals, and he killed and ate other men. The earth was a perilous habitat for all. Pestilence and famine were ubiquitous, and great numbers of people succumbed to them; mortality rates at birth and during the first year of life were prodigious, and the reproductive capacity of the human female was taxed to its limit in order to maintain the family, the clan and the tribe.

Then the first great transformation in the world population scene occurred. This affected Neolithic man and is known to historians as the Agricultural Revolution. The revolution is believed to have started in the Middle East in the area of the

Fertile Crescent, the site of modern Iraq and Iran. It spread slowly but inexorably to other parts of the planet reaching Europe by about 1500 BC. Man's horizons were broadening. He started to cultivate the soil and to gather its produce; he became aware of local flora and fauna, and he domesticated animals such as the horse and the ox for his own use. He obtained some respite from continuous hunting; now he tended to become a shepherd or a farmer and to settle in one place for longer periods of time. The Agricultural Revolution markedly changed the pattern of society. People came together in small communities, the forerunners of villages and townships. Wheeled vehicles made their appearance, and there was even time for some of the populace to turn their attention to new and exciting activities such as the mining of copper, tin and iron.

However, the earth was still an inhospitable place in which to dwell. The four famous horsemen of the apocalypse—famine, war, pestilence and death—still obtruded and the toll which they exacted was heavy. Famines remained widespread although on the whole they tended to become less severe as food supplies increased. Infectious diseases, especially bubonic plague and cholera, were prominent marauders and stalked the planet with impunity. There was much procreative activity. Birth rates remained high, but so also did death rates and infantile mortality rates; as a result life expectancy was short by modern standards, averaging only 20 to 25 years.

Following the Agricultural Revolution the world population took an erratic course, although the general trend was towards increasing numbers. When the Romans under Julius Ceasar invaded Britain in 55 BC there were reputed to be between 200 and 300 million people on earth. At the time of the invasion of England by William the Conqueror in 1066 and the compilation of the Domesday Book 20 years later, the world population was still in the same range. However, by 1600 AD with the reign of Elizabeth I drawing to its close, with the crowns of Scotland and England shortly to be united, and with Shakespeare's plays being widely performed throughout Britain, it had risen to some 450 million. However, the road to the increase had been rough and hazardous for amongst other calamities the Black Death had intervened. This was a deadly form of bubonic plague; it is primarily a disease of rodents and is transmitted to man by rat fleas. The disease probably had its origin in the Orient; thence it was transported across Europe by the black rat, killing thousands in its wake. By 1348 it had reached England and by 1350 Scotland. In these days British towns were squalid and insanitary and proved ideal for the activities of the carrier. The mortality rate amongst the people is difficult to compute but was certainly very high; indeed it has been stated that as much as one-third of the population of England perished from the disease. There were further episodes of plague in England in 1361, 1362 and 1369, and even as late as the seventeenth century sporadic outbreaks were still occurring. About this time Nature took a hand, and an epic contest ensued between the black rat and the brown rat. The latter was a sewer dweller; it wished to have no truck with plague fleas and it desired to live apart from man. It was the victor; it finally displaced the black rat and so was instrumental in reducing the incidence of plague.

In the years following 1600 AD the world population slowly crept upwards. By 1700 with William III on the throne of England, European exploitation of the North American continent in full swing, the parliaments of England and Scotland about to be united, and the great military campaigns of the Duke of Marlborough in the offing, numbers probably exceeded 600 million. Then at this stage history took a violent lurch which was to have effects on mankind just as profound as those of the Agricultural Revolution.

The eighteenth century ushered in the age of the Industrial Revolution. The term was not used at that time; indeed it is believed to have been coined as late as the nineteenth century by that doyen of French revolutionaries, Auguste Blanqui. The Industrial Revolution was the era of technological innovation; mercantilism flourished as did free trade; the merchant was king and the entreprenuer the idol of society. It was also associated with a large increase in world population, affecting particularly the industrial countries of the West. Between 1750 and 1850 the population of Europe doubled, this taking place in spite of sustained emigration to the North American continent, where numbers rose from 12 to 60 million in the same period. During the eighteenth and nineteenth centuries populations also increased in the non-industrialised continents of Asia, Africa and Latin America; however, the degree of expansion in these areas was less than that of Europe and North America, and it was not to be until the early 1920's that this situation was to be reversed. By 1800 with George III reigning in Britain, the American colonies irretrievably lost, the French Revolution receding into the background, and the containment of Napoleon Bonaparte becoming the dominant historical theme, the world population stood at over 900 million. By 1850 it had climbed to 1,000 million and by 1900 the total exceeded 1,500 million.

Why was the Industrial Revolution associated with a 'population take off' in the Western world? There has been much argument on this point amongst historians and demographers. Malthus attributed the increase to a rise in the proportion of persons marrying, and to a reduction in the average age of marriage; in his opinion both factors arose directly from the improvement in economic circumstances which had taken place. Others profoundly disagreed with these views, ascribing the rise in population during the eighteenth and nineteenth centuries solely to a fall in the death rate. To such authorities the triumphs of medical practice were paramount, and they extolled particularly the reduction in infantile and maternal mortality rates, the improvement of sanitation and the betterment of nutritional standards.

Up till the latter part of the nineteenth century the two great landmarks in the broad sweep of demography had been the Agricultural and Industrial Revolutions both of which had been associated with a rise in the world population. Now there occurred another quite remarkable change in the pattern of reproductive habits. This came to be known as the demographic transition; it followed in the wake of the Industrial Revolution and it was confined to the nations of the Western world. Up till then such countries had shown a fertility pattern typical of agricultural societies and consisting of high birth rates and high death rates. Now all was changed and there was substituted a pattern characterised by low birth rates and low death rates; such a model has remained up to the present day. What were the reasons behind the demographic transition? As with the population take off associated with the Industrial Revolution they were highly complex and still remain controversial. Perhaps a major factor was that in the industrial as opposed to the agricultural society people came to recognise that children no longer represented an economic bonus. Perhaps the increasing use of methods of birth control first by *coitus interruptus* and later by techniques such as the condom and vaginal cap played a significant role.

As the twentieth century opened the world population exceeded 1,500 million, but by now the contrast between industrialised and non-industrialised nations was becoming more striking. In the former the demographic transition was in full swing, but in the latter this change was not occurring and as a result they continued to show the high birth rates and high death rates characteristic of agricultural societies. In Europe birth rates continued to decline in the 1920's and 1930's during the time of the Great Economic Depression and the mass unemployment with which it was associated. Now demographers warned that the net reproductive rate of the industrialised countries of Western Europe could fall below unity and that such nations might face an actual decline in their populations. In France such a situation actually occurred during the 1930's and panic reigned amongst French politicians to whom the aggressive and revanchist policies being pursued by Nazi Germany constituted a continuous nightmare. In Britain people talked of the 'twilight of parenthood' and books such as *The Economics of a Declining Population* and *The Menace of Underpopulation* were widely read. The UK set up a Royal Commission on Population in 1944 and its findings were presented in 1949. The Commission had obviously been much influenced by the situation in the 1930's; its report was strongly pronatalist in type, recommending amongst other measures an increase in family allowances and raised maternity benefits. Even in 1972 when all thoughts of underpopulation in Britain have finally receded the ghost of this Royal Commission still haunts us as far as our legislation is concerned.

The fears of politicians that the population of Western countries would decline throughout the twentieth century proved to be without foundation. At the end of the Second World War a sharp upward surge in the birth rate took place. This was the so-called 'baby boom', no doubt caused by the return to civilian occupations of large numbers of servicemen. In Western Europe the baby boom had spent itself by the early 1950's, but in the USA its extent and duration were quite remarkable, the American level of fertility in the late 1940's and early 1950's being similar to that encountered 50 years previously before the demographic transition. It was anticipated that following the postwar baby boom birth rates in Western European countries would again fall. However, this was not to be. Society again surprised the demographer; birth rates started to rise in the mid-1950's, and it was not until the middle of the decade of the 1960's that this trend was to be reversed.

During the 1940's the fourth major watershed in the broad historical perspective of population trends took place. This was the Medical Revolution, and the Third World of Asia, Africa and Latin America was its principal stage. The Medical Revolution differed radically from the Agricultural and Industrial Revolutions and even from the demographic transition by the rapidity of its evolution. Within a mere 20 years the treatment of infectious diseases had been fundamentally altered and one by one, the formidable 'captains of the men of death' had been overwhelmed. Malaria was the prime victim of the Medical Revolution, this once great scourge of the planet yielding to drugs such as paludrine, mepacrine and chloroquine together with the direct attack on the mosquito made possible by insecticides such as DDT. In addition, the virulence of numerous diseases such as yellow fever, smallpox, cholera, plague and sleeping sickness was notably attenuated by the introduction of a whole spectrum of new antibiotics and by better techniques of vaccination. The health of women and children improved, and there was a corresponding fall in the infantile mortality rate.

As mentioned previously the effects of the Medical Revolution rapidly became apparent in the Third World. There was now control over death, and in the next few years death rates fell precipitously soon coming to resemble those of the industrialised West. But birth rates were not affected by the

Medical Revolution; indeed they remained stubbornly high, thus retaining the characteristic of an agricultural rather than an industrial type of society. The logic of the imbalance between birth rates and death rates was inescapable, and the result has been the biggest population explosion of all time.

Some examples from the Third World illustrate just how successful was the treatment of infectious diseases. In Mauritius starting in 1946 there was an intensive campaign to eliminate malaria from the island. Over a period of 10 years the infantile mortality rate fell from 150 to 50 per 1,000 live births; the death rate plummeted from 28 to 10 per thousand and the population of the island rose by 40 per cent! Now Mauritius with a population density of 428 persons per square kilometre is one of the most densely settled areas in the world, and during the late 1960's there were riots in the island resulting mainly from this cause.

In Ceylon in 1945 the death rate was 22 per thousand. DDT and antimalarial drugs were widely and successfully used and in less than 10 years the figure dropped to 10 per 1,000; in 1970 it had fallen even further to 8 per 1,000. In 1946 the expectation of life in Ceylon was 43 years; by the end of 1947 it had risen to 52 and by 1956 it stood at 61! Between 1953 and 1969 deaths from malaria in India fell from 800,000 to 10,000 per year; as a result there was a huge surge of numbers which governmental measures have been powerless to influence. In India in 1946 the life expectancy was 27; in the late 1960's it had risen to 40 or even more. Indeed, under present circumstances the average peasant tilling an Asiatic rice field can expect to live to a more advanced age than a tradesman or professional man living in Britain during the eighteenth century!

The decline in the death rate in the Third World was most marked in babies, children and young adults. Now the reckoning has come to these countries for one of their most damaging features is their high proportion of youth. Thus in most of the Third World over 40 per cent of the population is under 15 years of age as compared with 30 per cent in North America and only 25 per cent in Europe. The reproductive potential of these young people is enormous. The great majority of the males will be fertile, their ejaculates containing viable sperm; most of the females will have normal sex glands and will ovulate regularly at least 12 times per year. Furthermore, as will be emphasised later, family planning programmes in such countries have so far had singularly little impact, with the result that the great majority of acts of sexual intercourse will take place without any contraceptive protection. Small wonder therefore that our planet faces a grim prospect as today's seething mass of boys and girls in the Third World attain puberty, come into the reproductive era of life and procreate on a truly prodigious scale.

The excess of youth constitutes a millstone round the neck of the Third World. Education is a case in point. Illiteracy is rife particularly in Africa, where even in a country like Libya which under its new leader Colonel Gadaffi has ambitions to lead the Arab World, the figure stands at 90 per cent. At one time it was thought that increased educational facilities would solve the problem of illiteracy and would open up an exciting new world of opportunity for all. But this view was much too optimistic, and a recent survey published by UNESCO clearly indicated that the juggernaut of population growth was outstripping attempts to raise educational standards with the result that the number of illiterates throughout our planet was actually increasing. But education is by no means the whole story; the economic implications for the Third World of the explosion of youth are also profound. Children are basically dependent; they require schools, houses and health services. As a result a relatively high proportion of the Gross National Product in the countries of the Third World must be deflected to these needs, leaving less available for industrial investment and for improvements in the agricultural sector.

*   *   *

Following the Medical Revolution events moved swiftly. In 1940 the world population was approximately 2,300 million; by 1950 it had reached 2,500 million and by 1960 3,000 million. According to the Population Reference Bureau the world population in mid-1971 was 3,706 million; it was growing at a rate of 2.0 per cent annum, and was likely to double in 35 years.

During 1971 the human family gained 2.4 people per second, 142 per minute, more than 200,000 each day. The total gain for the year was 74 million, the great majority of these in the Third World, India alone contributing over 13 million. During 1971 Paul Ehrlich's 'population bomb' ticked on remorselessly, while Ritchie Calder's celebrated epigram to the effect that 'every time your pulse beats there are two more mouths to be fed' was also apposite. But how can we set the population gain for 1971 in its proper perspective? Perhaps by comparing it with what happened in wars and in national disasters.

The most traumatic events of the twentieth century have undoubtedly been the two world wars. The UN has provided the approximate casualty figures, and states that the First World War killed 10 million people and the Second World War 55 million. Yet the aggregate of these totals is a good deal less than the number added to the planet during 1971. In Britain the First World War was an agonising experience which maimed a generation. Yet the total British dead, amounting to some 750,000 was added to the planet in less than four days during 1971.

Vietnam in South East Asia has been involved in hostilities almost continuously for 30 years—first against the Japanese who were brazenly imperialist, then against the French who attempted to reinstate a colonial regime, and finally as a result of the American intervention. Casualties have been high in both North and South Vietnam, and it might therefore be anticipated that the population growth of the country would be relatively slow as compared with that of other areas of the world. But this has not been the case, for given a continuity of present trends numbers in both North and South Vietnam are likely to double in just over 30 years! Surely no better example can be given of the robustness of the human reproductive system in the face of adversity.

And what of natural disasters? In November 1970 there occurred in East Pakistan a cyclone which is reputed to have killed almost half a million people and which must be regarded as one of the greatest human tragedies of all time. Yet in order to place this event in its national and global perspective it must be remembered, firstly that it took little more than a month for

Pakistan to replenish this loss, and secondly that the number equivalent to that perishing from the cyclone was added to the planet in less than $2\frac{1}{2}$ days during 1971.

                    *   *   *

The central features of the world population crisis can be simply stated. It took until 1830 AD for Spaceship Earth to acquire its first 1,000 million inhabitants. Then the tempo of population growth accelerated and the next 1,000 million people were accumulated between 1830 and 1930. Since then the winds of population change have blown with hurricane force. In the 30 years between 1930 and 1960 the third thousand million was added; the fourth thousand million is likely to be accumulated between 1960 and 1975 and by the year 2000 AD the world total could well reach the 7,000 million mark. These sombre facts are depicted in the accompanying figure.

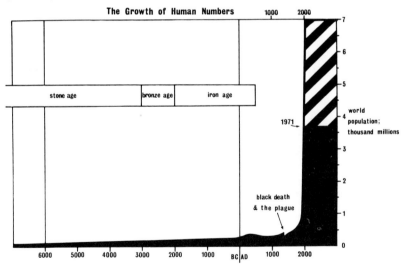

Gruesome forecasts have been made for the twenty-first century and beyond. Most of these will never come to fruition because, in the meantime, the horsemen of the apocalypse will have intervened and population growth will have ceased. Thus it has been stated that the world population could have reached 14,000 million by 2030 AD and 36,000 million by 2070. Another prediction is that some 250 years from now the overall population density of the earth will be similar to that now obtaining in Greater London, and yet another is that in 500 years there will be for each man, woman and child inhabiting the planet only one square metre of space on all the land masses of the earth including Antarctica and the Sahara Desert. Science fiction has surely never been outpointed by such prophecies as these!*

There has been no shortage of rhetoric about the population explosion. Indeed had executive action paralleled the flurry of laryngeal activity the problem might now be well on the way to solution. Instead we have had to be content with a veritable cascade of pronouncements from organisations concerned with overpopulation and from individuals in public positions who are deeply anxious about the future of mankind.

The Department of Economic and Social Affairs at the UN has proclaimed 'the growth of world population in the next 25 years has an importance which transcends economic and social considerations. It is at the very heart of the problem of our existence'. The US Academy of Science has bluntly stated 'either the birth rate of the world must come down or the death rate must go back up'. Lord Caradon, British Representative at the UN under the Labour Government of 1964-1970, commented 'if tackling the problem [of overpopulation] is left too late all our political and economic achievements will be swept away like sandcastles before the advancing tide'. Robert S.

* A much more realistic scenario is provided by Forrester of the Massachusetts Institute of Technology in his admirable book, *World Dynamics*. Forrester is associated with an organisation known as the Club of Rome, and his interpretations of future events are based on the behaviour of a series of computer models of the world scene which make it possible to interrelate factors such as population, capital investment, natural resources, environmental pollution and the quality of life. One of the models shows a continuing rise in population and capital investment. This triggers off a crisis of pollution and as a result the birth rate falls, the death rate rises and food production is depressed. The final outcome is best described as a 'population crash', numbers tumbling from the hypothetical figure of 6,000 million in 2030 AD to less than 1,000 million 20 years later.

MacNamara, President of the World Bank Group, speaking in Indiana in 1969, was convinced that 'the greatest single obstacle to economic and social advancement of the majority of the people of the underdeveloped world is rampant population growth'. Even Presidents had their say, and in 1969 Richard Nixon declared that 'one of the most serious challenges to human destiny in the last third of this century will be the growth of population'. Indeed support for population control has come from the unlikeliest of quarters, as indicated by the aphorism of Senator Gaylord Nelson, famed in the US Congress for his opposition to oral contraceptives, who asserted 'unless something is done about the population explosion, we will be faced with an unprecedented catastrophe of overcrowding, famines, pestilence and war'.

But the population explosion will never be solved by flights of oratorial brilliance. Deeds rather than words must be the order of the day. And in this sphere officialdom moves with leaden feet at a rate comparable to that of a tortoise whose joints are riddled with arthritis. Nineteen seventy four has been designated World Population Year, and in that year the third World Population Conference will be held under the sponsorship of the UN. It is to be greatly welcomed that the conference will be truly global in scope and that it will concern itself with population problems of developed as well as of underdeveloped societies. But what will have happened before the doors of the conference hall are flung open and the delegates file to their appointed stations? The world will have gained a further 200 million people, a figure similar to the present population of the United States and almost four times that of Great Britain!

References

CARR-SAUNDERS, A. M. (1936). *World Population.* Oxford, Clarendon Press.

CIPOLLA, C. M. (1964). *The Economic History of World Population.* London, Penguin Books.

EHRLICH, PAUL R. and EHRLICH, ANNE (1970). *Population, Resources, Environment.* San Francisco, W. H. Freeman and Co.

FLETCHER, T. W. and SINHA, R. P. (1965). 'Population Growth in a Developing Economy'. *J. of Development Studies,* 2, pp. 2-18.

FORRESTER, JAY W. (1971). *World Dynamics.* Cambridge, Massachusetts, Wright-Allen Press Inc.

INTERNATIONAL PLANNED PARENTHOOD FEDERATION (1971). 'Committee meets to plan World Population Conference'. *I.P.P.F. News,* No. 205, March/April.

LORAINE, J. A. (1970). *Sex and the Population Crisis.* London, Heinemann Medical Books.

PARK, C. W. (1965). *The Population Explosion.* London, Heinemann Educational Books.

POPULATION BULLETIN (1962). 'How many people have ever lived on Earth?'. 18, No. 1, February.

POPULATION BULLETIN (1971). 'Man's Population Predicament'. 27, No. 2, April.

POPULATION REFERENCE BUREAU (1971). *World Population Data Sheet.* June.

POPULATION REFERENCE BUREAU (1971). *Population Juggernaut keeps rolling along.* Press Release, Washington.

THE INTERNATIONAL UNION FOR THE SCIENTIFIC STUDY OF THE POPULATION (1971). 'International Population Conference, London 1969'. 1, Dorchester, Henry Ling Ltd.

UNITED NATIONS (1951). *Population Bulletin.* No. 1, December, New York.

WOLFERS, D. (1970). 'Problems of Expanding Populations'. *Nature,* 225, pp. 593-597.

XV

PEOPLE AROUND THE PLANET

Stirrings in Britain

Tuesday 18th May, 1971 gave no appearance of being exceptional. The weather throughout the country happened to be good, the cricket season was in full swing and there were hopes for a long hot summer. Newspaper headlines had as their dominant theme the tragedy of East Pakistan and there was apprehension lest a cholera epidemic would sweep through West Bengal and concentrate particularly on Calcutta. That old faithful the Common Market was prominent; the press bias in favour of Britain joining the Six was as strong as ever and, as before, the citizens of the country remained perplexed by and generally apathetic to the whole issue.

But there was a difference about May 18th, for on the evening of that day a report of a House of Commons Select Committee on Science and Technology was published. The Committee was chaired by Airey Neave, Conservative MP for Abington, and the document was concerned with the population of the United Kingdom. The whole situation was noteworthy because, for the first time in history, a body of *elected* representatives reached the conclusion that their country was overpopulated and requested the Government to take action to remedy the situation.

The report made a number of interesting points. It noted that between mid-1967 and mid-1968 births in the UK exceeded deaths by 292,000—a number roughly equivalent to the present population of cities such as Bradford, Nottingham or Hull. It commented on the avalanche of marriages which had recently taken place in the UK; it mentioned that the average age of marriage was falling thus increasing the span of reproductive life during which a woman was at risk from pregnancy. It emphasised the fact that the average number of children per family stubbornly remained at 2.5 whereas in order to stabilise the population a figure of 2.1 would be necessary. It quoted the former Chief Scientific Adviser to the Government, Sir Solly Zuckerman, who remarked that during the remaining 30 years of the present century provision might have to be made for as many additional people as had been accommodated in the first 70 years. It was fully aware of the fact that population projections must be interpreted with care; nevertheless it had no hesitation in stating 'the cardinal fact remains that all recent projections agree on a substantial and continuing increase in population'. It gave notice of its viewpoint that a high population density can adversely affect the quality of life, and it quoted freely in this context from a recent statement by the British Conservation Society entitled *Why Britain Needs a Population Policy*. Most important of all, it urged the setting up of a Special Office to report directly to the Prime Minister on population trends and their consequences.

The report had a varied press reception. *The Times* was antagonistic; but then it generally is whenever the concept of a population policy is mooted. The *Daily Telegraph* talked of 'Malthus in Committee' and described the report as imprecise and confused; *Nature* took a similar attitude emphasising the sociological uncertainties associated with population projections. But there was some support from other quarters. *The Guardian* praised the Committee for suggesting that the Government should be looking to the future and should be planning for 20 years ahead, while the *Lancet* agreed with the Committee that population growth in association with burgeoning technology was ruining the environment and was making life less and less tolerable for everyone inhabiting these islands.

How did the Government respond to the Select Committee's Report? Was there a clarion call for action? Did we witness the radical dawn of a population policy? Was the Special Office set up or was there at least agreement to appoint a Royal Commission? There were none of these things. The Government's reply came in July and it was profoundly disappointing. The timeworn clichés returned; a population policy was 'complex and controversial': such a question required 'careful and dispassionate analysis in depth'; 'gaps in our knowledge must be filled in' etc. The end result was the appointment of a panel of experts with 'broad and relevant experience', and with the 'necessary qualities' for objective assessment. Where one might rightly have expected an elephant the progeny turned out to be a mouse!

* * *

A population census was held in the UK during 1971. It disclosed that the population of the country had increased by more than 2½ million in the previous 10 years and now stood at a figure of 55,346,551; the main increase was in England but numbers in Wales, Scotland and Northern Ireland also rose. An extremely interesting facet of the census—and one which is diametrically opposed to that prevailing in the Third World— was the decline in population of the big cities, with a corresponding increase in the rural areas. Thus numbers in Greater London fell by over 600,000 in the 10-year period, the figure for 1971 being just under 7.4 million. Glasgow dropped from over a million to 896,958, Manchester from 661,791 to 541,468 and my native Edinburgh from 467,650 to 453,422.

The current birth rate of the UK is 16.3 per 1,000, the death rate 11.3 per 1,000 and the infantile mortality rate 18.6 per 1,000. Between 1968 and 1969 numbers grew by 0.45 per cent. The population projection for the year 2000 AD is 66.5 million, representing an increase of 20 per cent over the figure in 1971.* I have already emphasised (see Chapter IX) that the UK is the eighth most densely populated country in the world, England and Wales being second only to Formosa.

Traditionally the question of population has been given short shrift by British politicians as by their counterparts in other countries. The subject has been virtually taboo because of the widely held opinion that discussion of it will cause embarrassment, exacerbate religious differences and, worst of all, prove electorally damaging. At party conferences population has not featured; the Conservative Party has never debated it, and the Labour Party last discussed birth control in 1927! Overpopulation of the UK has not been an issue at any of the 19

* The projection for 2010 AD is 70.9 million.

general elections held in our country between 1900 and 1970. When the moderately liberal Abortion Act reached the statute book in 1967 it was expressedly stated that, of course, it formed no part of a population policy for Britain. Two MP's, one Labour and one Conservative, deserve much credit for their forward looking approach to population problems in the UK. The Labour representative is Douglas Houghton, Chairman of the Parliamentary Party and the member for Sowerby. Houghton, speaking in 1968, made a highly courageous statement. He equated large families with social irresponsibility and stated that in the future such procreative behaviour would come to be regarded as a form of social delinquency. As might be anticipated Houghton's statement had a mixed reception. Harold Wilson hastened to proclaim that Houghton's opinions were purely personal and did not represent the view of the Labour Party. Some of the press was antagonistic but, surprisingly enough, much of the comment was not unfavourable.

But in the field of population in the UK the pace-setter has undoubtedly been Sir David Renton, Conservative MP for Huntingdonshire. As long ago as 1967 Renton was in communication with the then Prime Minister, Harold Wilson, and the correspondence between the two men was published in the periodical *New Horizon*. Unfortunately the exchange of letters appears to have had little effect on Wilson because in the 836 pages of his recent book *The Labour Government 1964-70; a personal record*, neither the dialogue with Renton nor the general theme of population receives any attention whatsoever. Renton argued strongly for governmental support in discouraging the birth of large families and advocated the introduction of a population policy for the UK. Wilson's reply was discouraging. He stressed the element of personal choice in the number of children born, hesitated to involve the Government in a matter of such delicacy and doubted the ability of the legislative machine to influence population trends. But in spite of this setback Renton persisted. In 1968 he tabled an all party motion in the House of Commons calling on the Government to establish 'permanent and adequate machinery' to examine the difficulties associated with Britain's rising population. The outcome of the motion was surprisingly successful, 322 out of the total of 630 MP's attaching their signatures. During 1970 Renton gave evidence to the Select Committee on Science and Technology whose recommendations were discussed earlier in this chapter, and it is obvious from the report that his opinions carried considerable weight.

However, there remain many MP's, some of considerable seniority, to whom the views of Renton and Houghton are anathema. Thus Sir Keith Joseph, Secretary of State for Social Services, announcing in the House of Commons on 23rd February, 1971 an expansion of government grants towards family planning, advised Renton 'not to delude himself' into thinking that this had anything to do with a population policy for Britain. Reginald Maudling, Home Secretary, was quoted in the press as saying that a population policy for Britain would necessitate the presence of a 'policeman in every bedroom', while Peter Walker, Minister for the Environment, interviewed on television as recently as June, 1971, admitted the presence of a world population problem but denied that this applied to our own country.

What form would a population policy for Britain take? Here opinions are strongly divided. Some believe that a satisfactory slowing of population growth leading to a stabilisation of numbers would be achieved entirely through family planning; proponents of this viewpoint demand that facilities in this specialty be greatly increased and that they should be provided free within the framework of the National Health Service. However, another school of thought, while agreeing that family planning facilities should be extended, are very doubtful whether this activity *per se* will produce a significant effect on the population growth of these islands. Chapter XVII examines in more detail the pros and cons of these conflicting views.

Much of the debate centres around the problem of an optimum population for Britain. How is this defined? What is the magic number? These questions are exceedingly complex and so far no one has provided satisfactory answers to them. For the concept of optimum populations must take into account not only economic and nutritional factors but metaphysical parameters such as the 'quality of human life' and the 'degree of human happiness', and these are almost impossible to quantify. Some have equated an optimum population with 'the carrying capacity of the land', in other words the ability of the land to feed its people. Others regard the optimum population to have been exceeded when an imbalance exists between population density and available resources, and when a steady deterioration of the environment is taking place. This school of thought places much stress on what they term 'the carrying capacity of the environment', and emphasises the necessity for appraising the situation in the long as well as in the short term. Southwick, a noted British biologist, shares this viewpoint and has defined an optimal population for man as 'the maximum which can be maintained indefinitely without detriment to the health of individuals from pollution or from social or nutritional stress'.

Using criteria proposed by Southwick and others there can be little doubt that Britain is already overcrowded, and this was certainly the viewpoint taken by the great majority of the delegates who attended a symposium held on this subject in London in 1969 under the aegis of the Institute of Biology. But what is the appropriate number for the country? Here opinions are highly divergent. John Stuart Mill, writing 100 years ago, opted for 20 million; Malthus would have regarded this as excessive; so now does Paul Ehrlich. Sir Joseph Hutchinson, speaking as an agriculturalist, suggested an optimal figure of 40 million but said that this might take two centuries to achieve. Richard Crossman, giving evidence before the Select Committee on Science and Technology, opined that the archetype for the optimal population for Britain was best left in Heaven, while the prominent demographer, D. V. Glass, considered that it was impracticable to determine an optimum population for this country.

It is obvious that controversy on the theme of an optimal population for Britain is widespread and this situation is likely to persist for the forseeable future. But if one believes, as I do, that Britain is already overcrowded, what measures should the Government take to remedy the situation and thereby set an example to the rest of the world? As will be seen in Chapter XVII it has a formidable array of options at its disposal.

Apathetic Common Market

The great social issues which reverberated throughout Britain in the 1960's—the liberalisation of the abortion law, the provision of contraceptives for the unmarried, the improvement of the lot of the homosexual—left the countries of the European Economic Community largely unruffled. High economic growth rates and increasing material prosperity were the main concerns of the Six. The influence of the Roman Catholic Church remained all-pervasive. Discussion on population control was taboo, and even family planning made little impact; abortion laws remained amongst the most illiberal in the world, and, as a consequence, illegal abortion was rampant. Indeed in France the incidence of induced abortions was estimated to be half that of live births, while in Italy a one-to-one ratio was believed to prevail.

It is unfortunate that no dialogue on population exists within the Common Market for three of the participating countries— Belgium, the Netherlands and Federal Germany—are amongst the most densely settled in the world. Belgium has a population density of 316 persons per square kilometre; it is second only to Formosa and is on a par with South Korea. The Netherlands at 315 persons per square kilometre holds fourth place, while Federal Germany (237 persons per square kilometre) comes seventh in the world list. By the criteria applied to Britain and discussed in the preceding section of this chapter these countries must be regarded as considerably overpopulated. France (population density 92 persons per square kilometre), Italy (177 per square kilometre) and Luxembourg (130 per square kilometre) are less heavily settled, but here too the quality of life is being eroded through a mixture of affluence and population growth.

Birth rates throughout the Common Market countries remain relatively low. In 1971 they ranged from 13.5 per 1,000 population per year for Luxembourg to 19.2 per 1,000 for the Netherlands; death rates were a good deal lower than birth rates, ranging from 8.4 per 1,000 in the Netherlands to 12.6 per 1,000 in Luxembourg. Infantile mortality rates were also low, that for the Netherlands (13.2 per 1,000 live births) being second in world terms only to that of Sweden.

The low birth rates found in the Six are of considerable interest in view of the potent influence still exerted by the Roman Catholic Church in these countries. This Church is, of course, notoriously pronatalist in its attitudes and the technique of contraception which it continues to recommend—the so-called rhythm method—is one of the least reliable of those available. In spite of their avowed Catholicism the countries of the EEC experienced the demographic transition many years ago; since then their pattern of fertility consisting of low birth rates and low death rates has remained virtually unchanged. The Catholic hierarchy have been quite unable to reverse this trend, and even *Humanae Vitae*, that controversial Papal Encyclical of 1968, came and went leaving scarcely a ripple on the reproductive pool.

Any population policies which do exist within the Six have a pronatalist flavour. France is the prime example, for during the Presidency of Charles de Gaulle men and women were urged to procreate to the maximum of their capacity, and it was stated that the country could readily support 100 million people instead of its current 50 million. Family allowances in France are amongst the most generous in the world; they were increased in 1967 and now absorb almost 5 per cent of the national income. In Belgium, despite its high population density, there may soon be a drive for more people. In recent years the Belgian birth rate has tended to decline, and already the press of that country is bemoaning the dire consequences which are likely to ensue to the labour force as a result of this reduction.

The population of the Netherlands is growing at the rate of 1.1 per cent per year, and if present trends continue numbers could double in just over 60 years. Dutchmen of the future therefore face an awesome prospect in terms of overcrowding. Yet the Dutch Government of the day has as yet no official population policy, although it gives a certain amount of support to family planning activities and is now believed to be prepared to tolerate sex education in schools.

Adolf Hitler had no doubt that the country over which he ruled was overpopulated and this was one of the major reasons behind his strident cry for 'lebensraum'. His policy was to drive to the east—his famous *drang nach osten*—and with this aim in view he seized Austria and Czechoslovakia, invaded Poland in 1939 and thus started the Second World War. His continuing search for lebensraum led him to launch his ill fated 'operation Barbarossa' against the Soviet Union in the summer of 1941. But now he met an opponent of comparable stature, and his expansionist dreams eventually crashed in ruins. The Federal German Republic, which rose like a Phoenix from the ashes of the Third Reich, is now more densely populated than was the Nazi Germany of the 1930's. Indeed its total population of almost 59 million is not far short of the figure for the undivided country before the outbreak of the Second World War. However, the Federal Government in Bonn does not apparently consider the country to be overpopulated, has no official population policy and, although not antagonistic to family planning and permitting sex education in schools, it provides little financial support for either activity.

How will Britain's population be affected if she joins the EEC? The situation is highly enigmatic; it is largely ignored by politicians irrespective of whether they are pro- or anti-Marketeers, and in the 'Great National Debate' on the issue which was expected by some politicians to be a feature of the British scene in 1971, the voice of the demographer did not rise above a whisper. However, matters of population may well become of importance; for Article 48 of the Treaty of Rome permits the 'free migration of labour' within the EEC, and Britain, when she joins the Community, will obviously be expected to participate in such movements. What will be their effect? Some would argue that the result might be a mass exodus of skilled workers from Britain to Federal Germany which, with its high economic growth rate, has already acted as a magnet to other less prosperous areas of the Community notably Southern Italy. On the other hand, if as is so fervently desired by dedicated Europeans in Britain, our economic growth rate rises dramatically as a result of accession to the Market might the reverse not occur and might there not then be a flow of foreign nationals from Europe to the UK thus exacerbating our already grave population problem? The answer is in the lap of the gods. The future is as murky as in the case of the long term effects of pesticides, of nerve gases dumped in the Atlantic Ocean and of supersonic transport such as the Anglo-French Concorde. However, one can be sure that whatever the politicians of today proclaim, history will have the last laugh.

Perspectives in Eastern Europe

As mentioned in Chapter XIII classical Marxists regard over-population as an artefact of capitalist society which will vanish immediately the Utopian system envisaged under communism is established. For this reason official concern with over-population and rapid population growth is proscribed in Eastern Europe. Nevertheless, some of the countries in that part of the world have birth rates as low as anywhere on earth. How has this favourable situation come about?

Liberal abortion laws, and in particular the ability to perform an abortion for social as well as for purely medical and eugenic reasons, have undoubtedly been important. So has the wide-spread use of the relatively simple suction technique for abortion instead of the more laborious procedure of 'dilatation and curettage' practised until very recently throughout the Western world. In Hungary where the law is very liberal a woman during the first three months of pregnancy has the right to demand an abortion and the doctor cannot refuse to perform the operation. The birth rate in Hungary in 1971 was 15.0 per 1,000, the death rate 11.3 per 1,000; the population of the country was growing at the very slow annual rate of 0.4 per cent and would not double for 175 years. In Poland where a communist government rules a predominantly Catholic popula-tion, an abortion can be authorised by a certificate from a single physician; generally a 'difficult social situation', however defined, would be adequate grounds for a legal abortion. In Czechoslovakia a variety of social and medical indications make it relatively easy to obtain an abortion while the situation in Yugoslavia is not dissimilar. Abortion laws in the German Democratic Republic were restrictionist until the mid-1960's but since then have become much more liberal.

Prior to 1966 abortion laws in Rumania were liberal and the birth rate (14.3 per 1,000) was amongst the lowest in Europe.

Then the Government abruptly decided that the country was underpopulated and let it be known that it was alarmed lest the Rumanian nation would vanish from the face of the earth. Draconian legislation followed rapidly. Legal abortion was restricted to women over 45 years of age and to mothers supporting four or more living children; taxation on childless couples was increased, contraception was banned, powerful propaganda was mounted in favour of large families, and divorce was made more difficult. The result was predictable. During the first three months of 1968 the birth rate soared to 32.8 per 1,000, and by mid-1971 at 23.3 per 1,000 it was still high by Eastern European standards. The panic spread over the border and the Bulgarian government showed a similar but less drastic reaction. Since the late 1950's the Bulgarian abortion law had been liberal; however in 1968 there was alarm at the falling birth rate and the Government increased family allowances and made abortions more difficult to obtain. Since then the Bulgarian birth rate has increased *pari passu* with a fall in the number of legal abortions. Albania is unique in Europe. It has not yet experienced the demographic transition and it still has the high birth rates and low death rates characteristic of the Third World. Indeed if present trends persist the Albanian population could well double in as short a time as 26 years.

In Soviet Union the official policy towards abortion has oscillated between the extremes of liberalism and restrictionism. In 1920 after the Revolution with Lenin at the helm of state it was liberal and it remained so until the mid-1930's when during Stalin's hegemony and at the height of the show trials and purges, it became restrictionist. This situation persisted until the mid-1950's when in common with other countries of the Eastern bloc the USSR reverted to a liberal law; this has continued to operate up to the present time.

In mid-1971 the population of the Soviet Union was 245 million. Its birth rate stood at 17.0 per 1,000 and its death rate 8.1 per 1,000; between 1963 and 1971 the population grew at just over 1 per cent per annum and if this state of affairs continued it would double in some 70 years. However, birth rates varied greatly on a regional basis, and in the late 1960's some Soviet demographers were expressing anxiety about falling birth rates especially in European Russia. It remains to be seen whether the Soviet government will feel itself obliged to copy the example of its Rumanian and Bulgarian neighbours by attempting to stimulate the birth rate by a mixture of fiscal and social measures.

Rumblings in the USA

In contrast to the Common Market countries and the nations of Eastern Europe there is now a brisk dialogue in the USA on matters of population. As yet the country has no official population policy. However, the question is increasingly being asked whether continuing population growth will be good or bad for the nation. The seriousness with which the situation is viewed in high quarters is reflected in the fact that the Congress, acting at the behest of the President, recently established a Commission under the chairmanship of John D. Rockefeller 3rd with a remit to examine the probable course of population growth up to the year 2000 AD, and to attempt to assess the effect which this would have on the American economy, on resources and on the environment. The first report from the Commission appeared in March 1971; it was a model of its kind and is obligatory reading for those with an interest in this field.

The US decennial census of 1970 stimulated controversy and produced much fascinating information. The total population including Americans overseas was 204,765,770, and numbers were growing at a rate just exceeding 1 per cent per annum. Each day in the USA some 10,000 babies were born, 5,000 citizens died and 1,000 more people entered the country than left it. The net daily increase was 6,000 thus amounting to 2 million in one year.

An important point brought to light by the census was that between 1960 and 1968 the fertility rate amongst American females in the age range 15-44 declined, falling from 118 to 85.7 births per 1,000 women per year. Because of this finding the Census Bureau was forced to alter its population projections for the beginning of the twenty-first century. Whereas in 1967 the range for the country's population for 2000 AD had been from 281 million to 360 million, now the limits were revised downwards and were from 266 to 321 million. The salient point about both projections is, of course, the huge spread of the figures varying in one case over a range of 80 million and in the other of over 60 million. No better example can be found of the difficulties faced by demographers in predicting the reproductive habits of their citizenry.

However, on one point all US demographers were agreed, namely that there would be a marked rise in the population of the country by the end of the century. This will proceed with the inevitability of a Greek tragedy because the USA, like other nations, is a prisoner of its reproductive past and of the immutable law that population growth generates its own momentum. The ensuing decades will be dominated by the spectre of the baby boom which took place after the Second World War and as a result of which great numbers of young women are now reaching the prime of their reproductive life. Thus in 1975 there will be 5½ million more people between the ages of 20 and 29 than at present, and by 1985 a further 5½ million will have been added. Accordingly, if there were an immediate reduction in the US fertility rate to 2.1 children per woman—the so-called 'replacement level'—it would still take approximately 70 years for the population of the country to become stationary. Another factor that must be recognised is that small differences in family size produce large changes in population. Thus, if in the USA immigration continued at its present rate and families each had an average of two children the population in the year 2000 AD would be 266 million. However, if these same families opted for 3 children the total would leap to 321 million!

Apart from the census there were other notable events in the US population calendar of 1970. Family planning finally received the accolade of respectability and a Bill passed through the Congress authorising the expenditure of $382 million over a three-year period to make family planning available to women lacking such services, to train doctors in the specialty of birth control, and to encourage research in the general area of population. Abortion also had a reasonably good year during 1970. Certain states moved towards a liberalisation of their laws, the most outstanding example being New York where a restrictionist law dating back for 140 years and permitting abortion only to save the life of a pregnant woman was expunged from the statute book, and in its place was substituted a really liberal law authorising virtually all abortions within the first 24 weeks of pregnancy. However, some states in the Union continue to operate extremely illiberal laws with respect to the termination of pregnancy. A good example is Wisconsin which recently introduced bills aimed to outlaw all abortions. The official Family of the Year in Wisconsin had 12 members and in that state contraception for unmarried women remains illegal!

Perhaps the most outstanding feature of the early 1970's in the USA has been the expansion of an organisation known as Zero Population Growth (ZPG). Adherents to ZPG wish to see population growth stop immediately; they call for a dramatic fall in the birth rate; they laud the small family and campaign under the slogan 'stop at two'. By late 1970 ZPG boasted over 25,000 members in some 425 'chapters' spread throughout the nation. Already it had found a natural bedfellow in the Women's Liberation Movement and the two organisations were seen to be collaborating in a number of fields of related interest.

But the concept of ZPG did not go unscathed. The computer intervened and demonstrated that in order to produce an immediate cessation of population growth in the USA, the two child family would still be too large and instead parents would have to limit their reproductive capacity to one offspring. Bizarre effects would inevitably follow the institution of ZPG. In 10 years time the population under the age of 10 would be only 43 per cent of what it was today; as a result the whole educational system would be in danger of collapse and the labour force would be decimated. Furthermore, in order to maintain ZPG in later generations there would have to be wild oscillations in completed family size; indeed the whole pattern of fertility would come to resemble that of a concertina subject to alternate phases to expansion and contraction. ZPG, like homosexuality, pesticides, Concorde, sex education in schools and the fluoridation of water supplies is a highly emotive theme and arguments about it will rage for years to come. Many sections of the community will become enmeshed in its intricacies and eventually even politicians will be unable to ignore it.

Another major point of controversy in the USA in the early 1970's has been the relationship between population growth on the one hand and environmental pollution on the other. In the 1960's it had been generally assumed that the two factors were closely interwoven. Ehlrich argued strongly for this viewpoint in *The Population Bomb*: so did I in *Sex and the Population Crisis*, while Garrett Harden in his classical article entitled *The Tragedy of the Commons* went so far as to state that 'the pollution problem is a consequence of overpopulation'.

Now a different dogma was proclaimed. Ansley Coale stated that population growth had little to do with environmental degradation and that economic factors particularly the *per capita* increase in production were much more important in threatening the quality of American life. Wattenberry described Lake Erie and the Hudson and Potomac Rivers as 'ecological slums' and declared that if the US population did not increase by a single individual such waterways would remain in the same condition. The prestigious demographer, Philip Hauser, stated that if the aims of ZPG were immediately attained environmental pollution would still increase, and he proceeded to castigate what he termed 'angry ecologists' for merely 'using' the population explosion to obtain support for programmes designed to control environmental pollution.

But the counter attack was not long delayed. Ehrlich and Holdren in an article the content of which I found persuasive, argued that population growth had a 'disproportionate negative effect' on the environment with the result that a relatively small increase in numbers was capable of producing a large increase in the degree of pollution. Also Ehrlich, writing in the American *Saturday Review*, talked of '1,000 people discharging their raw sewage into a river with impunity but 10,000 people hopelessly polluting it'.

In the USA the arguments about population and pollution are tossed around in the literature like a shuttlecock on the badminton court. This is a healthy sign, and who would have it otherwise in a country which contains so many acknowledged experts and when the issues under debate are of such labyrinthine complexity? The introduction of a population policy within the USA could have far reaching effects for the rest of the world—indeed some might go so far as to say that the only hope for mankind depends on the emergence of such a policy. Will there be action in this field or will the timeworn technique of the 'intricate defensive' be so subtle that all efforts in this direction will be frustrated?

Paradoxical Japan

In mid-1971 the Japanese population was nearing 105 million; the birth rate was 18 per 1,000, the death rate only 7 per 1,000, and numbers were rising by just over 1 per cent per year. Early in the twenty-first century the population could be expected to reach a figure of 130 million; thereafter, if present demographic trends persisted, a decline in numbers could be expected. The current population density of Japan is 277 persons per square kilometre, placing the country fifth in the world list after Formosa, Belgium, South Korea and the Netherlands. But the density figure manifestly understates the case, for Japan far exceeds any other nation in the world for its numbers per habitable area of land. This is the reason why to Western eyes the congestion and overcrowding in Japan are truly phenomenal.

Japan has had a turbulent population history during the twentieth century. Birth rates were high up to the early 1920's; then a demographic transition from a predominantly agricultural to an industrial society took place, and thereafter birth rates started to decline. But the Japanese Government of the 1930's was militaristic, imperialist and strongly pronatalist. It backed procreation by rhetoric and by fiscal measures with the result that the fall in the birth rate was halted. Then after the Second World War the country experienced a marked baby boom due to the return home of servicemen and civilians from overseas.

By the late 1940's the population situation in Japan had become desperate. The country had been decisively defeated in war, and stemming from her defeat, she had been forced to witness the complete disintegration of her so-called South East

Asia Co-Prosperity Sphere which had been designed to provide an outlet for her expanding population. Now only the islands were left and the country was literally crammed with people. The Government was forced to take action, and in 1948 the Japanese Diet enacted its renowned Eugenic Protection Law which legalised abortion and sterilisation and which is generally given the credit for what has been described as Japan's 'population miracle'. The effect of the law on reproductive activity was striking. The number of legal abortions rose from 246,000 in 1949 to over a million in 1955, and between 1948 and 1959 it is estimated the number of female sterilisations performed topped the million mark; as might be expected the birth rate showed the opposite trend, plummeting from 34 per 1,000 in 1948 to 18 per 1,000 in 1959. What of Japan in the 1970's? There have been qualitative changes from the situation reigning 20 years ago. Female sterilisations, usually by tubal ligation, remain popular; family planning is on the increase although, surprisingly enough, oral contraceptives are still illegal as a method of birth control. On the other hand, the number of legal abortions is now tending to diminish.

In 1969 the Japanese Prime Minister, Eisaku Sato, surprised the world when he publicly proclaimed that his country should *increase* its birth rate. He made this statement as the result of the recommendations of a body known as the Population Problems Inquiry Council. The latter contained a number of demographers and it was concerned about a statistic known as the net reproductive rate, this providing a rough measure of the extent to which the female population in the reproductive era of life is replenishing itself with female babies. If the net reproductive rate remains at unity the population is likely to become stationary in the course of one generation. However, if the rate falls below unity numbers will eventually begin to decrease. Japan's net reproductive rate (0.9-1.0) is one of the lowest in the world, and the level has remained low since the late 1950's. The Population Council took the view that the continuation of this trend for a prolonged period of time would result in a severe distortion of the age composition of the population and—even more important to a country which boasts one of the highest economic growth rates in the world—there would eventually be a marked depletion of the labour force. The Council therefore proposed that the net reproductive rate in Japan should return to unity as rapidly as possible. To achieve this end it recommended that social conditions in the country should be improved in the hope that married couples would voluntarily decide to have more children!

The Japanese situation constitutes a classical example of the dilemma facing the world in the latter part of the twentieth century. Unfortunately the circle cannot be squared. For if the population is allowed to increase and the economic growth rate remains at its present high level, there will be more environmental pollution, more depletion of natural resources and a steady erosion of life's quality. Such a sequence of events is inevitable, and will follow just as naturally as night follows day, as one season follows another and as the growing plant seeks the sunshine.

Australia is Pro-People

The kaleidoscope of world politics and economics is in a continuous state of flux. Now Japan and Australia, once bitter enemies, are moving together in both spheres, and at present Japan, a nation very poor in indigenous resources, is the major importer of Australia's raw materials. Yet with respect to population the situation of the two countries could scarcely be more divergent.

In 1971 the Australian population stood at 12.8 million; the birth rate was 20 per 1,000, the death rate 9.1 per 1,000; the population was growing at a rate of 1.9 per cent annually and was likely to double itself in under 40 years. The population density of Australia (2 persons per square kilometre of land) is one of the lowest in the world, only Botswana, French Guiana, Libya, Mauretania, Mongolia and the Spanish Sahara being less densely settled. Family planning is extensively practised in Australia and the country has the highest *per capita* use of the Pill in the world. During 1970 abortion laws in South Australia were liberalised but elsewhere in the country they remain restrictionist.

Australian politicians desperately want growth—in economic terms and even more in terms of population. Indeed the 'frontier philosophy', so characteristic of the USA during the nineteenth century, is strongly favoured in Australia today. But what will be the future of the country? Can it really support a vast increase in its numbers, or will its optimum population in terms of the 'carrying capacity of the environment' soon be exceeded with a resultant deterioration in the quality of life?

The environmental scientists, D. H. F. Recher and F. H. Talbot, are amongst those who take a grim view of Australia's future. In a percipient article in the periodical *Walkabout* they provide their vision of their country in the year 2030 AD. They consider that by that time the Australian population could well exceed 50 million. However, far from being spread evenly throughout the land, numbers will be congregated in areas which already have a high population density. Undoubtedly urban agglomerations will have proliferated by 2030; thus Sydney could well have merged not only with Woolongong but also with Newcastle, the overall population of the megalopolis exceeding 13 million, while numbers in Greater Melbourne could have increased to over 10 million.

Australia in 2030 as portrayed by Recher and Talbot will not be the 'lucky country' of today. There will be a high degree of pollution affecting air, water and land. There will be frequent oil spills and leaks along the coasts impoverishing marine life and reducing recreational facilities. State parks will have become so crammed with people that in order to obtain holiday reservations a family will have to book over a year in advance. Open spaces will be found only at great distances from cities, public transport will have deteriorated dramatically and roads and highways will be clogged with motor vehicles of every description. Civil unrest will be commonplace as people herd together in large conurbations. The 'behavioural sink' of overpopulation—a term first coined by the American biologist J. B. Calhoun on the basis of experiments in rats—will be much in evidence as individuals become less and less tolerant of each other's frailties and violence erupts with increasing frequency.

Australian politicians, like those of other nations, frequently refer to the desires and aspirations of their 'children's children' and, as mentioned earlier, this phrase has now become one of the greatest political clichés of all time. But to cite the wishes of one's 'children's children' is utterly inappropriate because, of course, generations yet unborn are prevented from having any say in the type of country which their progenitors will leave them to inherit. If the voices of the Australian unborn could now be heard they would assuredly join with those of Recher and Talbot in attempting to slow the headlong drive for more and yet more people. Their plea would be both strident and poignant, for they would recognise with blinding clarity that although such a policy might have a short term appeal, its long term effects could only be disastrous. Unfortunately nowhere in the world will the politicians of today be summoned before the tribunal of history. Were they compelled to make such an appearance what proportion of their present policies would they be forced to abjure?

Reproductive Bonanza in the Third World

I firmly believe that the future hinge of history will be found not in Europe, North America and Australasia but in the underdeveloped and impoverished nations of the Third World. Already such countries are faced by gigantic problems. Year by year population pressures are mounting, living standards far from rising are tending to deteriorate, illiteracy is rampant, and in spite of the much vaunted 'green revolution' in agriculture the threat of massive famines still hangs over them like a veritable sword of Damocles.

In the past a certain passivity has reigned throughout the Third World. The lot of the populace in these areas has been miserable beyond belief; but there has been a degree of stoicism together with the acceptance of the belief that no betterment can be expected at least on this planet. Now there are stirrings. Old adages are being questioned; mutual toleration is diminishing; social unrest is on the increase and nowhere was this better exemplified in 1971 than in the series of happenings culminating in the Indian invasion of East Pakistan. At last some organs of the world press are rousing themselves from their self-imposed torpor, and in recent months a small number of professional journalists have begun to suggest that over-population may be a predisposing factor to revolutionary wars, that family planning will assuredly not cure the malady and that Armageddon may soon be discernible on the horizon. In the Third World the djinn of overpopulation has now been well and truly loosed from its bottle. Few thinking people imagine that it can be returned to its nidus without cataclysmic consequences.

THE ASIAN IMBROGLIO

In 1971 the overall population of Asia was 2104 million. Forty per cent of the population was under the age of 15; numbers were growing at a rate of 2.3 per cent per year and were likely to double in as little as 31 years. Asia contained four population giants—China, India, Pakistan and Indonesia—and of these the long term situation in India appeared to be the most critical.

India faces a demographic future which can only be described as bleak. During 1970 the Indian population passed the 555 million mark; by mid-1971 it had risen to 569.5 million. The birth rate was 42 per 1,000, the death rate 17 per 1,000, the population was growing at the rate of 2.6 per cent per annum and was likely to double in 27 years. By 2000 AD there could well be 1,000 million Indians on Spaceship Earth. The 'iron law' of demography affects India as it does other countries, for even if the pattern of family size in that country changed dramatic-ally so that by 1985 Indian couples were producing just enough children to replace themselves, the population would still rise to 1,000 million before flattening out.

India has a family planning programme which is the largest in the world. The programme started in the early 1950's and its tempo accelerated markedly during the sixties. Yet family planning has been singularly ineffective in reducing the Indian birth rate and in slowing population growth. Indeed since the programme was initiated the population has increased by almost 200 million, the birth rate has remained stubbornly high (40-45 per 1,000) and as mentioned earlier a *doubling* of the population is likely to take place in under 30 years' time.

The favoured method of contraception in India has been the intra-uterine device. Sterilisation in women by tubal ligation and in men by vasectomy are encouraged and the condom and more recently the Pill have gained some popularity. So far it has been estimated that 3.6 million intra-uterine devices have been inserted and 8 million sterilisations performed. Yet in spite of all the idealism, industry and dedication of family planning personnel in India it is still painfully obvious that only a relatively small proportion of the fecund population are making use of the contraceptive services provided. Moreover, there is disturbing evidence that the majority of the women seeking advice on birth control have already been much exposed to the treadmill of reproduction. Thus the average number of children born to women opting for the intra-uterine device is said to be 3.8 and to candidates for sterilisation 4.5. Other indications of the futility of current family planning measures in India are that only 8 per cent of the eligible women have so far been reached by the programme and that 32.5 per cent of all the females sterilised in the country have already had six living children. At the time of writing India's new abortion law is awaiting Presidential assent. It is moderately liberal, being similar to that in Britain; an important feature of the legislation is that it permits abortion in women in whom a contraceptive method has failed. Whether it will slow India's drift to a demographic disaster remains to be seen.

For India is a bottomless pit of overpopulation; no demographic transition is in sight and there appears to be no solution to the country's predicament. The enormity of the problem was well illustrated by Parkes when he commented on the Indian Government's proposal to sterilise all males who had fathered three or more children. Parkes calculated that some 40 million men would have to be subjected to the operation of vasectomy, and he estimated that if a thousand surgeons and para-surgeons each performed 200 operations a day for five days each week, it would take them eight years to deal with the existing candidates. In the meantime the relentless momentum of population growth would have dictated that large numbers of new candidates for vasectomy would have made their appearance. Parkes made his assessment in 1967; since then the population of India has increased by over 40 million.

*   *   *

The situation in Pakistan is grave. In 1971 the combined population of the two halves of Pakistan exceeded 140 million. There was the imbalance between birth rates and death rates so characteristic of the Third World, the respective figures being 50 and 18 per 1,000; 45 per cent of Pakistan's population was under 15 years of age; numbers were rising at a rate of 3.3 per cent per annum and were likely to double in less than 20 years.

Nineteen seventy one was a turbulent year for Pakistan. Elections were held in the country in late 1970. They acted as a catalyst to disturbances in East Pakistan which wished to break away from the western part of the state and to proclaim itself as the independent republic of Bangla Desh. Punjabi troops from West Pakistan invaded the eastern segment of the country; the revolt was brutally suppressed and the leader of the Awami league, Sheikh Mujibur Rahman, was imprisoned. Huge numbers of refugees, estimated at 10 million, crossed the Indian frontier into West Bengal and congregated in ramshackle and insanitary camps. The *Mukti Bahini* proceeded to mount guerilla activity in East Pakistan. Finally India, overwhelmed by the refugee problem in a highly vulnerable area of the country, invaded East Pakistan and recognised the independent state of Bangla Desh.

To India the crisis of overpopulation in West Bengal had proved intolerable; but undoubtedly population pressures had also contributed to the revolutionary situation in East Pakistan. This region contains 55 per cent of the total population of the country but has only 15 per cent of the land area. East Pakistan has about 400 persons per square kilometre as against 60 per square kilometre in the West; indeed the 75 million inhabitants of East Pakistan are crowded into an area smaller than that of England and Wales. East Pakistan has virtually no natural resources apart from natural gas and jute. What is the future for such a people whether independent in Bangla Desh or, as now seems most unlikely, still a part of a unitary state? Winston Churchill, speaking to the British nation during the Second World War, offered 'blood, sweat and tears', but in Pakistan today there must be added to this unholy trinity famine, disease and human degradation.

There has been family planning in Pakistan since the early 1950's; however, as in India, it has had singularly little effect in staunching the flow of births. The intra-uterine device has been the linchpin of contraceptive practice in Pakistan. Male and female sterilisations are now widely practised, and the market for condoms and oral contraceptives is rising; it is scarcely credible that the Pakistani law with respect to abortion remains illiberal! In spite of herculean efforts no demographic transition is on the horizon, and in its absence Pakistan, whether unified or dismembered, could well be the first area in the world in which the predictions of the doomwatchers have proved to be correct.

*   *   *

Indonesia is another Asian country with a very rapidly growing population. In 1950 there were 76 million Indonesians, in 1960 93 million and 1971 125 million; numbers are increasing by 2.9 per cent per annum and are expected to double in less than 30 years. The islands of Java, Madeira and Bali together comprise less than one-thirteenth of the total land area of Indonesia; yet together they contain almost two-thirds of the country's population.

Family planning has been in operation in Indonesia since 1957. However, its voice remained muted during the role of Achmed Sukarno because at that time the official policy of the state was strongly pronatalist. The military regime of General Suharto, which succeeded that of Sukarno, is firmly committed to family planning and is now supporting it financially. Yet the task of family planners in Indonesia is most unenviable. The birth rate of the country continues to soar, abortion is still legal only to save the mother's life, and even in the early 1970's it is reported that only some 14 per cent of the population know anything about birth control.

*   *   *

The People's Republic of China is the most populous country in the world. Unfortunately accurate statistics on its population are hard to obtain because no official figures have been released since the census of 1953; indeed the validity of that particular census is much in doubt because it was subsequently recognised that there were 133 million more people in the country than had actually been enumerated. All figures pertaining to the Chinese population scene are highly inaccurate and most of them are little more than inspired guesses.

However, one fact is certain, and that is that the Chinese population, like that throughout the rest of the Third World, is rising rapidly. In 1950 it was believed to be some 560 million; in 1960, 650 million, in 1966, 700 million and in 1971 the Population Reference Bureau estimated it at 773 million. By 1985 it could well be over 1,000 million, and by the beginning of the twenty-first century one out of every five persons in the world could be Chinese!

Since the communists assumed power in Mainland China in 1948 policies towards birth control have pursued a fluctuant course. Family planning commenced on a small scale in the early 1950's. However, it soon fell into disrepute, because this was the era of the Great Leap Forward which advocated an increase in manpower and was strongly pronatalist in its ethos. By the early 1960's the Great Leap Forward was seen to have been a failure, and family planning again became respectable. However, other political convulsions followed. In 1966 Mao Tse-tung launched his Great Cultural Revolution in which the Red Guards played such a conspicuous part. Family planning took a back seat; the air was full of jingoistic slogans and great power chauvinism held the stage. But birth control was not entirely forgotten. Indeed it was during this era that Chairman Mao introduced to an incredulous world his celebrated 'barefoot doctors' who, exposed to only three months of medical training, were reputed to be fanning out throughout the country and carrying the message of family planning even to the remotest village.

The Cultural Revolution ebbed and flowed. Finally it went into eclipse, and with the start of the decade of the 1970's there was evidence that China was again turning away from policies of introversion to those of internationalism. This viewpoint gained considerable credence with the announcement in July 1971 that the American President would visit China early in 1972, and with the admission of China to the UN during the current session.

The birth control programme in China has been eclectic in its scope. Indeed there is scarcely a method which has not been tried. At one time—and there is irony in this—the regime was much in favour of the rhythm method of contraception so beloved of the Catholic Church. This occurred in spite of the fact that at no time in its turbulent history could Mainland China ever have been said to be under Papal jurisdiction! Condoms were popular 10 years ago and are still in vogue; now the oral contraceptive pill is widely available. The Government requires pharmacists to 'maintain reasonable stocks' of contraceptives and all Chinese department stores, trading companies, drug stores and co-operatives must take part in the sale of such items. However, at the time of writing, contraception by the intra-uterine device, abortion and male and female sterilisation—all measures requiring medical attention—still hold pride of place in the hierarchy of birth control measures.

What has been the fate of the 'barefoot doctors'? They are being trained to insert intra-uterine devices and to perform vasectomies; thus it is hoped that these forms of birth control will be carried to the peasants and that this will materially slow the growth of population. China pioneered the suction technique for abortion, and indeed in that country abortion has never faced the legal and moral obstructions to which it has been exposed in the West. Tubal ligation in women is currently on the increase in China, but vasectomy in men has had more publicity. Indeed, as far back as 1963, the Chinese Prime Minister, that apparently indestructible warrior Chou En-lai, speaking while on a tour of Manchuria, uttered paeans of joy about vasectomy and stressed the responsibility of the male in the sphere of family planning. But what is the future of vasectomy? Will it ever produce a significant effect on the Chinese birth rate even if great numbers of 'barefoot doctors' become proficient in the procedure? Yuan Tien is one who is pessimistic about the eventual outcome. Writing in *Population Studies* in 1965 he emphasised that the Chinese population was increasing at a rate of just under 2 per cent per annum, a trend which has continued into the 1970's. Yan Tien calculated that

in order to depress population growth in China by a mere 1 per
cent per annum, some 43 million sterilisations would have to be
performed; put another way half the married men between the
ages of 20 and 44 would have to be vasectomised. The numbers
involved are truly formidable, and it can hardly be expected
that any group of 'barefoot doctors', however diligent, motivated and technically experienced, could reach this level of
activity!

Chinese Government propaganda now encourages family
planning, not only for the individual couple but also for the
benefit of the state. The Government favours late marriage and
recommends its postponement until the late 20's or early 30's.
It is against high procreative activity, two children being
regarded as the ideal family size. Large families are frowned
upon, and the legislative machinery indicates its disapproval by
failing to allocate rations of food and clothing to any child over
the accepted norm.

*　　*　　*

Indeed the record of family planners in Asia is bleak.
However, they do take some credit for falling birth rates in
countries such as Formosa (Taiwan), Ceylon, South Korea,
Singapore and Hong Kong.

Formosa is the country which *par excellence* is hailed as a
triumph for programmes of birth control. In 1951 its birth rate
stood at 50 per 1,000; by 1971 it had fallen to 26 per 1,000,
and the decrease has often been attributed to an active and
accelerating programme of family planning having as its linchpin
the intra-uterine device. However, there is another possibility to
account for the fall in birth rate in Formosa, and that is that the
island, like the Western European countries at the beginning of
the twentieth century and like Japan in the 1920's, was
undergoing a demographic transition from a predominantly
agricultural to a more industrialised type of society. Certainly
politics played a major part in the industrialisation of Formosa.
The process occurred during the era of John Foster Dulles, that
apostle of brinksmanship and communist containment, who
evinced an almost pathological hatred for the regime in
Mainland China. Lavish American aid was pumped into

Formosa to support their old ally Chiang Kai-shek.* As a result economic activity in Formosa sprouted and living standards rose. Given this set of circumstances it appears not unlikely that Formosan parents, like those in the West, recognised that children were an economic liability and took a decision to limit their family size.

What then caused the falling birth rate in Formosa? Was it family planning or was a demographic transition occurring? The matter will no doubt be hotly argued for many years. However, regardless of the precise cause, the situation in the island remains highly unsatisfactory. For Formosa with its current population density of 384 persons per square kilometre of land, is the most densely populated nation in the world. Furthermore, there is a strong possibility that if present trends continue, the island will have to support a population double that of 1971 in just over 30 years from now.

FERTILE AFRICANS AND LATIN AMERICANS

Numbers are rising steeply in Africa; in fact next to Latin America this is the most rapidly expanding region of the world. The growth rate in Africa is 2.7 per cent and each year almost 10 million individuals are added to that continent; birth rates remain high—generally from 40 to 50 per 1,000—and no demographic transition is yet in sight. Death rates are elevated as compared with those in Western countries; the lowest is 14 per 1,000 in Tunisia and Rhodesia and the highest 30 per 1,000 in Angola. Infantile mortality rates are amongst the highest in the world, but there is a strong likelihood that these will soon decrease as the overall practice of medicine improves. In most African countries numbers are likely to double in between 20 and 35 years. In mid-1971 the population of Africa stood at 354 million: by 2000 AD it is likely to exceed 800 million. In 1971 Africans contributed 9.6 per cent of the world's population; by 2000 the corresponding figure is likely to be as much as 12.6 per cent.

Like Latin America Africa is not densely populated when compared with Europe and certain parts of Asia. In the

* Between 1949 and 1961 the US Government allocated $1,300 million in aid to Formosa. This did not include direct military assistance (see Hensman, 1971).

mainland of the continent population densities range from 1 per square kilometre in Botswana and Libya, to 133 per square kilometre in Rwanda. Nigeria which with its current population of 56.5 million is the most populous state in Africa, has a density of only 69 persons per square kilometre. Egypt (34.9 million) holds second place to Nigeria in terms of total population; Egypt has an overall population density of 32 persons per square kilometre, but this figure is grossly misleading because the majority of the people are congregated in the Nile valley where crowding is intense and population pressures of all kinds are very severe.

One often hears the argument that because the population density of Africa is relatively low the continent could support many more people. This viewpoint is especially prevalent in nations south of the Sahara the governments of many of which adopt strongly pronatalist postures. Unfortunately, the opinion is an egregious fallacy because, as noted previously, population density *per se* is a poor guide to the optimum population of a nation or a continent. What is much more important is the so-called 'carrying capacity of the environment', and if one employs this index, a persuasive case could be made for the postulate that Africa is already overpopulated.

Some African nations are on record as wishing to increase their rate of population growth. Amongst these are the Central African Republic, Libya, Madagascar and Senegal; in such countries family planning is either proscribed or actively discouraged. However, some Black African States now offically sponsor family planning. In Kenya clinics sponsored by the Family Planning Association (FPA) have been available since 1965, and the avowed aim of the Government is to reduce the population growth rate from its current 3.3 per cent to 2.3 per cent per annum in 10 years; at the time of writing, it appears most unlikely that such a goal will be attained. The Federal Nigerian Government, following the cessation of hostilities in the breakaway province of Biafra, is no longer preoccupied with insurrectionary activity and is reported to be in the process of establishing a body which will be known as the National Population Council. Family planning activities are stated to be increasing in Nigeria; but the situation is far from satisfactory and it is estimated that 80 per cent of Nigerian women who currently practise family planning do so without their husbands' consent!

Ghana's population is rising at 3 per cent per annum and, at present rates of expansion, will double in 24 years. Surprisingly enough the Ghanaian Government appears to have some doubts about policies of pronatalism, and in 1969 it issued a statement to the effect that large populations *per se* did not make nations great and that in future generations the quality rather than the quantity of life would be the paramount consideration. Tanzania is growing at the rate of 2.6 per cent per annum and is likely to double its population in 27 years. Its family planning service is rudimentary, and training in this specialty is exiguous. Abortion is illegal and Zanzibar still prohibits the import of contraceptives! The Republic of South Africa follows the controversial policy of apartheid and has recently set aside some 12 per cent of its land area for the establishment of allegedly independent African states known as Bantustans. The first of these, the Transkei, has now been granted a very limited form of autonomy. The white population of South Africa has traditionally indulged in family planning activities and the FPA has been represented in that country for almost 30 years. Attempts are now being made to extend family planning facilities to the African population and to this end a clinic has recently been established in the Transkei. Future developments in this highly charged situation will be awaited with interest.

*   *   *

Within the term Latin America are included the land masses of South America, Central America and Mexico. The area has the doubtful distinction of expanding more rapidly in terms of its population than any other part of the world. During 1971 the overall growth rate of Latin America was 2.9 per cent, while that of Central America and Mexico reached the truly phenomenal figure of 3.4 per cent. Birth rates remain high (generally 40 to 50 per 1,000) and as in Africa and most of Asia there is as yet no hint of a demographic transition. Death rates and infantile mortality rates are a good deal lower than in Africa and in many other areas of the Third World due mainly to improved standards of medical practice. Most countries in

Latin America are likely to double their population in from 20 to 30 years. In mid-1971 the population of the area stood at 291 million; by 2000 AD it is likely to exceed 650 million, a prodigious increase of 124 per cent. In 1971 Latin America contributed 7.9 per cent to the world's population; by 2000 AD the corresponding figure is likely to be of the order of 10.0 per cent.

As in the case of Africa, the countries of Latin America show lower population densities than do those of Europe and Asia. For example, in South America densities range from 3 persons per square kilometre in Guyana to 21 persons per square kilometre in Ecuador. However, such figures paint a false picture for they completely obscure the fact that urbanisation in Latin America is proceeding at a quite staggering rate, far outstripping that of any other part of the world. Thus in Uruguay one half of the total population of the country live in the capital, Montevideo; in Venezuela the urban population in 1969 was estimated to be 75 per cent of the total, and in Mexico City between 1950 and 1960 the population grew by 59.6 per cent as compared with an increase for the whole country of only 35.4 per cent.

Some countries in Latin America perceive themselves to be underpopulated. One of these is Argentina which has living standards not too dissimilar to those of Western Europe and which has one of the lowest rates of population growth in the continent. Argentina is uneasy because she feels herself surrounded by nations indulging in an avalanche of procreation. Brazil, in spite of its transcendent problems resulting from excessive urbanisation and discussed in Chapter IX, also considers itself to be underpopulated; so do Bolivia and Peru. Chile has no overall policy to reduce its birth rate, and its population is likely to double in some 20 years, while in Mexico the recently elected President, Luis Echevarria Alverez, said of population growth in his country that 'we neither wish to, nor cannot stop it, but on the contrary wish to speed it up'!

As mentioned previously, numbers in Central America—that volcano ridden isthmus and the home of the notorious 'banana republics'—are growing more rapidly than in any other area on earth. In Costa Rica the population is expected to double in 19 years and in El Salvador, Honduras and Panama in 21 years.

During 1969 hostilities erupted between two Central American Republics, El Salvador and Honduras. The population density of the former is relatively high (158 persons per square kilometre) and of the latter quite low (22 persons per square kilometre). The fighting was on a relatively small scale and rapidly subsided as a result of the intervention of the Organization of American States (OAS). But the conflict was of great potential interest because for the first time in recorded history rapid population growth, and especially an imbalance of population between neighbouring states was cited by the OAS as a major cause of hostilities. One does not require to be clairvoyant to predict that in official pronouncements of the future such a cause will feature to an ever increasing extent.

The influence of the Roman Catholic Church is still widespread throughout Latin America. As a result abortion laws are amongst the most restrictionist in the world and illegal abortions run rampant, particularly amongst the urban poor. For example, in Santiago in Chile in the late 1960's it was estimated that there were 20,000 illegal abortions per year as compared with 77,440 births. The Marxist government in Chile, elected in 1970 under the leadership of Salvatore Allende, is reputed to be worried about the country's high incidence of abortion and is said to favour legislative changes of a liberal character.

The saga of family planning in South America presents a most uneven spectrum Chile encourages it and has the most advanced service in South America. Family planning is also receiving increasing support in Brazil and more recently in Venezuela; in Uruguay it is tolerated but is not supported by the government. In 1970 Colombia opened the first vasectomy clinic in Latin America, and the centre at Bogota is stated to be the largest family planning clinic in the world. In Argentina publicity about birth control is still illegal and family planning receives little encouragement. In Peru there were only 4 FPA clinics in the whole country in 1970, and the military junta which took office in 1968 has indicated that it is opposed to any form of birth control. Facilities for family planning remain miniscule in countries such as Bolivia, Paraguay and Ecuador, and no immediate change in this situation can be anticipated.

In Central America governmental reactions to family planning also vary considerably. There is a reasonable amount of support for it in Guatemala and Honduras but in Nicaragua the specialty is in an embryonic state. The government of El Salvador recognises that the country has a demographic problem but so far has taken little or no positive action. The Mexican government has no official policy in relation to family planning and the law prohibits propaganda in favour of contraception. In spite of this family planning services are available on a limited scale mainly from private sources.

Only a few miles east of the peninsula of Yucatan in Central America lies Cuba with its Marxist regime and with its economy heavily tied to the countries of the Eastern bloc. What is Cuba's population situation and what are its government's policies in this field? At first sight the demographic pattern in Cuba appears to be in no way different from that of its capitalistic neighbours. Cuba has a moderately high birth rate by world standards (27 per 1,000), and due to its relatively well developed medical services its death rate is as low as anywhere on the planet. Thirty-seven per cent of Cuba's population are under 15 years of age, and if current trends continue, the island's numbers will double in less than 40 years.

But there is one important difference in Cuba which sets it apart from the remainder of Latin America, and that is in the sphere of urbanisation. During the military dictatorship of Fulgencio Batista Cuba's citizens followed the general Latin American trend and crammed themselves into towns and cities; severe problems of overcrowding arose and reached their acme in the capital Havana. Soon after the Cuban revolution the Castro regime set out to check urban growth. It mounted strict controls over migration into cities and it provided financial incentives for those prepared to remain in rural areas. Such policies appear to have met with a marked degree of success, for the flow of the populace to cities has been staunched and the agricultural sector of the economy has benefited accordingly.

Officially Cuba, like other Marxist countries, is not concerned with population growth. Its government opposes birth control and still regards it as a 'capitalist-imperialist conspiracy' foisted by the developed nations on a reluctant Third World. However, there is now some evidence that this deeply entrenched attitude is weakening. Family planning is practised to some extent in Cuba, and in 1964 the intra-uterine device was introduced into the island. Cubans, like other Latin Americans, can take no pride in their abortion statistics, and it is currently estimated that in the country there is one abortion for every three or four live births.

In 1968 Pope Paul published his controversial Encyclical, *Humanae Vitae.* Here was no radical document providing a reappraisal of traditional Catholic attitudes to fertility control. Instead it was an extremely conservative tract declaring that abortion must continue to be 'absolutely illicit' as a method of regulating births and forbidding all forms of contraception apart from the notoriously unreliable 'rhythm method'. The Encyclical had a particularly unfortunate effect in Latin America, especially in countries such as Argentina, Brazil, Colombia and Peru, where it strengthened reactionary elements in the Catholic hierarchy and made the emergence of rational population policies even more distant. Perhaps the *New Scientist* had Latin America in mind when of *Humanae Vitae* it wrote in August 1968 'bigotry, pedantry and fanaticism can kill, maim and agonize those upon whom they are visited just as surely as bombs, pogroms and the gas chamber. Pope Paul VI has now gently joined the company of tyrants, but the damage he has done may well outclass and outlast that of earlier oppressors'.

References

BOFFEY, PHILIP M. (1970). 'Japan: a crowded nation wants to boost its birthrate'. *Science*, **167**, pp. 960-962.

COALE, ANSLEY J. (1970). 'Man and his Environment'. *Science*, **170**, pp. 132-136.

CONSERVATION SOCIETY (1969). *Why Britain needs a Population Policy?* Potters Bar, Conservation Society.

EHRLICH, PAUL R. (1968). *The Population Bomb.* New York, Ballantine Books Inc.

EHRLICH, PAUL R. and EHRLICH, ANNE (1970). *Population, Resources, Environment.* San Francisco, W. H. Freeman and Co.

EHRLICH, PAUL R. and HOLDREN, JOHN P. (1971). 'Impact of Population Growth'. *Science*, **171**, pp. 1212-1217.

FIRST REPORT FROM THE SELECT COMMITTEE ON SCIENCE AND
    TECHNOLOGY (1970-1971). *Population of the United Kingdom.*
    London, HM Stationery Office.
GAYLOR, ANNE (1971). 'Abortion in Wisconsin'. *Zero Population
    Growth*, **3**, No. 8, pp. 1-2.
HM STATIONERY OFFICE (1971). *Census, 1971, Scotland, England
    and Wales—Preliminary Report.* London.
HARDIN, GARRETT (1968). 'The Tragedy of the Commons'. *Science*,
    162, pp. 1243-1248.
HENSMAN, C. R. (1971). *Rich against Poor. The Reality of Aid.* London,
    Allen Lane, The Penguin Press.
INTERNATIONAL PLANNED PARENTHOOD FEDERATION—
    Situation Reports, March 1968—June 1971.
JOHNSON, STANLEY (1970). *Life without Birth.* London, Heinemann
    Books.
LEE, LUKE T. (1971). 'Law and Family Planning'. *Studies in Family
    Planning*, **2**, No. 4, pp. 81-89.
LEGUM, COLIN (1971). 'The explosion of a Nation'. *Observer*, 4th April.
LORAINE, J. A. (1970). *Sex and the Population Crisis.* London,
    Heinemann Medical Books.
PARKES, A. S. (1967). 'Can India do it?'. *New Scientist*, **35**, No. 555, pp.
    186-187.
POPULATION BULLETIN (1970). 'India, ready or not, here they come'.
    26, No. 5, November.
POPULATION BULLETIN (1970). 'Population Developments in 1970'.
    26, No. 6, December.
POPULATION BULLETIN (1971). 'The Future Population of the United
    States'. **27**, No. 1, February.
POPULATION OF THE UNITED KINGDOM REPORT FROM THE
    SELECT COMMITTEE ON SCIENCE AND TECHNOLOGY
    (1970-1971). *Observations by the Government.* London, HM
    Stationery Office.
RECHER, H. F. and TALBOT, F. H. (1970). 'Australia in 2030.
    Walkabout, **36**, No. 3 pp. 7-10.
RENTON, SIR DAVID (1967). 'The Population Problem'. *New Horizon*,
    January, p. 5, February, p. 7, April, p. 5, July, p. 5.
ROCKEFELLER, JOHN D. 3rd (1971). *Population Growth and America's
    Future*—Interim Report made to Congress, 16th March.
TAYLOR, L. R. (Editor) (1970). *The Optimum Population for Britain.*
    London and New York, Academic Press.
TIETZE, CHRISTOPHER (1969). 'Abortion Laws and Abortion
    Practices'. In *Advances in Planned Parenthood*, **5**, pp. 194-212,
    Excerpta Medica International Congress Series, 207.
UNITED NATIONS (1969). *Demographic Year Book.* New York.
WILSON, HAROLD (1967). 'The Population Problem'. *New Horizon*,
    February, p. 6, April, p. 5, July, p. 5.
YUAN TIEN, H. (1965). 'Sterilisation, Oral Contraception and Population
    Control in China'. *Population Studies*, **18**, pp. 215-235.

XVI

REPRODUCTION AND THE CONVENTIONAL WISDOM

> *But we, brought forth and rear'd in hours*
> *of change, alarm, surprise—*
> *What shelter to grow ripe is ours?*
> *What leisure to grow wise?*

In memory of the Author of 'Obermann'
Matthew Arnold, 1849.

The term conventional wisdom is not new. Galbraith made free play with it in *The Affluent Society* and elegantly catalogued its characteristics in the sphere of economics. The conventional wisdom has many facets but paramount amongst them is that it is widely acceptable; it is the music to which the ear is attuned; it is the reiteration of the familiar; in Galbraith's words it is 'an act of affirmation like reading aloud from Scriptures or going to church'. New concepts may shake the conventional wisdom but it will generally escape unscathed. Its ramparts will only be breeched when the ideas which it sponsors have become manifestly inappropriate to the aims and desires of contemporary society.

Specialist fields such as economics and foreign affairs have their conventional wisdoms; in Britain their record has often been poor as a few examples will illustrate. Thus during the Great Depression of the 1930's the economic wisdom preached the benefits of deflation and balanced budgets—policies subsequently shown by Keynes to be the precise antithesis of those necessary to remedy the situation. In the early 1960's the conventional wisdom had its colours firmly tethered to the mast of economic expansion; one result of this approach was mounting pressure on the British balance of payments leading to a deficit not far short of £1,000 million by the end of 1964. Similarly during 1971 the serried ranks of economists which traditionally surround our politicians were vociferous advocates of growthmanship and lauded to the skies the economic advantages which would accrue to Britain by our association with the Common Market countries. But there was no discussion from them or from their political overlords as to how this association would affect our environmental heritage or whether the enlarged EEC, with is avowed policy of economic expansionism, would exacerbate the international dilemma of resource depletion. Modern economists dislike rapid inflation, clearly recognising the hardship which it is likely to inflict on vulnerable sections of the community. Yet their conventional wisdom fails to associate inflation with population growth, and the silence of economists on matters such as birth control and pregnancy termination is impressive.

In British foreign policy the fallibility of the conventional wisdom has been striking. Thus in July 1914, some 10 days after the assassination of Archduke Ferdinand of Austria in Sarajevo and less than one month before the outbreak of the First World War, the then Chancellor of the Exchequer, David Lloyd George, said at the Guildhall 'in the matter of external affairs the sky has never been more blue'. During the 1930's politicians such as MacDonald, Baldwin, Chamberlain and Halifax consistently underrated the perils of German rearmament with grievous consequences for the nation. Even after the rape of Czechoslovakia and the outbreak of the Second World War such illusions persisted, and in 1940 Neville Chamberlain, commenting on the German invasion of Denmark and Norway, averred that Hitler had 'missed the bus'. When in 1956 this country made its ill-starred attack on the Suez Canal, the conventional wisdom of the Government thundered that Nasser was another Hitler and that we must intervene not only to 'separate the combatants and protect the nationals', but to maintain our authority throughout the Middle East. Even in the heat of the moment these aims failed to carry conviction with many people; now with the benefit of hindsight extending over 15 years their credibility has been completely eroded.

Has the record of conventional wisdom in the sphere of reproduction been any better than in economics and politics? My contention is that it has not.

For in respect of reproductive processes the conventional wisdom is far from neutral; indeed it is decisively and almost militantly pronatalist. It frowns on bachelors, urges them to marry without delay and has even been known to make disparaging remarks about their libido and sexual prowess. The wisdom assumes that for a male with normal sexual urges and normal psychological balance marriage is the inevitable and only natural desire. It cannot conceive that a man may choose to live unmarried, and it equates the bachelor status with sexual insufficiency and psychological disturbances. For spinsters the judgment is even harsher, and here the wisdom derives powerful support from virtually every woman's newspaper in the land, the latter extolling the virtues of marriage and childbearing within marriage. The conventional wisdom equates spinsterdom with failure; these women have 'lost the race'; their social status is inferior to that of their married counterparts and their old age will inevitably be lonely and miserable. In the Britain of the 1970's the pressures on women to marry remain monumental, and under such circumstances who can wonder that the fervent desire of every young girl is to enter into this state with maximum speed and at almost any cost?

For homosexuality in men and women the conventional wisdom has no truck. It is, of course, quite correct in condemning sexual assaults on young children and here it has behind it the full panoply of the legal system of the country. There is, however, the tacit assumption that all homosexuals would assault young children unless the law protected them, whereas heterosexuals would not do so. This is, of course, far from being the case, and indeed the nature and extent of attacks on young girls by heterosexual males, frequently culminating in murder, emphasise the need for the law to be completely impartial in its assumptions about the likelihood of assaults on children by homosexuals.

What of homosexual practices taking place in private between consenting adults? Here the conventional wisdom remains obdurate and appears to have been little affected by the compassionate and enlightened legislation in this field stemming originally from the Wolfenden Report of 1957. True there has been some advance from the days of the late Lord Kilmuir, that self-styled 'hammer of the homosexuals', who as Home Secretary was continuously denouncing the evils of 'sodomite societies' and 'buggery clubs'. Now the conventional wisdom is much less vociferous in its condemnation of the homosexual. Yet intransigence on this issue persists, for within the conceptual horizons of the wisdom there is no room for the thought that a proportion of men and women actually prefer homosexual to heterosexual relationships and that they will obstinately persist in such activities in spite of the most strident calls to sexual orthodoxy. Indeed the wisdom finds it exceedingly difficult to judge a man or woman by parameters other than his or her sex life; nor does it see fit to stress the contributions to civilisation of men such as Leonardo da Vinci, Oscar Wilde, John Maynard Keynes and Ivor Novello.

The monolithic pose of the conventional wisdom with respect to adult homosexuality will not endure indefinitely. The obsolescence of the approach will eventually become self evident, and it is even possible that some recent work performed by my research unit in Edinburgh may hasten the process. During 1970 my colleagues and I were able to demonstrate that functional abnormalities existed in the sex glands of male and female homosexuals and were especially prominent in the latter. Indeed lesbians were found to show a whole spectrum of hormonal abnormalities, this package being designated in the technical parlance of our specialty as a 'hormonal imbalance'. Thus the excretion in the urine of the lesbians of the male sex hormone, testosterone—a substance produced by females as well as by males—was grossly elevated, while levels of the female sex hormones—the oestrogens—were abnormally low. Moreover, there was evidence that the functioning of the pituitary gland—that so-called 'leader of the endocrine orchestra'—was disturbed in lesbianism.

There may be lessons for society arising from these findings, for traditionally the conventional wisdom has rightly been extremely tolerant of women showing other forms of hormonal imbalance. Thus there is no criticism of females who fail to menstruate and in whom menstruation is painful; there is no social stigma attached to the attainment of puberty and to the development of the climacteric; women who bleed from the womb and who become pregnant and deliver babies are free from the opprobrium of society. Yet the unfortunate lesbian, who also demonstrates a form of hormonal imbalance, remains the object of dislike and derision if not of actual persecution. She is the 'odd woman out', the prey of the silent majority, the prototype of the permissive society. It is evident that a fog of prejudice and bigotry still surrounds adult homosexuality. What period of time must elapse before the winds of change finally disperse it?

*   *   *

The conventional wisdom will defend with its dying breath the duty of a man to have only one wife; on the other hand it will be equally vehement in its protestations that the number of children born to a marriage is the couple's own affair and therefore cannot be brought into the arena of public debate. It shuns divorce 'for the sake of the children'; yet it does not shun endless procreation which may cause profound damage to the existing children. The wisdom looks with disfavour on childless marriages, and in the case of couples who make it clear that they do not desire to have any children it can be frankly abusive. Although the religious zeal of the conventional wisdom may have faded with the years, it will still support the portion of the wedding service which points to procreation as a prime purpose of marriage. The only child gets short shift from the conventional wisdom; thus he is described as 'spoiled' and 'wayward'; by definition he is a 'tragedy' and he must look forward to a life which will be greatly impoverished by the lack of brothers and sisters. But are such strictures on the only child justified? Almost certainly not; they arise mainly from folklore and have been perpetuated through the writings of some psychologists. There is little or no objective evidence to support them.

But in respect of the large family the conventional wisdom utters paeans of joy. Each new procreative enterprise—no matter how many have preceded it—is a matter for congratu-lation. Moreover, the question as to whether or not the parents actually desired the child is carefully avoided in spite of the now well recognised fact that even within marriage the proportion of unwanted children is relatively high. Faced with the birth of quintuplets and sextuplets which may follow treatment with 'fertility drugs' and which invariably receive the adulation of the press, the conventional wisdom will merely extol the marvels of medical science, and will make no mention whatsoever of the social and economic connotations of such an event to the family in question.

When as mentioned in Chapter XV the Labour MP Douglas Houghton described high reproductive activity as 'socially irresponsible' and 'verging on social delinquency' a howl of protest arose from the conventional wisdom. The circle had now been completed; from the reverence traditionally accorded to the matriarch a respected public figure was now prepared to question the pedestal to which society had raised her. Perhaps posterity will describe Douglas Houghton as one of the most percipient politicians of our time. At present he will no doubt take comfort from the fact that not infrequently the heresy of today becomes the accepted dogma of tomorrow.

No better illustration of the attitude of the conventional wisdom in Britain to reproduction is avilable than in the reception accorded to the television play of the 1960's, *Cathy, Come Home.* This play rightly excited great sympathy for a young mother, who, for economic reasons, had to be parted from her children; indeed an organisation such as *Shelter* which is concerned with the plight of the homeless, benefited considerably from its showing. But in the many articles and reviews of the play which appeared in the press of the time, the crux of the situation received no mention, for it was all too obvious that poor Cathy's plight could be traced to a high reproductive rate, three children having been born in the same number of years. Furthermore, reviewers failed to take cogni-zance of the fact that the whole tragic situation could readily have been avoided had responsible use been made of modern contraceptive technology by Cathy and her lover. But *Cathy, Come Home* is by no means exceptional, for looking back over the decade of the 1960's one can recall a whole host of television programmes concerned with bad housing, over-crowding, poverty and general human degradation. But never once can I remember hearing the conventional wisdom in the form of the interviewer offer the suggestion that such a state of affairs could be laid at the doors of excessive and unthinking reproductive activity and that it could readily have been prevented had reliable methods of birth control been employed.

The conventional wisdom is not only an ardent advocate of pronatalist policies; it also backs the rhetoric by fiscal measures designed to ease the load of reproduction. It pays family allowances—but paradoxically not for the first child—gives tax relief for children, provides maternity benefits including free antenatal and postnatal care and allows children free dental treatment and free education. The money to pay for such benefits comes out of the general pool of taxation; all of us contribute provided our salary is above a certain level—even bachelors, spinsters and childless couples. Were these sections of the community to complain that they were supporting 'other people's children' the conventional wisdom would be derisive, proclaiming that reproduction is sacrosanct to the individual and that those who voice a contrary view are both mean and selfish. Indeed selfishness in the eyes of the conventional wisdom is the attribute of those who criticise excessive reproductive activity in others. Yet is this a fair assumption? For in this grossly overpopulated world of the 1970's it could be argued with even greater force that the selfish in the community are those who, through their large families, are contributing disproportionately to the pollution of Spaceship Earth and are using up more than their share of our planet's finite and fast diminishing resources.

Unfortunately the rhetoric of the conventional wisdom on matters of reproduction is not matched by an equal knowledge of the processes of sex and conception. After all, most young men and women are fertile; in most of them the sex drive will be high, and I have commented on this point further in *Sex and the Population Crisis.* Accordingly, for the vast majority of couples, conception is not a process fraught with difficulty. Indeed procreation could probably be regarded as much too easy as the relatively high proportion of unwanted children born would tend to indicate.

*   *   *

The love affair between the conventional wisdom and family planning was slow to mature, and bitter acrimony attended the early days of the family planning movement in this country. Indeed those redoubtable women who pioneered birth control and who in a male-dominated world fought like tigresses for the dignity of their sex, were subjected to a degree of invective not far short of that accorded to Emmeline Pankhurst and her suffragettes in the years immediately preceding the outbreak of the First World War. But now all is forgiven. The conventional wisdom has finally taken family planning to its heart; Marie Stopes is now a national heroine and hospitals and clinics are named after her. Politicians of all parties currently support family planning, and increasing pressure is being put on local authorities to provide such services free under the National Health Service. We may well be witnessing the dawn of the golden era of family planning, and the only surprise is that the dawn has been so late in breaking. For the basic aims of family planning must be regarded as impeccable even by those indoctrinated with the conventional wisdom. It is voluntary; it can be neatly packaged within the practice of medicine; it concerns itself with the health of both mother and child; it stresses the 'inalienable right' of married couples to have as many children as they desire; it eschews even the mildest forms of coercion in reproductive processes; so far its reaction to abortion has been unfavourable, and its clinics traditionally provide facilities for the treatment of the infertile patient.

In accepting family planning the conventional wisdom has had perforce, also to swallow methods of birth control; for that is the main concern of the specialty. No longer are spermicides, jellies, caps and diaphragms classified as 'immoral agents'; the intra-uterine device after a stormy interlude in the 1930's has now gained the accolade of respectability. Even that elder statesman, the condom, which was no stranger to Casanova and from which 'no one ever died', no longer offends the wisdom.

The Pill, the doyen of them all because it is by far the most reliable, had a rough initial course but has now become acceptable, at least as far as married women are concerned; indeed some $1\frac{1}{2}$ million women in Great Britain are currently receiving this form of medication. Vasectomy in males has recently been added to the armamentarium of family planning clinics. Although some doctors are reluctant to perform it for reasons of conscience, the voice of the conventional wisdom will not be raised against this form of sterilisation, always provided, of course, that the family size has been 'completed' in advance of the operation.

However, towards that other major form of fertility control, namely abortion, the conventional wisdom, like the schizophrenic patient, presents a split personality. This is so because a violent controversy still rages in Britain and elsewhere between those who favour abortion and those who are violently opposed to the procedure. The catalyst to this controversy has been our moderately liberal Abortion Act which, following a series of highly acrimonious debates in the House of Commons, eventually reached the statue book in 1967. Since then the battle between the opposing forces has ebbed and flowed. The anti-abortionists, many of whom are influenced by religious dogma, have claimed that abortion is tantamount to murder, have cast the gynaecologist in the role of executioner and have produced lurid pictures of half-formed foetuses struggling valiantly for survival. They have stated that a liberal abortion law will cause a Gadarene slide into decadence, will undermine Christian morality, will destroy the whole basis of family life, will encourage promiscuity and may even produce a state of affairs reminiscent to that obtaining in Nazi Germany. The anti-abortionist campaign has been waged with dash and vigour, and in certain areas of the country, notably in cities such as Birmingham and Glasgow, it has been notably successful. To some extent the campaign has been bolstered by the conventional wisdom of the medical profession which can only save life and is precluded from taking a moral decision on life and death.

How do the pro-abortionists attempt to counter such a flood of emotive propaganda? They do so by a call to reason—by no means the best ally in such a highly charged situation. They deny the postulate of the anti-abortionists that the embryo is 'human' at an early stage of pregnancy and that it has a separate or existing persona. They hold firmly to the viewpoint that the woman herself, not the doctor and least of all an ecclesiastical authority, should decide whether or not a pregnancy should continue to term. Moreover, they stress the point—one which is carefully avoided by the anti-abortionist lobby—that if a woman is denied an abortion through official medical channels, she is then likely to seek the operation at the hands of a backstreet operator, to the detriment of her health and even to her survival. In answer to the criticism that a liberal abortion law will erode conventional morality, the pro-abortionists are on strong ground, for they can cite the examples of Japan and of Eastern European countries such as Hungary, Czechoslovakia and Yugoslavia, which have operated such laws for many years and in which there has been no objective evidence either of social decay or of moral decline.

To my mind, however, the trump card of the pro-abortionists is seldom played; yet it is there for all to see in the meticulous studies of Forssman and Thuwe from Göthenburg. These Swedish workers compared the characteristics of the children born to women who had been refused an abortion with those of wanted children who had gained the immeasurable advantages of a secure family life. The spectacle presented by the unwanted children in later life was a sorry one; thus they showed an increased incidence of drunkenness, delinquency and psychiatric disorders; they were frequently difficult to educate and many of them had to attend special schools; their health was often poor and they were frequently rejected for military service. Moreover—and this point merits special emphasis—they tended to marry young and produce more children than did the wanted group. The anti-abortionist lobby would do well to meditate on this important contribution to the medical literature.

One can readily see why the conventional wisdom is confused about abortion. But in the future, its confusion is likely to increase rather than diminish. Up till now it has had to deal with abortion produced by surgical means—either by the celebrated method of 'dilatation and curettage' or by the more modern suction technique. Now a new and quite different method of fertility control has raised its head. This involves a group of substances known as the prostaglandins which are widely disseminated throughout body tissues but which reach their highest concentration in the semen. Certain types of prostaglandin possess properties which could well give the conventional wisdom sleepless nights. Thus they could act as 'once-a-month' contraceptives and above all, they have been shown to be capable of producing an abortion once a pregnancy has become established. In women their activity is most marked when they are infused into a vein, but there are recent reports in the literature purporting to show that their abortifacient effect is still present when they are inserted into the vagina or placed between the foetal membranes and the wall of the uterus. The social effects of prostaglandins are likely to be far reaching. Perhaps at last medical science has produced an agent which if used on a sufficiently wide scale, could mitigate some of the evil effects of the population explosion.

*   *   *

The aim of this chapter has not been to trample on the susceptibilities of those who in the early 1970's find themselves to be parents of large families. After all, the crisis of human numbers is a relatively new phenomenon and to many in Britain as elsewhere the whole concept remains remote and academic. But if one accepts that a population explosion exists—and one might hope that perusal of this book might have persuaded even the most sceptical of this fact—then an alteration in traditional attitudes to reproductive processes must follow as naturally as night succeeds day. Only in that way will a more tolerable life be ensured for fewer children.

References

COOPER, WENDY (1971). 'Gender is a mutable point'. *Daily Telegraph Magazine,* 10th December, pp. 18-24.

FORSSMAN, H. and THUWE, INGA (1966). 'One Hundred-and-Twenty Children Born after Application for Therapeutic Abortion refused: Their Mental Health, Social Adjustment and Educational Level up to the Age of 21'. *Acta psychiat. neurol. scand.,* **42**, pp. 71-88.

GALBRAITH, JOHN KENNETH (1958). *The Affluent Society.* London, Pelican Books.

HARVEY, IAN (1971). 'The Homosexual's Plight'. *New Statesman,* 9th April, pp. 489-490.

HM STATIONERY OFFICE (1967). *Sexual Offences Act.* London, Ch. 60.

HOOD, ANDREW (1971). 'Anomaly of Homosexual Law; Unreformed and unenforced'. *The Scotsman,* 23rd September.

KARIM, S. M. M. (1971). 'Prostaglandins'. *Brit. J. Hosp. Med.,* **5**, No. 4, pp. 555-563.

LORAINE, J. A. (1970). *Sex and the Population Crisis.* London, Heinemann Medical Books.

LORAINE, J. A., ISMAIL, A. A. A., ADAMOPOULOS, D. A. and DOVE, G. A. (1970). 'Endocrine function in male and female homosexuals'. *Brit. med. J.,* **4**, pp. 406-408.

LORAINE, J. A., ADAMOPOULOS, D. A., KIRKHAM, K. E., ISMAIL, A. A. A. and DOVE, G. A. (1971). 'Patterns of hormone excretion in male and female homosexuals'. *Nature* **234**, pp. 552-555.

PEEL, J. and POTTS, M. (1969). *Textbook of Contraceptive Practice.* Cambridge, University Press.

THOMAS, PATRICIA and POWELL, GEORGE (1971). 'The One Child Family. *Zero Population Growth,* **3**, No. 2, pp. 6-9, 31-32.

XVII

A BRAKE ON OUR FERTILITY?

Winston Churchill wrote almost 40 years ago 'a vast fog of information envelops the fatal steps to Armageddon'. He was referring to the circumstances leading up to the outbreak of the First World War, but his aphorism is grimly apposite to the whole nexus of problems confronting Spaceship Earth in the last third of the twentieth century. Towering over them all is the dilemma of overpopulation, for unless a brake is applied to man's proclivity for reproduction there can be no tolerable future for the species. It has been said with truth before and it can be said again 'whatever your cause, it's a lost cause without population control'.

In one of his most famous phrases Keynes observed that we are ruled by ideas and by very little else. What ideas do we have to remedy the population explosion?

*   *   *

Will family planning do the trick? Certainly it is now widely accepted, and indeed a notable feature of the decade of the 1960's was the dissemination of the doctrine of family planning throughout the planet. In December of 1966 the UN Secretary General, U. Thant, issued a declaration on population signed by 12 heads of state, and a year later 18 additional heads of state signed the document. The aim of the declaration was two fold—firstly to stress the perils to mankind of the crisis of numbers, and secondly to recommend the widespread use of family planning to counter this all important threat to humanity. Accordingly, as the decade of the 1970's opens, the cure of the population explosion is indissolubly linked in the minds of heads of state, politicians and officials with the extension of family planning services. Family planning is the knight in shining armour, the hope for posterity, the darling of the conventional wisdom, the means whereby our 'children's children' will be accorded the 'good life'. But is this optimism justified? What does family planning stand for and above all what has it achieved so far?

I emphasised in Chapter XVI that much of family planning had to do with the provision of contraceptives. In the early stages of the movement vaginal caps and douches, jellies and spermicides held sway; now intrauterine devices and, above all, the oral contraceptive Pill, have moved to the centre of the stage. In the past the enthusiasm of family planners for the condom was muted, largely due to the overwhelmingly female orientation of the specialty; now, in the face of a worsening population situation, even the condom is emerging from the shadows. Prostaglandins are not prescribed in family planning clinics; nor is this likely to happen for a considerable period of time because of the swingeing regulations almost certain to be imposed on the use of such compounds by drug safety committees still operating in an era dominated by the emotionalism of the thalidomide tragedy. In recent years family planning has clasped vasectomy to its bosom, and now this operation is performed quite frequently in clinics under its jurisdiction. However, in the case of abortion—a method of fertility control of proved efficacy in reducing the birth rate as the examples of Japan and Eastern Europe illustrate—the traditional attitude of family planning has been antagonistic. Indeed, even as recently as the latter part of the decade of the 1960's much of the aid given by the USA to underdeveloped countries for purposes of family planning was provided on the understanding that such assistance would have as one of its major aims the reduction of the incidence of abortion!

It is a matter of intense satisfaction to politicians all over the world that the whole ethos of family planning is voluntary. Coercive measures in the reproductive sphere are vigorously opposed; the specialty is 'democratic'; it preserves the freedom of the individual; it loses candidates no votes at election time. It can be seen to be closely allied to the practice of medicine; it cares for the health of mother and child; it even provides for the treatment of the infertile patient. The family planning literature is studded with phrases such as 'couples must be able to have the number of children *they want*',* and the UN Declaration of 1967 expressly stated that the 'opportunity to decide the number and spacing of children is a basic human right'. In 1965 the Turkish Government passed a law dealing with population, an event of considerable interest in an underdeveloped country likely to double its numbers in under 30 years. Did the law recommend a brake on the procreative capacity of the nation? Not at all. Instead it proclaimed that population planning meant that individuals could have '*as many children as they wish whenever they want to*'.* What sort of population policy is this, and how on the basis of such statements can one take family planning seriously in the crowded world of the 1970's? Small wonder therefore that a certain degree of irreverance for family planning is widespread, the scepticism being summed up in the remark of a certain gentleman who said of the specialty 'family planning means that if we are going to breed like rabbits we should do so on purpose'!

All the criticism of family planning could be dismissed if it worked. But does it, and has the massive expenditure so far accorded to it been justified by the results? It is in the Third World of Asia, Africa and Latin America that family planning will eventually be judged. What has been its saga there?

I indicated in Chapter XV that the record of family planning in the Third World has so far been bleak. In India family planning started in the early 1950's; at that time the population was some 370 million and the growth rate was 1.3 per cent per annum. The momentum of family planning greatly increased during the 1960's; yet in 1971 the Indian population exceeded 550 million, was growing at the rate of 2.6 per cent per annum and was likely to double in 27 years. In Pakistan family planning took root in 1960; then the population was 99 million; now it is 141 million and is likely to double in 21 years. The People's Republic of China began to step up the dimensions of its family planning campaign in the early 1960's. Then the population was in the neighbourhood of 650 million; now it has risen to some 770 million and is expected to double in less than

* The italics are mine.

40 years! In Africa and Latin America a number of countries are now sponsoring programmes of family planning. But no slowing of population growth is apparent; indeed as stressed previously, these areas are experiencing a veritable avalanche of procreation with numbers rising more rapidly than anywhere else on earth. Only in a few countries—and none of them with large populations in world terms—is there any evidence that family planning activities may have contributed to falling birth rates. Islanders would appear to be more sensitive than mainlanders to the philosophy of family planning, and in a few islands such as Formosa and Puerto Rico and possibly also Ceylon and Mauritius, family planners would have us believe that their efforts have been responsible for the modest reduction in birth rates which has been observed in recent years; a similar claim has been made for South Korea and for the city states of Singapore and Hong Kong. But even in these areas the precise role of family planning in limiting fertility is in some doubt. Such nations are far from typical of the Third World as a whole, for as a result of their incipient industrialisation they could well be undergoing a spontaneous demographic transition from large to small families and could thus be following in the footsteps of Europe in the late nineteenth century and of Japan in the early 1920's.

The family planning literature is replete with aims and goals. Thus the government of India aims to reduce the birth rate of the country from 42 to 32 per 1,000 by 1974 and to 25 per 1,000 by 1978/79. In Pakistan the government is pledged to reduce the birth rate from 43 to 32 per 1,000 during the next 5 years. The Keyna government declares that it desires to decrease the annual rate of population growth from 3.3 to 2.3 per cent in 10 years, while in South Korea the intention in 1967 was to cut the rate from 2.9 per cent to 1.2 per cent by 1970. The outstanding feature of these aims is their modesty. There is no question of stopping the growth of numbers; indeed all that is offered is a slight deceleration of the present rapid tempo of procreation. Thus for Kenya a rate of increase of 2.3 per cent per annum would still allow numbers in that country to double in approximately 30 years, while in the case of South Korea—the second most densely settled nation on earth—a growth rate of 1.2 per cent per annum would permit the population to double in less than 60 years. If, as is sometimes stated, family planning programmes are merely the first step to a population policy then the step has so far been executed with leaden feet. Moreover, if this is the first step what is the next? No information on this vital point is provided in the family planning literature.

How have family planning programmes fared in developed countries where in some cases they have been operative for many years? Marie Stopes opened the first birth control clinic in Britain in 1921; since then, and particularly during the decade of the 1960's when the specialty became fashionable, services have multiplied. Many British politicians are now in favour of family planning programmes—just as they are in favour of economic growth and technological wizardry. What has been the effect of family planning in Britain and in particular has it slowed the rate of population increase? A definite answer to this important question cannot at present be provided, but it has been claimed that the increasing use of contraceptives, especially the Pill, contributed to falling birth rates during the decade of the 1960's.

To many people in Britain a population policy is synonymous with family planning. Protagonists of the viewpoint proclaim that in the UK, the excess of births over deaths each year lies between 250,000 and 300,000 and that this figure is of the same order of magnitude as that for unwanted births. Therefore, so the argument runs, all that is required in order to obtain zero population growth is to eliminate unwanted births through an effective family planning programme. Is this postulate likely to be true or is the whole concept unduly simplistic? The experience of the city of Aberdeen may give a pointer here. This was the home town of Sir Dugald Baird—that brightest of stars in the medical firmament of the twentieth century—who pioneered abortion for social reasons as early as the 1940's and who laid the basis of the most sophisticated family planning service in the UK, a service which has been continued and expanded by his able successors. What has happened to the birth rate in Aberdeen and in particular has it now attained replacement level? Unfortunately not. In 1970 the

Aberdeen birth rate stood at 14.5 per 1,000: admittedly this figure is well below the national average, but it is still too high for zero population growth.

In a percipient and hard hitting article published in *Science* during 1969 the American demographer, Judith Blake, took a highly critical view of current family planning policies within the USA. Blake devoted a considerable proportion of her paper to the position of the American urban poor, congregated in the squalid ghettoes of large conurbations and being constantly harried by the government to adopt methods of birth control. Blake regarded such governmental schemes as misdirected; the rhetoric was a waste of time, and in her opinion the programmes would not succeed in lowering the birth rate because already the majority of the parents in that section of the community had decided to have a relatively large family consisting of three or more children. But Blake went further. She argued that governmentally sponsored family planning programmes concentrating upon the urban poor would inevitably have a trivial effect on the nation as a whole. This is because the great bulk of American population growth—as of population growth in other developed countries including Great Britain—takes place in the affluent middle class who desire families of three children or more and so generate a rate of increase much in excess of that required to ensure zero population growth.

The argument of those who equate family planning with a population policy contains a fatal flaw, and this has been forcibly brought out by Davis in his truly admirable review of the subject. The flaw arises from the fact that the desired family size is all too frequently in excess of the two children which would be required to produce an eventual stabilisation of the population. The international evidence strongly supports Davis' contention. Thus in a survey conducted in Tunisia in the mid-1960's parents regarded as ideal a family size of 4.3 children; in a village near New Delhi in India the corresponding figure was 4.0 while in Bangalore the average figure desired by married women was 3.7 and by married men 4.1. In Latin America desired family sizes varied greatly; they ranged from 2.7 children in Rio de Janeiro to 4.2 children in Mexico City. In

the USA in the early 1940's in the wake of the Great Economic
Depression the most popular ideal was for only 2 children. By
1945 the figure had risen to 3.0 and by 1960 to 4.0; in the
latter part of the 1960's a decrease to 3.4 was reported. Britain
at present has an average family size of 2.4 children, but in
order to achieve a static population the figure would have to fall
to 2.2.

Family planning is a meritorious activity; it is good medicine
and as such should be encouraged. Nevertheless, it must be
recognised that it is manifestly failing to cure the disease for
which it has been prescribed as the antidote. Indeed according
to Davis the very factors which endear family planning to
politicians and officials—its emphasis on free choice, its basic
tenet that married couples have the 'inalienable right' to
produce the number of children which they desire—immediately
render it ineffective as a means of controlling human numbers,
because by placing the decision squarely in the court of the
individual it deprives the state and society as a whole from
regulating the size of the population. In *The Wealth of Nations*
Adam Smith enunciated the concept of the 'invisible hand'
which declared that each individual in pursuing his own
personal aims was driven as if by an invisible force to achieve
the best situation for society as a whole. As mentioned in
Chapter XIII this doctrine formed part of classical economic
theory; it held sway for many years but has now been
completely discredited. A modern equivalent of the concept of
the 'invisible hand' is recognisable in the doctrine of family
planning in which it is assumed that the aggregate of decisions
of countless couples with respect to family size will coincide
with the needs of the state in terms of its population. Such a
concept can only be described as naïve, and is scarcely one
which would stand up to critical examination.

Societal factors in the sphere of reproduction are highly
complex and little understood. In particular, we know almost
nothing of the reasons why parents opt to have a specific
number of children. Probably a whole host of diverse influences
are brought to bear on such decisions including, for example,
parental conditioning, the home environment, religion, the
economic climate, the desire of the male to prove his virility

and of the female to exercise her maternal instincts. Faced with such a web of complexity the approach of family planning can only be regarded as simplistic, for it aims to curb excessive human reproduction merely by the provision of more and better contraceptives. Furthermore, those who operate the specialty, although often highly motivated and idealistic, are generally somewhat limited in their conceptual horizons. Thus one cannot expect doctors, midwives, nurses and social workers to be trained in disciplines such as sociology, demography and economics. Yet the advice of individuals with such backgrounds is mandatory if the present ineffectiveness of family planning in the Third World is ever to be countered.

To attempt to remedy the population explosion by family planning alone ignores the deep societal changes which will be necessary before a solution to this most intractable of problems is forthcoming. Family planning is a blunt instrument which desperately requires to be refined. Up till now it has been the whitewash on the sepulchre, the splendour without the substance, the overture without the opera. Unless its ethos is radically altered in an antinatalist direction its chances of curing the world population crisis are slight—as meagre as those of an aspirin or of a single injection of penicillin in arresting the spread of a malignant tumour.

*   *   *

If family planning, as currently constituted, will not cure overpopulation what about education? Education like family planning has the inestimable advantage that it does not smack of coercion and is therefore politically acceptable in democratic societies.

John Stuart Mill once wrote that improvements in the lot of mankind would not be possible until great changes occurred in the fundamental constitution of their mode of thought. Such a metamorphosis can only be brought about by education. Nobody denies the benefits of education. But how are we educating the children of today about the vital themes of population, the environment and the depletion of the world's finite resources? The answer is that we are not; indeed in school curricula throughout the world teaching in these areas has not yet even got off the ground.

It is true that a number of governments and local authorities now permit sex education in schools. This is designed to inform youngsters about the function of the reproductive organs and may, in the hands of sufficiently courageous teachers, even grasp the twin nettles of contraception and abortion. But sex education is fundamentally different from population control. Sex education deals with the problems of the individual; it does not involve itself with the world scene; it makes no attempt to persuade the mothers of tomorrow to have fewer children; it is unidisciplinary rather than multidisciplinary. Moreover, sex education has already shown itself to be vested with highly emotive overtones just as have subjects like euthanasia, homosexuality, drug taking, the death penalty for murder and the fluoridation of water supplies. Indeed no topic has a greater propensity to rouse parents to paroxysms of rage than has sex education in schools. For to some adults it smacks too much of the permissive society; in their view it will inevitably undermine conventional morality, encourage premarital intercourse through the dissemination of contraceptives amongst teenagers, destroy parental influence and prematurely expose the child to the evils of pornography.

But for population education in schools there should be no comparable opprobrium from society; accordingly, the introduction of such a subject into the school curriculum should not prove to be difficult. Indeed there could be much support for it. For in the minds of countless numbers of ordinary people scattered throughout the planet there is currently a great unease. There is, for example, a growing realisation that the earth is already overpopulated, that pollution is rampant, that the environment is steadily deteriorating, that the chimera of security with which they have been wont to wrap their lives is being steadily eroded, that conventional politicians are capable of reacting only to instant problems and have no prescience or vision, and that as a result the earth is pilotless, is navigating perilous and inhospitable seas and can only end up by foundering on the rocks.

These views are still rudimentary and inchoate, and they manifest themselves particularly in protests about the environment. There are now numerous examples of such a reaction—the frenzied attempts of Japanese students to prevent another airport being built in Tokyo, the commotion in Stockholm over the preservation of elm trees, the roar from British conservationist groups at the government's decision to mine for copper in Snowdonia, and the furore on the quayside at Thorshavn in the Faroes which prevented the Dutch tanker, *Stella Maris*, carrying toxic industrial wastes, from refuelling there.

Indeed for many young people—who, after all, must suffer for the grievous errors of previous generations—the issues of population and the environment have become vested with a quasi-religious flavour. This is not surprising for the Christian religion has lost much authority and influence during the twentieth century; indeed it has never fully regained its poise since Darwin expounded his revolutionary concepts about the origin of man over 100 years ago. For the majority of people conventional religion seems strangely inappropriate to the pressing problems of the day. On overpopulation its voice is either muted or pronatalist; on environmental deterioration and resource depletion it scarcely speaks above a whisper. Manifestly it has failed to provide a moral and spiritual lead on contemporary issues. Many people require faith in something—otherwise to them life on earth becomes intolerable. Substitutes for conventional religion are being eagerly sought, and perhaps—who knows?—the answer for some will eventually be found in the concept that man is an integral part of a huge web of life which must be cherished and not degraded, preserved and not despoiled, protected and not betrayed.

For politicians education in matters of population should have considerable appeal. This is mainly because it carries with it no element of compulsion. For electoral reasons contemporary politicians fear and dislike any forms of coercion with respect to reproductive processes; indeed they would prefer to share a seat with a porcupine or with a boa constrictor rather than see them introduced. However, in a democratic society population education could find much favour. In contrast to coercive measures, which as someone once opined 'might bring down the Government rather than the birth rate', population education could form a plank in political manifestoes, could be proclaimed at the hustings and could be presented to the electorate without necessarily producing a salutary effect on the ballot box.

However, population education is not a panacea for the world's ills and, as emphasised in a recent article from the Population Reference Bureau, there remain formidable difficulties before it can become a viable option. The first and overriding consideration is that the dynamic behind such education will inevitably proceed at a slow tempo; thus the braking pressure applied to the world's fertility will be gentle, and in an era of exponential population growth may well prove to be inadequate. Difficulties will also arise with respect to the school curricula, for in the past educational systems have been arranged around specific disciplines; now an interdisciplinary approach will be essential. Furthermore, such curricula are already overcrowded, and to many professional educationists it may appear difficult or even impossible to introduce yet another course of study. Finally there is a very serious shortage of teachers and educators with experience in subjects such as demography and ecology; so much so that the demand for such individuals will far exceed their supply. Here colleges and universities will have a key role to play in the provision of the teachers of the future. Existing courses of study will have to be altered, and new courses continuously introduced in order to meet the needs of the times. The recently formed Environmental Quality Council in the USA pinpointed the dilemma in a statement issued in 1970. The Council bemoaned the great national shortage of trained professionals to teach subjects relating to the environment, and it recommended that the Federal Government should place high on its list of priorities the establishment of colleges geared to provide instruction in this area.

Have population educators made any impact at all so far? Again in America there is a faint glimmer of hope, for in April 1970 there took place at Manresa-on-Severn in Maryland the first ever Workshop on Population Education. Most of the participants in the Workshop were teachers who on their own initiative had taught population to their students without the aid of 'established curricula, tests or social administration'. The teachers issued a ringing affirmation of their credo at the end of the conference. They called for a massive expansion in the field of population education, for the provision of generous funds to ensure the health of the specialty, and for the increasing use of the mass media of communication in order to carry the message of population education into every home in the land.

The Workshop of Manresa was a start; nevertheless, the road to population education will be long, arduous and beset by many pitfalls. For what is desperately needed is an Educational Revolution, and this will be exceedingly hard to achieve. But were it to come to pass it could perhaps be the saviour of mankind for its effects might be as fundamental and far reaching as those of the Agricultural and Industrial Revolutions of bygone days.

*　　*　　*

The women of the 1970's are on the march. A new radicalism is stirring amongst them and is finding expression in organisations such as the Women's Liberation Movement. Potentially such radicalism, by channelling an increasing proportion of women out of the arena of conventional marriage, by exposing fewer of them to the treadmill of reproduction, and by guiding them towards alternative roles in society, could have a substantial effect on the world population crisis. What possibilities exist in this direction?

Radicalism amongst women is not new to the twentieth century. The suffragette movement was the first of the feminist surges, and it reached its zenith in Britain in the years immediately preceding the outbreak of the First World War. The women of England were incensed; constitutional action had failed to gain them the vote, and under the leadership of the indomitable Emmeline Pankhurst and her daughter Christabel they took the situation into their own hands. They set fire to pillar boxes and historical buildings; they smashed the windows of department stores; they slashed pictures in art galleries; they severed telegraph wires with long-handled clippers; they chained themselves to the railings outside Buckingham Palace; they threw themselves in front of racehorses. They consistently

harried the members of H. H. Asquith's Liberal cabinet. They
sent them letters filled with snuff and red pepper; they attacked
Mr. Asquith with a horse whip at Bannockburn, pilloried him
on the golf course, and continuously interrupted meetings
which he and his colleagues were attempting to address. The
men of the country scorned and derided the suffragettes; there
were however notable exceptions including Keir Hardie, George
Lansbury and George Bernard Shaw. But these women were
tough. They incited the police to considerable brutality and
they did not flinch at the repressive measures used. They
endured imprisonment without complaint; they went on hunger
strike and they bore with fortitude and restraint the torn gums,
lacerated gullets and general indignity of forced feeding by the
stomach tube. They became a mighty political force. For
together with the increasing militancy of the workers and the
revolt of the Conservative party over Ireland—a policy which
backed the wild men of the Orange Order, resulted in the
installation of Sir Edward Carson in Belfast and has finally
come home to roost in the agony of contemporary Ulster—they
wrecked the whole edifice of Asquithian Liberalism so carefully
built up since the beginning of the century. The Liberal Party
momentarily regained its poise at the outbreak of the First
World War; soon it was compelled to form a coalition with the
Conservatives, an association which indubitably hastened its
demise. When the First World War erupted in 1914 the then
Foreign Secretary, Sir Edward Grey, was heard to remark 'the
lamps are going out all over Europe'. But it was not only lamps
in Europe which were being extinguished. It was the lamp of
the once glorious Liberal Party—the party of Gladstone, of
Rosebery, of Campbell-Bannerman, of Asquith, of Lloyd
George, of Winston Churchill in his prime—and in the eclipse of
this seemingly indestructible bulwark of Victorian England the
suffragette movement had played a not insignificant role.

The Women's Liberation Movement of today espouses causes
which would have been foreign to the suffragettes of two
generations ago. Now man himself is the oppressor; he
dominates society and society is organised for him alone; he is
selfish and lascivious, and in sexual matters he is downright
irresponsible; he feels it essential to 'prove himself' by estab-

lishing his fertility; he may be possessed of an insensate desire to father a son and in order to achieve this end he will impregnate a woman time after time. The women are the second class citizens; in America they have sometimes been compared to the negro population. Whether they like it or not they are channelled into the marriage market and into pregnancy, child rearing and home management. From as early as they can remember—indeed from the time at which they handle their first doll—they are told that they have only two objectives in life—to snare a man and to bear his children. Mammoth propaganda is mounted on women to assume the reproductive role; women's magazines extol it, the mass media trumpet it forth, friends and relatives shout it from the rooftops and the conventional wisdom of religion supports it. Judith Blake summed it all up very well when, testifying to a US House of Representatives Subcommittee in 1969, she said:

'We penalise homosexuals, of both sexes, we insist that women must bear unwanted children by depriving them of ready access to abortion, we make people with small families support the schooling of others. We offer women few viable options to full time careers as wives and mothers, except jobs that are, on the average, of low status and low pay. In effect, we force a massive investment of human resources into the reproductive sphere—far more than we need to invest. It seems obvious that family life as we know it has been a forced march for more people than we usually care to admit, and that many people might be happier if they did not fill such roles'.

The Women's Liberation Movement wants free contraception and abortion on demand. It wants round-the-clock nursery facilities for children similar to those provided in some of the Eastern European countries. It wants equal educational facilities for men and women, and last but by no means least, it wants equal pay for women throughout the whole of the labour force.

The movement certainly has cause to be worried about the position of working women, for as Rhondda Levitt observes in a recent article in *Zero Population Growth* women are generally 'the last to be hired and the first to be fired'. Germaine Greer, in her erudite, highly polemical yet curiously moving book *The*

Female Eunuch, describes the plight of working women in England where they form 38 per cent of the labour force. The average weekly wage of women engaged in administrative, clerical and technical jobs is less than £12; on the other hand men in the same occupations earn as much as £28 per week. In manual jobs males earn an average of £20 per week, women only £10. What of equal pay for equal work? Will this be the solvent of all ills and will it open the gates to a feminine Utopia? Greer and others do not think so, for they consider that even if such legislation is introduced, the best jobs will continue to go to men. Indeed it has been argued that such a change in the law might make the situation even worse because employers who formerly were prepared to accept women at low wages in spite of the hazards of marriage, pregnancy and childbirth, might now refuse to do so because of the lack of any financial saving.

What will be the future of the Women's Liberation Movement? Will it grow and prosper or will it be an evanescent phenomenon reminiscent of the Scottish Nationalist Party in Britain between the general elections of 1966 and 1970? Only in the USA has Women's Liberation so far made any real progress. There it is a force to be reckoned with; it is radical and militant; it can stage protest marches down Madison Avenue and it can harry the Mayor of New York City. However, in other parts of the world including Britain the movement still remains in an embryonic state.

Will Women's Liberation be a significant factor in slowing the world's drift to a demographic disaster? No one knows—for it depends on the women.

*   *   *

The themes of this chapter so far have been family planning, population education and alternative roles for women in society. The common factor in these three options is the lack of any element of compulsion in the realm of reproductive processes. But there remain in the antinatalist armamentarium measures of a more coercive type, and it is when these come up for discussion that contemporary politicians become querulous and shake as though afflicted with the palsy.

Governments could make it known that they are in favour of the postponement of marriage. Such legislation would make good physiological sense for the span of reproductive life in women is limited. Fertility is higher in the early days of the childbearing era immediately following puberty; it tends to diminish with age as the incidence of anovulatory menstrual cycles increases; once the climacteric has supervened the women is infertile and remains so for the rest of her life. Later marriage might therefore tend to decrease the number of births by reducing the period of the woman's life during which she is 'at risk' from pregnancy. Furthermore, such a measure might have some effect on contemporary societal attitudes by deflecting a higher proportion of women than at present from life styles concerned with reproduction and child rearing into other types of occupation.

Objective evidence already exists that the postponement of marriage can act as a brake on population growth. The classical example is, of course, Ireland, where for a number of reasons, including a poor economic climate and the literal acceptance of a now anachronistic form of religious teaching, couples traditionally tended to marry at a relatively late age. As a result the Irish birth rate has until recently been lower than that of most other Western European nations. In the past few years, however, the winds of change have been blowing over the Irish Republic with almost hurricane force. Social mores have altered radically; the Catholic Church has been forced to adopt a defensive posture and is in some disarray; a Women's Liberation Movement has sprung up and there are now reports in the press of women fitted with vaginal caps and diaphragms and carrying the Pill crossing the border from Ulster and thus flouting the anti-contraceptive legislation of the Republic. The birth rate of a country is often a sensitive barometer of social change; therefore it is pertinent to note that in recent years the Irish birth rate has risen and is now very similar to that of other Western European states.

Undoubtedly the country which currently exerts most pressure on couples to marry late is the People's Republic of

China. In 1950 the Communist Government under Mao Tse-tung raised the minimum age of marriage from 18 to 20 in males and from 16 to 18 in females. In the early 1960's the campaign for late marriage was stepped up; now the state urged that men should not marry before the age of 28 and women before 25. Students were dismissed from schools if they married before graduation; in the communes marriage licenses for men were difficult to obtain before the age of 30. There were strong political overtones in this propaganda. Thus those who heeded the government's call for late marriage were the true patriots and were eulogised; those who did not respond were 'failing in their duty to the fatherland'. What effect, if any, has the propaganda drive in favour of late marriage had on the Chinese birth rate? It is very difficult to provide a meaningful assessment at present, but there exists the possibility that the somewhat slower rate of population growth in China as compared with, for example, India, Pakistan and Indonesia the governments of which do not sponsor such a policy, may have resulted partly from this cause.

Apart from actually postponing the legal age of marriage governments could take other forms of action, and some of the choices open to them have been reviewed by Berelson of the Population Council. Thus fees for marriage licenses could be substantially increased; incentive payments could be made if the couple agreed to delay their marriage, and governmental loans for wedding ceremonies could be provided if the bride were of sufficient age. Another suggestion which has been offered is intriguing. It is that there should be two types of marriage—the first childless and relatively easy to dissolve, and the second designed for procreation and therefore more long lasting.

What of changes in the fiscal system of the country with special reference to family allowances and tax relief for parents? Alterations of this type are certainly possible; undoubtedly they would be highly controversial. Politicians, brought up from their earliest days to regard their calling as 'the art of the possible', would classify such legislation as beyond the electoral pale, would eschew it for as long as possible and were it ever introduced would proceed to emasculate it with maximum speed. Indeed some of the revulsion felt by politicians in Britain and elsewhere at the concept of a population policy stems from the misapprehension that an integral part of such a system would necessarily be swingeing fiscal changes. It is when such changes are mentioned that hands are laid on political hearts, platitudinous utterances are made and there are pious declarations that elected representatives would never be party to the 'taxing of children'.

Throughout the world the official policy of most states is strongly pronatalist in that family allowances are paid to couples with children and tax relief is afforded to parents. In France, which leads the world in pronatalism, approximately 5 per cent of the national income of the country is devoted to family allowances; in Belgium the figure is just over 3 per cent and in Czechoslovakia 2.6 per cent. Currently the UK permits tax relief amounting to £155 on each child under 11 years of age, on £180 on each child between the ages of 11 and 15 and on £205 for each child over 16 years of age as long as he or she is still attending school. In addition family allowances are paid; ostensibly these are intended to assist the poorer sections of the community, and the taxation system 'claws back' this type of support from the more affluent. Surprisingly enough the first child does not feature in the British family allowance system, the rate being £0.90 per week for the second child and £1.00 per week for each subsequent child until the latter leaves school. British family allowances were last raised in 1968 and child allowances in 1971.

Family allowances and parental tax relief are essentially a relic of the days when an increase in population was regarded as beneficial to the state. In the overpopulated world of the 1970's such a view is manifestly inappropriate, and it is therefore scarcely surprising that in certain quarters suggestions have been made that this type of legislation should now be altered. Such proposals have been ably summarised by American authorities such as Davis, Berelson and Ehrlich, and to contemporary politicians speaking at the hustings and seeking re-election they must have an almost nightmarish quality. They include a reversal of tax benefits to favour the bachelor, the spinster, the childless couple and the couple with a small number of children, the complete abolition of family allowances or their withdrawal after an 'agreed' number of children have been born, increasing taxation for successive children, progressive reduction of maternity benefits as the family size increases, and avoidance of fiscal policies which discriminate against a married couple when the wife is in employment. The catalogue is grim indeed; yet one of the notable features of all the writings on this subject is the emphasis given by the authors to the necessity for protecting the very poor in the community from the icy blast of this reforming legislation. How this protection will be achieved has seldom been clearly defined, but possibly the provision of allowances in kind rather than in cash might go far to mitigate hardship as far as the individual family is concerned.

What relationship exists between the paying of family allowances and the procreative capacity of the community? No one knows precisely, and this is certainly an area in which there is a clamant need for future research. Lee, writing recently in *Studies in Family Planning*, suggested that when the size of the payment was in excess of the cost of delivering, rearing and educating the child a stimulus to fertility might be provided, and the example of Rumania quoted in Chapter XV where a large increase in family allowances together with other pro-natalist measures rapidly boosted the birth rate of the country would appear to lend support to this contention. If, on the other hand, as in Britain the family allowance payment is relatively small it seems unlikely that its withdrawal would have much effect on the birth rate. This is so because copulating couples throughout the world do not indulge in this activity in order to be awarded the glittering accolade of a family allowance and would not abstain from it were the payment withdrawn. High sex drive, inherent pronatalism, basic repro-ductive urges, societal pressures and the inability to recognise the existence of a world population crisis are undoubtedly much more potent spurs to procreation than are the payment of family allowances.

In a number of countries including Great Britain family allowances have become a basic rubric of society; indeed in the minds of many they are indissolubly linked with the concept of social justice. Any attempt to diminish or abolish them would be greeted with howls of anguish, and in Britain the reaction to such a proposal of a body such as the powerful and militant Child Poverty Action Group would verge on apoplexy. Politicians know this fact of life only too well; therefore, they tread warily and must at no time by word or deed be seen to be discriminating against children.

Instead of imposing penalites on the highly fecund in the community incentive programmes favouring those who abstained from reproduction might be more acceptable from the social point of view. Many ideas on this subject have been aired, and one which has received a good deal of publicity in Western countries was a proposal made by the Indian politician Chandrasekhar. His suggestion was that a transistor radio or a payment in cash should be given to subjects initiating the practice of contraception and that an award should also be provided for individuals agreeing to be sterilised; unfortunately the Indian government did not follow up Chandrasekhar's proposal, and his term of governmental office was brief. Manning, discussing the British scene, has urged the Government to launch a programme of positive incentives designed to reduce the birth rate. He calculated that each birth in the UK cost about £200 in direct grants and care, and he therefore suggested that an equivalent sum might be given to those prepared to offer themselves for sterilisation, particularly by the technique of vasectomy. Another proposal put forward by Manning was that annual tax-free bonuses should be paid to women of reproductive age who did not produce a child within the year.

*   *   *

From mildly coercive procedures designed to control reproduction we pass finally to really draconian measures. Here the contemporary politician blanches with terror; indeed his affection for such forms of legislation cannot be rated much higher than for the man-eating tiger athirst for his blood. For draconian measures carry with them the aura of compulsion, and although politicians would not, for example, object to their constituents being compulsorily educated, being forced to join a trade union, or being made to pay compulsory insurance, they would raise their voices in horror at the mere thought of mandatory sterilisation. To them sexual intercourse and pro-creation are personal and private matters and are not open for public debate. Indeed in the political vocabulary of the 1970's there could be no greater crime than compulsory sterilisation; thus it would be 'a gross interference with the liberty of the subject', 'a return to barbarism', 'a recrudescence of Hitlerism', 'a premature 1984'. Those in public life adept at the pejorative comment would never have had it so good!

The field of compulsory sterilisation presents many choices; all of them are highly unattractive when judged by the standards of contemporary society. Chandrasekhar has sug-gested that in India vasectomy should be compulsory after three living children have been born. Davis has proposed that an induced abortion should be made obligatory in an illegitimate pregnancy. Another authority has worked out a system involv-ing 'marketable licenses to have children' and has geared the system to the production of only two offspring per couple.

These are interesting proposals, but in the sphere of mandatory sterilisation most publicity has so far been accorded to the suggestion that a sterilising agent might be added either to water supplies or to a staple food. I discussed this concept in *Sex and the Population Crisis*, and in 1970 the prestigious American scientist, Carl Djerassi—co-discoverer with Gregory Pincus of the Pill—aptly designated such a compound an Orwellian contraceptive. What are the chances that an agent of this type will eventually be developed? Djerassi rates them as very low indeed, and lists a number of cogent reasons for his belief. In the first place, he promulgates the viewpoint that the substance would have to be active either in men and women but not in both; this would obviously limit its sphere of applica-bility. Moreover the substance would have to be completely non-toxic and devoid of side effects; it would have, of necessity, to be tasteless and, of course, it could not be allowed to interfere with the libido of either sex. If added to a food the substance would presumably have to be incorporated by the supplier; so all that would require to be done if one wished to avoid exposure to the contraceptive would be to eliminate that particular item from the diet. If the substance were added to water there would also be major problems. Presumably the addition could only be made in the case of water emanating from a central system. Accordingly, wells which provide water for at least half the world's population, would be immune, and it would indeed be ironic if the use of groundwater enabled millions to escape from a governmentally imposed programme of fertility control! But there would be a further dilemma for the effects of such a sterilising agent would have to be reversible by administering an antidote. No such antidote is on the scientific or medical horizon, and Djerassi is extremely doubtful if an agent with this property will ever be developed. Finally what sort of public reaction would follow the initiation of Orwellian contraception? Undoubtedly the furore would be prodigious, and compared with it the tumult over the fluoridation of water supplies would scarcely register one decibel.

*   *   *

It is apparent that a bewildering array of options would face a government intending to implement a population policy. Which method or combination of methods should be selected? How damaging would the choice of any method be to a party's political fortunes at the polls? How much coercion in reproductive processes would the electorate be prepared to tolerate? These are questions which will haunt politicians for the remainder of this century and beyond.

Had I the power of decision for which methods would I opt? The matter is one of almost labyrinthine complexity and the choice would have to vary depending on the area of the world.

In the developed countries of the West I would give pride of place to population education; high on my list also would feature a serious attempt to find alternative roles for women in society. These remedies appeal to me not only because they are basically democratic in nature, but also because they seem to offer some possibility of effecting the deep rooted and fundamental social changes which will be necessary before an acceptable population policy can evolve. I recognise only too well that both of these assaults on the bastion of overpopulation must, of necessity, proceed at a slow tempo, and that for this reason they may be unable to control the spread of the disease. Nevertheless, the measures are grounded in rationality and they should in my opinion be accorded an earnest and conscientious trial. Contrary to the views of world leaders, politicians and most officials, traditional family planning would not head my list; it would occupy a lower place because of my scepticism that the mere provision of contraceptives will significantly decrease birth rates. I am however prepared to be convinced that if conventional family planning is combined with a vigorous programme of abortion and sterilisation by vasectomy, a favourable effect on population growth might eventually be achieved. In Western countries the introduction of major coercive measures in the sphere of reproduction would almost certainly raise our volatile and indocile electorates to fury and would probably topple the government; for these reasons they are unlikely to come into operation in the foreseeable future. On the other hand, relatively mild coercive measures including, for example, changes in the fiscal system to favour the unmarried and those with small families, and alterations in the laws relating to marriage, might be tolerated by the citizenry provided that the reasons for such changes were adequately explained by governmentally sponsored propaganda of an antinatalist character.

What of the nations of the Third World? It would be pleasant to be able to state that the same series of options applied there. Unfortunately they do not. Much of the population in these areas remains illiterate, and therefore population education is utterly impractical; the role of the woman throughout the Third World is everywhere subservient to that of the man, and there is not even a glimmer of female radicalism on the horizon; family planning has manifestly failed to build a breakwater against the dangerous waves of overpopulation; abortion and vasectomy would have to be mounted on an unprecedented scale even to dent the colossus of population growth. So what are the prospects for the Third World? Must it continue to journey down the *via dolorosa*? Is there no light for it at the end of the tunnel? Alas, the outlook is melancholy indeed for already the situation has probably gone beyond a stage where repair can be contemplated. What then will happen eventually? Will there come a time when governments in the Third World, driven to distraction by population pressures, will introduce swingeing coercive measures in an attempt to limit fertility, or will the ultimate solution lie with the apocalyptic horsemen of Malthus—war, famine, disease and death—who will move from the wings into the centre of the stage and there extract their ineluctable toll?

The supreme world crisis of overpopulation desperately requires political leadership of the highest calibre. Yet this is singularly lacking and instead apathy, complacency, myopia and sheer lack of comprehension abound. Will it always be so? Or can one dare to hope that one day a real world leader will arise who will see it as his bounden duty to 'give history a push', to unfurl the banner of population control, to begin the long and perilous journey along the road of a global population policy, and once and for all to put an end to the gloomy lucubrations of doomwatchers like myself? At present there is no such leader in sight or even in prospect. However, were he to emerge and in the fullness of time to fulfil his mission on our tortured planet what better epitaph could be accorded to him than the immortal words of Sidney Carton in Dickens' *A Tale of Two Cities:*

It is a far, far better thing I do, than I have ever done; it is a far, far better rest that I go to than I have ever known.

References

BERELSON, BERNARD (1969). 'Beyond Family Planning'. *Studies in Family Planning,* No. 38, February.

BLAKE, JUDITH (1969). 'Population Policy for Americans: Is the Government being misled?'. *Science,* **164**, pp. 522-529.

DANGERFIELD, GEORGE (1966). *The Strange Death of Liberal England.* London, MacGibbon and Kee Ltd.

DAVIS, KINGSLEY (1967). 'Population Policy: Will current programs succeed?'. *Science,* **158**, pp. 730-739.

DJERASSI, CARL (1970). 'Birth control after 1984'. *Science,* **169**, pp. 941-951.

EHRLICH, PAUL R. (1968). *The Population Bomb.* New York, Ballantine Books, Inc.

GREER, GERMAINE (1971). *The Female Eunuch.* London, Paladin.

LEE, LUKE T. (1971). 'Law and Family Planning'. *Studies in Family Planning,* **2**, No. 4, April.

LEVITT, RHONDA (1971). 'In Pursuit of Freedom: Women in America'. *Zero Population Growth,* 3, No. 5, pp. 1-3.

LORAINE, J. A. (1970). *Sex and the Population Crisis.* London, Heinemann Medical Books.

MANNING, AUBREY (1970). 'No standing room'. *The Ecologist,* 1, No. 1, pp. 7-10.

POPULATION BULLETIN (1970). 'Population Education: A Challenge of the Seventies', 26, No. 3.

SPENGLER, JOSEPH J. (1969). 'Population Problem: In Search of a Solution'. *Science,* 166, pp. 1234-1238.

WORLD LEADERS DECLARATION ON POPULATION (1967). Presented at the United Nations on Human Rights Day, December.

EPILOGUE

And everything that is in the earth shall die.

Genesis, Chapter VI, verse 17

When Britain entered the twentieth century there were solid grounds for optimism. For her the Victorian era had been in many ways a golden age; it had been a time of mounting prosperity and notable achievement; above all, it had been an era of unprecedented peace. Britain had skilfully avoided major international entanglements in Europe; she had become adept at maintaining that delicate political equilibrium, commonly referred to as the 'balance of power', and as a result the recurrent revolutions and the mighty military campaigns which had surged throughout the land mass of Europe had left her unmolested and serene.

During the nineteenth century British power and prestige had been at their zenith. She had presided majestically over a great Empire; her authority was unassailable and secure from all attack; she was the cockpit of the civilised world. This was the time when Lord Palmerston, that archetypal symbol of the imperial age, could talk with truth of a 'pax Britannica' and in his celebrated 'civis Romanus sum' speech to Parliament could justifiably claim that 'a British subject in whatever land he may be, shall feel confident that the watchful eye and strong arm of England will protect him against injustice and wrong'. By the 1890's the whole world, including the European continent, was lapped in peace. So much so that in 1896 the young Winston Churchill, thirsting for adventure and scouring a placid planet for the merest hint of excitement, could find his heart's desire only in far off Cuba where a small and rather desultory guerrilla war was in progress between the Spaniards and the native islanders.

By the turn of the century there had been some erosion of Britain's hegemony. Powerful and thrusting competitors had made their appearance on the global stage in the form of Kaiser Wilhelm's Imperial Germany and the United States, then under the leadership of the flamboyant and charismatic President, Theodore Roosevelt. These countries were challenging for economic markets; they were bent on self-aggrandisement and they were determined to influence in a significant manner the *realpolitik* of the world. Britain had been compelled to abandon her traditional policy of non-alignment in Europe, and in 1904 the *entente cordiale* with France had been signed. Yet the overall British position remained strong. Her Empire was still intact, and indeed she had recently added to the territory under her suzerainty through the exploits of Kitchener in Africa and as a result of the Boer war. The Royal Navy policed the seas, and in so doing kept all antagonists at arms length; the City of London prided itself on being the commercial and business centre of the world; the social order seemed fixed and immutable and as unchanging as the planets in their courses.

The British political firmament of the early 1900's glowed with stars. For 1906 saw the election by a landslide majority of a Liberal government which in its intrinsic talent and sheer cerebral capacity far outranked any administration of past or present. The Cabinet was packed with illustrious names. There were Augustan figures such as Morley and Asquith, who had sat at the feet of Gladstone and had imbibed his wisdom. But, in addition, there were two new and exciting personages—David Lloyd George and Winston Churchill—men of outstanding intellectual ability, preordained to ride the deep and treacherous tides of destiny, to be in tune with the hour when their country sorely needed them, and to make their own indelible and highly specific imprint on the sweep of modern history.

What will be the situation when Britain together with the rest of the world enters the twenty-first century, a mere 30 years from now? It will undoubtedly be much more sombre than that obtaining 100 years ago. For the demons which already beset us in 1972 will not have been exorcised; rather will they have grown markedly both in stature and malignancy. By that time the developed countries could well be facing a state of affairs redolent of Pompeii in the shadow of Vesuvius. Their governments, spurred on by rising unemployment and intractable inflation, will almost certainly have prosecuted *à outrance* policies of economic growthmanship. Boulding's 'cowboy economy', referred to in Chapter XIII, will have been given free rein, and as a consequence the lot of politicians and officials will have increasingly become the difficult and unenviable task of steering their respective ships of state between the Scylla of environmental spoilation and the Charybdis of resource depletion. A grave food shortage is likely to hang over the developed countries like a veritable sword of Damocles, as the Third World, in the throes of starvation following the failure of the 'green revolution', becomes more and more reluctant to trade food for manufactured goods. The bloody spectre of social disintegration, having stalked the wings of the affluent nations for many years, could well be preparing to move into the centre of the stage, manifesting itself in such ills as violence, alcoholism, criminality, vandalism, drug addiction and rampant psychoneurotic illness.

But the overriding impression of the early twenty-first century will be that Spaceship Earth is bursting at the seams with people. The population will be in the neighbourhood of 7,000 million, and by far the most dramatic increase in numbers will have taken place in the Third World. By then some 80 per cent of our planet's inhabitants will be resident in Asia, Africa and Latin America. One in six people on earth will be Chinese; a similar proportion will be Indian; one in eight will be African and one in ten Latin American. The relative position of Europe *vis à vis* population will have been much weakened. Whereas in 1971 Europe plus the USSR accounted some 19 per cent of the world's population, by the early twenty-first century the corresponding figure will have fallen precipitously and will be less than 14 per cent of the total. By that time fewer than one in 100 people on our planet will be British, and the Market of the Ten—that enlarged Economic Community, so dear to the hearts of our fervent Europeans—will house no more than 5 per cent of the world community.

For it is in the Third World amongst that seething mass of fecund, starving, illiterate, underprivileged and intensely pathetic people that during the twenty-first century our planet will have its tryst with destiny. It is there that the fate of mankind will be decided; it is there that civilisation as we currently perceive it, could take its final lurch into oblivion. Faced with problems of such an overwhelming nature what courses are open to us in Britain? Can our actions have any influence whatsoever on the pattern of events and does it, for example, really matter in the long term whether we adhere to or remain aloof from the nations of the European Economic Community? Alas, by the early twenty-first century the hinge of history will almost certainly have moved decisively and irrevocably away from Europe towards the underdeveloped world, and in the comity of nations the role of Britain whether within or outwith the EEC, will at best be circumscribed. Indeed to historians of future years the rhetoric of the contemporary party politicians, advocating or opposing British entry in the Community, is likely to seem unreal and almost irrelevant.

To politicians is vouchsafed the decision as to whether or not the human race will survive, and it is a matter of grievous concern that on the transcendent issues of the latter part of the twentieth century—overpopulation, environmental degradation, depletion of finite resources—the dialogue of international politics, whether of left, right or centre, has little to offer. The themes are too new, too revolutionary, too broad in compass for most politicians to grasp, particularly if, as happens not infrequently, their intellectual granaries are replete with the harvests of the past. How much easier it is for them to deny that such problems exist, to utter euphoric statements about the glories of modern technology and to berate the doom-watchers for their alarmist prophecies. How much better to expunge such disagreeable problems from the inner recesses of the mind and, like the ostrich, to bury their heads in the sands of parochial affairs, day-to-day events and short term goals. For, make no mistake, politicians fear overpopulation as an electoral issue and therefore avoid its discussion; they stand ready to condemn environmental pollution, but alas, the condemnation loses much of its force because of their failure to equate pollution with overpopulation and burgeoning affluence; on the subject of resource depletion they either maintain an embarrassed silence or pin their pennon to the mast of technological wizardry.

But change must inevitably come, and from the maelstrom of contemporary politics a new grouping will ultimately arise. It will have as its basic tenets the control of population, respect for the environment, the conservation of finite resources and the substitution of the spaceman for the cowboy exonomy. It will be led by the young instead of being dominated by the old and the arteriosclerotic; it will look upwards to the heavens and will abjure the ground; it will harness the latent idealism of men and women all over the world; it will be exciting to belong to for it will be concerned with the problems of today and tomorrow and will not be shackled by the shibboleths of yesterday; it will provide Spaceship Earth with a much needed pilot; above all, its ethos will be international for it will be the embryo of world government. Initially, the movement will fare badly at the polls; it will be pilloried, castigated and subjected to all manner of pejorative comment. But in the long term it will triumph because amongst its supporters will be the greatest ally of them all—the future history of mankind.

Published by William Heinemann Medical Books Ltd, London

INDEX